Women Empowerment and Well-Being for Inclusive Economic Growth

Shailja Dixit
Amity University, India

Sana Moid
Amity University, India

I0894728

IGI Global
PUBLISHER of TIMELY KNOWLEDGE

A volume in the Advances in Religious and Cultural Studies (ARCS) Book Series

Published in the United States of America by
IGI Global
Information Science Reference (an imprint of IGI Global)
701 E. Chocolate Avenue
Hershey PA, USA 17033
Tel: 717-533-8845
Fax: 717-533-8661
E-mail: cust@igi-global.com
Web site: http://www.igi-global.com

Library of Congress Cataloging-in-Publication Data

Names: Dixit, Shailja, 1975- editor. | Moid, Sana, 1987- editor.
Title: Women empowerment and well-being for inclusive economic growth / Shailja Dixit and Sana Moid, editors.
Description: Hershey : Business Science Reference, 2020. | Includes bibliographical references and index. | Summary: "This book examines the role of women empowerment and well-being for inclusive economic growth"-- Provided by publisher.
Identifiers: LCCN 2019058361 (print) | LCCN 2019058362 (ebook) | ISBN 9781799837374 (hardcover) | ISBN 9781799837381 (paperback) | ISBN 9781799837398 (ebook)
Subjects: LCSH: Women--Employment. | Women's rights. | Women--Health and hygiene. | Women--Social conditions. | Women in sustainable development.
Classification: LCC HD6053 .W63846 2020 (print) | LCC HD6053 (ebook) | DDC 331.4--dc23
LC record available at https://lccn.loc.gov/2019058361
LC ebook record available at https://lccn.loc.gov/2019058362

This book is published in the IGI Global book series Advances in Religious and Cultural Studies (ARCS) (ISSN: 2475-675X; eISSN: 2475-6768)

British Cataloguing in Publication Data
A Cataloguing in Publication record for this book is available from the British Library.

For electronic access to this publication, please contact: eresources@igi-global.com.

Advances in Religious and Cultural Studies (ARCS) Book Series

Nancy Erbe
California State University-Dominguez Hills, USA

ISSN:2475-675X
EISSN:2475-6768

Mission

In the era of globalization, the diversity of the world and various cultures becomes apparent as cross-cultural interactions turn into a daily occurrence for individuals in all professions. Understanding these differences is necessary in order to promote effective partnerships and interactions between those from different religious and cultural backgrounds.

The **Advances in Religious and Cultural Studies (ARCS)** book series brings together a collection of scholarly publications on topics pertaining to religious beliefs, culture, population studies, and sociology. Books published within this series are ideal for professionals, theorists, researchers, and students seeking the latest research on collective human behavior in terms of religion, social structure, and cultural identity and practice.

Coverage

- Globalization and Culture
- Human Rights and Ethics
- Sociology
- Cults and Religious Movements
- Cultural Identity
- Group Behavior
- Cross-Cultural Interaction
- Stereotypes and Racism
- Politics and Religion
- Gender

IGI Global is currently accepting manuscripts for publication within this series. To submit a proposal for a volume in this series, please contact our Acquisition Editors at Acquisitions@igi-global.com or visit: http://www.igi-global.com/publish/.

The Advances in Religious and Cultural Studies (ARCS) Book Series (ISSN 2475-675X) is published by IGI Global, 701 E. Chocolate Avenue, Hershey, PA 17033-1240, USA, www.igi-global.com. This series is composed of titles available for purchase individually; each title is edited to be contextually exclusive from any other title within the series. For pricing and ordering information please visit http://www.igi-global.com/book-series/advances-religious-cultural-studies/84269. Postmaster: Send all address changes to above address.

Titles in this Series

For a list of additional titles in this series, please visit:
https://www.igi-global.com/book-series/advances-religious-cultural-studies/84269

Rising Voices and Experiences of Women in Leadership
Freda R. Russell (Cardinal Stritch University, USA)
Information Science Reference • © 2021 • 400pp • H/C (ISBN: 9781799822325) • US $195.00

Indigenous Language Acquisition, Maintenance, and Loss and Current Language Policies
Toru Okamura (Komatsu University, Japan) and Masumi Kai (University of Guam, Guam)
Information Science Reference • © 2021 • 302pp • H/C (ISBN: 9781799829591) • US $195.00

Memory, Conflicts, Disasters, and the Geopolitics of the Displaced
Clara Rachel Eybalin Casseus (Independent Researcher, France) Stevens Aguto Odongoh (Makerere University, Uganda) and Amal Adel Abdrabo (Alexandria University, Egypt)
Information Science Reference • © 2021 • 203pp • H/C (ISBN: 9781799844389) • US $185.00

Multidisciplinary Perspectives on Women, Voice, and Agency
Berrin Yanıkkaya (Yeditepe University, Turkey) and Angelique Margarita Nairn (Auckland University of Technology, New Zealand)
Information Science Reference • © 2021 • 333pp • H/C (ISBN: 9781799848295) • US $195.00

Handbook of Research on Social and Cultural Dynamics in Indian Cinema
Santosh Kumar Biswal (Symbiosis International University (Deemed), India) Krishna Sankar Kusuma (Jamia Millia Islamia, India) and Sulagna Mohanty (Amrita Vishwa Vidyapeetham, India)
Information Science Reference • © 2020 • 401pp • H/C (ISBN: 9781799835110) • US $235.00

Implications of an Evolved Christianity in the Modern World
James Patrick Byrnes (Temple University, USA)
Information Science Reference • © 2020 • 271pp • H/C (ISBN: 9781799854524) • US $195.00

Examining a New Paradigm of Heritage With Philosophy, Economy, and Education
António dos Santos Queirós (Lisbon University, Portugal)
Information Science Reference • © 2020 • 274pp • H/C (ISBN: 9781799836360) • US $195.00

Handbook of Research on New Dimensions of Gender Mainstreaming and Women Empowerment
Moly Kuruvilla (University of Calicut, India) and Irene George (Emirates Institute for Banking and Financial Studies, UAE)
Information Science Reference • © 2020 • 610pp • H/C (ISBN: 9781799828198) • US $255.00

IGI Global
PUBLISHER of TIMELY KNOWLEDGE

701 East Chocolate Avenue, Hershey, PA 17033, USA
Tel: 717-533-8845 x100 • Fax: 717-533-8661
E-Mail: cust@igi-global.com • www.igi-global.com

This book is dedicated all the Women in the World who are the Foundation stone and the Architect of the Society.

This book is dedicated to the constant source of positivity in my life and to all the Women for being so amazing and Wonderful!

Table of Contents

Detailed Table of Contents

Job satisfaction has fallen among doctors, and beyond lack of pay parity that averages 25%, female physician job satisfiers differ from male colleagues. Health systems can build upon female physicians' confidence in their abilities to communicate with patients, show empathy, build trust, and elicit patient compliance with treatment plans. Systems must attend to work conditions for young and female cohorts, thereby retaining half of the workforce offering critical care to 7.8 billion people. Ordinal logistic regression was used to analyze data gathered in the U.S. by the Center for Studying Health System Change. Data were used to build a predictive statistical model in concert with independent variables linked to generational and job satisfaction literature. This study revealed statistically significant correlations between factors not only by gender, but also by generational membership. Statistically significant factors affecting job satisfaction among female physicians include provision of quality care to all patients, adequate time spent with patients and income.

Indonesia has committed to embody gender equality in the labor market through gender mainstreaming programs in all sectors. Nevertheless, the reality indicates that gender inequality in the labor market still exists. This chapter aims to discuss various issues of gender inequality in the Indonesian labor market in the agriculture, manufacturing, and services sectors. The data used for the analysis is the 2016 national labor force survey. The survey covered 82,613 workers with 31,256 of them from the agricultural sector, 14,835 from the manufacturing sector and 36,522 from the services sector. The analysis shows the dominance of male labor in all the sectors with the lowest proportion of female workers occurs in the manufacturing sector (27.1%) followed by the agricultural sector (37.5%) and the services (46.5%). Based on the type of position, men are more dominant in strategic positions in all the three sectors. The highest wage disparity between women and men takes place in the agricultural sector followed by the manufacturing and the services.

The primary objective of this chapter is to focus on progress of literacy achievement in India and factors influencing literacy rate are identified with regression models. A gender disparity index is prepared to analyse trends in differentials among male-female literacy achievement. India is now facing the challenge of achieving universalization of primary education to achieve status of a 'literate country'. It is known fact that literacy and primary education are interdependent. A literate country will be a progressive-oriented country. It is observed that educational backwardness is due to various reasons like unsatisfactory progress of policy implementation, high level of illiteracy and dropout rates. Literacy rate is the best possible barometer to judge the level of educational awakening in a state, leading to a minimum capacity for self-learning. The empirical evidence substantiates the factors influencing educational achievement.

This study aims to find significant relationships between gender inequality and some economic indicators. More specifically, the labor force participation rate of females, maternal mortality ratio, and proportion of seats held by women in national parliaments are mainly used as gender inequality indicators while employment rate and GDP constitute the economy dimension. For this purpose, instead of using a single variable, multiple variables are mainly preferred, which will lead to a better understanding of the relationship between gender inequality and economic indicators. In order to measure these multiple correlations, canonical correlation analysis is performed which analyzes the relationship between two sets of variables. The rationale of using more than one variable for gender inequality and economy is that using only one variable is not sufficient to explain these concepts, so a variable set is needed.

Globalization has accelerated the pace of innovation and technology and has paved the way for new business across all countries. Gender (in)equality and empowerment of women is the most discussed and debated topic worldwide. To survive in a dynamic environment with enormous impediments in the form of societal, political, economic, legal, and technological environment is the biggest challenge. To prevail over this, there is an imperative need to discard old prejudices and accept innovative thinking and resolutions. The purpose of this chapter is to throw light on the subjugation of women across all sectors.

economic growth of the world. This chapter speaks about the government initiatives in empowering Uzbek women and bringing gender equality in the society. The data for the chapter was collected from secondary sources. The objectives of this article are to examine and analyse the initiatives taken by Uzbek government and other UN bodies for gender equality and women empowerment. The same strategies can be replicated in other parts of Central Asia where women are still not treated equally and can be empowered to contribute to the socioeconomic growth. The current research may suggest the authorities and civil society organizations to improve and implement inventive methodologies to attain gender equality, advancement, and peace.

Women are no less than men. She herself is on par with a man. WO-MAN empowering is not only a verbal concept; it should be in practical life. She is no less than a man in any work assigned to her. She is always ill-treated as a weaker sex. But in the real life, she is more powerful than a man. Her commitment towards her work is always dedicated. She always tries to prove herself in any task assigned to her. This movement of women empowerment is not a new one. When you look back into the prehistoric period, women were treated as equal warriors, better half to men. They were strong enough in mind and soul. Then when and where did she lose her identity? Why is she treated as a weaker sex? Why she is deprived of her right to respect, recognition, and remuneration in the outer world with reference to her male colleagues? Through this chapter, the author is trying to shed light on the rights of a women, which she is deprived of since ages.

Women's empowerment is much developed compared with the past. Women are working alongside men and making their own decision making in the situations like education, profession career, and lifestyle. It is clear that women can add incrementally to a developing nation's economy. However, the regulatory regime, narrow thinking, and conflict of work-life balance are some of the obstacles that are hindering the growth of women entrepreneurship. The chapter is an attempt to discuss issues like growth of women entrepreneurs globally and in India and contribution of women entrepreneurs. In spite of several obstacles faced by women entrepreneurs like lack of trust by the other party on their capabilities, struggles of managing work-life balance, proving their worth in a patriarchal society, with the increasing potential of women entrepreneurship, several initiatives taken by different authorities and organisations all over the world are playing a pivotal role in encouraging and supporting women entrepreneurs in different parts of the world. Need of the hour is the change in the mindset of the people and increase in the confidence on the capabilities of women entrepreneurs.

area. This chapter also finds that if a household receives international remittances, the level of household welfare may be increased by Tk. 3167.49. Therefore, this chapter calls for the policies for larger inflows of remittances and its proper utilization in productive purposes.

Health of the mothers is of prime concern for growth of any country, and their level of empowerment can be significantly related to the place of delivery selected for birth of a child. Janani Suraksha Yojana (JSY) is an astute attempt towards safeguarding maternal health by Government of India under the flagship health programme, National Rural Health Mission, to promote institutional deliveries among the poor pregnant women. Safe deliveries at the institutions are an indicator of women empowerment and inclusive growth, which paves the way towards economic growth by securing the health and well-being of mothers in rural areas, thereby sustaining productive capacities of women. The chapter assesses the rise in proportion of institutional deliveries among JSY beneficiaries with increased awareness under JSY in Punjab, after carefully assessing the situation of maternal health prevailing in the world, India, and state of Punjab. Further, policy measures have been recommended to augment women's health and empowerment, an inclusive economic growth parameter of country's growth trajectory.

This chapter presents an enquiry into the scourge of menstrual untouchability, which still pervades a large section of Indian society. An attempt has been made to understand the underlying dynamics of the social evil of menstrual untouchability through anecdotal evidence gathered through unstructured theme-based interviews of respondents in Uttarakhand, India. Social norms and the pressure to abide by them have been found major reasons for propagation of menstrual untouchability. The practice of menstrual untouchability has been found to be much less rigidly observed in urban communities and single adult-women households. Isolation during menstrual periods and consequent respite from household chores has also been discovered as a reason for some women submitting themselves to this practice. All these insights have formed the basis for suggestions made to rid the society of evil of menstrual untouchability.

In the past, Orang Asli women and men were considered equal, even though their roles were very different. As modernization slowly crept into their lifestyles, the gender divide has gotten a lot bigger and the paternalistic culture has taken a hold of many. Some researchers have said the skewed depictions was influenced by both Christianity and Islam, whereby women were considered to be created by supernatural powers alongside the male species. However, there have been accounts of women being the village chief, but as more anthropologists targeted their research on the Orang Asli, the role of a women in the

Foreword

Empowerment of women and economic growth are two directly proportional aspects and an inclusive development policy which focuses on elevating the economic status of women is imperative for sustainable growth of the country. The discourse on development of women has long focused on improving their social status without taking into consideration the role which economic growth can play towards ensuring a more equal society.

The development policies involving women focus more on the reproductive roles of women instead of investing in the economically productive works women can contribute. The increased involvement of women in the workforce will contribute in reducing the gender pay gap and gender-based inequality prevalent globally.

This book touches upon different aspects of gender disparity and provides a comprehensive outlook towards reaching a solution. The book has successfully managed to highlight the different dimensions of women empowerment and obstacles that women face in India and its neighbouring countries.

I extend my appreciation to Dr Sana Moid and Dr Shailja Dixit for the exemplary efforts put in preparing the book "Women Empowerment and Well being for Inclusive Economic Growth". I congratulate them and wish them a grand success. Hope this book becomes a resource-house for students and academics researching in the field of women empowerment.

Best wishes to the book. Keep working towards a more inclusive society.

Rekha Sharma
National Commission for Women, India

Preface

AN OVERVIEW

Improving the predicament of women and girls is one of the global morals, political and economic challenges of our time. Across developed and developing countries, women have been excluded from basic rights and do not enjoy the same opportunities as men nor do they get equal opportunity to contribute to the economic development of their countries. Gradually, world over policymakers in both developed and developing countries have understood that this is neither fair nor smart as this has created a vicious cycle: underinvesting in women limits development and leads to slows poverty reduction and economic growth. Only if policymakers consciously consider the differences in opportunities afforded to men and women can they use economic policy to narrow the gender gap – and can they take advantage of the full potential of their citizens.

According to a study by World Bank (Global development Women's rights and gender equality, 2018), Gender equality would enrich the global economy by an estimated \$160tn (£120tn) if women were earning as much as men in the workplace. Equal pay, equal hours and equal participation in the workforce could lead to a global wealth jump of \$23,620 a person, as well as creating knock-on benefits such as lower malnutrition and child mortality rates, said the report. According to a survey done by World Bank on Legal Discrimination of Women it was found that

- 45 out of 128 countries - women do not have the same legal capacity to act or to engage in economic transactions
- 49 out of 128 countries - women cannot work in all industries
- 32 out of 128 countries - women do not have equal inheritance rights

It has become widely accepted that promoting gender equality and women's empowerment is essential to achieving sustainable human development, poverty eradication, and economic growth specifically in the developing economies. Despite many international and national agreements set to promote women empowerment, gender equality, women still lag behind men in education, employment, politics, health, and access to public services. An important part of gender equality is empowerment for women, which focuses on power imbalances and giving women more control to manage their own lives. It is important for women to take ownership over their own empowerment, and this has increasingly been occurring across the African continent, as seen through a growing number of women's movements and grassroots women's organizations. It is important for women to take ownership over their own empowerment, and this has increasingly been occurring across the developing economies, as seen through a growing number of women's movements and grassroots women's organizations.

This book presents an important intervention in the debate between global economic and social sustainable development. It makes the case for understanding development in economic terms as well as in terms of well-being, empowerment and participation, uncovering the role of empowering women and achieving gender equality in the sustainable development.

Research work and cases related to participation of a women's labour force in the economic development of the country, the place of women in society, their contribution to the social development of their country and the problems faced by them are the key features of the book. In addition, research and cases related to women's rights and their violations, their authority in board room and politics are also highlights in the book. Apart from this the book focus on the holistic approach to women. Well-being which speaks about whole person's being – social, economic, and health related – and the ability to make important life choices. Well-being shall also entail a level of economic security, education, work life, housing, good family relations and social participation, feeling your contribution, having fun, feeling you are safe and in good physical and mental health.

This book presents an important intervention in the debate between global economic and social sustainable development. It makes the case for understanding development in economic terms as well as in terms of well-being, empowerment and participation, uncovering the role of empowering women and achieving gender equality in the sustainable development.

The book aims to focus on a number of inter-connected issues relating to pro-poor growth, e.g., while talking about the composition of growth and its relevance in the context of inclusive growth, it also analyses the causes of path differences and their impact on employment generation and levels of living, and well-being. The book talk about the issues of inclusive growth, women empowerment, well-being or economic growth in a consolidated way under one framework where these concepts are presented as one interwoven phenomenon where one variable leads to another. Present book talks about interrelating the concept of women empowerment and their well-being leading to inclusive economic growth thus benefiting the society.

The book focuses on a number of inter-connected issues relating to pro-poor growth, e.g., while talking about the composition of growth and its relevance in the context of inclusive growth, it also analyses the causes of path differences and their impact on employment generation and levels of living, and well being.

Book will cover issues like women empowerment, well being and their cumulative impact on inclusive economic growth and will cater to the following audience:

TARGET AUDIENCE

The target audience of this book is composed of professionals and researchers working in the field of social science, gender studies, health and well being, women empowerment, well being, Governance, Social Wellness and knowledge management in various disciplines, e.g. library, information and communication sciences, administrative sciences and management, sociology. Moreover, the book will provide insights and support executives concerned with the management of expertise, knowledge, policy making, public and private organizations information and organizational development in different types of work communities and environments.

The issues covered in the Book like women empowerment, well being and their cumulative impact on inclusive economic growth will be of relevance to following people also:

- Academicians & Researchers
- Business School Students
- Entrepreneurs
- Business Analyst
- Market Researchers
- Corporate for CSR initiatives
- Policy Makers
- National and international research agencies
- National and international management agencies
- National and international welfare agencies

COMPOSITION OF THE BOOK:

The book is divided into three sections, namely "Gender Inequality," "Women Empowerment," "Well-Being and Inclusive Growth."

Section 1: Gender Inequality

Chapter 1 talks about Inequality in Pay as a Factor Impacting Job Satisfaction Among Female Physicians in USA. Male and female physicians around the world report stress reduces their job satisfaction. This is worrisome for clinics, hospitals, national and international health organizations because research shows a direct link between physician job satisfaction and global health outcomes.

Chapter 2 is about Gender Inequality in the Indonesian Labor Market. Gender equality in the labor market is an important part of economic development in Indonesia. This equality refers to the fulfillment of the rights, opportunities and fair treatment of men and women of all age groups at all stages of life and work. To strengthen gender equality, Indonesia has ratified various ILO conventions for gender equality.

Chapter 3 involves the discussion on Gender Disparity In Educational Achievement In India. The primary objective of this chapter is to focus on progress of literacy achievement during 1951-97 and factors influencing literacy rate are identified with regression models. A gender disparity index is prepared to analyze trends in differentials among male-female literacy achievement.

Chapter 4 is about Application of Canonical Correlation Analysis to Gender Inequality and Economic Indicators and aims to find significant relationships between gender inequality and some economic indicators. More specifically, the labor force participation rate of females, maternal mortality ratio, and proportion of seats held by women in national parliaments are mainly used as gender inequality indicators while employment rate and GDP constitute the economy dimension.

Chapter 5 involves discussion About Upshot of Gender Inequalities Towards Labor Markets – A Macro Level Perspective. It presents the idea that Empowering Women To Contribute Completely In Economic Life Across Every Segment Is Crucial To Build Stronger Economies, Attain Internationally decided goals for growth and sustainability, and make progress with better quality of life for women, men, families, and communities altogether.

Section 2: Women Empowerment

Chapter 6 Assess the Performance of Female-Owned Enterprises and Highlighting Environmental and Social Obstacles to their Growth by discussing Case Study of Pakistani Female Entrepreneurs. Economic development is an ultimate goal of developing countries and utilization of human capital to achieve this goal is accepted as vital globally. Entrepreneurship, recognized as a central force to bring economic growth, needs more women to be involved in this context.

Chapter 7 presents Women Empowerment Initiatives And Socio- Economic Development- In Pursuit For Gender Equality In Uzbekistan. As a result of limited professional and career growth opportunities in Uzbekistan, insufficient remuneration and cultural restraints, women still represent a minority within the government and legal sectors. There is also a continued need to make sure women can benefit from vital government services. Initiatives aimed at empowering women and combating gender-based violence need to be implemented.

Chapter 8 talks about the idea of 3R`s of Women Empowerment i.e. Recognition, Respect and Remuneration which may change the situation to a great extent. Women is always a bridge between many situations which changed the history of many nations. Women always have the right to deserve Respect, Recognition and Remuneration for what she contributes to her family or office. In case this is a lacking point for her family or office the bondage and loyalty may start shaking.

Chapter 9 is An Observational Study on Women Empowerment in Marketing with reference to Chennai City which talks about Successful women Entrepreneur in India in Business. As observed, Women empowerment, in the truest sense, will be achieved only when there is attitudinal change in society regarding womenfolk, treating them with proper respect, dignity, fairness and equality.

Chapter 10 talks about A History of the United States Women's Bureau, 1917-1930 in the context of Economic Opportunity and Immigration. This chapter is presents an historical account of women's rights in the United States from 1917-1930 and its relationship to women immigrating to the United States for economic opportunity. It discusses the findings of the Women's Bureau and the perspective of Italian immigrant George La Piana about the integration of immigrant women into the American workforce relative to native-born women.

Section 3: Well-Being of Women and Inclusive Growth

Chapter 11 present Factors Affecting the Motivation and Productivity of Female University Teachers at Workplace. The study broadly focuses on a particular question of identifying the significant factors that affect the motivation and productivity of the female teachers at workplace. Besides the study also explores the demographic features of the respondents and the interrelationship of the significant factors affecting female teachers' performance.

Chapter 12 present International Remittances and Household Welfare taking Evidences from Naogaon, Bangladesh. This paper mainly explores the extent to what international remittances impact on household welfare in Bangladesh. Besides, a linear regression is applied to find out the impact of international remittances on household welfare.

Chapter 13 presents Janani Suraksha Yojana as an ardent approach to empower rural women for institutional deliveries: An Inclusive growth strategy in healthcare sector of India. Janani Suraksha Yojana (JSY) is an astute attempt towards safeguarding maternal health by Government of India under the flagship health programme - National Rural Health Mission to promote institutional deliveries among the poor pregnant women.

Chapter 14 is on Menstrual Untouchability: Socio-Psychological Factors Perpetuating the Social Evil. This study assesses the extent of the discriminatory practice in Kumaun region in Uttarakhand state. This chapter has also investigated various other aspects related to menstrual untouchability.

Chapter 15 talks about The Plight of the Orang Asli Women in Malaysia in the context of Promoting Wild Edible Plants through Street Food. It is important to highlight the contribution of Orang Asli women not just to the welfare of their families but also to the society in terms of leadership roles, their work ethics and just basic human rights as it cannot be denied that the key role in ensuring the continuity of both culture and tradition food system is highly dependent on the women.

The book covers varied aspects related to women from all parts of the world. It has been identified that Sustained inclusive economic growth embraces three distinct properties –efficiency, equity and sustainability – within a single framework. This might suggest a degree of internal inconsistency within the general definition of sustained inclusive economic growth. Women and girls require an enabling environment, including the mobilization of adequate resources, fair and equitable trade and technological progress for sustainable development and capacity-building, delivered through partnerships based on accountability and solidarity, and adequate data to monitor implementation for inclusion. All of these have important gender dimensions. Through the book concludes that inclusive development can be attained if women are empowered and their well-being is taken care of globally at micro and macro perspective.

Acknowledgment

This book bears the imprint of so many people.

From Shailja Dixit:

The Almighty God should be Thanked the first for this life. I could never have done this without the faith I have in You. My faith in You during this time of crisis has helped me to sail through these times when the whole world has come to a standstill. My overriding debt continues to be for my husband Anurag for providing me with the time, support and inspiration for writing this book. My loving children, daughter Shreshthi and son Yashvardan, who are a source of joy and happiness in my life, helped me to be lively during these times. I shall never have enough words to express my gratitude towards my in-laws, and my parents who have always supported and motivated me throughout my life personally and professionally.

The high energy & motivation levels and clear vision of My Co Editor Dr Sana Moid is worth appreciating. Her zeal helped in smooth sailing of the project.

From Sana Moid:

First and foremost I would like to thank God for giving me the power to believe in my passion and pursue my dreams. I would like to express my gratitude to the people who saw me through this book; to all those who provided support, talked things over, read, wrote, offered comments, allowed me to quote their remarks and assisted in the editing, proofreading and design. Nobody has been more important to me in the pursuit of this project than the members of my family. I would like to thank my parents and my in laws whose love and guidance are with me in whatever I pursue. Most importantly, I wish to thank my loving and supportive husband Zeeshan who supported and encouraged me in spite of all the time it took me away from him.

I am appreciative to my Co-Editor Dr. Shailja Dixit for continuous support and trusting me throughout the project.

My colleagues and associates at Amity University continue to have an important impact on my academic and research orientation.

From Both the Editors:

We owe a considerable amount of gratitude to our University Management. Foremost we are indebted to our most honourable President of the Amity Education Group and Founder of Ritnand Balved Education Foundation Dr. Ashok K Chauhan. It is his vision and motivation that faculty at Amity can do research with utmost passion. Our deepest gratitude to our Chairman and Chancellor of Amity University Dr. Aseem Chauhan, who inspires us constantly for achieving greater heights in academics. We cannot thank enough our Vice Chancellor, Prof. (Dr.) Balvinder Shukla whose energy and passion towards academics is contagious and she plays our role model for this profession. We are grateful to our Pro Vice Chancellor Prof. Dr. Sunil Dhaneshwar for his encouragement and to our Head of the Institute Prof (Dr.) Rohit Kushwaha for believing in our capabilities and for his unconditional support without which this book could not have been completed.

We are grateful to all our wonderful authors and reviewers who became part of this beautiful journey. Our sincere gratitude goes to the chapter's authors who contributed their time and expertise to this book. We also appreciate the valuable contributions of the reviewers regarding the improvement of quality, coherence, and content presentation of chapters. We thank them for their unrelenting support and promptness that has helped in the timely completion of the book. Most of the authors also served as referees; we highly appreciate their double task. Without their support, this book would not have become a reality

The talented staff at IGI deserves praise for their consistent support. We would like to thank our Project Manager for ensuring that everything is in proper way. We benefitted greatly from their seamless help.

We also thank the team at IGI Global for their excellent support and help in the publication of the book.

Shailja Dixit
Amity University, India

Sana Moid
Amity University, India

Section 1
Gender Equality

Chapter 1
Inequality in Pay Ranks Among Factors Impacting Job Satisfaction Among Female Physicians

Jaciel Elizabeth Keltgen
https://orcid.org/0000-0003-0465-1583
Augustana University, USA

ABSTRACT

Job satisfaction has fallen among doctors, and beyond lack of pay parity that averages 25%, female physician job satisfiers differ from male colleagues. Health systems can build upon female physicians' confidence in their abilities to communicate with patients, show empathy, build trust, and elicit patient compliance with treatment plans. Systems must attend to work conditions for young and female cohorts, thereby retaining half of the workforce offering critical care to 7.8 billion people. Ordinal logistic regression was used to analyze data gathered in the U.S. by the Center for Studying Health System Change. Data were used to build a predictive statistical model in concert with independent variables linked to generational and job satisfaction literature. This study revealed statistically significant correlations between factors not only by gender, but also by generational membership. Statistically significant factors affecting job satisfaction among female physicians include provision of quality care to all patients, adequate time spent with patients and income.

INTRODUCTION

Practicing medicine is taxing. Male and female physicians around the world report stress reduces their job satisfaction. This is worrisome for clinics, hospitals, national and international health organizations because research shows a direct link between physician job satisfaction and global health outcomes.

DOI: 10.4018/978-1-7998-3737-4.ch001

According to the United Nations, world population aged 80 years and older is projected to triple between 2017 and 2050 (Zhou, 2019). This demographic shift is due to declining fertility rates and rising survival rates and is predicted to jolt political and economic systems. Exacerbating this trend of aging citizens is a projected scarcity of physicians. The World Health Organization (Smith, 2019) has forecast a global shortage of 4.3 million physicians, putting more strain on current health professionals to deliver essential health interventions. The United States alone will suffer a shortage of more than 139,000 physicians by 2033 (Boyle, 2020). The current and forecast shortage is compounded by a cadre of physicians that is aging, too; 43 percent of physicians in the U.S. are older than 55 (Commins, 2017).

These health trends – as well as two global pandemics in the past two decades that rocked the economy, governments, citizens and health organizations – reinforce the imperative to recruit, train and retain physicians. But what if young generations simply aren't compelled to invest time and money in medical career demands? Generational research indicates young people aren't as interested in medical careers and younger physicians may have less commitment to a high-stress profession, are more concerned about their financial and physical wellbeing, do not enjoy administrative responsibilities and find the institutional nature of the healthcare industry unappealing (Cennamo & Gardner, 2008; Gursoy et al., 2008; Jurkiewicz & Bradley, 2002; and Pew, 2014). In fact, there is concern that young physicians, after years of training and with plenty of debt, may abandon their work altogether (Spector, 2018). In addition to generational differences, it is critical to consider how a physician's gender influences overall satisfaction at work. Research shows female and male physicians around the world attach great significance to salary and workload, but contributors to their satisfaction differ and depend upon work condition factors such as specialty, practice type, work culture, organizational commitment to quality care, having adequate time with patients, workload, clinical freedom and balancing obligations (Konrad, Douglas, McMurray, Pathman, Williams, Schwartz, Gerrity, Scheckler, Bigby & Rhodes, 1999; Lo Sasso, Richards, Chou and Gerber, 2011; McMurray, Linzer, Konrad, Douglas, Shugeman & Nelson, 2000; and Tyssen, Palmer, Solberg, Voltmer & Frank, 2013).

BACKGROUND

The study included in this chapter investigates which factors are most important to physicians – especially female physicians – engaged in delivering excellent care to an aging populace (Worldometers, 2019). Because forecasts show a formidable gap between the demand for healthcare to an older population and the inadequate supply of practicing physicians, it is important to develop a statistically significant model predicting satisfaction by gender as well as generation. Governments, employers, insurers, hospitals, medical professionals, taxpayers, and care recipients all have a substantial material stake in striking a balance between demand and supply.

Generations of doctors surveyed over the past two decades in Iceland, Norway, Germany, Switzerland, China, Saudi Arabia, Pakistan, India, Sudan, Turkey, Canada and the United States have weighed in on the factors impacting their multi-dimensional job satisfaction. Research reviewed here supports further exploration of the factors impacting physician job satisfaction as a public health issue that may be approached more effectively through modification of work condition factors – income, number of hours worked per week, having adequate time with patients, availability of technology, autonomy, status, effects of following protocols, eligibility for bonuses and incentives, providing quality care, administration and technological demands and consideration of patient costs when ordering diagnostic tests (Bawakid, Rashid, Mandoura, Shah & Mugharbel, 2018; Bovier & Pernieger, 2004; Bodur, 2002; Emmons, Nichols, Schulkin, James & Cain, 2006; Pathman, Konrad, Williams, Scheckler, Linzer & Douglas, 2002; Solberg, 2017; and Suliman, Eltom, Elmadhoun, Noor, Almobarak, Osman, Awadalla & Ahmed, 2017). Work conditions affect job satisfaction among young as well as experienced physicians. Increased administrative duties have reduced satisfaction because these responsibilities encroach on personal time and reduce time dedicated to direct care (Medscape, 2019). International efforts to reduce costs while increasing bureaucratic responsibilities related to insurance reporting have led to staff reductions, increased workloads and ultimately, threats to patient care (Medscape, 2019).

MAIN FOCUS OF THE CHAPTER

Gender, Pay and Workload

Physicians do not enjoy universal satisfaction, nor does satisfaction necessarily stem from identical variables. Gender has been the focus of voluminous empirical research that bears on the study at hand. Women have traditionally been care-oriented while men tend to be status-oriented. Women may not have the same societal pressures to earn high incomes. They also have a different set of demands than men, including homemaking and child rearing (Bobula, 1980; Lo Sasso et al., 2011; and Sasser, 2005). This means that flexibility and number of hours spent at work make a material difference in their wellbeing.

Prior research suggests female physicians likely derive greater satisfaction from spending more time with patients, practicing in specialties that offer flexibility and working fewer hours per week than male physicians (Keeton et al., 2007; Leigh et al., 2002; Linzer et al., 2000; and McMurray et al., 2000). Females generally communicate and interact well with patients in order to gain patient understanding and compliance with medical advice (Unwin et al., 2015). Females have been shown to seek intimacy and exhibit empathy (Kaldenberg, Becker & Zvonkovic, 1995; Reid et al., 2010; and Tannen, 1990); literature reveals this more openly expressed caring increases patient trust and reduces malpractice actions (Holder, 1979; and Unwin et al., 2015). Quality of care includes continuity of care; splitting care of one patient among multiple providers results in reduced patient conformance and therefore, negative health outcomes (DeVore et al., 1993). Literature has shown females derive greater satisfaction by spending more time with fewer patients (Collins et al., 1997; and Jovic et al., 2006). Resulting lower productivity also results in lower pay for female physicians and lack of awareness of individual patients' full health records reduces the ability to offer excellent care.

Work responsibilities impact female physicians differently than their male counterparts. Roughly one-third of the physician workforce is female with nearly half of all seats in American medical schools occupied by women (Kaiser Family Foundation, 2015). Women now comprise more than 60 percent of pediatricians and more than 51 percent of obstetricians/gynecologists in the United States (AAMC, 2015). This gender shift has led researchers to delve more deeply into how gender may affect satisfaction among physicians, especially because females have traditionally occupied caretaking roles in Western society (Bobula, 1980; Collins et al., 1997; Frank, McMurray, Linzer & Elon, 1999; Keeton et al., 2007; Linzer et al., 2000; McMurray et al., 2000; Sasser, 2005; and Taragin et al., 1992). While physicians of both genders are generally satisfied at work, studies show satisfaction is falling (Frank et al., 1999; Keeton et al., 2007; and McMurray et al., 2000).

Pay is a concern across the board. The bulk of the literature reinforces the importance of economic success as a source of physician job satisfaction (Bobula, 1980; Buchbinder et al., 2001; Grembowski et al., 2003; Katerndahl et al., 2009; Lichtenstein, 1984; Linzer et al., 2000; and Medscape, 2019). Economic success is influenced by income and ownership interests in the practice, as well as eligibility for bonuses and incentives.

Women tend to earn about 26 percent less than men around the world (Collins et al., 1997; Jovic et al., 2006; Langwell, 1982; Lo Sasso et al., 2011; Loury, 1977; and Medscape, 2019). "It has been suggested that the gender pay gap stems from leftover attitudes in a historically male-dominated profession, which fails to make allowances for maternity leave and family care responsibilities" (Medscape, 2019). According to the U.S. Bureau of Labor Statistics, female physicians earn an average of 67 percent less than male physicians or a median weekly salary of $1,667 vs. $2,513 (2018). Female physicians also express concern about the amount of time they can spend with patients (Collins et al., 1997; Jovic et al., 2006; Medscape, 2019; and Taragin et al., 1992). Langwell examined productivity and compensation between male and female physicians. This study showed female physicians receive 22 percent less salary than male physicians and see 38 percent fewer patients per hour (1982). Langwell's gauge of office productivity did not include emergency room visits, hospital inpatient visits, or house calls, and the researcher reports female physicians may be excluded from high-productivity practices. Langwell's work suggests female physicians provide "higher average quality office visits than do male physicians" (p. 273) and these findings complement those of other researchers who found female physicians are more empathetic, less likely to be sued for malpractice, less likely to take risks and more likely to score higher than males on measures of clinical quality (Cabot, 2015; Hojat, Gonnella, Nasca, Mangione, Vergare, & Magee, 2002; Reid, Friedberg, Adams, McGlynn & Mehrotra, 2010; Kaldenberg, Becker & Zvonkovic, 1995; and Tannen, 1990).

Women also reported more time pressures and higher volumes of patient load negatively impacted their satisfaction. It is not surprising that female physicians are less satisfied with more work and less pay. Women have historically accepted less pay in return for fulfilling work. In more complex and fractured work and personal roles, it makes sense that female physicians would seek not only pay parity but also positions allowing them to spend more time providing care for patients. Pay and patient load volumes are manipulable working condition factors and therefore can be adjusted with proper administrative focus.

According to Richardson and Burke (1991), males' satisfaction revolves primarily around income, number of hours worked per week, and time strains associated with seeing more patients. Females report different pressures affecting their satisfaction, including issues of having children at home, fulfilling multiple roles, salary inequity and less control over daily schedules that reduce their ability to provide high quality care (Frank et al., 1999). Additional responsibilities can affect female physicians' abilities to effectively balance demands, maintain confidence in providing high quality care to patients, and therefore, negatively impact their satisfaction on-the-job. Most job satisfaction studies point to pay and workload as the two most important variables impacting job satisfaction.

Generational Groupings

Research supports the appeal of a controllable lifestyle for younger generations. Controllable lifestyle includes being able to minimize workload pressures and malpractice concerns (Keltgen, 2016). Keeton et al. (2007) explored physician satisfaction, measuring differences across age, gender and specialty. Through factor analysis of 2,000 randomly selected physician surveys, researchers examined relationships between career satisfaction and demographics. The strongest predictor of satisfaction was control over schedule and hours worked. The researchers noted this finding corresponds to generational research showing that younger doctors value time off and lifestyle considerations more than older generations; therefore, controllable lifestyle was a factor in specialty selection more so than "traditional motivators such as remuneration and prestige" (p. 949). Controllable lifestyle has repeatedly been reported to be important to younger workers and supports the research shared here (Jurkiewicz & Bradley, 2002; Noble & Schewe, 2003; Parry & Urwin, 2011; Pew, 2010; Pew, 2014; and Smola & Sutton, 2002).

For the purposes of this study, physicians were grouped into gender and generational categories. Each generation has been born into a social environment characterized by distinctive values about social and family obligations (Winograd & Hais, 2008). These values are inconstant and cyclical, shaping each generation's values, behavior, and lifelong attitudes (Strauss & Howe, 1997). Each generation defines itself in comparison to preceding and succeeding generations (Winograd & Hais, 2008). As the size and force of the generation becomes more defined, primarily through positions of power and societal influence, it can demand that "the nation's institutions change to accommodate its beliefs and its values" (p. 2). There are four generations in the American workforce today, ranging in age from 14 to 100 (Strauss, 2014; and U.S. Bureau of Labor Statistics, 2014). Those who study social change often focus their work around generational time frames, as shown in Table 1.

Table 1. Commonly Held Generational Time Frames

Traditionalists	Baby Boomers	Generation Xers	Millennials
75 million people born 1900-1945 and lived through the Great Depression and World War II	80 million people born during the baby boom following World War II, 1946-1964	46 million people born between 1965 and 1980 in the "birth dearth" following the baby boom	76 million children primarily of baby boomers, born between 1981 and 1999

Lancaster & Stillman (2003) and Sparks (2012)

Traditionalists (TRADs) are committed and respectful of organizational structure and purpose. There are relatively few TRADs remaining in the American workforce, but those still working tend to be loyal and place work above recreational pursuits (Greer, 1984; and Smola & Sutton, 2002; and Strauss, 2014). They are concerned about patient costs and the overall availability and affordability of healthcare (Korn, Reichert, Simon & Halm, 2003).

Members of the TRAD generation are primarily retired, and each day for the next 14 years, 10,000 Baby Boomers will reach the age of 65 (Pew, 2010). This exodus from the American workforce puts pressure on younger generations – GENX and Millennials – to step in, not only into workforce roles, but also into citizenship roles. The preponderance of generational research points out that each generation behaves differently, a vital consideration if healthcare employers are to keep physicians fulfilled, remunerated and engaged (Ryder, 1965).

BABYBOOMers are results driven, exhibit commitment to their employers, find work central to their lives, give maximum effort and earn higher incomes (Burke, 2004; Cennamo & Gardner, 2008; D'Amato & Herzfeldt, 2008; Gursoy et al., 2008; Jurkiewicz & Bradley, 2002; Macky et al., 2008; Noble & Schewe, 2003; Parry & Urwin, 2011; Pew, 2010; and Smola & Sutton, 2002). Specifically, it is expected that economic variables offer the best explanatory power in predicting BABYBOOM physician satisfaction, based upon generational literature emphasizing this generation's priorities, attitudes and higher average household income. It should be noted that 22 percent of the BABYBOOM physicians surveyed for this study earned more than $300,000 in 2008. Only 14.5 percent of TRAD physicians and 16 percent of GENX physicians earned more than $300,000.

As a generation, GENXers are comfortable with technology and have come to expect efficiencies technology offers, learn quickly and dislike organizational hierarchy (Cennamo & Gardner, 2008; Noble & Schewe, 2003; and Smola & Sutton, 2002). Health systems acknowledge GENX physicians as an important group of service suppliers, especially now that healthcare is the largest single industry in the United States, TRADs are primarily retired and thousands of BABYBOOMers retire every day (Patel & Rushefsky, 2006; and Pew, 2010). Hallmarks of GENX include attention to life-work balance, social concerns, informality in appearance and personal relationships, comfort with technology and falling levels of trust. (Clark, 2014; Fabian, 2010; Pew, 2010; Pew, 2014a; Putnam, 1995; Robinson & Jackson, 2001; and Schwadel & Stout, 2012).

Millennials also seek life-work balance, express comfort with technology and experience low levels of trust (Pew, 2014b). They are generous with their time if impelled by organizations sharing their interests. This large demographic group has also seized new digital platforms — the internet, mobile technology, social media—as they construct personalized networks of friends, colleagues and affinity groups. Millennials have swiftly grasped new technological applications used for everything from communication to purchasing to managing projects. Traditionally, younger workers are expected to adapt to workplace traditions and expectations; however, the short supply of younger physicians may force administrators to more strongly consider generational values in hiring and retention decisions. Younger generations have already begun to infuse a medical workforce that is progressively less bound by professional norms, serving more often as employees of health systems and less often as partners in private practices (Survey of America's Physicians, 2014).

THESIS STATEMENT

Physician satisfaction is falling, eroding due to workload pressures and lack of remuneration. Increased pressures due to administrative workloads reduce satisfaction among older physicians, younger physicians desire a more controllable schedule that frees them for other interests, and quality of care standards are most important to female physicians. This research study hypothesizes job variables impact physician satisfaction differently, depending upon gender and generation (TRADS, BABYBOOMers, GENXers, and Millennials) and unless employers consider job satisfaction, there may not be enough qualified physicians to care for a growing population. It is hypothesized that TRAD physicians enjoy greater satisfaction when they provide excellent care, BABYBOOM physicians enjoy greater satisfaction when they earn a high income, and GENX and Millennial physicians enjoy greater satisfaction when they are able to use technology in diagnosis and treatment.

Model Development

Through development of models that best capture variables linked to satisfaction among physicians of a particular gender and generation, administrators can revamp policies and practices that encourage physicians to better serve the needs of society in a competitive environment. The primary objective of this analysis was to assist public administrators in healthcare settings to alleviate supply-and-demand issues by constructing satisfying jobs for physicians in a time of profound change. Based upon empirical research reviewed in an effort to better understand job satisfaction among younger physicians, several predictor variables were selected to construct a statistically significant model that contributes to greater understanding of satisfaction among generation and gender.

The researcher grouped 12 variables into three areas – Excellence of Care, Economic Success and Administrative – based upon literature review pertaining to generation and gender. Table 2 lists the seven control variables as well as the four variables included in each of the model's three sections.

Table 2. Variables Included in Model

Control Variables	Administrative Variables	Economic Success Variables	Excellence of Care Variables
Income	Availability and usage of technology	Eligible for bonuses and incentives	Provide high quality care to all patients
Years in Practice	Usage of patient reports	Practice is competitive	Hours spent in last month in charity care
Malpractice concerns	Effects of following Protocols	Ownership interest in practice	Being informed when patients consult other physicians
Number of hours worked per week	Receive patient condition reports	Practice is owned by physicians only	Consider patient costs when ordering diagnostic tests
Spending adequate time with patients			
Practice type			
Pediatric specialty			

Control Variables

Because the preponderance of preceding research into physician job satisfaction supported the statistical significance of income (Jovic et al., 2006; Leigh et al., 2002; and Lichtenstein, 1984), years in practice (Haas et al., 1998; Keeton et al., 2007), malpractice concerns (Becker et al., 2006; Carrier et al., 2010; and Katerndahl et al., 2009), number of hours worked per week (Bogue et al., 2007; and Linzer et al, 2000), spending adequate time with patients (DeVoe et al, 2002; and Katerndahl et al., 2009), practice type (Grembowski et al., 2003; Thomson-Reuters, 2011; and Warren et al., 1998) and pediatric specialty (Keeton et al., 2007; Leigh et al., 2002; and McMurray et al., 2000), these control variables were included and expected to be statistically significant. It was important to isolate these variables from the effect of the independent variables upon the dependent variable, job satisfaction.

Administrative Variables

Four administrative variables have been shown through literature review to be important in maintaining control over practice details as well as patients' health data (Bobula, 1980; Lichtenstein, 1984; Leigh et al., 2002; McMurray et al., 2000; and Smola & Sutton, 2002). This portion of the model includes utilization of information technology in the pursuit of global practice efficacy and reduced workweeks. Variables include availability and usage of technology, usage of patient reports, effect of following protocols and number of patient visits per week. Generational literature led the researcher to believe GENX physicians would be most satisfied in a more administrative and technology-rich employment situation (Cennamo & Gardner, 2008; Noble & Schewe, 2003; Parry & Urwin, 2011; Pew, 2014; and Smola & Sutton, 2002). Specifically, documented GENX comfort with technology and ability to learn quickly lend support for this model (Pew, 2014; and SHRM, 2004).

Economic Success Variables

The bulk of the literature reviewed for this study reinforced the importance of economic success as a source of physician job satisfaction (Bobula, 1986; Buchbinder et al., 2001; Grembowski et al., 2003; Katerndahl et al., 2009; Lichtenstein, 1984; and Linzer et al., 2000). Economic success is influenced by income and ownership interests in the practice, as well as eligibility for bonuses and incentives. It is expected that economic variables offer the best explanatory power in predicting BABYBOOM physician satisfaction, based upon generational literature emphasizing this generation's priorities, attitudes, and higher average household income. BABYBOOMers are results driven and find work central to their lives (Cennamo & Gardner, 2008; Gursoy et al., 2008; Jurkiewicz & Bradley, 2002; Noble & Schewe, 2003; Parry & Urwin, 2011; SHRM, 2004; and Smola & Sutton, 2002). Income is an important benchmark for physicians; salary is a relative measure of value, status and equity within the organization. Income is negatively correlated with age in that younger physicians tend to earn lower salaries. Younger physicians tend to feel less well compensated for their education, effort and time commitment, and also experience greater financial constraints through debt repayment obligations. It should be noted that 22 percent of the BABYBOOM physicians surveyed for this study earned more than $300,000. Only 14.5 percent of TRAD physicians and 16 percent of GENX physicians earned more than $300,000 in 2008. Literature reviewed here led to the hypothesis that BABYBOOM physicians would be most satisfied in an environment that fulfilled their financial goals.

Excellence of Care Variables

Variables associated with Excellence of Care have been shown to be important in providing optimal patient-centered care (Epstein & Street, 2011; Mead & Bower, 2002; and Mitchie, Miles & Weinman, 2003), including providing high quality care to all patients, donating hours to charity care, considering patients' out-of-pocket costs when ordering diagnostic tests and being informed, in the pursuit of continuity of care, when patients consult other. The Excellence of Care portion of the model is intended to most accurately reflect a participatory relationship that includes facilitating patient understanding and improved health outcomes through communication and interaction (Gerteis, Edgeman-Levitan, Daly & Delbanco, 1993; Epstein & Peters, 2009; and Lichtenstein, 1984). Literature reviewed for this study indicates doctors who entered the practice of medicine prior to the advent of many technologically advanced diagnostic tools likely entered the practice of medicine to help others. It is theorized male and female TRAD physicians will value settings where they can give maximum effort (SHRM, 2004) and converse one-on-one with patients rather than embrace a technology-mediated office visit (Czaja, Charness, Hertzog, Nair, Rogers & Sharit, 2006).

Data, Methods and Model Output

The researcher used STATA to perform an ordinal logistic regression (OLR) on data gathered by the Center for Studying Health System Change in 2008. The Center mailed a survey to a sample of American Medical Association (AMA) members. The survey collected personal and practice setting information for 4,720 physicians and was used to build a statistical model in concert with independent variables associated with generational and job satisfaction literature. The dependent variable is job satisfaction among U.S. physicians.

Data was analyzed in a step-wise fashion in order to ascertain how statistical significance changed and contributed to explanatory power as variables related to Administrative, Economic Success, and Excellence of Care were added to control variables. This process allowed the researcher to examine and analyze how significance of variables changed when gender and generation were included. Tables 3A and 3BCdisplay output used to test hypotheses related to gender and generation. Table 3A illustrates the full model for physicians of all ages and both genders. Table 3B runs the same model for female physicians only. One subsequent table (Table 4) and discussion will break out statistically significant variables for comparison and will reflect differences in generation and gender, as well as the suitability of the model in explaining manipulable variables contributing to job satisfaction.

Table 3A presents output for all physicians. Control variables are listed first, followed by four Administrative variables, then four variables associated with Economic Success, and finally, four variables associated with Excellence of Care.

Discussion of Control Variables and Model without Gender or Generation

It is clear when viewing output from Table 3A that control variables hold their statistical significance as additional variables are stepped into the full model. In accordance with earlier empirical findings, income, reduction in malpractice concerns, reduction in hours spent per week in medical care, adequate time spent with patients, and a pediatric specialty are important contributors to, and predictors of, job satisfaction among physicians participating in this study. Most of the variance in the model is attributed to these seven variables.

Not surprisingly, the odds of being satisfied increase by 19 percent for every one-unit ($50,000) increase in income, by 33 percent for a one-unit increase from 4 to 5 on a 5-point scale in having adequate time with patients, and by 74 percent if specializing in pediatrics. Income will also be examined by gender and generation later in this chapter for greater clarity in income's relationship with job satisfaction, as will the statistical significance for female physicians of spending adequate time with patients. These results are consistent with literature, and illustrate the importance to physicians of earning acceptable compensation while providing excellent care.

Both malpractice concerns and working more than 40 hours per week are negatively and significantly related to job satisfaction. The odds of being satisfied drop by 21 percent for a one-unit increase from 4 to 5 on a 5-point scale in fear of malpractice lawsuits, and 2 percent for every additional 10 hours (one-unit) spent at work per week. Clearly physicians are negatively and significantly impacted by their malpractice worries, and increasing pressure to work more hours per week likely exacerbates these fears.

Table 3a. Model Output for All Physicians

Control, Administrative, Economic Success, and Excellence of Care				
Career Satisfaction	**Odds Ratio**	**Std. Err.**	**Z**	**P>**
Control Variables				
Income	1.193744	.0336043	6.29	0.000***
Years in Practice	1.005417	.0041864	1.30	0.195
Malpractice Concerns	.7854806	.0351661	-5.39	0.000***
Hours spent per week in medical care	.9889369	.0027202	-4.04	0.000***
Time spent with patients	1.338688	.0469898	8.31	0.000***
Small practice	1.027472	.0351241	0.79	0.428
Pediatrics Specialty	1.738328	.2389713	4.02	0.000***
Administrative Variables				
IT available and used	1.1600489	.0655968	2.63	0.008**
Usage of patient reports	1.182379	.1068334	1.85	0.064
Effect of following protocols	1.005272	.0265988	0.20	0.842
Number of patient visits per week	1.001887	.0009761	1.93	0.053
Economic Success Variables				
Bonus	1.108518	.0879367	1.30	0.194
Competition Type	1.057879	.0469013	1.27	0.204
Practice Owner	1.042008	.126062	0.34	0.734
Practice Owned by Physicians Only	.7680003	.0907577	-2.23	0.026*
Excellence of Care Variables				
Provide high level of care to all patients	1.413265	.0560178	8.73	0.000***
Donate hours to charity care	1.000619	.0030314	0.20	0.838
Aware of all physicians caring for patient	.8934728	.0452558	-2.22	0.026*
Consider diagnostic costs to patients	1.085427	.039261	2.27	0.023*

N=2,541, Pseudo $R^2 = 0.0847$, Chi-square (19) = 510.12, p<0.0000

Control variables: Income, years in practice, malpractice concerns, hours per week spent in medical care, adequate time spent with patients, practice type, and pediatric specialty.

Administrative Model variables: Availability and usage of technology, usage of patient reports, effect of following protocols, being informed when patients visit other physicians.

Economic Success Model variables: Bonus, competition type, practice ownership, practice owned exclusively by physicians.

Excellence of Care Model variables: Providing high quality care to all patients, number of patient visits per week, donating hours to charity care, and considering cost of diagnostics to patients.

*Correlation is statistically significant at p<.05.

**Correlation is statistically significant at p<.01.

***Correlation is statistically significant at p<.001.

Two of the seven control variables are not statistically significant in the full output. Practice type and years in practice are not significant in the overall model, but the researcher expects these two variables to be significant when generational and gender output is examined. Literature has supported the hypothesis that years in practice will be negatively statistically significant for GENX male physicians and working in a small practice will be positively statistically significant for BABYBOOM female physicians.

Both access to technology and usage of patient reports are considered administrative tasks, and are therefore included among the Administrative variables. Only one variable is significant for the full population of physicians participating in this study: Availability and usage of IT. The odds of a physician being satisfied increase by 16 percent if IT is available and used rather than unavailable or available but not used. Most practices, hospitals, laboratories, and health systems require use of IT if it is provided as a mechanism for billing, patient records, prescriptions, etc. The requirement and use of IT can reduce autonomy as well as medical errors leading to malpractice suits. Physicians may also be less satisfied if they are not able to access IT as a way to reduce time devoted to administrative tasks. Researchers expected physician satisfaction to increase if they also utilize patient reports in the movement toward efficiency and accuracy in medicine, but it is not statistically significant. This finding is interpreted to mean physicians are displeased to have less time with patients. Spending more time producing and reading reports reduces time available for office visits. It is also surprising that following protocols and number of patient visits were not statistically significant, either positively for younger physicians or negatively for older physicians. It is reasonable to conclude that following protocols is required for malpractice insurance coverage, and that seeing more patients per week is a financial imperative for practices.

Only one Economic Success variable is statistically significant for all physicians. Physician ownership of the practice is negatively associated with satisfaction; the odds of being satisfied drop by 26 percent if the practice is owned solely by physicians. There are several possibilities for this finding. First, literature shows physicians are drawn into the profession to provide medical care. They are not trained to administer a business and may be frustrated in dedicating limited time to patient care and focusing more time on staffing, accounting, record keeping, risk management, operations and maintenance of buildings and equipment. Second, physician ownership increases economic uncertainty. While there is greater income potential when physicians do not share profits with other entities, there is greater risk involved individually as well. Greater risk most likely reduces satisfaction. Because financial incentives, competitive practices, and ownership have been linked to physician satisfaction in literature reviewed here, it is likely all four Economic Success variables will be statistically significant among BABYBOOM and TRAD males. This will likely not hold true for GENX male physicians because while they expect to earn an equivalent salary and salary may be part of the reason they initially pursued a medical career, they became physicians because they wish to provide excellent care and are idealistic about that calling.

Finally, three of the four Excellence of Care variables are statistically significant in the overall model. Because medicine is referred to as the ultimate caring profession this model was expected to reflect the original reason physicians are attracted to the profession. The odds of being satisfied rise by 46 percent per one-unit increase from 4 to 5 on a 5-point scale in the physician's belief that he/she provides high quality care to all patients. Odds also increase – but only by 1 percent – for each one-unit increase from 4 to 5 on a 5-point scale in considering patients' out-of-pocket costs for diagnostic tests. This relatively small increase may seem inconsequential but is reflective of a physician's concern for his/her patients' physical and financial wellbeing. Being informed when patients consult other physicians is negatively and statistically significant. The odds of being satisfied drop by 11 percent for a one-unit decrease from sometimes to seldom/never knowing when patients consult other physicians.

As has Table 3A, Table 3B displays the full statistical output but focuses only on satisfaction among female physicians. Differences due to being female will be gleaned through comparison of Table 3B (749 female physicians) to Table 3A (2,541 physicians of both genders). Generation is not included in this comparison of job satisfaction variables. Following Table 3B, discussion will compare and contrast statistical significance among variables as reflected by three generations of female survey respondents.

Table 3b. Model for All Female Physicians

Control, Administrative, Economic Success, Excellence of Care				
Career Satisfaction	**Odds Ratio**	**Std. Err.**	**Z**	**P>**
Control Variables				
Income	1.259791	.0748277	3.89	0.000***
Years in Practice	1.002369	.0096824	0.24	0.806
Malpractice Concerns	.8367323	.0705017	-2.12	0.034*
Hours spent per week in medical care	.9811607	.0054466	-3.43	0.001***
Time spent with patients	1.434108	.0933877	5.54	0.000***
Small Practice	1.118349	.067064	1.87	0.62
Pediatrics Specialty	1.638229	.3172041	2.55	0.011*
Administrative Variables				
IT available and used	1.113995	.1264123	0.95	0.341
Usage of patient reports	1.035485	.1779099	0.20	0.839
Effect of following protocols	1.011605	.0485827	0.24	0.810
Number of patient visits per week	1.002699	.0018329	1.47	0.140
Economic Success Variables				
Bonus	1.086723	.1624961	0.56	0.578
Competition Type	1.097346	.0919641	1.11	0.268
Practice Owner	1.004143	.2172026	0.02	0.985
Practice Owned by Physicians Only	.9058775	.1790747	-.050	0.617
Excellence of Care				
Provide high level of care to all patients	1.301729	.0956743	3.59	0.000***
Donate hours to charity care	.999414	.0048805	-0.12	0.904
Aware of all physicians caring for patient	.8785477	.0824333	-1.38	0.168
Consider diagnostic costs to patients	1.046397	.072207	0.66	0.511

N=749, Pseudo $R^2 = 0.0870$, Chi-square (19) = 156.04, p<0.0000

Control variables: Income, years in practice, malpractice concerns, hours per week spent in medical care, adequate time spent with patients, practice type, and pediatric specialty.

Model variables: Availability and usage of technology, usage of patient reports, effect of following protocols, being informed when patients visit other physicians, bonus, competition type, practice ownership, practice owned exclusively by physicians, providing high quality care to all patients, number of patient visits per week, donating hours to charity care, and considering cost of diagnostics to patients.

*Correlation is statistically significant at p<.05.

**Correlation is statistically significant at p<.01.

***Correlation is statistically significant at p<.001.

Discussion of Model for All Female Physicians

As expected, female physicians echo control variable findings in Table 3A. The same variables – income, malpractice concerns, hours worked per week, spending adequate time with patients, and being a pediatrician – are statistically significant in Table 3B. Just as with the general sample, malpractice concerns and number of hours worked per week beyond 40 are negative predictors. Literature shows that female physicians are paid less than their male counterparts, so it isn't surprising that the odds of satisfaction rise by 26 percent (compared to 17 percent in the overall sample) for each one-unit ($50,000) increase in income. This is important because equity is relative, not absolute, as illustrated by Brosnan and de Waal's capuchin monkey experiments (2014). A sense of fairness has developed in social institutions in order to ensure continued cooperation and must be considered by physician employers who wish to minimize conflict through proportionality, especially during a time of physician undersupply. Females are relatively less concerned about malpractice suits than males. The odds of being satisfied fall by 17 percent for women for each one-unit increase in malpractice worries, compared to 27 percent for males and 24 percent for the overall population of physicians. This finding illustrates that female physicians have more confidence in their abilities to communicate with patients, show more empathy, foster greater understanding, trust, and elicit patient compliance with treatment plans. Female physicians are also more likely to be satisfied by spending adequate time with patients. The art of healing requires a positive patient-physician relationship, and building such a relationship takes time. Literature reviewed here has highlighted this link between time with patients and satisfaction, and this study confirms these findings. Odds of satisfaction increase by 43 percent for each one-unit increase (10 hours per week) in time spent with patients, compared with 27 percent for men and 29 percent for the overall physician respondents. These findings point to essential differences in satisfiers between the sexes. Both are more satisfied when providing high quality care. However, male physicians derive greater job satisfaction in drawing a higher salary and less satisfaction when worried about malpractice, working longer weeks and sharing practice ownership. Female physicians find satisfaction in spending more time with patients and working fewer hours, likely in an effort to balance other responsibilities. Administrative variables are not statistically significant for female physicians, and contrary to the overall population of physicians as predicted for the Economic Success grouping of variables, their satisfaction is not reduced by being a practice owner. As for Excellence of Care, it was expected that female physicians would most closely fit this model. However, providing high quality care to all patients was the only statistically significant variable. Odds of being satisfied rise by 30 percent for each one-unit increase from 4 to 5 on a 5-point scale in the belief she is providing high quality care to all patients. This contrasts with a 40 percent increase in the combined sample and a 46 percent increase in the male physician population. This finding is interpreted to mean female physicians do not have enough time to spend with patients and this lack of time impacts their perception of quality of care. Table 4 shows statistical significance by both gender and generation.

Discussion of Overall Significance for Generation and Gender

Table 4 highlights several statistically significant generational findings. Younger physicians enjoy the same level of job satisfaction as older generations. Older physicians are less worried about malpractice and derive more satisfaction from income, spending adequate time with patients, and providing high quality care to all patients. Physicians generally are more satisfied with practices employing three or more physicians, and pediatricians are more satisfied than physicians in other specialties. Earning a higher income, spending adequate time with patients, and providing high quality care are important satisfiers and may be eroded by malpractice concerns and too many hours per week spent at work.

Table 4. Model Statistical Significance

	Gender and Generation					
	Males (N=1792)			Females (N=749)		
	GENX (N=510)	BABY BOOM (N=1096)	TRAD (N=186)	GENX (N=360)	BABY BOOM (N=370)	TRAD (N=19)
Control						
Income	✓	✓			✓	
Years in Prac	✓	✓				
Malpractice	✓	✓				
Hours		✓		✓	✓	
Small Prac					✓	
Adequate time	✓	✓		✓	✓	
Pediatrician		✓	✓		✓	
Administrative						
Technology						
Reports						
Protocols						
Patient visits						
Economic						
Bonus						
Ownership						
Competition						
Other owners		✓				
Excellence of Care						
High quality	✓	✓	✓	✓		
Charity care						
Aware of care						
Diagnostic $			✓			

SOLUTIONS AND RECOMMENDATIONS

Institutional arrangements affect women differently than men. Therefore, gender matters in workforce planning. Female physicians experience greater satisfaction not in income or other economic success factors necessarily, but rather in spending adequate time with patients and providing high quality care. Earning a higher income is a statistically significant satisfier for BABYBOOM females, but not for GENX female physicians. Therefore, attempts by employers to attract younger females solely with higher salary packages are not likely to succeed. This finding does not defend the standard practice of paying female physicians 26 percent less than their colleagues. In fact, satisfaction among female physicians rises with higher – not necessarily fair – pay.

Satisfaction is more complicated for female physicians. They deserve to earn the same as their male counterparts, and are motivated by the opportunity to provide higher quality care and by more flexibility so they can respond to other life demands. Older female physicians feel differently. They expect to be paid well, and their satisfaction depends somewhat on income; however, they are more likely to be pediatricians who are satisfied with smaller practices, and respond favorably to having adequate time for patients. BABYBOOM female physicians appear to be more businesslike and perhaps less idealistic in that providing high quality care to all patients is not statistically significant in this study. A lack of statistically significant malpractice worries indicates they believe their ability to communicate will alleviate patient dissatisfaction and prevent harm resulting in lawsuits.

Female physicians, unlike males, are not as accepting of long workweeks. Questions about other obligations were not included in this study; however, literature shows women have obligations outside of work that demand time and attention. While female physicians included in this study are generally satisfied with their jobs, they may feel overwhelmed with personal and professional responsibilities. BABYBOOMer female physicians may also have been influenced by traditional societal views of women as caregivers rather than as breadwinners. Employers may be able to assist in reducing stress by offering employment benefits designed to minimize distractions for all physicians. These benefits may include on-site and after-hours daycare, financial advice such as how to pursue loan forgiveness programs and health-related facilities such as fitness centers and counseling services.

Satisfaction for male physicians of all ages appears unaffected by Administrative and most Economic Success factors. Satisfaction factors are much easier to trace for BABYBOOM males. They are positively and significantly satisfied by income, being a pediatrician, and providing high quality care, and negatively and significantly impacted by malpractice concerns, number of work hours, and sharing practice ownership with other physicians. Constructing jobs for male physicians may be more straightforward for healthcare systems. Offering opportunities for mentoring and reverse mentoring, where younger physicians coach older physicians in how to use new techniques and technologies, may engage physicians of all generations, encourage interaction and reduce conflict.

LIMITATIONS

Data for this study were collected in 2008, a time when GENX physicians were just settling into their practices. The Center for Studying Health System Change data is the most recent full dataset available that reflects job satisfaction among a population that is difficult to survey. Physicians' work schedules are demanding and time is scarce. Participating in a survey represents a high opportunity cost to them. Physicians are also considered an elite population and consequently are frequently approached by surveyors. Gatekeepers may protect their time; therefore, physicians are 10 percent less likely to respond to surveys than the general population (Cummings, Savitz & Konrad, 2001; and Flanigan, McFarlane & Cook, 2008).

There is insufficient data collected about how changes wrought by the 2010 Affordable Care Act have impacted physicians' job satisfaction. From a workforce perspective, it is vital to collect timely data in order to measure satisfaction and forecast committed workforce membership; it is even more important during a pandemic. While a model predicting job satisfaction among GENX physicians in the U.S. is possible, the variables analyzed in this study may not be sufficient to make reliable predictions.

Moreover, it is likely that BABYBOOM physicians are retiring and have detached from day-to-day considerations of their career trajectories, which leaves GENX and Millennial physicians to cope with fast-paced changes in technology, integration and outside involvement (malpractice concerns, payor intervention, and policy evolution) when making decisions. Literature has revealed that physicians' autonomy has decreased due to protocols put in place in response to legal, financial and best-practices developments.

Perhaps the most important limitation is the generalizability of the study's findings to physicians practicing around the world. Physicians are the most respected and well paid profession in the United States (ValueWalk, 2019). They have been guided and safeguarded by the AMA since 1847. According to a survey conducted by the Varkey Foundation and the University of Sussex, licensed and certified physicians require years of education and training, stand between life and death and enjoy the resultant status and monetary compensation (ValueWalk, 2019). However, respect for physicians has dropped substantially in countries such as India and China. A 2019 article published in the *National Medical Journal of India* reported deteriorating doctor-patient relationships. "Several changes in the Indian medical care system, as well as society, have also affected the doctor-patient relationship. Pharmaceutical and medical device companies have become aggressive in marketing their wares. Corporate hospitals are taking over as medical care-providers in urban areas. Since healthcare affects everyone, it has attracted the attention of the government—to regulate it—and the media, which loves to use all those involved in healthcare as its favourite whipping boys" (Anand, 2019). In China, the percentage of young practicing physicians in public healthcare fell by 9 percent and the percentage of older doctors increased by 9 percent due to low pay, overwork and conflict with patients (Dandan, 2019). Approximately 100,000 violent incidents directed at medical professionals in China's public health system are reported annually (Dandan, 2019). In fact, the Chinese Medical Doctor Association published a white paper in 2011 disclosing that 78 percent of Chinese doctors did not want their children to choose the same profession (Cao, 2011).

FUTURE RESEARCH DIRECTIONS

There are many ways that pay gaps impact females generally and female physicians especially. Physicians take on enormous debt as they complete undergraduate and medical school training. Nearly 75 percent of medical school graduates borrow money for tuition and living expenses. The average student loan, according to the Association of American Medical College (AAMC), is $200,000 (2019). One of the long-term effects of the gender pay gap is that female college graduates are able to pay off 33 percent of their debt within five years of graduation. Male college graduates, by virtue of their higher salaries, are able to retire 44 percent of their student loans within five years of graduation (Whaley, 2018). Thus, college-educated females carry debt for longer periods. The other long-term effect is retirement income. According to an analysis of the U.S. pay discrepancy in 2017, UBS Wealth Management reports the lifetime income of females is 38 percent less than males at age 85 (Whaley, 2019).

Reviewing income inequality data by state or country has pointed researchers to the influence social environment plays in health (Marmot, 2002). It is possible that as physician income equalizes, the social environment and living standards may reduce health inequalities as well. Thus, income equality for physicians may improve health beyond physicians' abilities to supply high-quality care. We must continue to track income equality among physicians, investigate the important link between income equality and health outcomes and educate healthcare decisionmakers about inequalities.

Job satisfaction continues to be important as young generations move from job to job. Measuring their satisfaction and seeking ways to craft policies to meet their needs for work-life balance will also contribute to workforce maintenance. Through identifying and addressing emerging professional issues that impact women in medicine should be part of the AMA's efforts on behalf of female physician advocacy and policy.

CONCLUSION

Until gender pay gaps are addressed global health will continue to be an issue. Not only do pay gaps impact poverty levels and poverty levels affect wellbeing, but gaps influence societal wellbeing in myriad ways. In this chapter, research shows the pay gap may drive younger and female physicians away from choosing and persisting in the profession that is vital in delivering healthcare. Data analyzed in this chapter shows definitively – by generation and gender – which work variables affected job satisfaction among U.S. physicians before the Affordable Care Act was passed in the United States and today's Millennial physicians began their medical residencies. Some variables positively affect satisfaction and others negatively impact satisfaction. Data point out the importance of monitoring levels of satisfaction and implementing administrative approaches designed to build satisfaction during a period of profound change in an environment buffeted by a dearth of doctors in disease-ravaged regions, dependence upon technology, demographic change, complexity of care challenges, malpractice fears and even workplace dangers caused by pandemics.

Although other studies have noted physicians' growing dissatisfaction with their careers, the professionals who participated in the survey appeared satisfied. The points of dissatisfaction were inadequate remuneration, work invaded personal time and heavy workloads induced stress. Routinely, there is a need for organizations to examine the impact of their structures, policies, and procedures on quality of life for physicians.

Public health services and private health systems must pay attention to job satisfaction, implement human resource management strategies to protect their workers and recognize that professionals are autonomous individuals with rights and sometimes crushing responsibilities.

REFERENCES

Anand, A. (2019). Indian healthcare at a crossroads (Part 1): Deteriorating doctor-patient relationship. *The National Medical Journal of India*, *32*(1), 41–45. http://www.nmji.in/article.asp?issn=0970-258X;year=2019;volume=32;issue=1;spage=41;epage=45;aulast=Anand#ft22 PMID:31823941

Association of American Medical Colleges. (2018). An exploration of the recent decline in the percentage of U.S. medical school graduates with education debt. *Analysis in Brief*, *18*(4). Retrieved from https://www.aamc.org/system/files/reports/1/september2018anexplorationoftherecentdeclineinthepercentageofu.pdf

Bawakid, K., Rashid, O., Mandoura, N., Shah, H., & Mugharbel, K. (2018). Professional satisfaction of family physicians working in primary healthcare centers: A comparison of two Saudi regions. *Journal of Family Medicine and Primary Care*, *7*(5), 1019–1025. https://www.ncbi.nlm.nih.gov/pmc/articles/PMC6259539/ PMID:30598950

Bobula, J. (1980). Work patterns, practice characteristics, and incomes of male and female physicians. *Journal of Medical Education*, *55*, 826–833. PMID:7420390

Bodur, S. (2001). Job satisfaction of health care staff employed at health centres in Turkey. *Society of Occupational Medicine*, *52*(6), 353-355. Retrieved from https://bit.ly/37EsEhF

Bovier, P., & Perneger, T. (2004). Predictors of work satisfaction among physicians. *European Journal of Public Health*, *13*(4), 299–305. doi:10.1093/eurpub/13.4.299 PMID:14703315

Boyle, P. (2020). *U.S. physician shortage growing*. Association of American Medical Colleges. Retrieved from https://www.aamc.org/news-insights/us-physician-shortage-growing

Buchbinder, S., Melick, C., & Powe, N. (2001). Managed care and primary care physicians' overall career satisfaction. *Journal of Health Care Finance*, *23*(2), 35–44. PMID:11794755

Burke, M. (2004). Generational difference survey report. Society for Human Resource Management. Alexandria, VA: SHRM Research Department.

Cabot, R. (2015). Women in medicine. *Journal of the American Medical Association*, *314*(10), 1076. doi:10.1001/jama.2014.11972 PMID:26348764

Cao, X. (2011). The Chinese Medical Doctor Association: A new industrial relations actor in China's Health Services? *Relations Industrielles. Industrial Relations*, *66*(1), 74–97. doi:10.7202/1005106ar

Cennamo, L., & Gardner, D. (2008). Generational differences in work values, outcomes and person-organization values fit. *Journal of Managerial Psychology*, *23*(8), 891–906. doi:10.1108/02683940810904385

Center for Studying Health System Change. (2008). *Health tracking physician survey*. Retrieved from http://www.hschange.org/CONTENT/1085

Collins, K., Schoen, C., & Sandman, D. (1997). *The Commonwealth fund survey of physician experience with managed care*. Commonwealth Fund. Retrieved from http://www.cmwf.org/ programs/health_care/physrvy.asp

Commins, J. (2017). US physician workforce is getting old, fast. *HealthLeaders*. Retrieved from https://www.healthleadersmedia.com/strategy/us-physician-workforce-getting-old-fast

Czaja, S., Charness, N., Fisk, A., Hertzog, C., Nair, S., Rogers, W., & Sharit, J. (2006). Factors predicting the use of technology: Findings from the Center for Research and Education on Aging and Technology Enhancement. *Psychology and Aging*, *21*(2), 333–352. doi:10.1037/0882-7974.21.2.333 PMID:16768579

Emmons, S., Nichols, M., Schulkin, J., James, K., & Cain, J. (2006). The influence of physician gender on practice satisfaction among obstetrician gynecologists. *American Journal of Obstetrics and Gynecology*, *194*(6), 1728–1739. doi:10.1016/j.ajog.2006.03.012 PMID:16635457

Epstein, R., & Peters, E. (2007). Beyond information: Exploring patients' preferences. *Journal of the Medical Association*, *302*(2), 195–197. doi:10.1001/jama.2009.984 PMID:19584351

Frank, E., McMurray, J., Linzer, M., & Elon, L. (1999). Career satisfaction of US women physicians: Results from the women physicians' health study. *Archives of Internal Medicine*, *159*(3), 1417–1426. doi:10.1001/archinte.159.13.1417 PMID:10399893

Gerteis, M., Edgeman-Levitan, S., Daly, J., & Delbanco, T. (1993). *Through the patient's eyes: Understanding and promoting patient-centered care*. Jossey-Bass.

Grembowski, D., Ulrich, C., Paschane, D., Diehr, P., Katon, W., Martin, D., Patrick, D., & Velicer, C. (2003). Managed care and primary physician satisfaction. *Journal of the American Board of Family Medicine*, *16*(5), 383–393. doi:10.3122/jabfm.16.5.383 PMID:14645328

Gursoy, D., Maier, T., & Chi, C. (2008). Generational differences: An examination of work values and generational gaps in the hospitality workforce. *International Journal of Hospitality Management*, *27*(3), 448–458. doi:10.1016/j.ijhm.2007.11.002

Hojat, M., Gonnella, J., Nasca, T., Mangione, S., Vergare, M., & Magee, M. (2002). *Physician empathy: Definition, components, measurement, and relationship to gender and specialty.* Center for Research in Medical Education and Health Care. Retrieved from http://jdc.jefferson.edu/cgi/viewcontent.cgi?article=1003&context=crmehc

Jovic, E., Wallace, J. E., & Lemaire, J. (2006). The generation and gender shifts in medicine: An exploratory survey of internal medicine physicians. *BMC Health Services Research*, *5*(May), 55. doi:10.1186/1472-6963-6-55 PMID:16677387

Jurkiewicz, C., & Bradley, D. (2002). Generational ethics: Age cohort and healthcare executives' values. *HEC Forum*, *14*(2), 148–171. doi:10.1023/A:1020907731617 PMID:12141008

Kaiser Family Foundation. (2015). *Distribution of physicians by gender*. Retrieved from http://kff.org/other/state-indicator/physicians-by-gender/#table

Kaldenberg, D., Becker, B., & Zvonkovic, A. (1995). Work and commitment among young professionals: A study of male and female dentists. *Human Relations*, *48*(11), 1355–1377. doi:10.1177/001872679504801106

Katerndahl, D., Parchman, M., & Wood, R. (2009). Perceived complexity of care, perceived autonomy, and career satisfaction among primary care physicians. *Journal of the American Board of Family Medicine*, *22*(1), 24–33. doi:10.3122/jabfm.2009.01.080027 PMID:19124630

Keeton, K., Fenner, D., Johnson, T., & Hayward, R. (2007). Predictors of physician career satisfaction, work-life balance, and burnout. *Obstetrics and Gynecology*, *109*(4), 949–955. doi:10.1097/01.AOG.0000258299.45979.37 PMID:17400859

Keltgen, J. (2016). *The impact of generational and gender effects on physician satisfaction in the US* (Doctoral dissertation). University of South Dakota.

Konrad, T., Williams, E., Linzer, M., McMurray, J., Pathman, D., Gerrity, M., Schwartz, M., Scheckler, W., Van Kirk, J., Rhodes, E., & Douglas, J. (1999). Measuring physician job satisfaction in a changing workplace and a challenging environment. *Medical Care*, *37*(11), 1174–1182. doi:10.1097/00005650-199911000-00010 PMID:10549620

Lancaster, L., & Stillman, D. (2003). *When generations collide*. Harper Business.

Langwell, K. (1982). Factors affecting the incomes of men and women physicians: Further explorations. *The Journal of Human Resources*, *17*(2), 261–275. doi:10.2307/145472 PMID:7130708

Leigh, J., Kravitz, R., Schembri, M., Samuels, S., & Mobley, S. (2002). Physician career satisfaction across specialties. *Archives of Internal Medicine*, *162*(14), 1577–1584. doi:10.1001/archinte.162.14.1577 PMID:12123400

Lichtenstein, R. (1984). Measuring the job satisfaction of physicians in organized settings. *Medical Care*, *22*(1), 56–68. doi:10.1097/00005650-198401000-00005 PMID:6694460

Linzer, M., Konrad, T., Douglas, J., McMurray, J., Pathman, D., Williams, E., Schwartz, M., Gerrity, M., Scheckler, W., Bigby, J., & Rhodes, E. (2000). Managed care, time pressure and physician job satisfaction: Results from the physician worklife study. *Journal of General Internal Medicine*, *5*(7), 441–449. doi:10.1046/j.1525-1497.2000.05239.x PMID:10940129

Lo Sasso, A., Richards, M., Chou, C., & Gerber, S. (2011). The $16,819 pay gap for newly trained physicians: The unexplained trend of men earning more than women. *Health Affairs*, *30*(2), 193–201. doi:10.1377/hlthaff.2010.0597 PMID:21289339

Loury, G. (1977). A dynamic theory of racial income differences. In P. Wallace & A. Lamond (Eds.), *Women, Minorities, and employment discrimination* (pp. 153–186). Heath.

Marmot, M. (2002). The influence of income on health: Views of an epidemiologist. *Health Affairs*, *21*(2), 31–46. doi:10.1377/hlthaff.21.2.31 PMID:11900185

McMurray, J., Linzer, M., Konrad, T., Douglas, J., Shugerman, R., & Nelson, K. (2000). The work lives of women physicians. *Journal of General Internal Medicine*, *15*, 372–380. PMID:10886471

Mead, N., & Bower, P. (2002). Patient-centered consultations and outcomes in primary care: A review of the literature. *Patient Education and Counseling*, *48*(1), 51–61. doi:10.1016/S0738-3991(02)00099-X PMID:12220750

Medscape. (2019). *International physician compensation report 2019: Do US physician have it best?* Retrieved from https://www.medscape.com/slideshow/2019-international-compensation-report-6011814#5

Michie, S., Miles, J., & Weinman, J. (2003). Patient-centredness in chronic illness: What is it and does it matter? *Patient Education and Counseling*, *51*(3), 197–206. doi:10.1016/S0738-3991(02)00194-5 PMID:14630376

Noble, S., & Schewe, C. (2003). Cohort segmentation: An exploration of its validity. *Journal of Business Research*, *56*(12), 979–987. doi:10.1016/S0148-2963(02)00268-0

Parry, E., & Urwin, P. (2011). Generational differences in work values: A review of theory and evidence. *International Journal of Management Reviews*, *13*(1), 79–96. doi:10.1111/j.1468-2370.2010.00285.x

Pathman, D., Konrad, T., Williams, E., Scheckler, W., Linzer, M., & Douglas, J. (2002). Physician job satisfaction, job dissatisfaction, and physician turnover. *The Journal of Family Practice*, *51*, •••. https://www.mdedge.com/familymedicine/article/65406/physician-job-satisfaction-job-dissatisfaction-and-physician-turnover PMID:12160487

Pew Research Center. (2010). *Baby Boomers retire*. Retrieved from www.pewresearch.org/daily-number/baby-boomers-retire

Pew Research Center. (2014a). *Generation X: America's neglected middle child.* Retrieved from http://www.pewresearch.org/fact-tank/2014/06/05/generation-x- americas-neglected-middle-child/

Pew Research Center. (2014b). *Millennials in adulthood: Detached from institutions, networked with friends*. Retrieved from https://www.pewsocialtrends.org/2014/03/07/millennials-in-adulthood/

Reid, R., Friedberg, M., Adams, J., McGlynn, E., & Mehrotra, A. (2010). Associations between physician characteristics and quality of care. *Archives of Internal Medicine, 170*(16), 1442–1449. doi:10.1001/archinternmed.2010.307 PMID:20837830

Richardson, A., & Burke, R. (1991). Occupational stress and job satisfaction among physicians: Sex differences. *Social Science & Medicine, 33*(10), 1179–1187. doi:10.1016/0277-9536(91)90234-4 PMID:1767288

Ryder, N. (1965). The cohort as a concept in the study of social change. *American Sociological Review, 30*(6), 843–861. doi:10.2307/2090964 PMID:5846306

Sasser, A. (2005). Gender differences in physician pay tradeoffs between career and family. *The Journal of Human Resources, 40*(2), 477–504. doi:10.3368/jhr.XL.2.477

Smith, Y. (2019). *Physician shortage. News-Medical.net*. Retrieved from https://www.news-medical.net/health/Physician-Shortage.aspx

Smola, K., & Sutton, C. (2002). Generational differences: Revisiting generational work values for the new millennium. *Journal of Organizational Behavior, 23*(4), 363–382. doi:10.1002/job.147

Solberg, I. (2017). *Doctors' job satisfaction during early career and economic recession: Prospective and cross-national studies in Norway and Iceland*. Retrieved from https://www.duo.uio.no/handle/10852/57453

Sparks, A. (2012). Psychological empowerment and job satisfaction between Baby Boomer and Generation X nurses. *Journal of Nursing Management, 20*(4), 451–460. doi:10.1111/j.1365-2834.2011.01282.x PMID:22591147

Spector, N. (2018). The doctor is out? Why physicians are leaving their practices to pursue other careers. *NBC News*. Retrieved from https://www.nbcnews.com/business/business-news/doctor-out-why-physicians-are-leaving-their-practices-pursue-other-n900921

Strauss, V. (2014, January 10). America's oldest working teacher turns 100. *Washington Post*. Retrieved from http://www.washingtonpost.com/blogs/answer- sheet/wp/2014/01/10/americas-oldest-working-teacher-turns-100

Strauss, W., & Howe, N. (1997). *The fourth turning: What the cycles of history tell us about America's next rendezvous with destiny*. Broadway Books.

Suliman, A., Eltom, M., Elmadhoun, W., Noor, S., Almobarak, A., Osman, M., Awadalla, H., & Ahmed, M. (2017). Factors affecting job satisfaction among junior doctors working at teaching hospitals in River Nile State, Sudan. *Journal of Public Health and Emergency, 1*(17), 79. doi:10.21037/jphe.2017.09.04

Tannen, D. (1990). You just don't understand. Morrow: Academic Press.

Taragin, M., Wilczek, A., Karns, M., Trout, R., & Carson, J. (1992). Physician demographics and the risk of medical malpractice. *The American Journal of Medicine*, *93*(5), 537–542. doi:10.1016/0002-9343(92)90582-V PMID:1442857

Tyssen, R., Palmer, K., Solberg, I., Voltmer, E., & Frank, E. (2013). Physicians' perceptions of quality of care, professional autonomy, and job satisfaction in Canada, Norway, and the United States. *BMC Health Services Research*, *13*(1), 516. doi:10.1186/1472-6963-13-516 PMID:24330820

U.S. Bureau of Labor Statistics. (2014). *Occupational employment & wage estimates*. Retrieved from http://www.bls.gov/oes/current/oes_nat.htm#29-0000

U.S. Bureau of Labor Statistics. (2019). Women had higher median earnings than men in relatively few occupations in 2018. *The Economics Daily*. Retrieved from https://www.bls.gov/opub/ted/2019/women-had-higher-median-earnings-than-men-in-relatively-few-occupations-in-2018.htm

ValueWalk. (2019). *Professions in the world*. Retrieved from https://www.valuewalk.com/2019/03/top-10-most-respected-professions/

Whaley, N. (2018). 3 long-term effects the gender pay gap has on women. *Mic*. Retrieved from https://www.mic.com/articles/188833/3-long-term-effects-the-gender-pay-gap-has-on-women

Winograd, M., & Hais, M. (2008). *Millennial makeover: MySpace, YouTube & the future of American politics*. Rutgers University Press.

Worldometers. (2019). *Populations by gender, age, fertility rate, immigration*. Retrieved from https://www.worldometers.info/world-population/world-population-gender-age.php

Zhou, M. (2019). Aging population a global challenge. *China Daily*. Retrieved from http://global.chinadaily.com.cn/a/201904/09/WS5cabe02da3104842260b50cb_1.html

ADDITIONAL READING

Henry, T. (2019). Physician moms: More housework, higher career dissatisfaction. *American Medical Association.* Retrievable from https://www.ama-assn.org/practice-management/physician-health/physician-moms-more-housework-higher-career-dissatisfaction

Murphy, J. (2018). Most doctors are satisfied with their jobs despite eroding respect, survey finds. *MDLinx*. Retrievable from https://www.mdlinx.com/internal-medicine/article/1464

Pathman, D. (2002). Physician job satisfaction, dissatisfaction, and physician turnover. *The Journal of Family Practice*, *51*(7), 1. PMID:12160487

Schmit Jongbloed, L. J., Cohen-Schotanus, J., Borleffs, J., Stewart, R. E., & Schönrock-Adema, J. (2017). Physician job satisfaction related to actual and preferred job size. *BMC Medical Education*, *17*(1), 86. doi:10.118612909-017-0911-6 PMID:28494758

KEY TERMS AND DEFINITIONS

Baby Boom Generation: Those individuals born between 1946 and 1964, after the Traditional Generation and before Generation X.

Economic Success: For individuals, having a high enough income to live comfortably in a given economy.

Generation X: Individuals born between 1964 and 1980, after the Baby Boom Generation and before the Millennial Generation.

Generational Cohort: A group of people born in the same time and identified with having experienced similar world events

Global Health: An area of study, research and practice focusing on improving health and achieving equity in health for the world population.

Income Inequality: The gap between the wealth of one population segment in comparison to another.

Information Technology (IT): The use of systems (especially computers and telecommunications) for storing, retrieving, and sending information. This system includes electronic health records.

Job Satisfaction: A feeling of fulfillment or enjoyment that a person derives from their job.

Millennial Generation: Individuals born between 1981 and 1996, after Generation X.

Quality of Care: The extent to which health care services provided to individuals and patient populations improve desired health outcomes.

Traditional Generation: Individuals born between 1922 and 1945, before the Baby Boom Generation.

Work Conditions: The working environment and all existing circumstances affecting labor in the workplace, including job hours, physical aspects, legal rights, and responsibilities.

Work-Related Stress: The adverse reaction people have to excessive pressures or other types of demand placed on them at work.

Workload: The amount of work to be done by someone.

Chapter 2
Gender Inequality in the Indonesian Labor Market

Ngadi Ngadi
https://orcid.org/0000-0002-5249-0860
Indonesian Institute of Sciences, Indonesia

Devi Asiati
Indonesian Institute of Sciences, Indonesia

Ade Latifa
Indonesian Institute of Sciences, Indonesia

Nawawi Nawawi
Indonesian Institute of Sciences, Indonesia

ABSTRACT

Indonesia has committed to embody gender equality in the labor market through gender mainstreaming programs in all sectors. Nevertheless, the reality indicates that gender inequality in the labor market still exists. This chapter aims to discuss various issues of gender inequality in the Indonesian labor market in the agriculture, manufacturing, and services sectors. The data used for the analysis is the 2016 national labor force survey. The survey covered 82,613 workers with 31,256 of them from the agricultural sector, 14,835 from the manufacturing sector and 36,522 from the services sector. The analysis shows the dominance of male labor in all the sectors with the lowest proportion of female workers occurs in the manufacturing sector (27.1%) followed by the agricultural sector (37.5%) and the services (46.5%). Based on the type of position, men are more dominant in strategic positions in all the three sectors. The highest wage disparity between women and men takes place in the agricultural sector followed by the manufacturing and the services.

DOI: 10.4018/978-1-7998-3737-4.ch002

INTRODUCTION

Gender equality in the labor market is an important part of the economic development in Indonesia. This gender equality refers to the fulfillment of the rights, opportunities and fair treatment of men and women of all age groups at all stages of life and employment. Gender equality means that all human beings are free to develop their personal abilities as well as to choose without being constrained by stereotypes and prejudices against gender roles or characteristics of men and women. But the concept of gender equality does not mean that men and women are the same or have become the same. Instead, it means that their rights, responsibilities, social status and access to their resources are independent of their gender

To strengthen gender equality, Indonesia has ratified several International Labor Organisation (ILO) conventions for gender equality, i.e.: (a) ILO Convention No. 100, 1951 on the allotment of equal pay for work of equal value between men and women; (b) ILO Convention No. 111 on the prohibition of discrimination and the promotion of equal opportunity and treatment in employment and position based on origin including sex; (c) ILO Convention No. 156 on workers with family responsibilities which promotes equal opportunity as well as treatment for men and women with family responsibilities; (d) ILO Convention No. 183 of 2000 on the expansion of outreach to women workers as stated by the convention and the extension of leave rights to 14 weeks.

The government has also explicitly regulated the equality between men and women in the labor market as stipulated in the Labor Law No.13 of 2003. This law clearly states that all workers must have the same rights and opportunities to choose work, obtain work or move to another employment and receive a decent income. Subsequently, job placement must also be based on transparency, independency, objectivity, justice and equal opportunities without discrimination (Article 31 and 32).

While the struggle for gender equality has been enforced for quite a long time, discrimination of men and women still exists in Indonesia. A report from the ILO (2015) showed that women in Indonesia tended to get less wages than men. In 2015, the level of participation of women in the labor force was only 50.9%, which was lower than men. Similarly, in wages, women earned 79% of the men's income. The Indonesian Central Bureau of Statistics also finds a considerably high inequality of wage between men and women in the agricultural sector. The same condition is also found in the service sector businesses, where the average wage for women is only 50.18% of their counterpart.

These facts show that the struggle for gender equality in the labor market in Indonesia still requires time and continuous effort. For that matter, comprehensive information on the reality of gender inequality in the labor market has become an important part of the struggle. Therefore, this paper aims to discuss various issues of gender inequality in the labor market in the agriculture, manufacturing and services sectors. This paper is useful as a reference in order to achieve the Sustainable Development Goals (SGDs) i.e. to increase the growth of inclusive and sustainable economy, to provide productive and comprehensive employment opportunities, and to lay out decent work for all.

BACKGROUND

Economic restructuring that occurs in the globalization era lead to a shift in the sectors of manufacturing, technology, banking and managerial work from the industrial to developing countries. This also offers employment opportunities especially for women to fill job openings in those sectors, with lower wages. While this process opens employment opportunities for women, it also shows a phenomenon laden with issues of gender inequality, one of which, among others, is in the context of the wage gap between female and male workers.

Indonesia, as a developing country, has also experienced quite a rapid economic growth in line with the progress of globalization. The process of economic growth is also generally followed by an increase in population movement from rural to urban areas (urbanization) in search of better income. An interesting fact about this matter, based on the results of the Taniguchi and Tuwo (2014) study in Indonesia, showed that there was a gender wage gap as an implication of economic growth. According to Taniguchi and Tuwo (2014), the gender wage gap widened when there was an increase in income levels triggered by the migration of people from villages to cities. This phenomenon was also recognized when the World Bank report also identified that women's participation as workers did not translate into equal employment opportunities and/or equal income between male and female workers.

Gender analysis provides a deeper understanding of the relations of processes, markets, transactions and political movements, including a fundamental understanding of the causes of these processes. Through gender analysis it can be understood that the social construction of gender understanding is manipulated, conserved and negotiated at every level in the process of economic development. Through social institutions occur a process of legitimacy of gender understanding that is 'assumed' to be more related to men/ masculinity, as opposed to women/ femininity. The implication of this can be observed from the differences in treatment experienced by women and men in the labor market. This also possibly reinforces inequality between groups and both sexes.

In developing countries, the process of gender legitimacy reinforces the depiction of a gender ideology that puts women in their traditional roles. For instance, there is more demand for female workers in the flower packaging industry because women are more dexterous and skilled at cutting and arranging flowers. Furthermore, in the manufacturing industries that are spread across Batam, Riau Islands, for example, the job vacancies as production operators, tend to prefer female workers. In addition to being skilled, women were also considered to be more thorough, disciplined and able to stand for hours. In contrast, male workers, were considered physically stronger than women, and therefore, were more in demand in the assembly industries, such as in shipbuilding companies. They were considered more suitable for jobs that required physical strength, such as climbing ships, painting, and doing underwater welding (Malamassam, et. al. 2017).

Placing women in jobs that are considered 'soft' or not at high risk, becomes a discourse to disguise the level of danger from the job itself. Women who are 'forced' to stand for hours to become operators, face a negative risk to their health conditions. Ironically, women with low wages often accept jobs that are classified as 'dangerous' without rights or additional wages. The involvement of women in the work environment also tends to be entailed in temporary work, hence wage received is considered only to fulfill things that are not basic needs, such as 'lipstick' and 'powder'. In other words, the wage received by women from work is not seen as the means to support the family income. This description of female workers, working only 'temporarily', not the main breadwinner, often conditions women as parties that do not demand long-term investment to improve their education or skills. As a result, access towards education and training for women is very limited. The result of the Taniguchi and Tuwo study (2014) in Indonesia showed that men tended to have higher levels of education than women.

When referring to the initial formation of the concept of gender, it can be understood why such work segregation occurs. When the concept of gender was first introduced in the late 1980s, it was seen as an 'appropriate' activity carried out by women and men in relation to production. This approach or concept that sees 'doing gender' emphasizes more on behavior. In other words, men and women are expected to behave according to characteristics that are different from one another. This concept of gender includes how people's perceptions, interactions and micro political activities which also contain the values of masculinity and femininity in them. Thus, the concept of gender is perceived as something that is constructed by the community, the outcome and rationality of various social agreements while also the means to legitimize the division of society that is considered the most important/ influential. Gender is a dynamic concept, not static, because it is continuously constructed and used in interactions.

Gender inequality faced by female workers has also gained legitimacy from global institutions. Women are also encouraged to fill jobs as public service providers because they are considered 'female' domain, this too is conceptualized at various levels: household, family and community. What interesting is, that as individuals, women are suspected of not being able to 'choose' for occupations/ career that is suitable for them, the decision has already been made for them. The decisions on 'work' that were made for women, accoding to the study of Ford and Parker (2008), were influenced by cultures that had the ideological or symbolic systems related to what was 'good' for women and men.

The participation of women in the labor market has brought about a gradual change in gender relations. Women who work as formal workers, in large numbers throughout the world, are considered to have 'destroyed' the depiction of men having a special role in the family as the main breadwinner. The process of globalization is also said to have given women access to low-paid jobs while at the same time has 'shaken' the position of men in the labor market. Barker (2005) as quoted by Ford and Parker (2008), noted that the involvement of women in formal economic activities was a path to women's emancipation and empowerment. However, this is not entirely captured in the discourse of discussion related to patriarchy. While the developments of the current situation have facilitated social transformation through gender construction and gender roles, it may seem too unassuming to conclude that the inclusion of a large number of women in the labor market, can equate relations between men and women in both work and domestic spheres.

Studies show that while women have access to resources, it is not a guarantee that women can also control resources. Traditions, norms and constructions of gender are interrelated in influencing access to resources and power relations. This process was what shaped gender ideology and behavior, because women and men had different positions in relation to access to resources, power systems, responses to changing roles and ideologies (Ford and Parker, 2008). Many factors were influential and therefore could not simply be equated for all sexes. Lopes, Coelho and Ferreira (2015) stated that while Portuguese women had equal access to men in the labor market, women were not politically considered, and even had to endure double or treble duties. It was also identified that women faced various obstacles to fully enjoy their rights as part of the community, including discrimination in the work environment, barriers to accessing higher work positions, heavier workloads in the household and lack of social support, such as receiving leniency of working hours for female workers who have to breastfeed their babies.

The position of women in the work environment in countries that have implemented Industrial 4.0 is apparently not much different. Referring to the Piasna and Drahokoupil study (2017) quoted by Howcroft and Rubery (2018) regarding the transformation of occupational structures accros Europe the study seen there are positive development in the ability of women to outperform men in the occupation that require analytical skills. Women have succeeded in the areas that were previously dominated by men such as medical. However, women remain under presented in jobs related to sciences, technology, engineering, mathematics and have a tendency to be involved in a low paid income.

Ford and Parker (2008) outlined the importance of a holistic approach, both from the economic and political perspective. In order to comprehend the women in the work environment, simply making gender disaggregated data was not enough. On the other hand, to understand the issue comprehensively using a gender analysis knife, a holistic approach was also needed to see how women or men exist in relation to society, within the household, gender roles and norms applicable in the society, including the construction of ideologies on the division of labor. In some feminist studies, it is even explained that to understand women in work it is necessary to deconstruct binary analytical tools, such as formal and informal work, production and reproduction, public and private. An interpretive approach to women's work becomes an approach to understand the relationship between concepts of gender with empirical conditions.

Without an in-depth analysis on how women and men receive and interact with global economic forces, what left are simply pieces of understanding on the matter. Gender analysis is an important key to understanding the interaction between economic restructuring in various labor sectors and the problems faced by female workers. The following is an explanation of the phenomenon of gender inequality in Indonesia, which is focused on agriculture, manufacturing and service sectors.

GENDER INEQUALITY IN INDONESIA

Gender Inequality in Agriculture Sector

Indonesia is an agricultural country where the agricultural sector holds an important role in the development, especially concerning employment's absorption. In 2018 the agricultural sector absorbed 35.7 million workers (28.8%). Among these, women played an important role because of their large numbers that added to the majority of agriculture in Indonesia was managed by households. Data from Beureu of Statistic showed that the number of female workers in the agricultural sector in 2018 was 12.8 million people (35.9%), while men amounted to 22.9 million (64.1%). The role of women in the agricultural sector in Indonesia was stated by Food and Agriculture Organization (FAO) that agricultural production activities in Indonesia were mostly carried out by family units, so that all household members including women were involved in agricultural activities (FAO, 2019). Multani et. al. (2017) found that women in rural areas had to manage multiple activities like maintaining home, making food, arranging water while working in farms also.

Various gender equality programs have been carried out by the Indonesian government, especially after the Presidential Instruction No. 9/2000 on gender mainstreaming in the national development. The implementation of gender mainstreaming in the agricultural sector was followed up with a Decree of the Minister of Agriculture on the Establishment of the Gender Mainstreaming Coordinating Team, since 2003. Although gender equality has become a national consensus in the agricultural sector, gender inequality in this sector still occurs. There are still several labor issues that show disparities between men and women in this sector such as the work positions, wages, hours of work and work facilities.

Low Position of Women in Agriculture Sector

In general, the position of women in agriculture sector is still lower than that of men. The weak position of women in the workplace is reflected in the large number of women who are positioned as unpaid/contributing family workers, in addition to small number of women in strategic positions. The 2016

Sakernas data showed that more than half of female workers in the agricultural sector in Indonesia were characterized as unpaid/ contributing family workers (60.1%). With this status, women were more positioned as the supporting forces in the agricultural sector while the responsibilities and decision makers were carried out by men. With this position, women, participated in managing agriculture, but most did not take part in determining decisions in agricultural activities. The multitude number of women as unpaid/ contributing family workers related to patriarchal culture in Indonesia. The patriarchal ideology characterized that men were the heads of the family and the breadwinners who were seen in productive work outside the home as well as the successor to progeny (Sihite, 2007).

Figure 1. Male and female workers in the agricultural sector by main employment status (%)
Source: National Labor Force Survey, 2016

The weak position of women in the labor market also reflected from the dominance of men in strategic positions in the agricultural sector, especially in the managerial positions. National labor force survey data in 2016 showed that most managerial positions in the agriculture sector were taken by men, namely 75.0% while women were only 25%. Men appeared to have better opportunities to occupy important positions in the workplace such as managers or supervisors. This related to the low opportunity for women in the agricultural sector to receive training (Mariyono et. al. 2013). In addition, there were differences in the transition period between women and men when reaching adulthood. Doss et. al. (2019), stated that young women and men experienced the transition to adulthood differently. Across all structural and rural transformation categories, young women were more likely to be married and lived with their spouses, and less likely to be in school or employed.

The more men holding managerial positions, the more decisions and policies in the agricultural sector that are determined by men. The weaker position of women has implications for the low participation of women in determining opinions both for decisions in farmer organizations and at the household level. FAO (2019) showed that women often had no control over valuable resources and assets such as land, labor and new technologies. Elmhirst (2017) found that the opportunities of women to engage in institutional arrangements were limited because of the prevailing gender and family norms. Furthermore, Mulyoutami et. al (2012) found that female participation in decision making was indicated as very low. Some women workers in agriculture also did not have adequate facilities and protection. Li, TM (2015) illustrated the weak position of women in palm oil plantations in West Kalimantan by mentioning women workers from the enclaves who reported that they cried at home every night with injuries, exhaustion and quiet

Table 1. Male and Female Workers in the Agriculture Sector by Type of Occupation

Occupation	Proportion (%)		N
	Male	Female	
Professional, technician, and related occupations	96.7	3.3	30
Managerial and supervisory occupations	75.0	25.0	4
Clerical and related occupations	67.2	32.8	61
Sales workers	50.0	50.0	20
Services workers	68.7	31.3	67
Agriculture, forestry, hunting, and fishing workers	62.1	37.9	30,639
Production workers, operation of machinery workers, and laborers	83.4	16.6	435
Total	62.5	37.5	
N	19,522	11,734	31,256

Source: National Labor Force Survey, 2016

fury. The position of woman in agriculture sector is differing among several countries in Southeast Asia. Akter et, al. (2017) found that women in Thailand and the Philipines play an active role in agricultural groups, but men is dominant in Indonesia and Myanmar

Women's Wages in Agriculture Sector Are Only Half of Men

The low wage of women workers is a gender problem in the agricultural sector in Indonesia. In 2018, National Labor Force Survey showed that women's wages in the agricultural sector were only 30.7% of men's wages. The average wage of men in the agricultural sector was US$ 45.6 (IDR 603,720), while women was US$ 14.0 (IDR 185,420). This showed that the mainstreaming program needed to continue to be encouraged in Indonesia. This result was in line with the research of Surbakti (2015) which showed that the average wage received by women was lower than that received by men.

Wage disparities between men and women differ according to their level of education. At the diploma and above, the proportion of wages of women to men is 64.1%, but at the level of senior high school education and below, the proportion of wages of women to men is still low. Therefore, raising the educational attainment is one way to increase the equal pay of men and women workers in the agricultural sector. This is in line with the research of Surbakti, 2015 who found that the lowest wage of agricultural sector workers was that for workers who had no schooling, even in this group the average wage received by women was inferior to that received by men, women's average wage was only 56.9 percent that of men's. Furthermore CIDES (2015) found that women's higher education attainment was successful in reducing the wage gap.

The problem of wage disparity between male and female workers cannot be defined by simply using the education improvement approach. It will take time for Indonesia to only utilize the education approach since most of the workforce in Indonesia are still low educated. In 2018, there were 58.8% of the workforce with only junior high school and below. The large number of low education workers was found in rural areas (74.4%), while in urban areas was at 45.5% (Central Bureau of Statistics, 2019).

Table 2. Wages of Male and Female Workers (IDR) in Agricultural Sector by Education Attainment

Education	Male (M)		Female (F)		Total		(F/M)*100
	Mean	N	Mean	N	Mean	N	
Elementary and below	532,093.1	12,461	176,645.1	8,935	383,657.5	21,396	33.2
Secondary School	685,923.4	3,580	191,359.6	1,629	531,259.5	5,209	27.9
Tertiary school	760,303.2	3,145	218,382.0	1,089	620,919.1	4,234	28.7
Diploma I/II and above	918,639.9	336	589,271.6	81	854,661.9	417	64.1
Total	603,720.6	19,522	185,409.7	11,734	446,680.0	31,256	30.7

Source: National Labor Force Survey, 2016

The Low Working Hours of Woman

The working hours of workers in Indonesia were specifically regulated in Law No. 13 of 2003 on manpower. Article 77 paragraph 1 required every employer to implement the provisions of working hours. However, most workers in the agricultural sector worked under predetermined working hours. The total hours of work a week for male and female workers in 2016 was 34.54 hours per week. In general, women's working hours were lower than men's respectively by 29.26 hours a week and 37.71 hours a week, bringing the women's working hours to only 81.2% of men's working hours. The lower working hours of women was in accordance with the findings of Surbakti (2015) who found that generally men worked more hours than women.

Low working hours in the agricultural sector are related to the dual tasks of women in agricultural households. In the agricultural sector, women generally have two roles at the same time, which are to help earn a living and take care of the household. These double tasks cause women's working hours to be lower than men's since they have to divide their time to work and take care of the household. This was in accordance with Surbakti (2015), that on top of working to earn income, women had domestic duties such as taking care of children and maintaining the household. Therefore, women's working hours in the agriculture sector are generally lower than men.

Table 3. Average of Working Hours in Previous Week (hours) in Agricultural Sector by Education Attainment

Education	Male (M)		Female (F)		Total		(F/M)*100
	Mean	N	Mean	N	Mean	N	
Elementary and below	37.97	12461	29.48	8935	34.42	21396	77.6
Secondary School	37.08	3580	28.67	1629	34.45	5209	77.3
Tertiary school	37.73	3145	28.44	1089	35.34	4234	75.4
Diploma I/II and above	34.95	336	28.38	81	33.67	417	81.2
Total	37.71	19522	29.26	11734	34.54	31256	77.6

Source: National Labor Force Survey, 2016

Gender Inequality in Service Sector

The services sector plays a significant role in the Indonesian economy, this can be seen from its contribution to GDP and the provision of the employment opportunities. The contribution of the service sector to the economy is in line with the economic transformation which has taken place in Indonesia. The economy was initially supported by the primary agricultural sector before shifting to the industrial sector and finally to the services sector. Since 2000 the service sector contribution to GDP has increased from 45% to 54% in 2017, bigger than the agriculture and manufacturing sectors. The important role of the services sector in providing employment opportunities has been perceived since the economic crisis in 1998. The weakening of the exchange rate during the economic crisis caused industries that use imported components to experience shocks which resulted in the reduction in labor. Service sectors such as trade then became the alternative employments for workers who lost their jobs. The services has already been a major source of growth in Asia. The share of service sector in employment is greater than the manufacturing sector employement in 12 major Asian economies are PRC, Hongkong, China, India, Indonesia, Republik of Korea, Malaysia, Pakistan, Philipine, Singapore, Taipei, China, Thailand and Vietnam (Park, D and Shin K, 2012).

The service sector provides large employment opportunities for women workers. Data from Beureu of Statistic (2016) showed that the proportion of women employed in the service sector was 44.2%, greater than the agriculture and manufacturing. The large participation of women in the service sector was a contribution of the increasing employment opportunities in the service sector (Rendall, M., 2013). The development of the service sector opened new access and opportunities for women to join the labor market. The service sector was relatively more friendly to women due to the nature of the work of the service sector which was more service oriented thus required more interaction with consumers (Setiawan, 2011). However, based on gender differences, women's participation in the labor market has been lower than men with tendencies to stay stagnant, namely 50.2% in 1990 to 51.4% in 2013 while men were in the number of 81.1% to 84.4%. The small increases in women's participation was due to low participation of married women and women with young children. The presence of children under the age of two reduced the chances of women in participating in the labor market by 8% (AIPEG, 2017).

The employment opportunities in the service sector tend to increase, in addition to employment created from the service sector activities themselves or linkages with the industrial sector[1]. In this case, the output of the traded goods industry, could launch employment opportunities in the service sector, such as trade, transportation services, financial services and business. The diversity of jobs in the service sector is distinguished by the characteristics of its workers, like 'modern' services that involve highly educated professional workforce, or traditional or informal services that do not require a high level of education, such as retail and street vendors and other services. The characteristics of both jobs in the service sector went hand in hand with the characteristics of their respective workforce (Manning, 2012).

The Domination of Male Workers in the Service Sector

From a gender perspective, employment in the service sector is still dominated by male workers. The 2016 Sakernas data noted that out of 36.5 million employment in the service sector, 53.6% of them were male and 46.4% were female (Figure 2). The dominance of male workers happens in the employment with a modern nature that requires expertise, high skills and capital intensive, while women dominate more in the traditional jobs. Manning (2012) showed that more than 60% of employees graduating from tertiary education, including the women who worked as civil servants or teachers/ lecturers in schools and colleges. At least 80% of women in Japan, Korea, Hongkong (China) and Macau are involved in the services sector and at least 66% of women in Malaysia dan Philippines, while Indonesia, Thailand, Timor Leste, Sri Langka, Vietnam, Pakistan India, Nepal services sector dominated of men (OECD, 2014)

Figure 2. Male and female participation in services sector in Indonesia, 2016
Source: National Labor Force Survey, 2016

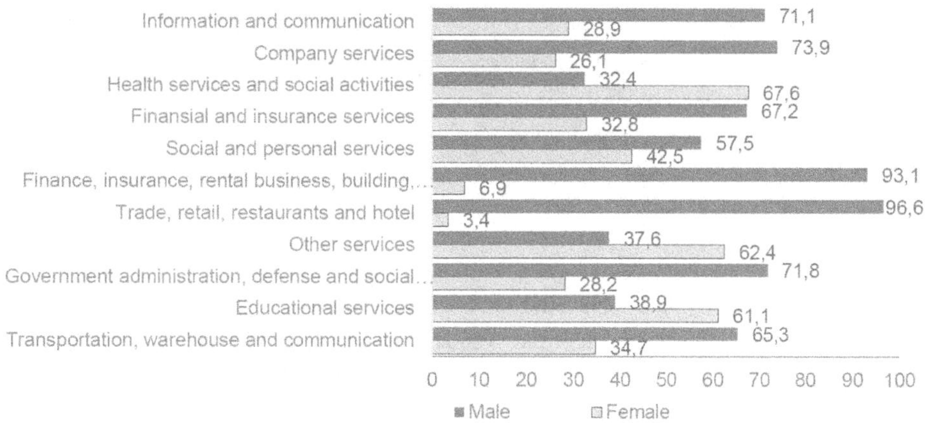

Low Position of Women in Service Sector

Women's work position is lower than men in workplace in service sector. Men dominate jobs that require higher managerial skills and expertise as employer assisted by permanent worker (Table 4). Likewise, in jobs that require special skills in the service industries as an employee, the proportion of men is 54.3% which is more than women that is of 48%. The weak position of women in service sector also could be shown from dominance of women with jobs as unpaid/contributing family worker by 13.7%, much higher than men only 4.3%, and in positioned as employer assisted by temporary worker/unpaid worker, which is 12.6%, while men are 10.7%. While both jobs are household-based businesses, usually done at home or around the residence with the help of household members, like trading at home. It is easier for women, especially those with low education, to make small-scale businesses because they do not require large capital nor special expertise. The data shows that more women are absorbed in traditional household-based jobs that lack managerial skills as well as higher education.

The low position of women in service sector could also be seen from dominance of men in positioned managerial and supervisory occupation with 2.8% higher than women with 1.0%. Most of female's worker work as sales worker of 44.3% higher than male worker was 30.8% (Table 5). The type of businesses that have been developing in Indonesia are small-scale trading businesses that generally do not require a large amount of capital and higher education making it easier for women to get involve. Economic Census 2016 showed that 70.8% of total 26.7 million non-agricultural business, was a bussiness category non occupying buildings, such as peddlers, street vendor and small business in home.

Table 4. Male and Female Workers in Services Sector by Main Employment Status

Status	Sex		Total
	Male	Female	
Own-account worker	22.1	21.5	21,8
Employer assisted by permanent worker	5,0	2.2	3.7
Employee	54.3	48.0	51.3
Employer assisted by temporary workers/ unpaid worker	10.7	12.6	11.6
Casual agricultural worker	0.0	0.0	0.0
Casual non-agricultural worker	3.7	2.0	2.9
Unpaid/contributing family worker	4.3	13.7	8.7
Total	100	100	100
N	19560	16962	36522

Source: National Labor Force Survey, 2016

The development of trading business has been started since the 1998 economic crisis until now. During the economic crisis, the trade business was the savior of the household economy for workers who were laid off. Those affected by layoffs, both with high and low level of education, enter the small trade businesses because they do not need large capital. In the current digital era, the development of the small and retail trade sector and the transportation transportation businesses have increased significantly. The automation of production equipment in the manufacturing industry resulted on the reduction on the unskilled workers in the workforce. Those who lost their jobs in the industrial sector then turned to service jobs, such as trading businesses or online transportation (Asiati, et al, 2019). This caused a shift in labor from the industrial sector to the service sector. The current trend, online sales and even re-sellers are mostly done by women. This work can be done at any time while doing most household chores.

Table 5. Male and Female Workers in Services Sector by Type of Occupation

Occupation	Sex		Total
	Male	Female	
Professional, technician, and related occupations	11.5	20.7	15.8
Managerial and supervisory occupations	2.8	1.0	2.0
Clerical and related occupations	13.6	12.2	13.0
Sales workers	30.8	44.3	37.1
Services workers	6.3	12.8	9.3
Agriculture, forestry, hunting, and fishing workers	0.1	0.0	0.0
Production workers, operation of machinery workers, and laborers	35.0	8.9	22.9
Total	100	100	100
N	19560	16962	36522

Source: National Labor Force Survey, 2016

Low Level Income of Female Worker

In general, the average wage level in the service sector is US$ 139.0 (1,839,889 IDR) per month, which is higher than the agriculture and industrial sectors. However, there is a wage gap between men and women, where the level of women's wages is lower than men's. Based on National Labor Force Survey (2016), the average wage of women workers in the service sector was US$ 110.8 (1,466,497 IDR) per month, lower than the average wage of male workers of US$ 163.5 (2,163,687 IDR) per month. The low wages of women transpire in almost all areas of employment in the service sector, except for the wholesale trade, retail, restaurants and hotels. Some significant wage differences were found in the community services sector, education services, and government administration, and defense (Figure 3).

Women are more vulnerable when economic shocks, such as inflation, take place which cause the declining of the purchasing power. The wage differences that were not too large was found in the information and communication sector with a ratio of 94% and company services with a ratio of 98%. There were no wage differences between women and men in the financial, insurance and rental business sectors with a ratio of 100%. Many of the activities in these three sectors are classified as modern sectors occupied with professionals and higher education workers, where the wage system is usually in accordance with the competency standards without gender differentiation. On occupations based on specific knowledge and skills, there were no significant differences between men and women (Stieger, 1995).

Figure 3. Male and female wages in services sector in Indonesia (million IDR), 2016
Source: National Labor Force Survey, 2016

Based on the level of education, the proportion of female workers with low education is lower than male, which is 28% of women and 22% of men. This shows that service sector employment opportunities do indeed absorb more female workers with little education. Hence, the traditional or informal service jobs, such as retail traders or other services, are mostly filled by women. What interesting is that the proportion of female workers with a higher education is also higher than that of men, which is 28% of women and 21% of men. This condition shows that the service sector also absorbs a large workforce of women with high education. However, they are less engaged in the managerial and leadership areas, and mostly taken in the work of sales and professional staff, such as teachers or nurses.

Table 6. Wage of Male and Female Workers in Services Sector by Education Attainment

Education	Male		Female		Total	
	Mean	N	Mean	N	Mean	N
Elementary and below	1,329,012.5	4286	708,672.5	4740	1,003,241.2	9026
Secondary school	1,451,096.5	3242	757,006.2	2571	1,144,111.1	5813
Tertiary school	2,051,669.7	7887	1,203,164.5	4911	1,726,071.3	12798
Diploma I/II and above	3,797,250.9	4145	2,881,987.5	4740	3,308,973.1	8885
Total	2,163,687.4	19560	1,466,497.6	16962	1,839,889.89	36522

Source: National Labor Force Survey, 2016

When it comes to inequality of wages, women at all levels of education experienced this condition. At all levels of education, the average wage received by women is lower than that of men, either it is in jobs with low elementary education qualification level or the academy/ university (Table 6). Greater wage differentials are found at low level education, such as senior high school, where men's wages are almost double the women's. At the higher education level, wage differences are getting smaller with the ratio of wages between women and men is at 76%. This condition coincides with the notion that women even with higher education are still less engaged in jobs that require expertise and high managerial level.

Gender Inequality in Manufacturing Sector

The manufacturing sector is the main motor that drives the Indonesian economy aside from the oil and gas. This sector has been able to contribute an average of 20% year to the acquisition of Indonesia's Gross Domestic Product (GDP). The manufacturing sector is also one of the mainstays of job creation for job seekers in urban areas due to its labor-intensive nature. Some of the industries included in the labor-intensive category in this sector are textile, garment, footwear, electronic assembly, leather processing, wood products and its derivatives. The development of the manufacturing sector characterized the economic transformation from a country that was initially based on its natural products towards an industry that processed natural products while at the same time utilized a more modern technology (World Bank, 2012: 2).

The manufacturing sector also has a strategic role in the formation and development of other business activities, especially in the processing of agricultural products and trade services. In the field of social development, the development of the manufacturing sector also had a positive impact on the increase participation of the female workforce (World Bank, 2012). This meant, efforts to develop manufacturing industries were not only positive for the development and achievement of gender equality in Indonesia, but also became part of efforts to improve the economy and the welfare of women and their families.

The Dominant of Male Workers in the Manufacturing Sector

Indonesia's manufacturing industry employment is still dominated by male workers with quite a lopsided proportion of male and female workers. Of the 14.2 million employed in the manufacturing sector, around 72% of them are male. One of the reasons of the relatively low women's participation in the manufacturing sector is that married women with children are 'incapable' of meeting the job requirements attached to this sector. Most of the job opportunities in the manufacturing sector tended to require specific marital status, with single women enjoyed the wider access than married women in the sector (Tadjoeddin, 2016).

With long hours and lack of support system such as childcare, these conditions further reduce the opportunities for married women with children to participate in the manufacturing sector. Consequently, married women in Indonesia mostly take part in the informal sectors such as in agriculture and service sectors with low quality of working conditions with low wage, no social security and even often unsafe conditions (Pinagara and Bleijenbergh, 2010).

The dominance of male workers in the Indonesian manufacturing sector is especially noticeable in the types of jobs that fall into the category of processing industries such as machinery, electronics, wood processing and chemicals. The kinds of works in these industries generally require physical strength which bring the dominance of male workers to be even more substantial. Meanwhile, the female workers generally dominate the types of work that require speed and accuracy in completion. Some manufacturing industries that absorb a lot of female workers are textiles, garments, footwear and electronic assembly. This type of industry is a labor-intensive industry that productivity is highly dependent on the amount of labor involved. That is, to increase productivity in this sector, the use of more work will increase the output produced.

The requirements to be involved in the labor-intensive industries were known to be more accessible than that of the capital-intensive industries. Similarly, the use of modern technology was relatively low, and the level of labor input and turnover tended to be high (Tadjoeddin, 2016). This meant, that female workers in the Indonesian manufacturing sector tended to be involved in jobs that did not require too much of a physical strength with a relatively high labor turnover. The opposite applied to male workers.

Based on the employment status, most workers in the manufacturing sector work as laborers/employees. This can be understood given that most of the industrial activities in Indonesia's manufacturing sector are labor-intensive industries. Judging by the type of job based on position, most jobs in the Indonesian manufacturing industry are dominated by jobs in the production and manual work types. This condition generally applies, for both male and female with difference only in a very small percentage, which is 90.8% and 89.9% for female and male workers respectively.

Table 7. Male and Female Workers in the Manufacturing Sector by Type of Occupation

Occupation	Sex		Total
	Male	Female	
Professional, technician, and related occupations	2.2	0.6	1.8
Managerial and supervisory occupations	3.1	0.5	2.4
Clerical and related occupations	2.66	4.9	3.2
Sales workers	1.0	2.0	1.3
Services workers	1.2	1.2	1.2
Agriculture, forestry, hunting, and fishing workers	0.0	0.0	0.0
Production workers, operation of machinery workers, and laborers	89.8	90.8	90.1
Total	100	100	100
N	10816	4019	14835

Source: National Labor Force Survey, 2016

When it comes to the type of work that requires higher managerial expertise, the proportion of male workers compared to their counterpart is relatively much greater. For instance, in the employment areas that require leadership, the proportion of male workers holding the position are greater than the female, which are 3.1% and 0.5%, respectively. Meanwhile, the proportion of female workers dominating the types of work associated with administrative work such as in sales and administration is significant. This can be interpreted that women workers in the Indonesian manufacturing industry tend to be more on demand for the type of employment that requires patience and high accuracy while male workers are generally related to regulation and leadership.

Gap of Working Hours, Level of Income and Educational Attainment

The average working hours of workers in the manufacturing sector reaches 45.1 hours per week, which is higher than the normal working hours limit (35 hours per week). This means that most workers in the manufacturing sector either work longer hours or are involved in work that requires overtime. Based on the gender differences, the male workers in the manufacturing sector work longer than the female workers. On average, male workers work 47.71 hours per week, while female workers clock in 38.34 hours per week. The length of work certainly affects the level of income earned by both the male and female workers.

The level of income of workers in the manufacturing sector is higher than that of the agricultural sector workers, although is still lower than the service sector. In the manufacturing sector, male workers have higher average income than the female with the difference in income of the men and women that is more than double. In average the income of male workers in the manufacturing sector reaches US$ 145.5 (IDR 2,163,687) while female workers take home US$ 75.3 (IDR 997,115). This condition causes female workers to be more at risk from the economic shocks of (for example rising inflation) than male workers. This, furthermore, emphasizing the lower income of female workers compared to male workers in Indonesia.

The low level of income of female workers compared to male workers in the manufacturing sector is strongly suspected to be related to the characteristics of the type of industry. Female workers are generally involved in the labor-intensive industries with lower wage rates than men who work in the capital-intensive industries. In this labor-intensive industry, wage rates are usually determined from the targeted job completion based on units of yields or output.

Table 8. Average of Working Hours in Previous Week (hours) by Education Attainment of Workers in Manufacturing Sector

Education	Male (M)		Female (F)		Total	
	Mean	N	Mean	N	Mean	N
Elementary and below	47.57	4417	37.11	1911	44.41	6328
Secondary School	47.80	2466	37.96	904	45.16	3370
Tertiary school	48.03	3425	40.84	1009	46.39	4434
Diploma I/II and above	46.42	508	39.33	195	44.45	703
Total	47.71	10816	38.34	4019	45.18	14835

Source: National Labor Force Survey, 2016

Table 9. Wage of Male and Female Workers in Manufacturing Sector by Education Attainment

Education	Male		Female		Total	
	Mean	N	Mean	N	Mean	N
Elementary and below	1,511,080.3	4417	569,012.2	1911	1,226,584.1	6328
Secondary school	1,653,717.7	2466	964,359.8	904	1,468,797.9	3370
Tertiary school	2,226,265.1	3425	1,437,287.4	1009	2,046,725.6	4434
Diploma I/II and above	4,836,326.8	508	3,066,774.4	195	4,345,483.6	703
Total	1,926,250.2	1911	997,115.6	4019	1,674,535.2	14835

Source: National Labor Force Survey, 2016

As argue by Pinagara and Bleijenbergh (2010) women faced structural disadvantages in the labour market in Indonesia, particularly related to negotiation to advocate for better working conditions at work. Women in Indonesia generally have low access to trade unions which further reduce their access to get better hiring rates, fair work agreement and contracts. Consistent with these findings, Feridhanusetyawan, Aswicahyono and Perdana (2001) and Alisjahbana and Manning (2006) found that men occupations in the manufacturing sector were associated with higher productivity and wage, which further implied the reason for the higher wages received by men in comparison to women.

Similar condition also found in other developing countries such as women in the Philippine, Cambodia and Bangladesh. In the Philippine for instance, employers tend to foster long-term loyalty among their workers by recruiting women in rank-and- file position', especially married women with children (Chant 2010). In Bangladesh, Paul-Majumder and Begum (2000:24) found that women are recruited in the manufacturing industries to 'exploit the comparative advantages of their disadvantage'. Thus, in Bangladesh's manufacturing industries, 'tension and ambivalence are more prevalent among female workers than male workers (Paul-Majumder and Begum 2000:7). Meanwhile in Cambodia, the low labor productivity and infrastructure deficits in manufacture sector led women this country are more likely to be employed in the vulnerable sector 'which offers the least opportunities for decent work' (Asian Development Bank, 2013). Recognizing these conditions gender inequalities underpin women recruitment in the manufacture sector in many developing countries, which further reaffirms women disadvantage in the working lives.

The gap between the educational attainment of men and women in the manufacturing sector also reflects what is happening to the Indonesian labor market in general. The educational attainment of male workers working in the manufacturing sector seems to be better than that of female workers, especially those with secondary and higher educational attainment backgrounds. This condition also responds to the reality of the fulfilment of job positions in Indonesia's manufacturing sector, where positions that are managerial and professional tend to be dominated by male workers.

The managerial and professional positions usually require work experience and a certain level of education. In the meantime, female workers fill the job positions that require middle and low skill jobs which are mainly found in the textile, garment and footwear sectors. To be involved in these industries, workers generally do not need a level of education that is too stringent, however, prior work experience is required. For instance, the apparel and footwear industry require their workers to have sewing skills. In addition, the characteristics of these kinds of jobs are normally do not have career advancement opportunities and that the length of work does not affect the level of income or the career of the women who work in this labor-intensive industry.

Therefore, it can be understood if in the types of jobs in the manufacturing sector, men generally occupy the supervisory positions while women do the operational work. In the long term, efforts to improve quality through developing the skills of female workers will be very important. Developing the skills level of female workers will present opportunities for their inclusion in various types of manufacturing sector jobs that are not only in the managerial positions, but also with higher income levels.

The data related to the education level of workers in Indonesia's manufacturing sector also shows interesting conditions, especially for the average workers with low level of education, namely junior and elementary school level and below. In this level, the proportion of the male workers are greater than the female workers. This condition shows that male workers with low education levels can still obtain jobs more easily in the manufacturing sector compared to the female with the same educational status.

In the type of work that is menial, it is certain that employment opportunities in the manufacturing sector for male workers will be greater than female workers. This condition also responds to the high absorption of women workers in the agricultural sector, which generally does not require more stringent educational requirements than the manufacturing and services sectors.

It can be stated that the manufacturing sector is one of the economic sectors that can create a choice of opportunities for the Indonesian women to access the labor market and, as a result, earn an income. The development of this sector is expected to accommodate the excess of female workers in the agricultural sector, which are characterized by the low income to the manufacturing sector with better earning. However, the strong stereotypes of Indonesian people who generally see the differentiation of types of work based on gender (gender bias), have an impact on the segregation of jobs in the manufacturing sector to be increasingly visible, with the dominance of male workers in all indicators.

Women workers in the manufacturing sector are generally taken in the labor-intensive activities with low wage rates and even lower career advancement opportunities. Women workers in the manufacturing sector are involved in manual jobs and their productivity is determined by how many workers are involved. This means that the absorption of women workers in manufacturing sectors is greatly determined by the output demand which is the target of every labor-intensive industry. The increase of the output targets will allow the absorption of women workers more, while the decrease in the output targets will have implications for the reduction of women workers involved in the production activities. Meanwhile, the education level of female workers which is relatively lower than that of men impacts the limited access of the female workers in the manufacturing sector to obtain better types of work and higher incomes. For this reason, the ongoing efforts to raise awareness on gender equality and improve educational outcomes for women are key. Improving access to education for women will not only increase the skills and knowledge of the female workers, but also increase their bargaining power in the labor market, especially in the manufacturing sector.

FUTURE RESEARCH DIRECTIONS

The efforts to materialize gender equality in the work environment have become a national consensus, and therefore, data and research on gender reality in the labor market are needed. Some of the gender research themes that will be required include the position of women in the work environment in the era of the industrial revolution 4.0, the specific gender reality in the agriculture, manufacturing or services sectors, as well as the gender equality in highly educated workforce.

The industrial revolution 4.0 has given a rise to various types of jobs and new work patterns in the work environment. This can create implications for gender disparity in the work environment. Only workers who have the expertise and skills in accordance with the demands of the workforce can adapt to technological progress. Therefore, the reality on how women and men face the technological advances needs to be analyzed comprehensively.

The gender analysis in this paper includes analysis of the whole sectors. In order to get more in-depth data on the matter, gender analysis research needs to be done specifically in the agriculture, manufacturing and services sectors. Even more so since each sector has many interesting cases to be analyzed in depth, especially the sector that absorbs a lot of women workers.

With more access to education for women and better formal education achievements, the research on the participation of Indonesian women in the labor market is increasingly crucial. The research will not only open further explanation on how to re-position women workers in certain posts in the labor market, but also their role and position in the domestic economy, especially in the household decision making.

CONCLUSION

Women in Indonesia face structural and cultural challenges in the labor market as well as the still unfair treatment and inadequate working conditions of employment. These conditions may influence the way younger generations of women in Indonesia in recognizing their role in the labor market while at the same time affecting their decision on education, occupation and future career. This further affects the segregation of occupations by gender resulting in women being subordinated by men because women are often employed in the low level and manual jobs, work less hours with less wages, deal with lack of facilities to support working women with children, receive little to none social security that further take women to a more vulnerable position than men in the Indonesia's labor market.

The analysis of National Labor Force Survey (2016) shows that in the agriculture, manufacturing and services sectors the proportion of male workers is greater than women. The lowest proportion of female workers to men occurs in the manufacturing sector (27.1%) followed by the agriculture sector (37.5%) and services (46.5%). The low number of female workers brings the implications of the male dominance in the strategic positions, especially the managerials. With this condition, women lack the opportunity to make decisions at work. The biggest inequality is seen in the agricultural sector because 60% of the female workforce is unpaid/ contributing family worker. The low position of women in the agricultural sector has led to a decrease in the interest of young women to work in this sector which then further legitimized the decline in the proportion of the women workers in the agricultural sector.

The non-strategic position of female workers makes the average wage of women in all sectors to be lower than that of men. The highest wage disparity between women and men occurs in the agricultural sector as well as in the manufacturing and the services with the proportions of female to male wages in the three sectors were 30.7%, 51.8%, and 67.8%, respectively. There is a huge gap between the average wages of women and men in the agricultural sector. Based on the existing inequality shown, the lowest inequality happens in highly educated workforce. Hence, higher education is a way to reduce wage inequality between men and women in Indonesia.

The service sector is a sector that has the potential to accommodate workers, especially the women. The characteristics of the service sector's job descriptions that consist of the traditional or the informal sector and the modern sector go hand in hand. Each requires the quality of workers in accordance with their needs so that this sector can be entered by workers with low and high education. Women are more absorbed in jobs that require less in expertise and education. However, increasing the level of education for women needs to also be accompanied with equal access for both men and women to participate in the employment that is appropriate with their level of expertise. It is important to reduce the income gap between men and women.

REFERENCES

AIPEG. (2017). *Gender Inequality in Indonesia. A report prepared in a collaboration between the Australian-Indonesian Partnership for Economic Governance (AIPEG), the Australian Department of Foreign Affairs and Trade (DFAT) and Monash University's Centre for Development Economics and Sustainability*. CDES.

Akter, S., Rutsaert, P., Luis, J., Htwe, N. M., San, S. S., Raharjo, B., & Pustika, A. (2017). Women's empowerment and gender equity in agriculture: A different perspective from Southeast Asia. *Food Policy*, *69*, 270–279. doi:10.1016/j.foodpol.2017.05.003

Alisjahbana, A. S., & Manning, C. (2006). Labour market dimensions of poverty in Indonesia. *Bulletin of Indonesian Economic Studies*, *42*(2), 235–261. doi:10.1080/00074910600873674

Asian Development Bank. (2013). *Gender Equality in the Labor Market in Cambodia*. International Publications: Cornell University ILR School.

Asiati, Aji, Ngadi, Triyono, Ningrum, Edi, Aruan, & Purba. (2018). Transformasi Digital dan Ketenagakerjaan di Indonesia. P2K-LIPI, Jakarta.

Blau, F. D., & Kahn, L. M. (2001). *Understanding International Differences in The Gender Pay Gap*. NBER Working Paper No.8200. National Bureau of Economic Research.

Central Bureau of Statistics. (2019). *Keadaan Angkatan Kerja di Indonesia Agustus 2018 (Labor Force Situation in Indonesia August 2018)*. BPS-Statistics Indonesia.

Cepeda, L. (2013). Gender Wage inequality in Indonesia. In T. W. Bank (Ed.), *Presentation*. The World Bank Office Jakarta.

Chant, S. (2010). Gender and Export Manufacturing in the Philippines: Continuity or change in female employment? The case of the Mactan Export Processing Zone. *Journal of Gender. Place and Culture.*, *2*(2), 147–176. doi:10.1080/09663699550021991

Chevalier, A. (2007). Education, Occupation and Career Expectations: Determinants of the Gender Pay Gap for UK Graduates. *Oxford Bulletin of Economics and Statistics*, *69*(6), 819–842. doi:10.1111/j.1468-0084.2007.00483.x

Doss, C., Meinzen-Dick, R., Quisumbing, A., & Theis, S. (2018). Woman in agriculture: Four Myth. *Global Food Security*, *16*(1), 69–74. doi:10.1016/j.gfs.2017.10.001 PMID:29552461

Elmhirst, Siscawati, Basnett, & Ekowati. (2017). Gender and generation in engagements with oil palm in East Kalimantan, Indonesia: insights from feminist political ecology. *The Journal of Peasant Studies*, *44*(6), 1135-1157.

FAO. (2019). *Country Gender Assessment of Agriculture and the Rural Sector in Indonesia*. Food and Agriculture Organization of the United Nations Jakarta.

Feridhanusetyawan, T., Aswicahyono, H., & Perdana, A. A. (2001). The male-female wage differentials in Indonesia. *Economics Working Paper Series, 59*.

Fitrania, S. N. (2013). *The Impact of Globalization on Gender Wage Gap in Indonesia: A Sub-National Level Analysis* (Master's Thesis). Tilburg University.

Ford, M., & Parker, L. (2008). Thinking about Indonesian Women and Work. In M. Ford & L. Parker (Eds.), *Women and Work in Indonesia* (pp. 1–16). Routledge. doi:10.4324/9780203932360

Howcroft, D., & Rubery, J. (2018). *Gender Equality Prospects and The Fourth Industrial Revolution.* https://policynetwork.org/opinions/essays/gender-equality-prospects-fourth-industrial-revolution/

Li, T. M. (2015). *Social impacts of oil palm in Indonesia: A gendered perspective from West Kalimantan*. Occasional Paper 124. Bogor, Indonesia: CIFOR.

Lopes, M., Coelho, L., & Ferreira, V. (2015). *Civil Society Organisations and Gender Equality: Mainstreaming and Empowerment in the Public Policies towards Civil Society*. Paper for the ISTR Eight International Conference and 2nd EMES-ISTR European Conference, The Third Sector and Sustainable Social Change: New Frontiers for Research, organized by ISTR, EMES in partnership with CINEFOGO, Barcelona, Spain.

Malamassam, A., Latifa, A., Setiawan, B., Hidayati, I., & Romdiati, H. (2017). *Optimalisasi Modal Manusia Tenaga Kerja Melalui Migrasi: Kasus Kota Batam*. LIPI.

Manning & Aswichyono. (2012). *Perdagangan di Bidang Jasa dan Ketenagakerjaan: Kasus Indonesia*. ILO.

Mariyono, Latifaha, & Dewia. (2013). *Diskriminasi Jender di Sektor Pertanian Pedesaan di Jawa dan Bali: Kasus Masyarakat Petani Sayuran*. Komnas perempuan dan Program Studi Kajian Gender Program Pascasarjana Universitas Indonesia.

Multani, N., & Sanghvi, A. (2017). Women Workers in Agricultural Sector: A Literature Review. *IRA-International Journal of Management & Social Sciences*, *6*(1), 24–30.

Mulyoutami, E., Martini, E., & Khususiyah, N. (2012). *Agroforestry and Forestry in Sulawesi series: Gender, livelihoods and land in South and Southeast Sulawesi.* Working paper 158. Bogor, Indonesia: World Agroforestry Centre (ICRAF) Southeast Asia Regional Program.

OECD. (2014). Gender Eguality in the "three Es" in the Asia/Pacific region. Society at a Glance Asia/Pacific 2014.

Park, D., & Shin, K. (2012). *The Service Sector in Asia: Is It an Engine of Growth?* Asian Development Bank.

Paul-Majumder, P., & Begum, A. (2000). *The Gender Imbalances in the Export Oriented Garment Industry in Bangladesh.* Policy Research Report On Gender And Development Working Paper Series No. 12. The World Bank.

Pinagara, F. A., & Bleijenbergh, I. (2010). *Understanding the Low Proportion of Women in Employment in Indonesia: A System Dynamics Approach.* Academic Press.

Rendall, M. (2013). *The Service Sector and Female Market Work: Europe vs US.* The University of Zurich.

Setiawan, S. (2011). Kontribusi Industri Jasa dan Perdagangan Jasa Lintas Batas Bagi Rumusan Strategi Baru Pertumbuhan Ekonomi. *Catatan hasil pertemuan APEC SOM.*

Stieger, T. L., & Wardell, M. (1995). *Gender and Employment in the Service Sector. Oxford Journals, 42(1).*

Surbakti & Devasahayam. (2015). *Women and Girls in Indonesia: Progress and Challenges.* UNFPA Indonesia Monograph Series: No.5.

Tadjoeddin, M. Z. (2016). Productivity, wages and employment: Evidence from the Indonesia's manufacturing sector. *Journal of the Asia Pacific Economy.*

Taniguchi, K., & Tuwo, A. (2014). *New Evidence on the Gender Wage Gap in Indonesia.* Asian Development Bank Manila. doi:10.2139srn.2512096

Trask, B. S. (2010). Globalization and Families: Accelerated Systemic. *Social Change.* Advance online publication. doi:10.1007/978-0-387-88285-7_3

World Bank. (2012). *Why the Manufacturing Sector Still Matters for Growth and Development in Indonesia. Policy Note.* The World Bank Office Jakarta.

ENDNOTE

1 The service sector consists of several sectors, i.e.: 1) Transportation, warehousing and communication; 2) Educational services; 3) Government administration, defense and mandatory social security; 4) Wholesale trade, retail, restaurants and hotels; 5) Finance, insurance, rental business, building, land and business services; 6) Community, social and personal services; 7) Financial and insurance services; 8) Health services and social activities; and 9) Company services.

Chapter 3
Gender Disparity in Educational Achievement in India

Satya Sekhar Venkata Gudimetla
https://orcid.org/0000-0002-0320-6608
GITAM University (Deemed), India

ABSTRACT

The primary objective of this chapter is to focus on progress of literacy achievement in India and factors influencing literacy rate are identified with regression models. A gender disparity index is prepared to analyse trends in differentials among male-female literacy achievement. India is now facing the challenge of achieving universalization of primary education to achieve status of a 'literate country'. It is known fact that literacy and primary education are interdependent. A literate country will be a progressive-oriented country. It is observed that educational backwardness is due to various reasons like unsatisfactory progress of policy implementation, high level of illiteracy and dropout rates. Literacy rate is the best possible barometer to judge the level of educational awakening in a state, leading to a minimum capacity for self-learning. The empirical evidence substantiates the factors influencing educational achievement.

1. INTRODUCTION

Universalization of elementary education and total literacy campaigns are really two sides of same coin. No literacy campaign can be successful if a programme of compulsory primary education is not implemented. The need for education awareness can be generated through national literacy campaign.

India is now facing the challenge of achieving universalization of primary education to achieve status of a 'literate country'. It is known fact that literacy and primary education are interdependent. Literate country will be a progressive oriented country. It is observed that educational backwardness is due to various reasons like: unsatisfactory progress of policy implementation, high level of illiteracy and dropout rates. Literacy rate[1] is the best possible barometer to judge the level of educational awakening in a state, leading to a minimum capacity for self-learning. The empirical evidence substantiates the factors influencing educational achievement and gender disparity in south Indian states. A meaningful national policy on education must bring clear objectives, priorities, available resources and modalities of action into close relationship for comprehensive and integrated design for change.

DOI: 10.4018/978-1-7998-3737-4.ch003

1.1. Definitions

- **Literate**: A person who is able to read and write along with understanding it in any language is treated as literate. Literacy can be achieved through different levels of education and different modes of education systems.
- **Literacy rate:** The United Nations Educational Scientific and Cultural Organization (UNESCO) [2] defined literacy as follows:
    - "Ability to identify, understand, interpret, create, communicate compute and use printed and written materials associated with varying contexts. Literacy involves a continuum of learning in enabling individuals to achieve their goals to develop their knowledge and potential, and to participate fully in their community and wider society."

2. BACKGROUND

The philosophical view of education is based on various approaches and each approach may be identified with some eminent scholars, as given below:

- Idealism: Plato, Immanuel Kant, Goerg Wilhelm Fredric Hegel
- Realism: Aristotle, Avicenna, Ibn Tufail, John Locke, Jean-Jacques, Rousseau, Mortimer Jerome Adler, Harry S. Broudy
- Pragmatism: John Dewey, William James, William Heard Kilpatrick, Richard rorty
- Essentialism: William Chandler Bagley
- Progressivism: Jean Piaget, Jerome Bruner

This section deals with the various viewpoints given by a select eminent scholars like: Aristotle, Plato, Rousseau, Benjamin Franklin, Mahatma Gandhi, Jawaharlal Nehru, Dr. Sarvepalli Radhakrishnan etc.

Franklin (1747) reveals that - "men should be taught as if you taught them not, and things unknown proposed as they forgot". According to Franklin, 'the Tutor encourages his pupil to initiate good example'. He makes faculties and encounters positive for the correct molding of the understudy's conduct and to his groundwork forever. The kid feels and encounters great for the correct molding of the student's conduct and to his groundwork forever. On the off chance that the kid detects this consideration without feeling frustrated by it, he produces for his guide an increasingly elevated and more close feeling of regard than would ever be made by any outer power. After the eleventh year of the life, this solid sort of instruction makes away for an increasingly scholarly kind". Thus, the entire of instruction for Franklin is equivalent with the one's life. As water can't run tough, school can't spare a degenerate human progress. A few plans and proposition identifying with uncommon instructive foundations were completely connected with these general thoughts regarding the improvement of society. This is actually the summit of instructive shrewdness. Instruction is simply the sign of the flawlessness. Training which doesn't assist the normal mass with equiping themselves for the quality of character, a feeling of generosity, and the boldness of lion, isn't worth. The very substance of instruction is convergence of brain, not the gathering realities. We need that instruction by which character is framed, quality of psyche is expanded, the acumen is extended, and by which one can remain on one own feet.

Francis (1941) states that instruction is the way toward drawing and controlling youngsters towards that standard which is articulated right by the law and affirmed as genuinely directly by the experience of the most established and generally just. The soul of Plato's ideas as a genuine savant was a long ways into the great beyond of the school in. In this manner, his view can not to be squeezed into the run of the mill educational systems upheld by guardians who need their youngsters to be adjusted to the common social or expert gauges. During seventeenth century, thinkers made an idea which shocked instructors out of their smug routine is 'Retournez A ' La Nature' changed instructive strategies and impacted the demeanor of guardians to such an extent, that an adolescence was not, at this point thought about a simply second rate condition of adulthood. Training is considered as a successful apparatus for accomplishing the goals, to such an extent that it is professed to be 'incredible equalizer' and a substitute to radical rebuilding without including slaughter and brutality, all the more so in a system where radical measures have been limited.

Aristotle philosophy provided not only the logical tool but also the wisdom which enabled such men as Albetus Magnus and Thomas Acquinas to create a systematic Christian philosophy during the period of 384 BC - 322 BC. He states that "the educator can be successful only if he works with a discipline that is willing to absorb suggestions". Plato wishes that all means of education be concentrated systematically towards bringing about a full and mature personality. For this purpose a forming power within the human personality is necessary and strong enough to harmonize the body with the mind aesthetic with moral demands. According to Aristotle, "education must count on sound physique of the educand. Therefore right diet and proper gymnastic are basic needs of educand. But they cannot do all, for the development of an individual is largely determined by hereditary factors not only physically, but also with respect to psychological qualities, what we call `a healthy nature', in the broadest sense of the word healthy, is mixture of endowment and accomplishment".

Ulich (1967) clarifies the grassroots of instructive way of thinking. Collins (1976) centers around Rousseau's way of thinking of training that ought to be 'negative' nature, however the guideline is on a very basic level contrary with the continually interceding authority "Mentor".

Charles Humme (1993) cites the meaning of training given by Aristotle that 'the objective of instruction is indistinguishable with the objective of man'. Clearly all types of instruction are expressly or verifiably coordinated towards a human perfect. In any case, Aristotle thinks about that instruction is basic for the total self-acknowledgment of man. The preeminent great which all strive for is joy.

Charles Hummel (1993) quoted Aristotle's definition of education and states that, "the goal of education is identical with the goal of man. All forms of education are either explicitly or implicitly directed toward a human ideal. However, Aristotle considered education to be essential for the complete self-realization of man."

Swami Vivekananda (2002) stated that "Education is not the amount of information that is put into the brain to rot there undigested all your life. We must have life-building, man-making, character-making, assimilation of ideas. The donkey carrying a load of sandalwood knows only the weight and not the value of the sandalwood. If education is identical with information, libraries are the greatest sages around the world, and encyclopedias are rishis. Therefore, the education of our entire country should be spiritual and secular, and these changes should be incorporated at a national level, through national methods, as far as practical".

3. GENDER DISPARITY INDEX IN INDIA

Tanushree (2019) examines the literacy landscape in India between 1987 and 2017, focusing on the gender gap in four age cohorts: children, youth, working-age adults, and the elderly. It finds that the gender gap in literacy has shrunk substantially for children and youth, but the gap for older adults and the elderly has seen little improvement. The main thrust of this section is to examine the gender disparity in literacy achievement during 1951-91, based on India's census data. The India's census estimates of literacy rate considered population belonging to above 5 years up to 1971. From 1981 onwards, population belonging to above 7 years is considered. In order to make them comparable, the literacy rates of earlier periods are divided by the ratio of population of 7 years and above to the population 5 years and above age. In order to see the trends in gender differential in literacy rates, the following index (I) is:

$$I = 100 - \frac{Percentage\ of\ literacy\ among\ females}{Percentage\ of\ literacy\ among\ males}$$

The index will be zero if the literacy rate of males and females is the same and it will be 100 if the literacy rate of females is zero. Hence a decline in the index indicates that the literacy rates of females are getting closer to those of males.

The table 1 shows the gender disparity index in educational achievement during 1881-2018. In 1881, only 8.45 percent of India's population was literate. The improvement in literacy rate from census to census reveals that a significant growth in fifties, there is slackness in sixties and seventies. The improvement in literacy is again high from 1981 onwards. During the period 1951-61, literacy rate increased from 20 per cent to 30 per cent. In the next two decades, literacy rate is increased to 44 per cent.

When the educational achievement of males and females is considered, male literacy increased at a high rate in the fifties while female literacy was almost stagnant. But in 1960s and 1970s, despite slow growth in overall literacy, there is less disparity between males and females. In 1980s, literacy improvement of males is lower than that of females. Thus, the literacy rate of males is improved from 43 in 1961 to 64 percent in 1991. The corresponding improvement for females is 16 percent to 39 per cent. Thus, there is still a wide gap in literacy achievement between males and females. The disparity index which stood at 18.3 percentage points in 1951 raised to 25 percentage points in 1961 and declined gradually during 1970's and 1980's. It came down to 16.9 percentage points in 2018. When the literacy achievement is analyzed for the four decade period, male literacy rate was increased 10 times. On the other hand, female literacy rate was increased six times. Hoping, in very near future the disparity will become zero.

4. FACTORS INFLUENCING LITERACY RATE

Literacy rate is influenced by several factors. Some of these factors are analyzed by the PROBE team (1999). PROBE team states " what needs to be considered is not just physical distance but also various barriers that may prevent a willing child from the reaching the local school. In many areas, for instance, villages are divided into separate hamlets, and children from one hamlet may be reluctant or unable to go to school in another hamlet, Only half of all hamlets in rural India have a primary school. In case of schooling for girls, restricted freedom of movement further enhances the problem of social distance."

Table 1. Gender disparity index in educational achievement 1881-2018 (population aged 7 years and above)

Year	Male	Female	Disparity
1881	8.1	0.35	7.75
1891	8.44	0.42	8.02
1901	9.8	0.6	9.2
1911	10.6	1.0	9.6
1921	12.2	1.8	10.4
1931	15.6	2.9	12.7
1941	24.9	7.3	17.6
1951	27.16	8.86	18.3
1961	40.4	15.35	25.05
1971	45.96	21.97	23.99
1981	56.38	29.76	26.62
1991	64.13	39.29	24.84
2001	75.26	53.67	21.59
2011	82.23	65.73	17.5
2018	84.5	67.60	16.9

* Excluding Assam where census could not be conducted in 1981
** Excluding Jammu & Kashmir where census could not be conducted in 1991

The table 2 shows that there are six independent variables are considered to indentify regression equation, as important in influencing literacy rate in India viz., 1) Urbanization, 2) Percentage of Scheduled Castes and 3) Percentage of Scheduled Tribes, 4) Proportion of Child Labour, 5) State Domestic Product and 6) Lagged Literacy.

The table 3 shows the correlation matrix of data. Among these factors per capita income, urbanization and lagged literacy are expected to have a positive influence on the literacy rate. On the other hand, the shares of scheduled castes and scheduled tribes and the incidence of child labour assumed to have a negative impact on the literacy rate, using combinations of these variable from different equations are estimated and are results are presented.

Table 2. Factors influencing literacy rate in 1981-1991: India

STATE	LITERACY RATE (%) IN 1981	LITERACY RATE (%) IN 1991	URBANISATION (%)	SCHEDULED CASTES (%)	SCHEDULED TRIBES (%)	CHILD LABOUR (%)	SDP in 1991 Rs.
ANDHRA PRADESH	35.7	44 .1	26.9	15.9	6.3	15.7	10634
BIHAR	32.0	38.5	13.1	14.6	7.7	8.0	5944
GUJARAT	52.2	61.3	34.5	7.4	14.9	4.2	13329
HARYANA	43.9	55.8	24.6	19.8	0.0	1.3	15432
HIMACHAL PRADESH	51.2	63.9	8.7	25.3	4.2	0.5	11182
KARNATAKA	46 .2	56.0	30.9	16.4	4.3	8.7	10607
KERALA	81.6	89.8	26.4	9.9	1.1	0.6	9631
MADHYA PRADESH	34.2	44.2	23.2	14.6	23.3	12.3	8746
MAHARASTRA	55.8	64.9	38.7	11.l	9.3	11.3	16425
ORISSA	41.0	49.1	13.4	16.2	22.2	4.6	7597
PUNJAB	48.1	58.5	29.6	28.3	0.0	1.6	19267
RAJASTHAN	30. 1	38.5	22.9	17.3	12.4	5.3	8935
TAMILNADU	54.4	62.7	34.2	19.2	1.0	7.8	11398
UTTAR PRADESH	33.3	41.6	19.8	21.0	0.2	11.2	7885
WEST BENGAL	48.6	57.7	27.5	23.6	5.6	4.7	10696

When all the variables are introduced in Model 1, the R value is found to be very high. But only lagged literacy and per capita income are statistically significant. This indicates that multi-collinearity is high.

In model-2, independent variables viz., urbanization and per capita income are deleted. In this case the percentage of scheduled tribes has got a proper sign, but it is statistically insignificant. The co-efficient of percentage of child labour is statically significant. But it has an undesirable sign. This model is also rejected. In model-3, three variables i.e., per capita income, urbanization and lagged literacy are used. In this case, all the co-efficient values are significant. But urbanization has got a negative sign. This model reveals that initial literacy and per capita income are the major determinants of literacy rate. Urbanization has no positive impact as generally expected. This indicates that even though urbanization is high the rural literacy rate is very low and dominates the positive effect of urbanization.

Table 3. Correlation matrix

	LR 81	LR 91	URBN.	SC	ST	CL	SDP
LR 81	1.0	0.99	0.373	-.239	-.3405	-.487	.336
LR 91	.99	1.0	0.3565	-.1814	-.3545	-.5249	.3912
URBN .	.373	.3565	1.0	-.3165	-. 1658	.2184	.5904
SC	-.2399	-. 1814	-.3165	1.0	-.4398	-.2711	.2375
ST	-.3405	-.354	-.1658	-.4398	1.0	.2482	-.3457
CL	-.487	-.5249	.2184	-.2711	.2482	1.0	-.2801
SDP	.336	.3912	.5904	.2375	-.3457	-.2801	1.0

LR 81: Literacy rate in 1981
LR 91: Literacy rate in 1991
URBN: Urbanisation
SC: Scheduled castes
ST: Scheduled tribes
CL: Child labour
SDP: State domestic product

In model-4, independent variables viz., percentage of scheduled castes, percentage of scheduled tribes and incidence of child labour are used. Though R^2 is slightly lower in this case all the co-efficient values are statistically significant with proper sings. All the three variables have a negative impact on literacy rate. However, the incidence of child labour has the least impact followed by percentage of scheduled tribes.

5. INTER-STATE VARIATIONS IN LITERACY ACHIEVEMENT

This section deals with analysis of variations in literacy achievement across states in India and to analyze rural- urban disparities in literacy achievement. Comparable data are available only from 1971. The data are available from Census estimates of 1971, 1981 and 1991 and NSS survey conducted during 1997 was also considered. During 1981 Census enumeration was not conducted in the Assam state. Hence, average growth between 1971and 1991 is applied for 1981. All-India average literacy rate nearly doubled during the period 1971-97. For instance, All- India average literacy rate was 37 percent in 1971 was increased to 62 percent in 1997.

The table 4 represents the data is segregated into two groups i.e., major and minor states based on achievement in literacy rate. The educational performance of major states is further into four quartiles. In 1971, Rajasthan, Bihar, Uttar and Madhya Pradesh states can be grouped into first quartile, as their educational performance is very poor. While best performing states are Guajarat, Maharastra, Tamil Nadu and Kerala, grouped in fourth quartile. Relative ranks on the basis literacy achievement in 1971 and in 1997 are given for all the states to analyze trends in the performance of different states during the period 1971-97. In 1971, Rajasthan had the lowest literacy achievement of 21 per cent among major states and Arunachal Pradesh with 14 per cent among minor states. But, during the period 1971-97, Rajasthan's performance was improved as its relative ranking improved from 1st in 1971 to 4th in 1997. Arunachal Pradesh sustains the same position even in 1997.

Table 4. Ranking of states based on literacy rate during 1951-97

STATE	LITERACY RATES				IMPROVEMENT DURING			RANK	
	1971	1981	1991	1997	1971-81	1981-91	1991-97	1971	1997
MAJOR STATES :									
RAJASTHAN	21	30	39	55	9	9	16	1	4
BIHAR	26	32	38	49	6	6	11	2	1
UTTAR PRDESH	28	33	42	56	5	9	14	3	5.5
MADHYA PRADESH	28	34	44	56	6	10	12	4	5.5
ANDHRA PRADESH	31	36	44	54	5	8	10	5	3
WEST BENGAL	33	49	58	72	16	9	14	6.5	10
ORISSA	33	41	49	51	8	8	2	6.5	2
HARYANA	35	44	56	65	9	12	9	8	11
ASSAM	38	45	53	75	7	8	12	9	8
KARNATAKA	40	46	56	58	6	10	2	10.5	9
HIMACHAL PRADESH	40	51	64	77	11	13	13	10.5	15
PUNJAB	41	48	59	67	7	11	8	12	11
GUJARAT	45	52	61	68	7	9	7	13	12
MAHARASTRA	49	56	65	74	7	9	9	14.5	14
TAMILNADU	49	54	63	70	5	9	7	14.5	13
KERLA	75	82	90	93	7	8	3	15	16
MINOR STATES :									
ARUNCHAL PRADESH	14	26	42	60	12	16	18	1	1
SIKKIM	24	42	57	79	18	15	22	2	5
NAGALAND	33	50	62	84	17	12	22	3	6
MEGHALAYA	38	42	49	71	4	7	28	4	4
TRIPURA	39	50	60	73	11	10	13	5	2
MANIPUR	42	50	60	76	8	10	16	6	3
ALL INDIA	**37**	**44**	**52**	**62**	**7**	**8**	**10**		

Census estimates are not available for Assam. Hence, average growth between 1971-91 is assumed for 1981.

Among states belonging to first quartile in 1971, Uttar Pradesh and Madhya Pradesh could show better results. Hence, they jumped into second quartile in 1997, while Orissa and Andhra Pradesh states' performance was deteriorated. Hence these two states are entered into first quartile in 1997. When coming to states belonging to fourth quartile in 1971, their relative position marginally changed. For instance, Maharastra state's rank in 1971 is 14.5 and it is 14th in 1997. Tamil Nadu rank in 1971 is 14.5 and it is 13th rank in 1997. Gujarat position was deteriorated from 13th rank in 1971 to 12th rank in 1997 and Himachal Pradesh entered into fourth quartile in 1997 with 15th rank.

6. URBAN RURAL DISPARITY IN LITERACY ACHIEVEMENT (1991-2014)

The table 5 states that during the period 1971-81, some states could show better literacy improvement viz., West Bengal (16%), Himachal Pradesh (11%), Rajasthan(9%) and Haryana (16%). When the literacy improvement situation is analysed for the period 1991-97, the least performing states are, Orissa (2%), Karnataka (2%) . While best performing states are: Rajasthan(16%), Uttar Pradesh(14%), and Himachal Pradesh(13%). Andhra Pradesh state literacy improvement during 1980's and 1990's resembles all-India average literacy improvement i.e., 8 percent in 1980's and 10 per cent in 1990 's. Disparities in literacy achievement between the urban and rural areas, which are still quite high. Because of the literacy achievement in rural areas is very less and they are lagging behind the urban areas with a variance of nearly 30 percentage points during 1961 to 1991.Thus literacy in urban areas increased from 54.43 per cent in 1961 to 73.08 per cent in 1991. When it is examined in rural areas, its relative position is margina.lly improved. Rural literacy achievement in 1961 is 22.46 improved to 44.69 per cent during 1991.

Table 5. Gender disparity in urban literacy rates during 1991-2014 in India (population above 7 years of age)

Year	Urban			Rural		
	Male	Female	Gender disparity	Male	Female	Gender disparity
1991	81.09	64.09	17.00	57.87	30.62	27.25
2001	86.27	72.86	13.41	70.7	46.13	24.57
2011	88.76	79.11	9.65	77.15	57.93	19.22
2014[1]	91.1	80.8	10.3	79.8	61.3	18.5

Source: Towards a Literate India, National Literacy Mission, Ministry of Human Resource Development.
* Excludes Assam
** Excludes Jammu & Kashmir

7. GENDER DISPARITY ACROSS STATES -2011-2018

The table 7 indicates the gender disparity in education achievement across states in the year 2011. It is observed that disparity is least in Meghalaya with 3.4 per cent and highest in Rajasthan with 27.8. In addition to this, educational backwardness among females is found very high in Jharkhand (22.3 per cent), Chattisgarh (20.9 per cent), Madhya Pradesh (20.5 per cent) and Bihar (20.2 percent). Whereas, in some states, women are more or less equally achieving literacy rate with Men, for instance: Kerala (4 per cent), Mizoram (4.3 per cent) and Lakshdweep (7.9 per cent).

Table 6. Rural literacy in southern states: 1991

STATE	MALE	FEMALE	TOTAL
ANDHRA PRADESH	47.28	23.72	35.74
KARNATAKA	60.30	34.80	47.70
KERALA	92.91	85.12	88.92
TAMILNADU	67.19	41.84	54.59
ALL INDIA	57.87	30.62	44.69

Source: Final Population Total, Paper-2 of 1992 Registrar General, India.

The table 8 shows the disparity in literacy rate during 2017-18. It is found that educational backwardness among women is high in Rajasthan (29 per cent) and Uttar Pradesh (23 per cent). While, the disparity index is very low in states of Meghalya and Mizoram (2 per cent only).

8. RELATIONSHIP BETWEEN LITERACY AND GENDER DISPARITY

Literacy achievement among male is more than that of female in India. The gap in educational achievement is treated as gender disparity in literacy. The reasons are explained below:

1. Girls are often dropping out from school to share the family responsibility.
2. Girl child from low-income families are forced to learn skills and work and not encouraged to go to school.
3. Early marriage and child marriage is still preventing girls in achieving literacy.
4. Priority to son's education compared to daughter education.
5. Non-availability of schools in backward areas. Lack of transport facilities to reach school.
6. It is found that poor health, hygiene conditions at school are also hampering girl education.
7. Child-labour and migrant labour problems are also one of the reasons for low-literacy in female.
8. In India, dowry system and religious beliefs are also causing low literacy.
9. Lack of safety, eve-teasing and male-domination are obstacles to achieve literacy for female.

Table 7. Gender disparity in literacy rate, 2017-2018

S.NO	STATE	DISPARITY %
1	MEGHALAYA	2
2	MIZORAM	2
3	KERALA	5
4	TRIPURA	6
5	SIKKIM	7
6	ASSAM	8
7	NAGALAND	8
8	PUNJAB	9
9	GOA	10
10	WEST BENGAL	10
11	MANIPUR	12
12	TAMIL NADU	13
13	DELHI	13
14	HIMACHAL PRADESH	14
15	MAHARASTRA	14
16	ORISSA	14
17	KARNATAKA	15
18	ANDHRA PRADESH	16
19	UTTARAKHAND	16
20	TELANGANA	19
21	ARUNACHAL PRADESH	19
22	HARYANA	19
23	CHATTISGARH	19
24	MADHYA PRADESH	20
25	GUJARAT	20
26	JAMMU AND KASHMIR	20
27	BIHAR	21
28	JHARKHAND	21
29	UTTAR PRADESH	23
30	RAJASTHAN	29

9. SUMMARY

The primary objective of this chapter is to focus on progress of literacy achievement during 1881-2018 and factors influencing literacy rate are identified with regression models. A gender disparity index is prepared to analyse trends in differentials among male-female literacy achievement.

The regression results reveals that the factors like per capita income, literacy in 1981 and urbanization have positive influence. While percentage of Scheduled castes and Scheduled Tribes and Child labour factors are barriers in the improvement of literacy rate.

The table 6 shows the rural literacy achievement examined among south-Indian states, Andhra Pradesh is still educationally backward. At the same time there are variations in literacy achievement among social groups, males and females, urban and rural areas. It may be because of various social forces which are responsible for educational backwardness of the scheduled tribes and Scheduled castes . So they are isolated from main stream. For instance, female literacy among scheduled tribe women is abysmally low with 8 percent even in 1991.

Further, recent statistical evidence (2011-2018) on gender disparity in literacy achievement is also analyzed. The Government of India should take necessary steps to improve literacy among women in Rajasthan, Uttar Pradesh, Jharkhand and Bihar.

Table 8. Gender disparity in education achievement across states: 2011

S.No	State	Male Literacy Rate (2011 Census)	Female Literacy Rate (2011 Census)	Disparity
1	Andaman & Nicobar Islands	90.1%	81.8%	8.30
2	Andhra Pradesh	75.6%	59.7%	15.90
3	Arunachal Pradesh	73.7%	59.6%	14.10
4	Assam	78.8%	67.3%	11.50
5	Bihar	73.5%	53.3%	20.20
6	Chandigarh	90.5%	81.4%	9.10
7	Chattisgarh	81.5%	60.6%	20.90
8	Dadra & Nagar Haveli	86.5%	65.9%	20.60
9	Daman & Diu	91.5%	79.6%	11.90
10	Delhi	91.0%	80.9%	10.10
11	Goa	92.8%	81.8%	11.00
12	Gujarat	87.2%	70.7%	16.50
13	Haryana	85.4%	66.8%	18.60
14	Himachal Pradesh	90.8%	76.6%	14.20
15	Jammu and Kashmir	78.3%	58.0%	20.30

REFERENCES:

Bhattacharjee, Hnatkovsa, & Lahiri. (2015). The Evolution of Gender Gaps in India. *India Policy Forum, 11*(1), 119-156. https://faculty.arts.ubc.ca/vhnatkovska/Research/GenderGap.pdf

Chandra, T. (2019). *Literacy in India: The Gender and Age Dimension. ORF Issue Brief No. 322*. October, Observer Research Foundation.

Collins. (1976). Rousseau's Philosophy (or Philosophies?) of Education. *The Irish Journal of Education, 2*, 51-80.

Cornford, F. M. (1941). The Republic of Plato. Oxford University Press.

Franklin. (1747). *Proposals relating to the Education of Youth in Pennsylvania 1747*. National Humanities Center Resource Toolbox Becoming American: The British Atlantic Colonies, 1690-1763.

Hummel, C. (1993), Aristotle (384-322 B.C.). PROSPECTS: The Quarterly Review of Comparative Education, 23(1-2), 39-51.

The Complete works of Swami Vivekananda. (2002). Advaita Ashram.

Ulich, R. (1967). History of Educational Thought. Eurasia Publishing House(P) Ltd.

ENDNOTES

1 The percentage of persons literate among total population.

2 "The Plurality of Literacy and its implications for Policies and Programs", *UNESCO Education Sector Position Paper: 13. 2004.*

Chapter 4
Application of Canonical Correlation Analysis to Gender Inequality and Economic Indicators

Ozge Dinc-Cavlak
Ankara Haci Bayram Veli University, Turkey

ABSTRACT

This study aims to find significant relationships between gender inequality and some economic indicators. More specifically, the labor force participation rate of females, maternal mortality ratio, and proportion of seats held by women in national parliaments are mainly used as gender inequality indicators while employment rate and GDP constitute the economy dimension. For this purpose, instead of using a single variable, multiple variables are mainly preferred, which will lead to a better understanding of the relationship between gender inequality and economic indicators. In order to measure these multiple correlations, canonical correlation analysis is performed which analyzes the relationship between two sets of variables. The rationale of using more than one variable for gender inequality and economy is that using only one variable is not sufficient to explain these concepts, so a variable set is needed.

INTRODUCTION

The relationship between gender inequality and economic development has been widely investigated by using several variables and applying different models. This effort is very critical since, in the countries where gender equality does not seem, severe economic problems may come into question. Further, the differences between economic behaviors of men and women may have an influence on macroeconomic policies including the tax system, social insurance program, regulatory policies, and structural reforms (Stotsky, 2006). Therefore, to be able to reveal the underlying reasons for gender inequality, and reveal the economic factors that can represent economic development is essential in order to understand the relationship between those two concepts.

DOI: 10.4018/978-1-7998-3737-4.ch004

Gender inequality defined as "gaps in opportunities (education, the legal system, access to finance) as well as outcomes (employment and political empowerment)" by Hakura et al. (2016) is a long term phenomenon nearly for all countries and nations since it is closely related to the development levels of the countries. The phenomenon which is also defined as a major barrier to human development by the United Nations Development Program (Gaye et al., 2010) is observed in several dimensions such as health, education, political representation, labor market. Moreover, women and girls face unfavorable consequences about the development of their capabilities and freedom of choice due to discrimination. In this direction, the United Nations Development Program (UNDP) has started to report the gender inequality index since 1990 for several countries. While building this index, three dimensions are mainly considered, which are health, empowerment and labor market, and their indicators are identified as maternal mortality ratio, adolescent birth rate, female and male population with at least secondary education, female and male shares of parliamentary seats, female and male labor force participation rates.

Further, Van de Kerk and Manuel (2008) form the sustainable society index (SSI) by using three dimensions which are human, environmental, and economic wellbeing. While forming the economic wellbeing dimension, two different categories are used namely, transition (organic farming and genuine savings) and economy (GDP, employment, public debt).

In the light of this information, the present study aims to reveal the associations between the concepts which are gender inequality and economic development by considering several indicators. In this direction, to measure gender inequality, the labor force participation rate of females, maternal mortality ratio, and proportion of seats held by women in national parliaments are mainly while employment rate and GDP are considered as economic indicators. While creating the gender inequality index, UNDP determines three main aspects of human development as health, empowerment, and labor market. In line with these aspects, the present study chooses some of the indicators of each aspect, which are labor force participation rate of females, maternal mortality ratio, and proportion of seats held by women in national parliaments. In several types of research, the labor force participation of females is mostly considered as an indicator of gender inequality, and the other indicators are neglected. However, it is only related to the labor market dimension. To be able to obtain strong representativeness, one should also consider other aspects of gender inequality which are health and empowerment, so the present study also considers the indicators of these aspects which are maternal mortality ratio and proportion of seats held by women in national parliaments, respectively. On the other hand, Van de Kerk and Manuel (2008) develop the sustainable society index (SSI) which consists of three main dimensions (human welfare, environmental welfare, and economic welfare). From these dimensions, the economic welfare dimension consists of two different sub-dimensions which are transition and economic development. While transition sub-dimension composes of organic farming and genuine savings, economy sub-dimension composes of the indicators of GDP, employment, and public debt. The SSI is considered to be a well-suited tool informing the decisions regarding achievement of human and economic growth (Saisana and Philippas, 2012). They also assert that the SSI is formed as a comprehensive method that can measure and monitor the health of coupled human-environmental systems. It also approaches sustainability in its broad sense by considering 21 indicators, 8 policy categories, and 3 dimensions (human, environmental, economic) for 151 countries which accounts for 99 percent of the world population.

From the indicators of the economic welfare dimension, the present study considers GDP and employment as indicators of the economy, however, public debt is not taken into consideration in the scope of the present study since the data of public debt is not available for several countries.

This study aims to find significant relationships between gender inequality and some economic indicators. More specifically, the labor force participation rate of females, maternal mortality ratio, and proportion of seats held by women in national parliaments are mainly used as gender inequality indicators while employment rate and GDP constitute the economic development dimension. For this purpose, instead of using a single variable, multiple variables are mainly preferred, which will lead to a better understanding of the relationship between gender inequality and economic indicators. In order to measure these multiple correlations, canonical correlation analysis is performed which analyzes the relationship between two sets of variables. The rationale of using more than one variable for gender inequality and economy is that using only one variable is not sufficient to explain these concepts, so a variable set is needed.

In the present study, the labor force participation rate of females, maternal mortality ratio, proportion of seats held by women in national parliaments, employment rate, and GDP per capita variables are mainly utilized for the year 2017, and the data are obtained from World Bank for 181 countries.

In the next section, the background of the issue is summarized. Then, the main focus of the chapter is briefly explained. Next, the methodology part is mentioned. Finally, findings, conclusion, implications, and future research directions are mainly presented and discussed.

MAIN FOCUS OF THE CHAPTER

Several studies examine the relationship between gender inequality and economic development by considering a single variable, mostly the labor force participation rate of females or education levels of women are used to measure gender inequality, and GDP growth rate is mostly used to represent economic development. However, the current research tries to catch a more comprehensive viewpoint by using multiple variables to examine the relationship between gender inequality and economic development. Instead of using a single variable, to use multiple variables that captures more dimensions enables to obtain of more realistic and detailed analysis results.

There are also some controversies concerning the association between gender inequality and economic development. Several researchers examine the relationship between gender inequality and economic development from the labor market viewpoint, and they analyze the effect of labor force participation rate of females on economic growth (Choudhry and Elhorstand, 2018; Tsani et al., 2013; Tam, 2011; Cagatay and Ozler, 1995; Erturk and Cagatay, 1995; Goldin, 1994). Their findings support the view that there is a U-shaped relationship between those variables. On the other hand, some researchers assert that there is a negative relationship between gender inequality and economic growth (Klasen, 2000; Hakura et al., 2016) while Seguino (2000) finds a positive correlation between GDP growth and gender inequality. Last, Lahoti and Swaminathan (2013) could not find a significant relationship between the level of economic development and the labor force participation of females.

When these contradictory findings are considered, the present study aims to look at the relationship between gender inequality and economic development from a broader perspective by using multiple variables that can represent gender inequality and economic development.

BACKGROUND

There is extant literature investigating the relationship between gender inequality and economic activity. Particularly, the labor force participation rate of females, maternal mortality ratio, and proportion of seats held by women in national parliaments which are considered as gender inequality indicators and employment rate and GDP per capita which are considered as economic indicators have been commonly addressed by researchers. Several studies have reported that gender inequality is negatively associated with the per capita GDP. Hakura et al. (2016) find a negative relationship between gender inequality and per capita GDP growth by performing dynamic panel regressions and time-series data for 115 countries. When they examine this negative relationship between gender inequality and per capita GDP growth for the countries at different levels of development, it is mainly seen in lower-income countries. Klasen (2000) analyzes to what extent gender inequality in education and employment may decrease growth and development by using cross-country and panel regressions. The findings indicate that gender inequality has a remarkable impact on economic growth. More specifically, gender inequality directly affects economic growth by reducing the average quality of human capital while it implicitly affects economic growth through investment and population growth. Elborgh-Woytek et al. (2013) find ample evidence that women can make crucial contributions to economic development by enhancing their labor market potential, increasing the school enrollment, and controlling income. Stotsky (2006) also investigates the gender differences in economic behavior by reviewing the related literature in order to maintain the macroeconomic policy. He also specifies that since the economic behaviors of men and women are different, these differences might affect public policies. The findings also propose that in order to decrease gender inequality and moving forward the status of women might improve economic growth and provide economic stability.

Further, the relationship between fertility on female labor force participation and economic growth is examined by using cross-country panel data (Bloom et al., 2007). Their results reveal that fertility and female labor force participation are negatively correlated with each other. As fertility increases, the labor force participation of females decreases, which has a negative impact on economic growth. Kumari (2018) aims to analyze the relationship between economic growth and women's economic activity by reviewing the related literature deeply. The findings of the review propose that there is a U-shaped relationship between economic growth and female labor force participation rate during the process of economic development, which is also supported by several researchers (Choudhry and Elhorstand, 2018; Tsani et al., 2013; Tam, 2011; Cagatay and Ozler, 1995; Goldin, 1994). Kim et al. (2018) examine the effect of gender inequality on long-term economic growth by using an endogenous-growth model for Korean data. The simulation results demonstrate that when the incongruities between males and females at domestic and in the labor market are totally removed, both the female labor force participation rate and the growth rate in per capita income increase.

Erturk and Cagatay (1995) examine the relationship between feminization in the labor market and economic growth for Latin American countries. They suggest that an increase in the female labor force participation stimulates investment while a rise in the intensity of female household labor has a positive impact on savings. Also, Rodriguez (2018) indicates that the feminization of the labor force is positively related to economic growth while it does not with the labor supply. Mukherjee and Mukhopadhyay (2013) investigate the effects of gender inequality in education and labor force participation on economic growth by using cross country regressions. The findings of the study reveal that gender inequality in education has a negative impact on economic growth while gender inequality in labor force participation positively affects economic growth. Forsythe et al. (2000) investigate the relationship between economic growth and gender inequality by developing a new set of data in both cross-sectional and longitudinal levels. As a measure of women's status and the dependent variable, they use the gender-related development index whose individual components are the achievement of women with regard to life expectancy, education, and access to income. They also use the level of economic development, gender empowerment, the weight of patriarchal institutional arrangements, and structural adjustment as the independent variables. Their findings propose that there is a positive and linear relationship between the level of economic development and the status of women measured by the gender-related development index. They find that the status of women is higher in wealthy nations and lower in poorer ones in the cross-sectional analysis while such a relationship can be observed in the countries with the highest rates of economic growth. Moreover, Lagerlof (1999) points out a strong link between gender inequality in education, high fertility, low investments in human capital, and thus economic growth. Accordingly, lower gender inequality in education leads to lower fertility and higher economic growth.

Contrary to several findings, Seguino (2000) suggests that GDP growth is positively correlated to gender inequality. Accordingly, gender inequality which works to reduce women's wages relative to men's promotes both investment and the productivity of investment, and thus growth in export-oriented economies.

On the other hand, Lahoti and Swaminathan (2013) examine the association between economic growth and women's economic activity in India by using dynamic panel models. They could not find a significant relationship between the level of economic development and the labor force participation of females.

METHODOLOGY

Canonical correlation analysis developed by Hotelling (1936) is a multivariate technique that aims to examine the relationship between two sets of variables. These sets include more than one variable and canonic correlation analyzes how these sets relate to each other (Tabachnick and Fidell, 2013). Canonical correlation analysis is adequate when the underlying dimensions which represent the combinations of variables are unknown (Tabachnick and Fidell, 2013). The linear combination of the variables in a set is defined as a variate which can also be considered as a dimension. In each set, there might be more than one variate and these variates maximize the canonical correlation between the linear combination of the first variable set and the linear combination of the second variable set.

According to the purpose of the researcher, one of the variable sets can be defined as the predictor set and the other one is the criterion set to check the possible causality between variables sets (Sherry and Henson, 2005). In other words, one set of a variable can be considered as a dependent variable set while the other can be defined as independent variables set.

In the present study, gender inequality indicators which are labor force participation rate of females, maternal mortality ratio, and proportion of seats held by women in national parliaments are considered as independent variables set while economic indicators which are employment rate and GDP are considered as dependent variables set. In Figure 1, the conceptual model is portrayed, and a_{x1}, a_{x2}, and a_{x3} state the loadings which show the correlation with each gender inequality indicator on canonical variate X, and a_{y1} and a_{y2} state the loadings which show the correlation with each economic indicator on canonical variate Y, and r_{c1} indicates the canonical correlation for the first pair of canonical variates (Tabachnick and Fidell, 2013).

Figure 1. The conceptual model

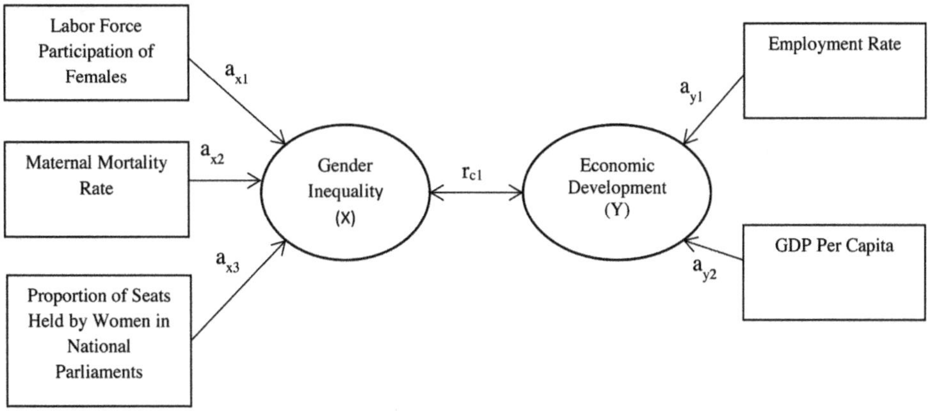

Let's assume there are two sets of variables *X* and *Y*. The variable set of *X* includes *p* variables while the variable set of *Y* includes *q* variables.

$$X = \begin{pmatrix} X_1 \\ X_2 \\ \vdots \\ X_p \end{pmatrix} \tag{1}$$

$$Y = \begin{pmatrix} Y_1 \\ Y_2 \\ \vdots \\ Y_q \end{pmatrix} \tag{2}$$

Then, the linear combinations from the observed variables are formed by creating U and V variates denoting as below;

$$\begin{aligned} U_1 &= a_{11}X_1 + a_{12}X_2 + \ldots + a_{1p}X_p \\ U_2 &= a_{21}X_1 + a_{22}X_2 + \ldots + a_{2p}X_p \\ &\vdots \\ U_p &= a_{p1}X_1 + a_{p2}X_2 + \ldots + a_{pp}X_p \end{aligned} \tag{3}$$

$$\begin{aligned} V_1 &= b_{11}Y_1 + b_{12}Y_2 + \ldots + b_{1q}Y_q \\ V_2 &= b_{21}Y_1 + b_{22}Y_2 + \ldots + b_{2q}Y_q \\ &\vdots \\ V_p &= b_{p1}Y_1 + b_{p2}Y_2 + \ldots + b_{pq}Y_q \end{aligned} \tag{4}$$

Thus, canonical variates could be defined that are the linear combinations in a variable set and created canonical variate sets that maximize the correlations between the variate pairs. Then, the variance of the variable U_i, the variance of the variable V_j, and covariance of U_i and V_j are computed as below;

$$VAR\left(U_i\right) = \sum_{k=1}^{p}\sum_{l=1}^{p} a_{ik} a_{il} cov(X_k, X_l) \tag{5}$$

$$VAR\left(V_j\right) = \sum_{k=1}^{p}\sum_{l=1}^{q} b_{jk} b_{jl} cov(Y_k, Y_l) \tag{6}$$

$$COV\left(U_i, V_j\right) = \sum_{k=1}^{p}\sum_{l=1}^{q} a_{ik} b_{jl} cov(X_k, Y_l) \tag{7}$$

When the canonical correlation is computed, the variances and the covariance of the canonical variate sets are utilized for the ith set that maximizes the correlation between the linear combination of variables in Set 1 and Set 2.

$$\rho_i = \frac{COV(U_i, V_i)}{\sqrt{VAR\left(U_i\right) VAR\left(V_i\right)}} \tag{8}$$

The null hypothesis asserts that there is no significant relationship between variable sets meaning that p canonical variate pairs are uncorrelated.

$$H_{0=}\rho_{1=}\rho_{2=} \ldots\ldots = \rho_p = 0 \tag{9}$$

FINDINGS

In the data set, gender inequality consists of three variables and economic development consists of two variables, so the number of the relationship between variates will be the minimum of the variable set which is equal to two in this case. Table 1 indicates the number and significance of canonical correlations between two sets of variables.

- The results show that there is a correlation between gender inequality and economic development variables which is 82.9 percent indicating a quite larger relationship between the sets of variables. This canonical correlation coefficient cannot be negative since the weights in the linear equations are standardized (Sherry and Henson, 2005).
- Also, there is 68.2 percent (the square of canonical correlation) overlapping variance for the first pair of canonical variates. In other words, it expresses the proportion of variance shared by two variates. The null hypothesis asserts that there is no significant relationship between variable

sets. However, the Wilks Statistic suggests that the relationship between the variates is significant ($p<0.001$) implying that there is a significant relationship between gender inequality and economic development, and the magnitude of this relationship is observed as 82.9% which is substantially larger.

- Furthermore, the canonical functions named as variate specify a set of standardized canonical function coefficients for the observed predictor and criterion variable sets. Every function is orthogonal to any other function, meaning that each set of synthetic predictors and criterion variables is entirely uncorrelated to all other synthetic predictors and criterion variables from other functions (Sherry and Henson, 2005).

Table 1. Canonical Correlations

	Correlation	Eigenvalue	Wilks Statistic	F	Num D.F	Denom D.F.	Sig.
1	0.829	2.200	0.155	90.483	6.000	352.000	0.000***
2	0.711	1.020	0.495				

Note: ***p<0.001

Table 2 demonstrates the standardized canonical correlation coefficients for gender inequality variables. The weights are formed in z-scores to maximize canonical correlation.

- Since the standardized coefficient is larger, providing the highest contribution to the first canonical variable is the labor force participation rate of females, and since only the first canonical correlation is available, only the coefficients of the first function are interpreted.

Table 2. Standardized Canonical Correlation Coefficients for Gender Inequality Variables

Variable	1	2
Parliamentary Seats Held by Women	0.098	-0.095
Labor Force Participation Rate of Females	-1.029	-0.143
Maternal Mortality Ratio	0.078	0.999

Table 3 demonstrates the standardized canonical correlation coefficients for economic development variables.

- Since the standardized coefficient is larger, providing the highest contribution to the first canonical variable is the employment rate, and since only the first canonical correlation is available, only the coefficients of the first function are interpreted.

Table 3. Standardized Canonical Correlation for Economic Development Variables

Variable	1	2
Employment Rate	-1.005	-0.038
LogGDP Per Capita	-0.071	-1.003

Table 4 demonstrates the canonical loadings of gender inequality variables. since only the first canonical relationship is found to be significant, only the coefficients of the first function are interpreted.

- As the coefficients suggest, providing the highest contribution to set 1 variate is the labor force participation rate of females.

Table 4. Canonical Loadings for Gender Inequality Variables

Variable	1	2
Parliamentary Seats Held by Women	-0.113	-0.265
Labor Force Participation Rate of Females	-0.994	0.049
Maternal Mortality Ratio	-0.153	0.983

Table 5 demonstrates the canonical loadings of economic development variables. since only the first canonical relationship is found to be significant, only the coefficients of the first function are interpreted.

- As the coefficients suggest, providing the highest contribution to set 1 variate is the employment rate.

Table 5. Canonical Loadings for Economic Development Variables

Variable	1	2
Employment Rate	-0.998	0.07
LogGDP Per Capita	0.037	-0.999

Table 6 illustrates the cross loadings identifying the correlation between gender inequality variables and economic development variate.

- Accordingly, the most correlated variable with the economic development variate is the labor force participation rate of females.

Table 6. Cross Loadings for Gender Inequality Variables

Variable	1	2
Parliamentary Seats Held by Women	-0.094	-0.188
Labor Force Participation Rate of Females	-0.824	0.035
Maternal Mortality Ratio	-0.127	0.698

Table 7 demonstrates the cross loadings identifying the correlation between economic development variables and gender inequality variate.

- Accordingly, the most correlated variable with gender inequality variate is the employment rate.

Table 7. Cross Loadings for Economic Development Variables

Variable	1	2
Employment Rate	-0.827	0.050
LogGDP Per Capita	0.031	-0.710

Table 8 portrays the proportion of variance explained and the redundancy analysis that indicates how much of the variance in Set 1 and Set 2 can be explained by opposite variates.

- Set 1 by Self column indicates that the proportion of variance of Set 1 explained by its own canonical variables meaning that 34.1 percent of the variation in gender inequality can be explained by the labor force participation rate of females, maternal mortality ratio, and proportion of seats held by women in national parliaments.
- Set 1 by Set 2 column means the proportion of variance of Set 1 explained by opposite canonical variables. Accordingly, the first canonical variate in economic development explains 23.5 percent of the variance in gender inequality.
- Set 2 by Self column suggests that the proportion of variance of Set 2 explained by its own canonical variables. In other words, the first canonical variate in economic development extracts 49.8 percent of variance from its own variables.
- Set 2 by Set 1 column means the proportion of variance of Set 2 explained by opposite canonical variables. Accordingly, the first canonical variate in gender inequality explains 34.3 percent of the variance in economic development.

Table 8. Proportion of Variance Explained and Redundancy Measures

Canonical Variable	Set 1 by Self	Set 1 by Set 2	Set 2 by Self	Set 2 by Set 1
1	0.341	0.235	0.498	0.343
2	0.346	0.175	0.502	0.253

CONCLUSION

The present study aims to reveal the associations between the concepts which are gender inequality and economic development by considering the multiple indicators. In this direction, to measure gender inequality, the labor force participation rate of females, maternal mortality ratio, and proportion of seats held by women in national parliaments are mainly while employment rate and GDP are considered as economic indicators. For this purpose, instead of using a single variable, multiple variables are mainly preferred, which will lead to a better understanding of the relationship between gender inequality and economic indicators. In order to measure these multiple correlations, canonical correlation analysis is performed which analyzes the relationship between two sets of variables. The rationale of using more than one variable for gender inequality and economy is that using only one variable is not sufficient to explain these concepts, so a variable set is needed. In the present study, gender inequality indicators which are labor force participation rate of females, maternal mortality ratio, and proportion of seats held by women in national parliaments are considered as independent variables set while economic indicators which are employment rate and GDP are considered as dependent variables set.

Canonical correlation analysis results suggest that the correlation between gender inequality and economic development variables is 82.9 percent indicating a quite larger relationship between the sets of variables, and there is 68.2 percent (the square of canonical correlation) overlapping variance for the first pair of the canonical variates.

When examining the canonical correlation coefficients, it can be observed that the variables providing the highest contribution to set 1 variate is the labor force participation rate of females and employment rate. In addition, when the cross loadings are examined, the most correlated variable with the economic development variate is the labor force participation rate of females, and the most correlated variable with the gender inequality variate is the employment rate.

The results of the current research support the previous findings proposing that the labor force participation of females and economic development are highly correlated. Accordingly, the most correlated variable with economic development is the labor force participation rate of females. Also, the variable providing the highest contribution to the gender inequality dimension is the labor force participation rate of females.

IMPLICATIONS

The present study mainly aims to focus on the linear relationship between gender inequality and economic development by performing canonical correlation analysis. Consistent with the previous researches, the findings of the study assert that the highest contribution to gender inequality comes from the labor force participation rate of females which is also positively correlated with economic development. This finding implies that promoting women's labor force participation rate enhances economic development which is also supported by Tsani et al. (2013). They emphasize that to remove the barriers to the entry of women in the labor market supports economic growth implying that region-specific barriers should be removed to maintain economic benefit.

Even though the relationship between maternal mortality ratio and proportion of seats held by women in national parliaments and economic development seems weak, Pearson correlation results suggest that there is a negative significant relationship between maternal mortality ratio and GDP per capita (r=-0.702), and the relationship between proportion of seats held by women in national parliaments and GDP per capita is positive (r=0.185). These findings highlight that the importance of women's status in several areas, and reveal that women's activity either in the labor market or in the political arena has an essential influence on economic development which is an important implication for policymakers. For instance, Revenga and Shetty (2013) assert there is a gender gap in earnings and economic productivity between men and women, and they propose certain policies to be removed the women's access to economic opportunities by providing health care or improving the access of women to credit. They further suggest that implementing quotas for women's favor in workplaces promotes the productivity of women.

FUTURE RESEARCH DIRECTIONS

The study has also some limitations. Canonical correlation analysis assumes that all variables and all linear combinations of variables should be normally distributed, and the relationships between variables should be linear since canonical correlation analysis can capture only the linear relationship between variables, and it misses the nonlinear relationships (Tabachnick and Fidell, 2013). Accordingly, the logarithmic transformation of GDP per capita is used to reduce the departure from normality and linearity. Even so, the analysis results cannot capture nonlinear relationships which should be investigated for further research by using nonlinear analysis techniques.

Further, the present study includes only some variables that can represent gender inequality and economic development dimensions. However, there could be also some other variables that are associated with these dimensions. For instance, the education level of females or public debt may also be investigated for further research.

"This research received no specific grant from any funding agency in the public, commercial, or not-for-profit sectors".

REFERENCES

Bloom, D. E., Canning, D., Fink, G., & Finlay, J. E. (2007). Fertility, Female Labor Force Participation, and Demographic Dividend. *Journal of Economic Growth, 14*(2), 79–101. doi:10.100710887-009-9039-9

Cagatay, N., & Ozler, S. (1995). Feminization of the labor force: The effects of long-term development and structural adjustment. *World Development, 23*(11), 1883–1894. doi:10.1016/0305-750X(95)00086-R

Choudhry, M. T., & Elhorst, P. (2018). Female labour force participation and economic development. *International Journal of Manpower, 39*(7), 896–912. doi:10.1108/IJM-03-2017-0045

Elborgh-Woytek, K., Newiak, M., Kochhar, K., Fabrizio, S., Kpodar, K., Wingender, P., Clements, B., & Schwartz, G. (2013). *Women, Work, and the Economy: Macroeconomic Gains from Gender Equity. Staff Discussion Note 13/10.* International Monetary Fund.

Erturk, K., & Cagatay, N. (1995). Macroeconomic consequences of cyclical and secular changes in feminization: An experiment at gendered macromodeling. *World Development, 23*(11), 1969–1977. doi:10.1016/0305-750X(95)00090-Y

Forsythe, N., Korzeniewicz, R. P., & Durrant, V. (2000). Gender inequalities and economic growth: A longitudinal evaluation. *Economic Development and Cultural Change*, *48*(3), 573–617. doi:10.1086/452611

Gaye, A., Klugman, J., Kovacevic, M., Twigg, S., & Zambrano, E. (2010). Measuring key disparities in human development: The gender inequality index. *Human Development Research Paper*, *46*, 41.

Goldin, C. (1994). *The U-shaped female labor force function in economic development and economic history*. NBER Working Paper No. 4707.

Hakura, M. D. S., Hussain, M. M., Newiak, M. M., Thakoor, V., & Yang, M. F. (2016). *Inequality, gender gaps and economic growth: Comparative evidence for sub-Saharan Africa*. International Monetary Fund.

Hotelling, H. (1936). *Relation between two sets of variates*. Biometrica.

Kim, J., Lee, J. W., & Shin, K. (2018). Gender inequality and economic growth in Korea. *Pacific Economic Review*, *23*(4), 658–682. doi:10.1111/1468-0106.12181

Klasen, S. (2002). Low Schooling for Girls, Slower Growth for All? Cross Country Evidence on the Effect of Gender Inequality in Education on Economic Development. *The World Bank Economic Review*, *16*(3), 345–373. doi:10.1093/wber/lhf004

Kumari, R. (2018). Economic growth, disparity, and determinants of female labor force participation: A research agenda. *World Journal of Entrepreneurship, Management and Sustainable Development*, *14*(2), 138–152. doi:10.1108/WJEMSD-03-2017-0009

Lagerlof, N. (1999). *Gender Inequality, Fertility, and Growth*. Department of Economics, University of Sydney.

Lahoti, R., & Swaminathan, H. (2013). *Economic Growth and Female Labor Force Participation in India*. Indian Institute of Management Bangalore, Working Paper, (414).

Mukherjee, P., & Mukhopadhyay, I. (2013). Impact of Gender Inequality on Economic Growth: A Study of Developing Countries. *IOSR Journal of Humanities and Social Science*, *13*(2), 61–69. doi:10.9790/0837-1326169

Revenga, A., & Shetty, S. (2012). Empowering Women Is Smart Economics-Closing gender gaps benefits countries as a whole, not just women and girls. *Finance and Development-English Edition*, *49*(1), 40.

Rodriguez, A. V. (2018). Economic growth and gender inequality: An analysis of panel data for five Latin American countries. *CEPAL Review*, *2017*(122), 79–106. doi:10.18356/73d010ed-en

Saisana, M., & Philippas, D. (2012). Sustainable Society Index (SSI): Taking societies' pulse along social, environmental and economic issues. *Environmental Impact Assessment Review*, *32*, 94–106.

Seguino, S. (2000). Gender inequality and economic growth: A cross-country analysis. *World Development*, *28*(7), 1211–1230. doi:10.1016/S0305-750X(00)00018-8

Sherry, A., & Henson, R. K. (2005). Conducting and interpreting canonical correlation analysis in personality research: A user-friendly primer. *Journal of Personality Assessment*, *84*(1), 37–48. doi:10.120715327752jpa8401_09 PMID:15639766

Stotsky, J. G. (2006). *Gender and its Relevance to Macroeconomic Policy: A Survey* (No. 6-233). International Monetary Fund.

Tabachnick, B. G., & Fidell, L. S. (2013). *Using multivariate statistics* (6th ed.). Pearson.

Tam, H. (2011). U-shaped female labor participation with economic development: Some panel data evidence. *Economics Letters*, *110*(2), 140–142. doi:10.1016/j.econlet.2010.11.003

Tsani, S., Paroussos, L., Fragiadakis, C., Charalambidis, I., & Capros, P. (2013). Female labour force participation and economic growth in the South Mediterranean countries. *Economics Letters*, *120*(2), 323–328. doi:10.1016/j.econlet.2013.04.043

Van de Kerk, G., & Manuel, A. R. (2008). A comprehensive index for a sustainable society: The SSI-the Sustainable Society Index. *Ecological Economics*, *66*(2-3), 228–242. doi:10.1016/j.ecolecon.2008.01.029

ADDITIONAL READING

Bloom, D. E., Canning, D., Fink, G., & Jocelyn, E. F. (2009). Fertility, female labor force participation and the demographic dividend. *Journal of Economic Growth*, *14*(2), 79–101. doi:10.100710887-009-9039-9

Boserup, E. (1970). *Women's Role in Economic Development*. St Martin's Press.

Clark, R. (1991). Culture, gender, and labor force participation: A cross-national study. *Gender & Society*, *5*(1), 47–66.

Lim, L. L. (2001). *Female Labor Force Participation*. ILO.

Mishra, V., & Smyth, R. (2010). Female labor force participation and total fertility rates in the OECD: New evidence from panel cointegration and Granger causality testing. *Journal of Economics and Business*, *62*(1), 48–62. doi:10.1016/j.jeconbus.2009.07.006

Schultz, T. P. (1990). Women's changing participation in the labor force: A world perspective. *Economic Development and Cultural Change*, *38*(3), 457–488. doi:10.1086/451811

Tansel, A. (2002). *Economic Development and Female Labor Force Participation in Turkey: Time Series Evidence and Cross Province Estimates*. Economic Research Center.

KEY TERMS AND DEFINITIONS

Employment Rate: The degree of the extent to which available labor resources are being utilized. The proportion of the employed to the working age population.

GDP per Capita: The degree of a country's economic output that accounts for its number of people. It separates the country's gross domestic product by its total population. That creates it a great estimation of a country's standard of living.

Gender Inequality: The gaps in opportunities (education, the legal system, access to finance) as well as outcomes (employment and political empowerment).

Labor Force Participation Rate of Female: The rate of the female population ages 15 and older that is economically active: all individuals who supply labor for the production of goods and services during a specified period.

Maternal Mortality Ratio: The number of maternal deaths during a given time period per 100,000 live births during the same time period.

Proportion of Seats Held by Women in National Parliaments: The number of seats held by women members in single or lower chambers of national parliaments, communicated as a rate of all occupied seats; it is determined by partitioning the entire number of seats involved by women by the total number of seats in parliament.

Chapter 5
Upshot of Gender Inequalities Towards Labor Markets: A Macro Level Perspective

Gayathri R.
SASTRA University (Deemed), India

Vijayabanu C.
https://orcid.org/0000-0002-0125-4534
SASTRA University (Deemed), India

ABSTRACT

Globalization has accelerated the pace of innovation and technology and has paved the way for new business across all countries. Gender (in)equality and empowerment of women is the most discussed and debated topic worldwide. To survive in a dynamic environment with enormous impediments in the form of societal, political, economic, legal, and technological environment is the biggest challenge. To prevail over this, there is an imperative need to discard old prejudices and accept innovative thinking and resolutions. The purpose of this chapter is to throw light on the subjugation of women across all sectors. The reports from various countries are scrutinized. The chapter studies the linkage of various aspects that hinder the progress of oneself and the economy at large and to put forward different techniques for inclusive growth of women with enhanced economic growth. To accomplish gender equality, we need to focus on the gaps that have remained as an impediment for further development

INTRODUCTION

"All growth depends upon activity. There is no development physically or intellectually without effort, and effort means work". - Calvin Coolidge

A nation's progress depends on the level of economic activity primed by the people. Labor constitutes the prime factor in the production process and this determines the intensity of economic movement in the

DOI: 10.4018/978-1-7998-3737-4.ch005

country. Productivity is a process to assess the efficiency of an effort done either by a person, machine, system etc. The optimization of the existing natural, human or capital resources depends on the ideal blend of technology with the constraints. The work force participation rate signifies the proportion of working population to total population and this depends on diverse aspects like gender, location age, ability to work, job opportunities, the type of economy etc and this varies across countries. The total area of India is 32,87,469 sq.kms inhabited by 62,32,70,258 males and 58,75,84,719 females and the number of people residing in the rural areas is 83,30,87,662 and that in the urban areas is 37,71,05,760 according to the census 2011.Majority of the women actually spend more time than men in economic activities but these are not captured and recognized in the actual framework. In rural areas, where the main occupation is agricultural activities, tiny and cottage based industries or construction activities, women involve themselves into such labor market as they believe that it's appropriate for them to do something at their level of understanding and knowledge. In the due course, the society had defined a pattern for labor utilization. In certain countries, women and children are employed due to cheap labor as their bargaining power is negligible.The Census 2011 in India shows that the work force participation for males is 53.26% and for females is 25.51%. In rural India, women's participation in the economic activities is on the rise with 30.02% females compared to 53.03% males. India is positioned at 112th place out of 144 countries in the Global Gender Gap Index 2019 (Global Gender Gap Report, n.d.). Wage packages diverge across countries, livelihoods, amongst all businesses, genders etc as there exist a factor of discrimination involved in all these aspects. A statistical analysis on work force participation in India shows that women participate in the economic activities both at the formal and informal sectors of the economy and thus contribute to the development of the economy.

A SCRUTINY OF THEORETICAL LITERATURE

An analysis of some of the research studies pertaining to gender (in) equality and economic growth shows that women abstain from the active participation in labor market; education due to various aspects like societal restrictions, shorter duration of employment, pay packages, sexual discrimination, time schedules etc that has been detrimental to economic development. Further, examining the work of researchers is crucial to identify the statistical association amid societal beliefs and gender which would pave way in providing suitable policy interventions aimed at gender equality.

Seguino (2000) illustrated that gender wage inequality might be a positive factor for economic development. Gender inequality consecutively reduces the potential of the work force, human capital investments and affects the economic growth rates. AnandSwamy, Omar Azfar, Stephen Knack and Young Lee (2001) have identified that females in the most powerful designation are more reputable than men. Psacharopoulos and Patrinos (2004), Nafukho & Brooks (2006) believed that education will pave way for efficiency and financial payments would increase considerably along with health. Baliamousne –Lutz and Mc Gullivray (2007) recommended that trade stimulated economies may be linked with higher levels of gender inequality. Mark Blackden et al (2007) have identified in their study that skilled women leave the labor market due to gender inequality in employment and this decreases their performance and economic growth would decline. Klasen and Lamanna (2009), Esteve-Volart (2009), (Baldwin & Johnson, 1992). Gender equality results in positive economic growth (Ali 2015).Increase in women's participation in the workforce upsurge the family's income and accelerates demand (Vaughan-Whitehead 2016). Though development persists (Davis and Greenstein 2009), argument could be made that gender disparity in the

United States (US) continues. A study found that in the US, people are no more becoming egalitarian with regards to gender role attitudes (Cotter et al. 2011). A research study was undertaken to examine the role of society in the social stratification through the gender beliefs (Guiso et al. 2003; Morrisson and Jutting 2005; Sen 2007). An interesting study was related to the societal attitude towards fertility (Cunningham et al. 2005) educational ambition (Davis and Pearce 2007), and other outcome (Whitehead 2012; Silverstein and Giarrusso 2012).

Why Are We Focusing on Women's Issue?

From the beginning of human civilization, agriculture was the prime occupation and societies thrived on the prosperity of agriculture. From then onwards men and women occupied different roles in the society: women took the position of a concierge in private sphere, while men took their position in the public sphere. In the due process, male domination and all sorts of gender inequalities continued to prevail in dissimilar stages in the context of religion, cultural norms, and socio political rights across various countries. Informal social norms and practices lead to the development of social institutions which restricts the choices, the decision making capacity and behavior of the individuals and communities. The social institutions set the constraints of what behavioral decisions and choices are to be accepted and therefore played a key role in influencing gender roles. The social institutions are not permanent and they often vary across communities, regions and countries and they also change over time. Social institutions exert their influences directly and indirectly on women and men. An example of indirect influence by the social institutions on women's economic and social role is the community norms which attribute greater societal value to sons over daughters, and thus has the consequence in early marriages and vast gap in the age of spouses, high fertility rates, and underinvestment in health care, high infant mortality rates and education of girls. Certain common troubles related to women's issues across countries are due to the limited or no role in decision making related to education, early/late marriages, choice of a child, legal rights, financial security etc and are subject to domestic violence and sexual harassment which are never reported due to the reason that women are blamed for their 'behavior or family honor'. Social institutions are intrinsically not bad, but when they confine or eliminate women and girls' access to education, resources and power they become discriminatory social institutions which have a negative impact on the development upshot of a country. These discriminatory social institutions replicate gender powered relations.

A lot of qualitative research work has been undertaken by researchers worldwide to divulge on the different patterns of economic growth across nations and some of the prominent factors influencing economic growth are the investment and saving rate, technology, efficient utilization of human resource development, trade induced growth strategies etc have paved the path to development. The linking of emerging socio-economic and demographic aspects depends on how women contribute to the work is versatile. The necessity to work depends on two major factors; one is driven by poverty and the other by enhancing the educational accomplishments they contribute to the economy. An additional significant aspect of gender related studies that have garnered the attention of academicians and policy makers pertain to the decision making ability of women within the family circle. The shoddier the countries, fewer likely are the women to influence in the decisions related to expenditure. Participation and acknowledgement of women's decision making capacity in the family related to investments, savings, education etc, is itself a healthy trend.

A significant consequence of relentless gender gaps is that the competence of women towards economic contribution and decision making remains untapped in many countries. Women are indulged as succeeding citizens in many of the societies even today. Some of the common quandaries voiced out from the suppressed and oppressed women across the world are associated with torment which relates to both physical and mental crimes, kidnapping, human trafficking, suicides, discrimination at every stage, societal & political restrictions, low morale, work life imbalance, pay related issues, motherhood, dowry etc. The focal point of the chapter is to emphasize the context of existing gender inequality prevalent across various countries accumulating as a result of the societal structure, labor laws and markets' productivity, pay checks, promotion, education, skill levels and other factors and to present different theories and research pertaining to the gender inequality in the country and to provide a wider scope for policy makers, academicians, international establishments, researchers etc in understanding the various facets of gender inequality and framing suitable polices to reduce gender inequality in the economy.

Does Gender Inequality Endure Across Continents?

Obviously, in spite of the progress achieved by the countries, women and men do not have access to equal opportunities in career, wages, rewards, benefits etc due to diverse issues. It is estimated by the World Economic Forum (2017) that it will take 217 years to seal the overall global gender gap and in providing equal opportunities. Owing to low wages and lesser participation of women in the workforce, India has moved to the 112th position in the Global gender gap index (WEF). (IMF, n.d.)

Diverse Facet of Inequality Across Continents

The effects of gender inequality related to labor markets are widespread, pertaining to different continents and across varied sectors have raised certain crucial questions on the gendered influenced relations which include discrimination, structural inequalities, violence, gender pay gaps, widespread atrocities and harassments, gender biased employment opportunities, education and so on. The effects of inequalities have brought in lop sided development. Let's analyze a few gaps from varied dimensions and countries.

Inequality in Distribution of Income

Disparity in the distribution of income is rampant and widespread. Inequality in income has augmented more or less among all the countries at diverse phases due to the policies and decisions taken by the respective governments. According to the World Inequality report 2018, inequality persists among all the countries and the share of national income varied across different countries and among the best 10 percent earners of national income, Europe had a share of 37% whereas China had a share of 41% compared to that of India which had a share of 55 percent (WIR, 2018).

Women in Parliament

Women's active role in political arena positively reflects to their contribution in economic growth and more the number of people in employment, further is the decision making capacity and additional are the parliamentary seats occupied by women.

A highly successful country is one where the highest decision making authority which governs the people or represents them i.e., is the parliament does not discriminate itself of the population it represents. Mere percentage of reservation of seats for women does not promote equality nor does it bridge the gap between gender inequalities. It's just not right to equality but it's about acknowledging women's resources in ***decision making*** that benefits societies across communities. Men outnumber women in politics across all countries. Only 23.97% of women parliamentarians' are found across all regions and all forms of political structures in spite of the progress and development made by the countries .(IPU, n.d.)

Women and Financial Services

Financial services occupy a very prominent position in the creation of credit, output and employment opportunities in the economy and have significant linkages with the country at large, providing essential inputs for all the activities pertaining to the individual and the industry. Optimization and appropriate allocation of financial resources starts from home and women play a prominent role in balancing them amidst budget constraints.

In spite of the key role played by women in contributing and managing the income of the household in terms of sending or receiving money, they are less likely to be empowered than men and even now in certain societies they have no control over managing their own resources at home. With the commencement of latest innovations in banking services and other payment options, women trail behind men when it comes to financial transactions.

Transmitting money through digital channels can lower the costs of financial transactions as much as 90 percent when compared to the transactions that are done physically in banks. It's viable and lucrative for digital financial contributors to offer their services in places wherever banks and automatic teller machines are unable to serve. It ought to be equally important that the vulnerable sections of the society are not exploited from unfair and fraudulent practices.

Across the world, merely 65 percent of the women have formal access to the banking services when compared to 72 percent of men, with the gap widening amongst under developed and developing economies. (World Bank Global Findex, 2018)(World Bank, n.d.a). There are also gaps in the use of smart cards (debit and credit cards) and financial services. (Delechat and others, 2018). Financial self-determination would pave the way for women to take apt decisions in terms of enhanced healthcare for their health as well as for their families.

Women and Law

The nonexistence of fundamental constitutional rights in certain countries averts women from participating completely in business and political opportunities. A country when it restricts women from participating in the labor markets is also restricting the revenue and the potential of the work force. More than 2.7 billion women face restrictions on employment globally, according to the 2018 Women, Business and the Law Report (World Bank, n.d.b). Furthermore there are no laws existing in 59 countries against sexual harassment in the work place. Societal norms also contribute to gender inequality and negatively impact the efficiency of the work force. Adding to their owes, many countries still restrict women from access to property and inheritance.

Women and Mobile Services

Technology transforms lives and mobile empowers women to experience safety, stays connected and surf for any information or services and thereby influences community decision making and transforms themselves as agents of change. Mobile services surpass topography, civilizations, culture, socio-economic status and provide extensive advantages to women and society. While mobile connectivity is spreading rapidly, it's not extending uniformly. The dimension of the gender gap in mobile possession and mobile internet utilization diverge considerably across all regions.

Lack of awareness connected with the potential benefits result in fewer women using the digital technology. Women, in general do not engage themselves in online activities as they perceive that they do not gain any benefit from internet usage. Moreover illiteracy, lack of interest, low expectations related to the usefulness, lack of local languages etc additionally hampers women's capability to access online services. The socio cultural factors play a prominent role in identifying the causes for digital gender divide. Only one fifth of women in India and Egypt believed that internet usage was not suitable for them due to various cultural reasons and 12 percent of women in India do not make use of the internet due to the pessimistic societal perception associated with it and 8 percent due to restrictions from family members. Active encouragement and confidence from their families would contribute to more women accessing the internet. Vigorous women internet users are three times probable to have families that approve their internet usage and women non users are six times most probable exposed to opposition and prohibition from their families. (Intel, n.d.) Another prominent reason for the restriction of internet usage cited by families interrelates to safety issues. Additional risks in the form of cyber stalking, harassments online, abusive audio and video clippings, sexual trafficking etc prevents women in reaping the fullest benefits of technology. In rural areas especially, the capability of women to access digital technologies is unswervingly affected by factors generally associated with the extent of investments, regulations and installation of network towers etc in less commercial areas. In spite of the advancement made, women have fewer accesses to technology than men in low and medium developing countries. Even though to be in possession of a mobile phone does not result in reaping the fullest benefits of technology to users, as women are less likely to use the additional services than men. Further affordability to the mobile packages widens the gap among men and women.

Gender gap related to basic models and latest smart phone ownership exists in small and regular income countries. On an average 10 percent of the women are fewer likely to own a basic mobile and 26 percent are less probable to own a smart phone. Particularly in South Asia 26 percent of the women own a basic mobile phone and 70 percent are less probable to own a smart phone that can hook up to the mobile internet . Certain parts in Saharan Africa have a gender gap of 14 percent of women who possess a basic mobile and 34 percent of women have a smart phone.[8]

According to the GSMA mobile gender gap report 2018, conducted across 23 countries, it was found that women and men used the voice calling at related levels. The use of SMS was found to be low amongst women in around half of the countries. In more than a few countries, the usage of internet was found to be tremendously low among women. For example, a meager of 13 percent of women in India had used mobile internet in the last three months when compared to 31 percent among males, whereas China had a better usage rate of mobile internet than that of India(GSMA, n.d.). According to the Gender Gap Report on mobile usage 2019, towards closing the gender gap in owing a mobile phone and improved usage would result in added revenue of $140 B in profits for the mobile industry in the low and middle income countries by the next five years. Fastening the gap in internet usage by 2023, would add further $700 B in GDP growth rate in these countries.(Guiso et al., (2003).

Gender Diverse Boards

A business corporation to be further flourishing should recognize gender diversity as the key to their accomplishment. Gender diversity in workplace is concerning more than gender, it's all about acceptance, respect, promotion of both males and females in an organization and creating an equal opportunity at all levels that works for everybody without any discrimination in any form. Creating a diverse workforce is everybody's responsibility and a successful strategy depends on the level of responsiveness, attitude and actions of all employees and organizational heads. Gender diversity necessitates that workplace guidelines and practices assimilate the diverse needs and knowledge of women and men. In an OECD Business survey, the data on the number of registered small and medium enterprises registered with Face book (April 2018) reveals that the top most management designations are apprehended by men. Only one in three, attributes to women management in small and medium enterprises, and barely one in four had a more gender balanced team. (Future of Business Survey, 2018). There are ample researches conducted by (Prof.Michel Ferrary, 2013, MSCI 2015), to establish that female representation on boards improves the financial performance of the company and ensues enhanced corporate governance. In a study conducted across 91 countries by Peterson Institute for International Economics in 2016 states that firms progress depends on the proportion of female executives in the corporate management. A new research conducted by McKinsey in 2018 shows that there exists a statistically positive relationship between a diversified team and monetary outperformance persists to be true. Globally, the contribution of women in the informal sectors of the economy is high and quite stumpy when it comes to senior leadership positions. Despite all the progress made so far and the research studies undertaken, regrettably there are very few women as CEOs of the world's biggest corporations. As per the reports of 2018 Fortune List only 24 women (4.8 percent) were the CEOs of Fortune 500 companies. (Catalyst, Historical List of Women CEOs of the Fortune Lists: 1972-2018, 2018). Women represent for a fewer than a quarter (24%) of higher position worldwide.(Thornton, 2018). To further sustain contribution of women on corporate boards, countries like India, Germany, France, Italy, Norway, Netherlands, Finland etc have a proportional share of the seats for women in public companies.(Eastman, 2017)

Women and Education

In terms of underprivileged or oppressed sections of the society lacking basic human rights, women would top the list obviously in almost all the countries. Discrimination of women from cradle to grave is well known and still prevails in many countries. Women have to battle against all the obstacles to gain acceptance in the society. Regrettably everyone knows the significance of women in her varying roles as a child, daughter, friend, sister, wife, mother etc but still people do not acknowledge their contributions as a decision maker. This has led to underrating women in all walks of life. To shatter all the myths, education plays a key role in building confidence and empowering women. Education augments labor market efficiency and earnings for everyone, however educating and empowering women has favorable consequences on communal well-being. Although educational advancement had benefited both the genders, it has failed to eliminate the gender inequality. Globally, the statistics across different countries divulge that school enrollment ratios and literacy rate are gender biased. In the emerging economies girls lag behind boys at all stages of education. Governments should ensure that all children should be compulsorily enrolled in schools. Inequality in school completion rates vary among the poorer children in Eastern and Southeastern Asia and in Latin America and the Caribbean, further deprived females than underprivileged males' finished lower and upper secondary education. In countries with low income, just 2 percent of the deprived females and 3% of the underprivileged males completed upper secondary education.(UNESCO, n.d.). A study on literacy rates of adult and Gender Parity Index among varied inference years amongst the SAARC countries reveals that adult female literacy rates are very low when compared to that of male. The adult literacy rates (age group of 15+) in 2011 in Afghanistan among the female was 17.61 percent and 45.42 percent amongst male. Afghanistan had the lowest female literacy rates and Maldives had the highest female adult literacy rates among the SAARC countries. The adult literacy rates in Bangladesh during 2016 amongst the females were 69.90 percent and 75.62 among the male. The adult literacy rates in Bhutan during 2012 among the females were 48.02 percent and with that of males were 66.0 percent. In 2011, India had 59.28 percent of women and 78.88 percent of men as adult literates. Nepal in 2011 had 48.84 percent female literates and 71.71 percent males. Maldives in 2014 had 98.69 female literates and 98.52 male literates. In 2014, Pakistan had 44.28 percent female literates and 69.07 male literates. Sri Lanka in 2010 had 89.96 percent women and 92.58 percent men as adult literates. (UNESCO, 2018). In a study undertaken in the OECD countries reveals that girls generally in the age group of 15 years, have an aversion for subjects like STEM (Science, Technology, Engineering, Mathematics) and ICT (Information Communication & Technology) and are less probable to opt for a profession as a software developer, scientist, architect, engineer etc. One interesting fact observed in certain countries is that parents encourage boys to take up STEM studies and such societal stereotypes are passed on from one generation to another in spite of girls outperforming boys in STEM. (OECD, 2017b).

During the last five year period, nearly 90 percent of the open resource software packages were authored by men. Merely 20 percent of the women graduates had opted for ICT related studies which holds prominence in the digital age. Girls learning STEM further head out into scientific careers with a dream to make it big in scientific professions, but in reality very less proportion of women reach to higher-ranking positions. A latest study undertaken, related to the scientific publication of authors reveals that only 21 percent of the women are recognized as "corresponding authors". There are only 20 percent of the women who are on editorial boards as members and these plunge to fewer than 15 percent when their activities are compensated. Even though citations, proceedings and other outputs are being published, their impact is less recognized in various platforms. The highest contribution of women as corresponding authors in social sciences is above 30 percent and lesser than 15 percent in the areas of engineering, physics and material science. This obviously reflects to gender inequality in the academic world. In 2015, 80 percent of patents filed across the world were from men which have remained unchanged over the previous decade. During 2010 to 2015, the numbers of patents filed by women were merely 4 percent. Patents filed by men and women as teams were 17 percent from 2010 to 2015. (International Labour Organization (ILO), 2017).

Gender Pay Gaps

Skill is one of the most indispensable constituent for the swift growth of a country and the futuristic economy depends on the talented workforce. A society with gender bias loses on ideas, skills, growth rate etc that are very crucial for tackling global issues and binding innovative prospects. In several countries, development has transpired in situations of comparatively sluggish economic growth, while in few countries it has happened in spite of accelerating financially viable conditions and diminishing unemployment rates. With the onset of digital revolution, the nature of jobs, time and skills required have transformed absolutely. The relevance of certain skills like creative thinking, problem solving ability, cognitive skills, speed etc are some of the required ability to sustain in this digitally transformed era. Labor markets reward a variety of skills based on the demand and this may diverge across genders and all regions. To reap the fullest benefits of training and education, consequent policies are required by families to maintain work life balance. A study by ILO estimates 3.3 billion individuals are actively engaged in employment worldwide with the average world workforce participation rate stands at 62 percent of the working age population. Majority of the workers depends on these wages for their household consumption. The global earnings rate in 2017 was at its lowest when compared to that of the financial crisis of 2008.The global wage growth rate adjusted for price inflation declined from 2.4 percent in 2016 to just 1.8 percent in 2017(ILOSTAT; ILO, 2017) (ILOSTAT, 2017). Countries with the higher income levels have the lowest levels of wage inequality and countries with low or middle income have the highest levels of wage inequalities. In low- and middle-income economies, development in average wages has generally been vigorous, however with much diversity across countries and regions. While wages have enlarged swiftly over the past decade in some countries, most predominantly in China, in many other countries normal wages remain low and inadequate to effectively cover the needs of people. Overall, in low- and middle-income economies, a probable 50 per cent of all income earners persist to work in the informal economy, moreover in the informal segment or as informal workers in the formal segment (ILO, 2018a).(ILOSTAT, 2018).

Gender and Health

Gender impacts the welfare and health of every one in a country. Gender, not only establishes our uniqueness as individuals, but has a foremost impact on our outlook, career stability and progress, and to the possibility of living a healthy life. Accomplishing gender equality necessitates that everybody enjoys the right to comprehend their fullest potential to guide healthy lives and contribute to vigorous societies. Gender influences further in deciding the need for efficient health care services. Men and women are consistently exposed to health risk and the consequences may vary across gender due to biological differences, geographical disparity, hormones, ageing process, reproductive cycles, behavioral attitudes, society, status etc. These dissimilarities are to a great extent owing to the societal phenomenon of sexual characteristics. Gender traverses with additional drivers of disproportion, prejudice, marginalization and communal segregation, which have multifarious consequences on vitality and welfare. Certain communities compel women to early marriages and consequentially domestic violence, miscarriages, abortions etc prevails and finally damages their decision making ability to seek health care for themselves. In many countries, malnutrition, poor awareness of health emergencies and inadequate health care remain a hindrance to development and leads to dearth conditions in providing treatment for even the most essential health services. The life expectancy gap among men and women typically is 4.6 years globally, with women surviving longer than men in all the countries and sometimes even with a gap of 10 years. (Life Expectancy, n.d.).Worldwide in terms of disability adjusted life (Compare, 2016) from time to time women last longer than men enduring disability. (Gender and Blindness, 2002). The percentage of women as board members in Fortune 500 health care companies remains only at 22 percent in 2018 and a very small proportion of women that is only 10.2 percent of them are in the digital health care as

CEOs. (Statnews, 2018). In low and middle income countries, there is a severe deficiency in health care facilities related to maternal and child care. The maternal mortality rates remain high in many parts of Africa. (WHO, n.d.).

Women Entrepreneurs

Entrepreneurs contribute by playing a dominant role in shaping the fortune of a company and the economy as well. These are the people who blend creative and innovative initiatives in the market and make precise decisions to turn their ideas into profits. Any woman who organizes and manages any business venture with shrewdness is a "women entrepreneur". Women entrepreneurship describes the position of women and the role of entrepreneurship in the society. Entrepreneurship is an indispensable mechanism for emerging economies as it is a social engine for the inclusion of women in new innovative ventures. Unfortunately, women are yet to cash in the opportunity formed by the wave of globalization and digitalization. Certain factors that are most likely to hinder the entrepreneurship skills are lack of awareness about entrepreneurial activity in the early stages of education, policies related to R&D, tariffs, bureaucracy, technological transfers, taxation, regulation etc. Perception plays a prominent role in decision making as only 37 percent of the women within OECD countries consider that they have the relevant skills to initiate a big business when compared to 51 percent of men. Only 11 percent of the new start ups looking for investments are from women across diverse sectors. In many countries, banks are sluggish and cautious in financing new innovative business firms especially led by women, as the risks involved in such business are high and are less likely to be funded. Women have to look for venture capitalists for their businesses to take off but it's relatively tiresome to access funds from them. Women are less probable to engage in international exports and business operations due to such skepticism. (OECD, 2015). Innovation and entrepreneurship are closely interconnected with each other. By monitoring the market trends and fluctuations, entrepreneurs introduce new innovative products that disrupt the market equilibrium and jostle out the firms that are less innovative. A few points on the global entrepreneurship monitor survey 2017 reveals that from 2016 onwards there have been considerable improvements in efficiency driven economies related to supportive entrepreneurial conditions from the government, financial sectors and the academic community. The innovation driven economies are benefited by the quality of education and have shown substantial developments. In the factor-driven economies, the section of improvement-driven opportunity entrepreneurs, as contrasting to necessity-driven entrepreneurs, has become twofold since 2016, demonstrating a transformation concerning the nature of entrepreneurship in these economies. Countries that has the most favorable entrepreneurial framework is North America and the least supportive being Africa, Caribbean and Latin America.(Global Entrepreneurship Monitor Report, 2017).Technological modernization paves way for safer and green techniques by rapid productivity and brings in enormous opportunities which would benefit the entire economy. But the prevalent apprehension is about automation and considerable job wage and loss, especially in the manufacturing sector. While the risk of automation is conventionally high in manufacturing sectors where men dominate, and comparatively less in certain industries like retail, health care social work etc where women are predominant. The risk of automation persists on an average, across all industries and countries but the degree may vary depending on the level of economic development.

The Digital Wave

The new buzz word that everybody uses is the word 'skill' that has garnered the attention of the corporate. However, digital transformation depends upon the pace at which industries would cash in the opportunities. An understanding of the digital wave is imperative to assess the skillfulness of women and men. In the changing scenario, implementing new technologies requires people to be capable of equipping themselves with certain expertise like numerical ability, communication and managerial skillfulness that would help them to cope up with the digital transformation.

A survey conducted by OECD on Adult Skills reveals that the gender related pay gap in digital concentrated sectors has decreased considerably. On an average, men earn between 3 percent and 27 percent more than women in elevated digital sectors, and 2 percent to 28 percent more in low intensive digital sectors. If women lag behind men in the required skills set then the already existing gender divide would further escalate gender inequality.[27]

Can We Prevail Over the Effects of Gender Inequality?

The gender inequality across different countries affects the entire economy and not merely individuals or societies. Women actually work longer hours than men, both in the household as well as in the corporate sector, but still lands up paid very inadequately. Statistically there are many reports that show that gender inequality still prevails in every country in one form or the other. This unfortunately hinders the economic growth and development of a nation as half of its labor resources are not productively employed. Practically, in all the countries around the world, women still face obstacles to cross the threshold of the labor market in spite of the progress made under the UN Millennium Development Goals. For instance the World Bank has reported that nearly 2.7 billion women across the world are prohibited by law from working in certain sectors and this result in a potential income loss of $160 trillion. Yes, to prevail over the effects of the gender gap and to attain gender equality we need to focus on sustainable development and equal access to educational services, job opportunities healthcare etc to start with. Gender equality has persuasively shown to inspire economic growth, which is vital for the developing countries. It is acknowledged that in the Organization for Economic Co-operation and Development (OECD) of member countries, better access to school education among the boys and girls have resulted in the financially viable growth over the past 50 years (GVI, n.d.). Unless policy makers strive to bridge the gender gap countries will find it very tough to develop.

Women Empowerment and Gender Equality

"When a woman moves forward, the family moves the village moves and the nation moves." - Pandit Jawaharlal Nehru

As we progress on from an epoch of Liberalization, privatization and globalization (LPG) to an era of vigorous skillfulness, the next echelon of strategic decision making for the most part is crucial for companies, organizations and industry as a whole. In this context, incorporating women into the team of resources becomes prerequisite. Women's financial empowerment connotes growth together with the direct impact on productivity and efficiency. The emphasis is now on gender equality as it promotes better development activities and in turn supports the Gross Domestic Product (GDP) of the country.

Gender equality is one among the UN Sustainable Development Goals for enduring peace and prosperity across countries.Gender equality should ensure fairness in opportunities' provided to men or women to unleash their fullest potential and thereby contribute to economic, socio-cultural and political development. Governments in partnership with private entities and voluntary organizations across continents ought to ensure equality in wages, access to employment opportunity, health care, education, social security measures etc which will narrow down the gap on gender inequality. Several of the experiential studies undertaken by leading organizations have recommended that improving gender equality might result in momentous economic surplus, which may diversify depending on the type of economy and the challenges that they confront. Some of the remarkable estimates imply that economic gender equality may perhaps add on further US$250 billion to the GDP of United Kingdom, US$320 billion to France's, US$1,750 billion to that of the United States,US$550 billion to Japan's and US$310 billion to the GDP of Germany.(OECD, 2017a).Other studies suggest that there would be an increase of US$2.5 trillion to China and this may well be achieved by improving gender equality.(PwC, 2017) In addition, the world's GDP would increase by US$5.3 trillion by 2025 if gender prejudice in economic participation is immediately abridged by 25 percent in a similar phase.(McKinsey & Company, 2015).

The Way Forward

There has been substantial development in addressing the issues and challenges that women face in terms of maternity and paternity paid leave, flexible workplace and timings, tax incentives for additional income earners, unpaid work, pension schemes, elderly care etc across the world. However, as the global trends emerging from countries to reduce gender gap in the work place are laudable but are inadequate. The precise resolutions and strategies that we frame currently would provide an opportunity for women to escalate further. Digital technologies are a resolution for the people to get better with social and economic outcomes, and may perhaps facilitate the right jobs for individuals situated in various parts of the world by harmonizing the demand and supply of labor in a more flexible way. Trendiest companies like Blablacar, Amazon, Task Rabbit etc have harnessed the digital enabled potential to the most advantageous level and have generated flexibility, mobility, additional income for the workers to thrive on, thus creating "just in time demand", "gig economy" and so on. However the greatest challenge lies in the access and utilization of these technologies by women transversely in all the regions. As more number of women participates in the labor market, the economies can expand more rapidly in response to high labor inputs. At a similar time, as countries develop, the standard of living of the people also increases and this provides a good impetus for women to develop their skills and actively participate in the opportunities that the organization stipulates. Education and equivalent learning opportunities would unquestionably lead to transition of individuals amidst professions and sectors thereby assisting the people to reap the gains of digital revolution while diminishing its community cost. Access to free online courses especially for women on a wide range of topics can help them to achieve more.

To uphold digital literacy, policies encouraging initiatives in the field of education, information technology and other disciplines should be accessed by women at affordable price. Further enhancing cyber security would instill the confidence in women and facilitate them in exploring the plethora of opportunities that the digital era offers.

Innovative policies on child and elderly health care, flexible work, maternity leave, health, infrastructure, financial inclusion, abolishing tax on women who are additional income earners, tax credits to low income earners etc can pave way for maintaining a healthy work life balance. Economic policies can play a prominent role in redesigning the structure of the labor force. Brilliant policies and schemes of the government should integrate latest inclination like gender budgeting which has met with tremendous success in Morocco. Fiscal policies inculcating gender budgeting can augment the macroeconomic stability of the country which is indispensable to provide jobs and income to all the people.

Mere implementation of policies and diverse initiatives would not resolve the problem of gender divide. The learning from the outcomes of diverse programs necessitates the systematic compilation of data intended at recognizing priorities, identifying crucial information and monitoring key outlines for action. Promoting the gender-related facets in official statistics is imperative in this respect as this would enable in the equitable sharing of benefits of development.

CONCLUSION

"We cannot all succeed if half of this are held back." —Malala Yousafzai

Only when we respect women and acknowledge their contributions across all sectors of the society we can shatter the notion of gender inequality. Empowering women to contribute completely in economic life across every segment is crucial to build stronger economies, attain internationally decided goals for growth and sustainability, and make progress with better quality of life for women, men, families, and communities altogether.

REFERENCES

Ali, M. (2015). Effect of Gender Inequality on Economic Growth: Case of Pakistan. *Journal of Economics and Sustainable Development, 6*(9), 10-10.

Baldwin, M., & Johnson, W. G. (1992). Estimating the employment effects of wage discrimination. *The Review of Economics and Statistics, 74*(3), 446–455. doi:10.2307/2109489

Baliamousne-Lutz & McGullivray. (2007). Does Gender Inequality Reduce Growth in Sub Saharan African and Arab countries? *African Development Review*, 224–242.

Blackden, M., Canagarajah, S., Klasen, S., & Lawson, D. (2007). Gender and Growth in Africa: Evidence and Issues. In Advancing Development: Core Themes in Global Development. WIDER and UNU-WIDER Research Paper No. 2006/37.

11Catalyst, Historical List of Women CEOs of the Fortune Lists: 1972-2018. (2018). Academic Press.

21Compare, G. B. D. (2016). *Data visualization hub*. Institute for Health Metrics and Evaluation, University of Washington. Available from https://vizhub.healthdata.org/gbd-compare

Cotter, D., Hermsen, J. M., & Vanneman, R. (2011). The end of gender revolution? Gender role attitudes from 1977 to 2008. *American Journal of Sociology, 117*(1), 259–289. doi:10.1086/658853 PMID:22003521

Cunningham, M., Beutel, A. M., Barber, J. S., & Thorton, A. (2005). Reciprocal relationships between attitudes about gender and social contexts during young adulthood. *Social Science Research*, *34*(4), 862–892. doi:10.1016/j.ssresearch.2005.03.001

Davis, S. N., & Greenstein, T. N. (2009). Gender ideology: Components, predictors, and consequences. *Sociological Perspectives*, *50*, 249–271. doi:10.1525op.2007.50.2.249

Deléchat, C., Newiak, M., Xu, R., Yang, F., & Aslan, G. (2018). *What is Driving Women's Financial Inclusion Across Countries?* IMF Working Paper 18/38, International Monetary Fund.

13Eastman, M. T. (2017). Women on Boards: Progress Report. MSCI.

Esteve-Volart, B. (2009). *Gender discrimination and growth: Theory and evidence from India. mimeo.* York University.

10Future of Business Survey. (2018). *Explore the Future of Business*. https://eu.futureofbusinesssurvey.org/manager/Storyboard/RHViewStoryBoard.aspx

22Gender and Blindness. (2002). *Gender and health information sheet*. Geneva: World Health Organization. Available from: https://www.who.int/gender-equity-rights/knowledge/a85574/en

26Global Entrepreneurship Monitor Report. (2017). Global Entrepreneurship Monitor.

1Global Gender Gap Report. (n.d.). In *Wikipedia*. https://en.wikipedia.org/wiki/Global_Gender_Gap_Report

8GSMA. (2018). *Connected Women – The Mobile Gender Gap Report 2018*. https://www.gsma.com/mobilefordevelopment/wpcontentuploads/2018/03/GSMA_The_Mobile_Gender_Gap_Report_2018_Final_210218.pdf

9GSMA. (n.d.). https://www.gsma.com/mobilefordevelopment/connected-women/the-mobile-gender-gap-report-2018/

Guiso, L., Sapienza, P., & Zingales, L. (2003). People's opium? Religion and economic attitudes. *Journal of Monetary Economics*, *50*(1), 225–282. doi:10.1016/S0304-3932(02)00202-7

28GVI. (n.d.). https://www.gvi.co.uk/blog/why-is-gender-equality-important/

Hunt, Prince, Dixon-Fyle, & Yee. (2018). *Delivering Through Diversity*. McKinsey & Company.

18ILOSTAT. (2017). World Employment and Social Outlook: Trends for Women. Geneva: Author.

19ILOSTAT. (2018). *World Employment and Social Outlook: Trends*. Geneva: Author.

2IMF. (n.d.). https://www.imf.org/external/pp/ppindex.aspx

7Intel. (n.d.). https://www.intel.com/content/dam/www/public/us/en/documents/pdf/women-and-theweb.pdf

17International Labour Organization (ILO). (2017). Economic Impacts of Reducing the Gender Gap (What Works Research Brief No. 10). ILO.

4IPU. (n.d.). http://archive.ipu.org/parlinee/WomenInParliament.asp?REGION=All&typesearch=1&LANG=ENG

Klasen, S., & Lamanna, F. (2009). The impact of gender inequality in education and employment on economic growth: New evidence for a panel of countries. *Feminist Economics*, *15*(3), 91–132. doi:10.1080/13545700902893106

20Life Expectancy. (n.d.). *Global Health Observatory (GHO) data*. Available from: https://www.who.int/gho/mortality_burden_disease/life_tables/situation_trends_text/en/

31McKinsey & Company. (2015). The Power of Parity: How Advancing Women's Equality Can Add $12 Trillion To Global Growth. Author.

Morrisson, C., & Jutting, J. (2005). Women's discrimination in developing countries: A new data relationships between attitudes about gender and social contexts during young adulthood. *Social Science Research*, *34*, 862–892. doi:10.1016/j.ssresearch.2005.03.001

Noland, Moran, & Kotschwar. (2016). *Is Gender Diversity Profitable? Evidence from a Global Survey.* Peterson Institute for International Economics.

25OECD. (2015). *The ABC of Gender Equality in Education: Aptitude, Behaviour, Confidence*. OECD Publishing. doi:10.1787/9789264229945-

29OECD. (2017a). *Entrepreneurship at a Glance 2017*. OECD Publishing. doi:10.1787/entrepreneur_aag-2017-

16OECD. (2017b). *OECD Science, Technology and Industry Scoreboard 2017: The Digital Transformation*. OECD Publishing. doi:10.1787/9789264268821-

27OECD Calculations Based on OECD. (2017). *Survey of Adult Skills (PIAAC).* www.oecd.org/skills/piaac/

Psacharopoulos, G., & Patronos, H. A. (2004). Returns to Investment in Education: A Further Update. *Education Economics*, *12*(2), 111–134. doi:10.1080/0964529042000239140

30PwC. (2017). *Women in Work Index.* https://www.pwc.co.uk/services/economics-policy/insights/women-in-work-index.html

Seguino, S. (2000). Gender Inequality and Economic Growth: A Cross-Country Analysis. *World Development*, *28*(7), 1211–1230. doi:10.1016/S0305-750X(00)00018-8

Sen, G. (2007). Informal institutions and gender equality. In J. Ju¨ tting, D. Drechsler, S. Bartsch, & I. de Soysa (Eds.), Informal institutions: How social norms help or hinder development (pp. 49–72). Paris, France: OECD Set for Better Policies.

Silverstein, M., & Giarrusso, R. (2012). *Continuity and Discontinuity in Aging Families*. Johns Hopkins Univ. Press.

23Statnews. (2018). https://www.statnews.com/2018/08/01/gender-inequality-health-care-leadership-women/

Swamy, Azfar, Knack, & Lee. (2001). Gender and Corruption. *Journal of Development Economics, 64*(1), 25-55.

12Thornton, G. (2018). Women in Business: Beyond Policy to Progress. Academic Press.

14UNESCO. (n.d.). https://unesdoc.unesco.org/images/0026/002615/261593E.pdf

15UNESCO. (2018). *Gender parity index*. UIS (UNESCO Institute of Statistics).

Vaughan-Whitehead, D. (Ed.). (2016). *Long-term trends in the World of Work: What effects on inequalities and middle-income groups?* ILO and EC.

Whitehead, A. L. (2012). Gender ideology and religion: Does a masculine image of god matter? *Review of Religious Research, 54*(2), 139–156. doi:10.100713644-012-0056-3

24WHO. (n.d.). https://www.who.int/reproductivehealth/publications/monitoring/maternal-mortality-2015/en/

3WIR. (2018). https://wir2018.wid.world

5World Bank. (n.d.a). https://globalfindex.worldbank.org

6World Bank. (n.d.b). https://documents.worldbank.org/curated/en/926401524803880673/Women-Business-and-the-Law-2018

Section 2
Women Empowerment

Chapter 6
Assessing the Environmental and Social Obstacles to Women Entrepreneurs:
A Case Study of Pakistan

Nazima Elahi
Foundation University, Pakistan

Qaisar Ali Malik
https://orcid.org/0000-0002-6488-2204
Foundation University Islamabad, Pakistan

ABSTRACT

Economic development is an ultimate goal of developing countries and utilization of human capital to achieve this goal is accepted vital globally. Entrepreneurship, recognized as a central force to bring economic growth, needs more women to be involved in this context. Studies on female-entrepreneurs are missing for developing countries, especially in the context of Pakistan. Therefore, this study is aimed to find the social and environmental factors acting as hindrance to female-entrepreneurship development in Pakistan. Primary data is collected from five major divisions of Pakistan involving 200 social entrepreneurs engaged in running their businesses and contributing towards the social well-being of society. The findings highlighting the major environmental and social factors are generalized and presented against each division in results section. It is concluded that access to finance, social norms, lack of adequate infrastructure, registration facilities, access to marketing, and acknowledgment are among the major factors, which deter their entrepreneurship development.

DOI: 10.4018/978-1-7998-3737-4.ch006

BACKGROUND AND RESEARCH PROBLEM

Women entrepreneurs constitute human resource meant to overcome the economic challenges globally. As argued by Kalim (2019), female entrepreneurs are an important human resource that helps meeting the economic challenges in modern high tech world and empowering women. They diversify the production services, Stevenson and Onge (2005). Role of this sector in poor countries is different from developed world. literature cites that contribution of female entrepreneurship vary from country to country and region to region depending upon a number of factors including their cultural and ethical beliefs, their access to natural resources and policies pursued at national level to promote female entrepreneurship.

As far the Pakistan is concerned, it is ranked as 132 out of 134 countries in terms of economic activities pursued by women Nadgrodkiewicz (2011). On the same lines, Global Entrepreneurship Monitor GEM (2018) reports female entrepreneurship is approximately 4% less than male activity of entrepreneurship in Pakistan. A government of Pakistan survey conducted revealed that approximately 6.6 million of people are employed in the household and out of them approximately 0.5 million are women. 15% of these employed females are proprietors and self-employed, while 30% are serving as unpaid workers, and rest of all (55%) are paid workers. Like other developing regions, in Pakistan female-owned businesses are in sub sectors like fresh designing, food retailing, knitting and dressmaking. Against this backdrop, there is little evidence on the research based on the issue of female entrepreneurs as per developing countries and specifically Pakistan is concerned.

INTRODUCTION

Utilization of human capital in positive and productive manner guarantees the economic growth. Developing nations seek for the ways to promote their growth and bring them in line with the rest of developed world. A number of drivers are responsible for this development, the one is discussed in this study i.e. contribution of women as entrepreneurs. Schumpeter (1934) contended that, business cycles and economic development is caused by entrepreneurship. Similarly, Barretto (1989) was of the view that economic development comprises of a series of steps in which new markets, and new organizations are developed by the entrepreneurial efforts. Hence, the concept of entrepreneurship was introduced as defined by Haque (2007), as a process of identification, and development of innovative ideas and opportunities into business.

There are differences across the male owned and females owned firms. This phenomenon has been widely discussed for developed countries, but the literature still lacks discussion for developing countries. It is considered as a key to growth, and therefore, most of the financing programs are focusing on the promotion of female entrepreneurship in developing countries. Due to wide differences across the geographical and regional location, cultural constrained, religious beliefs. Business world has gained benefits from the emerging and developmental idea of entrepreneurship. Historically the concept was confined to males, but over the time a turn up has been observed, due to increasing needs and challenges. The concept of women entrepreneurship has been a widely discussed issue in developed countries[1]. However, for developing nations of the world, this is still a topic to be discussed yet. A review of government policies and many microfinance programs shows that, they encourage women access to credit and women- entrepreneurship to raise their contribution in economic growth.

Various studies in the context of studying the barriers or the obstacles to women entrepreneurship highlighted factors, which are of variety of nature. Asli and Nour (2018) classified these factors into two broad categories i.e. entrepreneurial environment & factors of individual concern. In some advanced economies, the remaining barriers are subtle. In many parts of the emerging world, the basics of legal protection, self-determination and access to essential services remain elusive for millions of women. The analysis of 95 countries finds that female labors are contributing about 37% to the world's GDP, which is quite lower than the 50% of the globally working people. The global average masks large variations among the world's ten regions (Exhibit 1). The contribution of regional GDP produced by women is only 17% in India, 18% in MENA, and 24% in South Asia (excluding India). The share is highest at 40 to 41 percent in North America and Oceania, China, and Eastern Europe and Central Asia. (Barch and Yee, 2012.)

Depending on the situations of developing countries, there is almost declining trend in employment opportunities for female workers. Therefore, they are encouraged to create jobs for themselves and become entrepreneurs. There is a long way to go for female entrepreneurs to compete and achieve the level of men owned enterprises. It is a commonly observed phenomenon that female owned businesses are smaller compared to men-owned businesses (Blank, 2010 and Bruhn & Zia, 2011). The encouragement of female entrepreneurs requires a detailed analysis of environmental and social factors affecting them, and policies pursued by government to promote them. A deep analysis will help government to formulate policies, identify gaps in policies and social set up.

Over the time, innovation is thus introduced in entrepreneurship together with risk bearing due to technological advancement. Over the time, it has been taken as a driver to accelerate economic growth, a mean to bring employment opportunities, profitability and innovation in the long run. The idea developed from the thinking that introducing and promoting new business brings employment generation, innovation, and high welfare and improvement in living standard (Brush *et al.*, 2009). It is observed that economic integration and globalization stream into developing countries brought the idea of women entrepreneurship there. However, this concept has been a diminished idea before this[2]. Ghani *et al.* (2011) stated that women constitute a group of major driver to economic growth since last a few decades. Hence, an idea of women entrepreneurship emerges right after the success of male entrepreneurship.

Specific Objectives of Study

The study aims to find the performance of female owned enterprises in Pakistan and tried to explore as maximum as possible factors particularly environmental and social which act as a hindrance to the growth of female owned enterprises. In addition, it also compares the performance of male owned and female owned enterprises.

Organization of Study

The study is organized as follows: following introduction in section one. Section 2 reviews the studies for Pakistan, and rest of South Asian countries. Section 3 is a comprehensive description of state of Women entrepreneurship in Asian region. Section 4 explains how women contribution towards business helps to reach sustainable development goals. Section 5 states methods and material and key findings are discussed in section 6. Final section concludes the study.

REVIEW OF LITERATURE

Since the magnitude of impact of women, entrepreneurship varies across different areas; Vedamani (2018) discussed the effect of women empowerment in urban and rural areas of India. The study has analyzed the empirical and theoretical dimensions of women empowerment in the new era. It has tried to explore the challenges in urban and rural India. A data collected through various sources has been analyzed and examined using graphs and tables. The findings showed that with the changing era, the women have taken over the industry and Females are now in top management. Hence, the rise in women empowerment have helped a lot in educating women of urban and rural areas and increased in feminizing. In particular, this research deals with the problems of women who are not the sole earners and the fact that men are the bread earners so now the women have taken half of the world by empowering themselves through their profitable businesses.

On the same lines, another study by Patterson et al. (2009) have investigated the provocation faced by women when starting a business or when being an entrepreneur. Problems faced by women are different from men in magnitude and dimension in social and cultural reasons but the major stages of entrepreneurial process that are creating, nurturing and nourishing are same for both men and women. Women are leaving corporate employment in increasing number, as their need for challenge achievement and status is left exasperated. Holmen et al. (2011) studied that credit institutions seek tangible collateral for loans, and women have always been kept aside from many institutions, they are not given access to finances. Mattis (2004) focused that women are facing invisible barriers in attaining carrier advancement. Policymakers or researchers while designing policies had a small focus on access of women to businesses. The added responsibility of society on women as mothers and wives distinguish women from men counterparts and their lack of knowledge is a barrier for women in policymaking. The burden of these social responsibilities directly affect the conduct of women in business and these factors do not effect men of south Asia. Women of south Asia *i.e.* Bangladesh, India, Pakistan etc. has had to face various difficulties in doing their own businesses. They have financial barrier as well as a burden of households on them, looking after the children are also a task done by them. Harassment and discriminating attitude are some of the problems that women entrepreneurs face in south Asia.

Mitchelmore and Rowdey (2013) states that entrepreneurial competencies have a great impact and can influence the growth and performance of an entrepreneur firm. The study aims to observe, analyze and investigate the skills of female entrepreneurs that were stated by the hard working and dedicated women entrepreneurs who are devoted towards their business growth. To achieve the goal of the Study a questionnaire was developed and survey of women entrepreneurs was conducted in the cities of Wales and England. The questionnaire had the list of all skills that were already researched and observed in different researches and theoretical frameworks. Researcher selected the Likert scale, which allowed the respondents to rate their skills and abilities relative to each of the competency. Then collected data was analyzed through SPSS. Study then identified and made four major groups of skills as individualism and associations, occupation and administration, business and human relational abilities in comparison to the previous researches. Women entrepreneurs as compared to the men entrepreneurs have given the skills identified in these groups. This research then concluded that identification of these clusters would be beneficial for the development of effective educational programs for women entrepreneurs. Thus, the main beneficiaries of the study were identified as the government training institutes who works for the growth of women entrepreneurship and the entrepreneurs themselves.

Frayal (2018) tried to measures the factors that affects entrepreneurships in women, particularly social, political, individual and economic. The data was collected from 240 registered women entrepreneurs of Peshawar, KPK, and Pakistan and list of entrepreneurs were from three different businesses. To check the measurement effect of predictor on response variable it used regression model technique. The study reveals that the entrepreneurial factors including (social, political, individual and economic) has significant effect on business performance. Women are facing disadvantage especially owing to their gender, social-cultural factors and religious factors also. According to "women are not facing discrimination in the professional fields but also in the entrepreneurial world". Conducted that reports research studies published related with social, economic, political, and personal entrepreneurial factors in Pakistan are minimal. Pardah and izzat are also the most significant factors in Pakistan. Roomi & Parrott (2008) investigated and found that women entrepreneurs encounter a variety of hurdles, which includes but are not limited to economic and social restrictions, management and networking limitations. Some of the difficulties can be resolved through targeted state strategies and policies. These include the allotment of adequate budgeted resources to assist female business owners.

Parvin *et al.*, (2012) examined those factors, which influence the development of female micro-entrepreneurship in the rural part of Bangladesh. The analysis was based on experimental investigations and was conducted in north side of Bangladesh. It measured female entrepreneurship's determinates which were based on three selected indicators; their individual qualities, family matters and exterior settings & situations. Both female micro-entrepreneurs and non-business women were selected as a sample for this study. Data collected through complete survey techniques comprehended through graphical and econometric techniques and then interpreted in order to find out the factors which affects the female entrepreneurship. Estimation of proposed model using Probit model concluded that among personal attributes; academic knowledge, liberty to do the business, wish for earning more, having good income and a yearning for developed societal status were considered to be the influencing factors for females in becoming the part of micro-entrepreneurships. Difficult family phases have also proved to be the triggering factor for females to be involve in entrepreneurship. The study recommends that adjustment in rights policy and its true implementation by the government will positively affect the women entrepreneurship development, which will lead towards balance socio-economic development. These policies will not only empower women economically but will significantly contribute to national economy.

Rahmatullh and Zaman (2014) investigated the restrictions the female face due to work and family conflict and the initial stages of operation of their business ad pointed that problems that female entrepreneurs face are universal. It highlighted that females are now trying to be more innovative in their businesses because they are now unable to cope the conflicts they face when they are in top management. The female entrepreneurship development of Bangladesh from the perspectives of birth, growth and success is highlighted. The females who are doing businesses have the barriers of family, access to market and no financial support by their spouse. Thus for female entrepreneurship social and cultural norms should be supported.

Malika Das (2000) studied how females are managing and owing small and medium sized enterprises and how they set up, operate their business with the family, and work conflict. The females are own more focused toward the idea of starting new businesses as they are unable to cope with the injustice done in organization when a female is in top management. Thus the researcher have studied that there are resemblance and differences between the birth growth success rate of female entrepreneurs of developing and developed countries. Similarly, Khan (2014) in this research identified both human and social capital factors, which affects the female entrepreneur's performance. It has also explored the key reasons for the variation of business performances of female entrepreneurs. The study used an interpretive approach in order to; explore the aspects that affects the performance of female entrepreneurs, investigating the reasons, the causes and the objectives of women to initiate a business and then lead it as top manager and focuses on different ways and styles that female entrepreneurs' practice. For this purpose, data was collected from focus group discussions and individual interviews.

Researcher investigated these factors through an explanatory viewpoint. The research focused the women entrepreneurs of Pakistan, specifically the Punjab area. A qualitative research technique based on multiple designs was used. The study employed focus groups and a case study design. The earlier was conducted to know more about the current situation with regard to Pakistani female entrepreneurship and was followed by individual in-depth interviews with selected entrepreneurs using a purposive sampling technique. The research has concluded that inspirations, societal education, networking associations, human as wealth in terms of experience and professional & technical edification and the effects of environment are the most important in measuring and describing the performance of Pakistani female entrepreneurs. These results indicated that the environmental and social factors influenced women's desire to initiate a venture and the reasons identified were the yearning to have better financial situations for the families, better life opportunities, a wish to improve societal status and woman's desire to assure the financial protection to the family of her own.

A study by Arasti *et al.* (2012) explained that regardless of impressive development of female entrepreneurship, most female run businesses in Iran are small scale, and the rate of growth for female run businesses has not increased at the same pace as that of male run businesses. These limited growth prospects can be explained by many factors, the most important of which is the "growth factor". There is ample evidence in entrepreneurship literature that points to the fact that compared to men business initiatives taken by women tend are often smaller. Many personal, organizational level and environmental factors could be attributed for such differences. More than half of Iranian population is female, and there is an upward trend of pursuing higher educational opportunities and contributing to social causes among the new generation of Iranian women. Due to this, the challenges faced by Iranian women are manifold compared to their male counterparts. Therefore, being attentive to factors that influence growth orientation of female business ventures is akin so attention to the factors affecting growth orientation of their ventures is the same as intentional economic progress and the country's income. This qualitative research also quantifies environmental components that affect female entrepreneurs' growth orientation in the long run into three groups economic group, social and cultural group and the legal group.

While exploring the normative context for women's entrepreneurship in Pakistan, a critical analysis" by Roomi, Rehman & Henry (2018) the authors investigate how informal institutional components effect entrepreneurship prospects for women within Pakistan. The authors further analyze ways in which female entrepreneurs use agency for dealing with the restrictions imposed on them due to these factors. In qualitatively exploring the normative context and real-life experiences of female entrepreneurs, the authors explain how social and cultural belief systems and prevalent attitudes affect career and entrepreneurial drive among women in Pakistan. The findings of this research point out that the choice to pursue entrepreneurial initiatives by women is deeply intertwined with existing cultural and social factors. Female entrepreneurs from Pakistan use agency for dealing with gender roles and negative stereotyping within their families and the society that greatly affects the performance and outputs of female owned businesses and SMEs in Pakistan. These women often use religion to support their choices and explain them to peers as they navigate their entrepreneurial activities.

Based on the literature review conducted, it has been observed that following are the factors affecting women entrepreneurship.

- Financial factors i.e. finance as barrier of women entrepreneurship (Zeb A *et al.,* (2019))
- Socio-cultural factors (Khan 2014)
- Education and Experience i.e. the entrepreneurial competencies (Mitchelmore S *et al.*, 2013)
- Environmental Factors i.e. the skills to start a business, societal links and family support. (Lee & Rogoff 1998), (Brush *et al.*, 2009)
- Personal factors (motherhood i.e. family commitment) (Brush *et al.,* 2009)
- Government support i.e. lack of supportive policies and training programs for women-entrepreneurship (Lee & Rogoff, 1998).

STATE OF WOMEN ENTREPRENUERSHIP IN ASIA

Pakistan is a developing country having an estimated population of 207 million in 2017. Women make up almost 49% of the population. Unfortunately, there is a low percentage of women (28.85%) who get formal education with fewer of them attaining higher education (1.18%). However, according to World Bank data the percentage of women labour force participation in Pakistan has increased from 14 percent in 1990 to 25.12 percent in 2018[3]. Overall, the labour participation rate for Pakistan stands at 54.51 percent (Nasir *et al.,* 2019).

Subohi, (2006) highlighted that females of Pakistan are facing great barriers in managing or running their own businesses because of the culture and traditions. Females are facing issues regarding gender, attitudes and routine inadequate structural support. The major barriers includes lack of access to finance, access to markets of women and lack of technical knowledge. Various studies highlighted the state of women empowerment and its contribution towards achieving the Millennium Development Goals (MDGs) Jawad, (2010) studied that Pakistan is a developing economy, which suffers from decades of internal and international political disputes and economic instability since its independence in 1947. Taking in account the religion and cultural aspects Pakistan is an economy, which faces barriers, which faces many barriers like this. Pakistan is a signatory of the Millennium Development Goals, thus affirming its commitment to empower women and eliminate gender inequality by 2015.

Zeb *et al.,* (2019) examined the political situations in Pakistan and its effects on female entrepreneurial performances. It has also discussed that stable political environment is very much important for the progress and flourishment of entrepreneurial activities. It conducted the study, registered group and Non-Registered groups of female entrepreneurs for data collection, adopted a self-administered questionnaire method, and then represented it in tabular form. The quantitative method of research has been used. Multiple regression analyses were carried out. This study engages inferential and graphical statistical analyses in order to determine the respondent's characteristics. The results showed that initiatives taken by the Government and the way it encourages the female entrepreneurs are very much important and plays a significant role in women development. Study then concluded that Government is not properly supporting the female entrepreneurs in terms of financial aid, moral supports and adequate support programs. If the women of Pakistan provided such an environment, the economy of the country can progress in a much better way. Colaco (2018) studied the challenges that women of India faced in female's entrepreneurship. The analysis emphasized particularly the role and challenges that female entrepreneurs faced in the urban parts of India. The study has the objective to analyze new scopes and dimensions of entrepreneurship theoretically and empirically; and to inspect the prospects and challenges for strategic entrepreneurship in urban India. In order to examine these objectives, secondary data was collected from various reputed publications. Graphs and tables were made to analysis the data through t-test of mean and regression analysis. The study proved that there is no significant difference in proprietary ownership by female in the rural and urban setup of India. Women can succeed in their new ventures if the perception of societal values does not harm them.

Wellalge & Locke (2017) investigated the gender equality in assessing the capital market for SMEs in South Asia. The objectives of this study were to explore the likely constraints and inequalities faced by women- owned enterprises in South Asia. The data of approximately 9,000 SMEs in South Asian economies has used to conduct the study by using the IV-Probit modeling to investigate the credit constraints between male and female enterprises. The results found that female-owned enterprises are 3% less likely to face difficulties in availing credit opportunities than male-owned enterprises. In addition, it also reported that this study proved a timely signal for promulgation of new rules and policies to enhance the opportunities for female population of the South Asian Region.

Cabrera & Mauricio (2017) probed the barriers in the success of women entrepreneurs with the purpose to identify the barriers influencing the each stage of entrepreneurial process using the Meta analysis approach and analyzed 108 articles produced since January 2010 to October 2015. The findings of this meta- studies indicated that several factors including human capital, education and experience, and access to financial sources were significantly influenced the performance of female-owned enterprises. The literature review further suggested that change in policies and procedures regarding female education system are highly needed. It will not only help to empower them, but also help to alter the socio-cultural perceptions that are hindering their way to get accessibility towards resources to manage and grow in entrepreneurial environment. Khan *et al* (2018) examined the challenges faced by the young women entrepreneurs in Pakistan. This state-level study focused on the challenges affecting female is success in business and indicates the problems being faced by them as an entrepreneurs. This research paper based on the primary as well as secondary data collection from labor Force Survey (2014-2015), Pakistan Bureau of Statistics (2015), Women Economic Participation & Empowerment Status Report (2016-2015). The factors are highlighted as financial instability, lack in family support, business regulatory process, and male-dominated culture are those crucial factors that inhibits the performance of female-owned enterprises. The findings of the research paper further suggested to Federal as well provincial governments to legislate new laws to introduce women friendly business environment and to reduce the gender biases to ease the entrepreneurial environment for the female population of the country.

Jabeen & Ahmad (2018) investigated the factors hindering the intent to start a female owned enterprise, explored the hurdles in accessing capital and training and identified the socio-cultural barriers and trends that impede the ways of female entrepreneurs in the Pakistan. The study is based on social constructionist approach and an in-depth data analysis in QSR Nvivo of the interviews of ten female entrepreneurs. The results indicated the socio-cultural norms surely impacts and acts as obstacles that women's business owners faced and may give a portrayal of a few female owned enterprises in the Pakistan. The authors' recommended for the future research studies a larger sample size to cover more aspects and barriers to further generalize the recommended thoughts on different cities of Pakistan. Yunis, *et al* (2019) examined the enablers and restraints of female social entrepreneurship within the perspective of Pakistan. This provincial level study conducted using an interpretive qualitative approach based on interviews of ten female social enterprises in Peshawar, Pakistan. The study findings showed a novel and innovative insight to cultural impacts of gender as a restraint towards female owned social enterprises within the context of developing country both theoretically and empirically. The study recommended that this social entrepreneurship is innovative, that endorses purpose of entrepreneurial as social value creation. It plays redemptive role for women in the context of KP and helps to realize their strengths and value with a hope for change.

Dissanayake (2018) highlighted the environmental factors on women led SMEs in the Asian region by unveiling the macro-level pictures of regulatory, cognitive, and normative environments. The study comprised on the conceptualization of facts based on institutional theory and found that environmental factors has a significant impact on women-led enterprises and also on policy and decision makers to draw an appropriate knowledge to adopt necessary measures. In addition, the extent of enterprise competition, corruption and bureaucratic procedural hurdles in the entire South Asian region inhibited females to opt entrepreneurship as a career line.

Role of Entrepreneurship for Sustainable Development

Sustainable Development (SD) means meeting the present needs without compromising on ability of future generations. SDGs address three central aspects of sustainability: economic prosperity, social equity and environmental protection. Taking a multi-level approach, the factors influencing SMEs in sustaining the environment for future generations and caring about the well-being of society are explored. Entrepreneurship plays an important role towards achieving SDG's but it has to deal with social economic and environmental factors both on local and international level. Sustainable development is often communicated through the concept of Corporate Social Responsibility (CSR). It is also defined as "Social Responsibilities of the Businessman". This defines the social responsibilities of the businesspersons to overcome the challenges they are facing. Now a day the biggest factor is to overcome the social and environmental factors. The magnitudes of social and environmental factors at the global scale are beyond the abilities of individuals and require more powerful anchors to overcome these factors.

SD have different dimensions that include economic, social and environmental dimensions. Job creation, promotion, profitable work, sustainable agriculture are the economical dimension that helps the entrepreneur to drive economic growth. On a wider scale, social factors play a positive role in entrepreneurship by promoting social cohesion, reducing inequalities and expanding opportunities for all including women, young people with disabilities and others. Environmental factors help to address the challenges faced by the environment through the introduction of new climate due to global warming and the adaptation of new technologies. SDG development helps in substantially increasing the number of young and old people who have technical and relevant skills for attaining jobs to start a new business.

The millennium development goals in 2015 were replaced by the sustainable development goals (United Nations, 2015). Resolutions to put an end to poverty and hunger, building of peaceful societies, empowerment of women and girls in order to protect the planet were the part of sustainable development goals (Apostolopoulos et al., 2018). Sustainable development has different scales of measurements that include economic, social and environmental dimensions, which help entrepreneurship to progress that eventually contributes to SDGs achievement.

Another important catalyst for sustainable and innovative economy even in challenging environments is the Corporate Social Responsibility (CSR). By implementing, the new technologies that lead to monetary addition in the developing economies can work efficiently against scarcity. Implementation of aforementioned factors by the prospect investors can effectively fuel their actions towards the achievement of SDGs. Moreover, the current modern societal, environmental and fiscal challenges could be met by building new sustainable business models, adopting new practices, measures and technologies. Further, it is also important to discover the continuing involvement and contribution of female entrepreneurs in this challenging environment, as these businesses can prove to be a driver for equivalence and equal opportunities whilst contributing the potential for better situations in disadvantaged societies (Apostolopoulos *et al.*, 2018).

WOMEN ENTREPRENUERSHIP AND SUSTAINBLE DEVELOPMENT GOALS

United Nations Conference on Trade and Development (UNCTAD) has worked to address the influence of technological innovation on SDG implementation and focus on the gender divide in science and technology (Carpentier, *et al* 2019). Therefore, women-entrepreneurship can be proved as a driving force in attainment of equality and equal opportunities by offering the potential for better conditions in underprivileged communities and helps in improvement of livelihood of the deprived people.

Women entrepreneurship development is a challenging fact, however in many developing countries this factor is increasing rapidly with special support from government and financial industry. The women involvement in businesses are helping them to contribute for the country's economy and family income. Female involvement in the enterprises are being a challenge in a society that is more towards male, the policies of government and financial institutions are a big challenge for women. The living conditions have improved and females are earning more respect in society and family. However, lack of access to credit, limited access to market information, infrastructure and utility services, traditional technology, bureaucratic complexity are the big challenges that females are facing. Gender, class and location are determined on the bases economic, political and social recognition. The city areas have greater opportunities for business development while countryside areas lag behind. Meanwhile, good number of NGO-MFIs offers microfinance services to the women involving actively in micro, small and medium enterprises. Direct or indirect supports to women are provided by different types of organizations, entrepreneurs, besides the government point of 0.80, 0.30 and 0.50, respectively, which implies that women are getting more access to loans than other assets (BBS, 2009). In fact, these resource mobilizing institutions motivated and encouraged rural women, and made them entrepreneurs, that is, agricultural entrepreneurs (crops, livestock and fisheries), small business owners, tailors, handicraftsmen and so on (Rahman et al., 2011).

Entrepreneurship through small scale businesses can support the achievement of SDGs". However, the negative insights about women entrepreneurs in society has created institutional and financial barriers for women empowerment in economy. These circumstances created an economic trap and made women labor force misdirected. There are numerous ways of taking actions that can fortify the position of women in the economy to achieve the Sustainable Development Goals (SDGs) and increase women`s activity. Some of them include the improvement in social conditions that will allow more women to take tactical positions in decision-making and by forming such policies, which makes the financial assets available to women entrepreneurs and made them able to actively participate in the labor market. Further, the use of better information, communication and technology will also empower the women (UN Commission: Economic Empowerment of Women to Achieve Sustainable Development Goals 2015).

It is stated that women out of 57.7 million people constitute 51% and 35.4% of the country's economically active population (Stats SA, 2018). Women entrepreneurship can be a main contributor towards gender parity and enhancement of female authority in the economy. They can contribute to the economic growth and is a feasible approach for addressing the sustainable development objectives, reducing inequality and fostering the social inclusion. It is well documented that increased in female labor involvement is directly related to the economic growth.

Women entrepreneur can yield significant economic benefits through increased female entrepreneurship participation. Other than contributing to economic development through job creation and their economic empowerment by increasing income, women entrepreneurs can contribute in social development by promoting gender equality and by exercising this authority, it can help women to reduce their dependence and break the cycle of poverty.

Comparison of Male and Female Enterprises in Pakistan

Appended table displays gender based early stage entrepreneurial activity (TEA) rates region wise in Pakistan. It is evident from the table that KPK has the highest Male TEA rate whereas Sindh has the highest female TEA rate. (Source: GEM 2012)

Table 1. Gender wise TEA

Province	Male	Female
Sindh	14.60%	3.20%
Punjab	20.50%	0.90%
Baluchistan	30.50%	-
Khyber Pakhtoon khowa	37.50%	-

(GEM report 2012)

Table 2. Male-Female Labor Force (% of Participation in Pakistan)

Years	Male	Female
2006-07	83.1	21.3
2007-08	82.4	21.8
2008-09	82.0	23.1
2009-10	81.7	24.1
2010-11	81.9	24.4
2012-13	81.1	24.3
2013-14	81.0	25.0
2014-15	81.4	25.0
2017-18	81.1	22.8

Source: *Pakistan Bureau of Statistics (2018)*

METHODS AND MATERIALS

The study adopted qualitative method and collected data through purposive sampling. The sample consists of women entrepreneurs who own small and medium enterprises and contributing towards the well-being of our society. It is an exploratory study, data is collected through questionnaires, and semi structured interviews conducted through one on one interviews, telephone and emails. The entrepreneurs thus selected has been successfully running businesses in the field of textiles, beauty, education and vocational training. Data is collected from 200 individuals and findings are generalized.

KEY FINDINGS

Table below pinpoints the factors acting as hindrance to the development or operations of female entrepreneurs in five major administrative units of Pakistan.

Table 3. A snapshot of Key Factors causing Hindrance to Development of Women Entrepreneurship

No.	Environmental Factors	Social Factors
Punjab	1. Access to capital 2. access to networks 3. Lack of guidelines and interaction with successful entrepreneurs. 4. Low priority given by bankers to provide loan to women entrepreneurs.	1. access to information 2. Social un-acceptance as women entrepreneurs. 3. Family responsibility. 4. Gender discrimination, missing network.
Sind	1. Financing 2. security	1. The effort to balance work and family 2. Gender biased role of society
Baluchistan	1. Exporting their product overseas 2. Increasing the volume of production 3. security 4. Lack of operational and managerial skills. 5. Women's inexperience of negotiating with the banks 6. Access to the essential abilities, skills and experiences for business 7. Lack of abilities, skills and expertise in certain business matters	1. Cultural constraints 2. Constraints and barriers to obtaining money to start and grow their own business. 3. Their dual (household) and triple (community) roles and responsibilities 4. lack of key dedicated "time" to be able to explore and nurture their own resources 5. Lack of exposure to the world of business
KPK	1. accessing credit from formal institutions in view of their limited access to formal education, ownership of property, and social mobility 2. include business experiences, 3. limited knowledge of marketing strategies, 4. weak business associations, 5. lack of networking facilities 6. training programmes	1. The prevailing social and cultural gender-base 2. Inequalities and biases 3. Unequal access to opportunities and markets 4. Poor access to education and
Islamabad Capital Territory	1. Inadequate financing 2. Competition 3. Obtaining quality raw materials.	1. Gender discrimination 2. Balancing time between the enterprise and the family
Azad Kashmir	1. lack of training and advisory services 2. lack of managerial and technical skills 3. weak infrastructure 4. Difficulties in accessing loans, and 5. Complicated company registration processes. 6. the willingness to take risks	1. Cultural constraints 2. Gender discrimination

CONCLUSION AND RECOMMENDATIONS

Current study is conducted to explore and highlight the factors responsible for hindering the growth of female owned enterprises. The female entrepreneurs in Pakistan are facing various difficulties and deterrents while running their businesses. The major data collected through primary data collection methods showed that the common factors include less access to finances, lack of training, cultural constraints, availability of inadequate infrastructure, lack of support and guidance for registration and advisory services, lack of networking facilities and weak marketing. Moreover, dual household roles, lack of experience and skills have also been highlighted among the many other factors.

Since female entrepreneurship is an important engine to promote economic growth and social development. Theories postulate it as a cultural, psychological, technological and economic event, which takes place in an appropriate environment. This is a process, which for its development, needs attention of multiple bodies including family, society, governmental and training. In case of Pakistan, there is still a room space for its development and women needs to be encouraged to participate in economic activity and enhance economic growth. There are various sides for example provision of financing, training, support for governmental efforts to raise awareness and starting campaigns for women entrepreneurship development at large scale.

ACKNOWLEDGMENT

The studies is conducted with the financial support of Foundation University Islamabad, Pakistan, under Internal Funded Research Grant (2018-2019).

REFERENCES

Apostolopoulos, N., Al-Dajani, H., Holt, D., Jones, P., & Newbery, R. 2018). Entrepreneurship and the Sustainable Development Goals. In Entrepreneurship and the Sustainable Development Goals (Contemporary Issues in Entrepreneurship Research, Volume 8) (pp. 1-7). Emerald Publishing Limited.

Asli, A., & Nour, H. (2018). Female Entrepreneurship in Morocco, Obstacles and Ways to Overcome Them. *6th International OFEL Conference on Governance, Management and Entrepreneurship. New Business Models and Institutional Entrepreneurs: Leading Disruptive Change. April 13th - 14th, 2018, Dubrovnik, Croatia, Governance Research and Development Centre (CIRU)*, 390-401.

Barretto, H. (1989). *The Entrepreneur in Microeconomic Theory: Disappearance and Explanation.* Routledge.

Barsh, J., & Yee, L. (2012). Unlocking the full potential of women at work. *McKinsey & Company/ Wall Street Journal.*

Blank, R. M, (2010). *Women-Owned Businesses in the 21st Century.* Report prepared by US. Department of Commerce, Economics and Statistics Department, for White House Council of Women and Girls.

Bruhn, M., & Zia, B. (2011). *Stimulating managerial capital in emerging markets: the impact of business and financial literacy for young entrepreneurs*. The World Bank. doi:10.1596/1813-9450-5642

Cabrera-Gil-Grados, E. M., & Mauricio, D. (2017). *Factors affecting the success of women's entrepreneurship: a review of literature*. Academic Press.

Colaco, V., & Hans, V. (2018). *Women Entrepreneurship in India–Changes and Challenges*. Academic Press.

Das, M. (2000). Women entrepreneurs from India: Problems, motivations and success factors. *Journal of Small Business and Entrepreneurship*, *15*(4), 67–81. doi:10.1080/08276331.2000.10593294

Dissanayake, K. (2018). Environmental effects on women-LED SMEs in Asia: From institutional perspective. *The Journal of Business*, *5*, 1.

Ghani, E., William, K., & Stephen, O. (2011b). *Spatial Determinants of Entrepreneurship in India*. NBER Working Paper 17514.

Hans, V. (2018). *Women Entrepreneurs in Modern Era–Opportunities*. Trends and Challenges.

Haque, N. (2007). *Entrepreneurship in Pakistan. Pakistan Institute of Development Economics*. Working Paper, 20.

Holmén, M., Min, T. T., & Saarelainen, E. (2011). Female entrepreneurship in Afghanistan. *Journal of Developmental Entrepreneurship*, *16*(03), 307–331. doi:10.1142/S1084946711001860

Jabeen, S., & Ahmad, F. (n.d.). *Culture and Barriers to Women's Entrepreneurs in Pakistan*. Academic Press.

Kalim, A. (2019). Women Entrepreneurship the Emerging Workforce in 21st Century: Turning Challenges to Opportunities. *Proceeding of 2nd International Conference on Business Management*.

Khan, A. A. (2014). Factors affecting the performance of female entrepreneurship: evidence from Punjab, Pakistan. Pakistan.

Khan, G., Naveed, R. T., & Jantan, A. H. B. (2018). Status of Wonder Women: Challenges for Young Future Women Entrepreneurs in Pakistan. *International Journal of Experiential Learning & Case Studies*, *3*(1), 97–109. doi:10.22555/ijelcs.v3i1.1838

Mattis, M. C. (2004). Women entrepreneurs: Out from under the glass ceiling. *Women in Management Review*, *19*(3), 154–163. doi:10.1108/09649420410529861

Mitchelmore, S., & Rowley, J. (2013). Entrepreneurial competencies of women entrepreneurs pursuing business growth. *Journal of Small Business and Enterprise Development*, *20*(1), 125–142. doi:10.1108/14626001311298448

Nadgrodkiewicz, A. (2011). *Empowering Women Entrepreneurs: The Impact of the 2006 Trade Organizations Ordinance in Pakistan*. Center for International Private Enterprise. Available at http://www.cipe.org/publications/fs/pdf/042911.pdf

Nasir, M., Iqbal, R., & Akhtar, C. (2019). Factors Affecting Growth of Women Entrepreneurs in Pakistan. *Pakistan Administrative Review*, *3*(1), 35–50.

Parker, S. C. (2009). *The Economics of Entrepreneurship*. Cambridge University Press. doi:10.1017/CBO9780511817441

Parvin, L., Rahman, M. W., & Jia, J. (2012). Determinates of women micro-entrepreneurship development: an empirical investigation in rural Bangladesh. *International Journal of Economics and Finance*, *4*(5), 254-260.

Patterson, N., & Mavin, S. (2009). Women entrepreneurs: Jumping the corporate ship and gaining new wings. *International Small Business Journal*, *27*(2), 173–192. doi:10.1177/0266242608100489

Rahmatullah, M., & Zaman, F. (2014). Female Entrepreneurship in Bangladesh: Constraints, Motivation and Success. *Bangladesh e-Journal of Sociology*, *11*(2).

Roomi, M. A., & Parrott, G. (2008). Barriers to development and progression of women entrepreneurs in Pakistan. *The Journal of Entrepreneurship*, *17*(1), 59–72. doi:10.1177/097135570701700105

Roomi, M. A., Rehman, S., & Henry, C. (2018). Exploring the normative context for women's entrepreneurship in Pakistan: A critical analysis. *International Journal of Gender and Entrepreneurship*, *10*(2), 158–180. doi:10.1108/IJGE-03-2018-0019

Schumpeter, J. (1934). *The Theory of Economic Development*. Harvard University Press.

Stevenson, L., & St-Onge, A. (2005). *Support for Growth-oriented Women Entrepreneurs in Tanzania*. ILO.

Subohi, A. (2006, Oct. 16). Competition driven sustained growth. *Daily Dawn*.

Syed, J. (2010). *Women and small business entrepreneurship in Pakistan*. Academic Press.

Wellalage, N., & Locke, S. (2017). Access to credit by SMEs in South Asia: Do women entrepreneurs face discrimination. *Research in International Business and Finance*, *41*, 336–346. doi:10.1016/j.ribaf.2017.04.053

Yunis, M. S., Hashim, H., & Anderson, A. R. (2019). Enablers and Constraints of Female Entrepreneurship in Khyber Pukhtunkhawa, Pakistan: Institutional and Feminist Perspectives. *Sustainability*, *11*(1), 27. doi:10.3390u11010027

ENDNOTES

1. See Parker (2009), containing studies for developed countries of the world.
2. Annual evaluation report of ILO (2006), found on www.ilo.org
3. www.theglobaleconomy.com

APPENDIX: ACRONYMS

CSR: Corporate Social Responsibility
GEM: Global Entrepreneurship Monitor
KPK: Khyber Pakhtunkhwa
MDGS: Millennium Development Goals
NGO: Non-government organization
SDGs: Sustainable Development Goals
SMEs: Small and Medium Enterprises
UNCTAD: United Nations Conference on Trade and Development

Chapter 7
Women Empowerment Initiatives and Socio-Economic Development:
In Pursuit of Gender Equality in Uzbekistan

Anviti Gupta
Sharda University, Uzbekistan

Alok Gupta
Sharda University, Uzbekistan

ABSTRACT

Empowered women encourage economic development and assist in making stable societies, and everyone benefits from the growth and stability that empowered women add to the economy. According to a study by McKinsey, if the economic participation of women is promoted globally, especially in developing countries, then it might enhance world economic growth by $28 trillion dollars by 2025. In Uzbekistan disparities exist between men and women in education, health, employment and income opportunities, control over assets, personal security, and participation in the political process in the country. The women come across significant barriers which deter her to participate fully and freely in contributing to the economic growth of the country. The stereotypical image of women, where we revere her mainly as a mother, the guardian of family wellbeing, is rooted in the minds of people; it is true, but in today's world, she should not be an inactive bystander, but an active and proactive contributor in the currently going on democratic transformations in the country. There is no denying the fact that Uzbek women have made a considerable progress in the last few years, but they have to struggle against many handicaps and social evils in the male-dominated society. The empowerment of women is one of the solutions to the problems of inequality, subordination, and marginalization. A critical problem and a high priority for the Government of Uzbekistan are to improve women's role and empower them to take part in the economic growth of the world. This chapter speaks about the government initiatives in empowering Uzbek women and bringing gender equality in the society. The data for the chapter was collected from

DOI: 10.4018/978-1-7998-3737-4.ch007

secondary sources. The objectives of this article are to examine and analyse the initiatives taken by Uzbek government and other UN bodies for gender equality and women empowerment. The same strategies can be replicated in other parts of Central Asia where women are still not treated equally and can be empowered to contribute to the socioeconomic growth. The current research may suggest the authorities and civil society organizations to improve and implement inventive methodologies to attain gender equality, advancement, and peace.

1. INTRODUCTION

Women empowerment is explained as a state in which women freely participate in social, political and economic domains of life (Sushama, 1998). Through empowerment people gain social, economic and political power to free themselves from inequalities in the community (Wallerstein, 1992). Empowerment is a state in where people, organisations exercise control to tackle their problems (Rappaport 1987; Zimmerman, 1995) The notion of empowerment is comprehended in terms of explicit needs of the people who are longing for enablement (Kabeer, 2005). Women empowerment is enabling women to take decisions by giving more opportunities of education. (Pathak2003). The economic empowerment of women denotes the initiatives taken to make women self-sufficient, contribute in home income and earn to fight against poverty. (Elliot 2008). On the other hand the political empowerment of women is giving opportunity to women folk to participate in governance of the state by pursuing their political careers. (Pam Rajput, 2001; Tiwari, 2001).

The UN Women's view of women's empowerment is focused around the active participation of Government in ensuring gender equality, no discrimination at work between men and women, fair treatment, no violation of human rights, considering wellbeing of women, ensuring health, safety and growth of women folk and maintaining records of implementation of initiatives towards gender equality, (Hawk and Mills, 2011).

The struggle for gender equality is an old battle, amidst prejudices and biases against women, unequal opportunities to education and jobs, unfair treatment, discrimination and cultural biases, countries are struggling to protect the rights of women and empower them so as to uplift their status in the society. A World Bank study (2018)has found that In 104 countries working in specific jobs for women is legally prohibited, and more than 2.7 billion women are barred from doing the same jobs by men. Unfortunately, in Uzbekistan the situation is no different Uzbekistan too confronts such conditions related to discrimination and gender biases.

In 1991, after being part of the former Soviet Union since 1924, the Republic of Uzbekistan gained independence and it began its transition to a market economy. Uzbekistan is a presidential republic. It is a country rich in resources, doubly landlocked, strategically located in the heart of Central Asia. Country's population is of approximately 32 million (as recorded in early 2017), out of which approximately half lives in urban areas. The population of Uzbekistan accounts for roughly 46 percent of the 68 million population of Central Asia. The World Bank reclassified Uzbekistan from a low-income country to a low-middle-income nation in 2011.

Since declaring independence in 1991, gender roles in Uzbekistan had been conditioned by Soviet policies on equality and traditional Uzbek values and culture. These factors caused hardship while transitioning to an independent, sovereign state, limiting women's growth and empowerment in Uzbekistan.

Traditions of the Soviet Union tended to give men and women formal equality when it came to employment, health, and political offices. Nevertheless, because of household tasks and child care, women were often relegated to unpaid work or lower-paying jobs. There remains unequal division of labor. The Uzbek government has established programs in the country to increase women's participation and empowerment.

Uzbekistan's government ratified the Convention on the Elimination of All Forms of Discrimination against Women (CEDAW) in May 1995, through legislation to address the gender issues in the country. The government also continues to work to improve the economic status of women by allowing companies to hire women workers and also give them opportunity to have special access to credit. In an effort to maximize the political roles of women, the government made it compulsory for political parties to include some percentage of women candidates.

2. OBJECTIVES

The purpose of this article is to review the status of women in Uzbekistan and to highlight the initiatives undertaken by the Uzbek Government and other organisations in empowering the women of Uzbekistan. It also mentions the gender equality in context of Uzbekistan and also focuses on various steps undertaken to ensure equal status to Uzbek women.

This article appreciates the initiatives of Government of Uzbekistan which recognizes that reforms are desirable in governance to improve participatory decision-making, transparency and openness. Challenges include enhancing public awareness and following human rights principles, ensuring that justice is done to the groups who are susceptible and endorsing gender equality.

3. RESEARCH METHODOLOGY

Secondary data from various sources were analysed, including articles from peer reviewed journals, international statutes, government policies and publications.

4. WOMEN IN UZBEKISTAN

After Uzbekistan separated from USSR the women were badly affected by the transition .The people of Uzbekistan faced a lot of hardships post-soviet economic transition. Education and professional opportunities were less for women but due to reduced family support services the education became less affordable for women in Uzbekistan. Women who are divorced, unmarried mothers, from large families are affected more by poverty than men. 63% of women remain unemployed after transition. Unemployed women are mostly unskilled or can only work in the agricultural field or low paid jobs. Most of the women who are employed are serving predominantly in health and education sectors and face hardships because they are paid less, women also lack entrepreneurial or business skills for small businesses, they also lack access to credit. Moreover many organizations prefer men over women because the expense of engaging females is costlier to them because the women are guaranteed a number of rights such as maternity benefits and other benefits. Many societies treat women unequally and unjustly. The fundamental rights of women are violated from centuries in many cultures including Uzbekistan. Uzbekistan being a male-controlled society has inherent flaws including discrimination against women.

Uzbekistan acquired Independence in 1991 and since then it has faced many difficult situations. The republic has undergone social, political and economic transformation during the last 19 years of Independence. The country has tried to restore the original ethno-national culture and traditions and imbibed the principles of the modern world. It has come a long way in the steady development of democracy, nation building and socially oriented market economy. Traditions are blended with modernity in Uzbekistan. Traditionalists expect women to be at home and liberals want to give equal status to women and encourage their participation in building the nation Currently Uzbekistan Is treading on the path of revivalism. These dichotomies exist in the constantly developing neo modern society of Uzbekistan which makes the task for empowering women more challenging. The Republic Of Uzbekistan after disintegrating from Soviet Union has initiated a new chapter of enhancing the equal status for women. The government made number of changes in Constitution where emphasis is made in giving equal status to the women.

4.1 Overview of Status of Women in Different Periods

4.1.1 Pre-Soviet Period

The strict customs and tenets of Islam influenced the roles, responsibilities and status of women in Central Asian culture. Previously the authors from the west who visited Central Asia portrayed a miserable depiction of their society. They mentioned in their writings that the women folk of Central Asia particularly, were subdued and were treated like slaves by male clan and religious leaders, They were treated as mere possessions, were forced into suffocating matrimony .The literature also depicted the negative image of traditional culture with their imperialist ideology. The lack of gross knowledge of the family structure in Central Asia led them to look at women folk only as slaves, subject to their lords and were at their masters ‘ whims and fancies.

4.1.2 Soviet Period

From the start of the Soviet era, Soviet leaders started working towards women liberation, with the purpose of uplifting women in all areas of cultural, social and political life. Robust efforts were made during the same time to include women in the process of political administration. Female delegates were elected at local and republican level to represent their communities in public meetings. Since the start of 1929 more than 1000 Uzbek women became members of the political party. Although their membership remained low as they lacked previous political exposure. In order to empower women the government introduced promotion and also a quota system, where women were granted around one-third of government and party roles in various administrative bodies.

4.1.3 Post-Soviet Period

The Post-Soviet period witnessed main political, social and economic changes in Central Asia. Five independent states came into being in the region which further led to the drastic changes in the previous ideologies. One of the newly independent states promoted the revival of the ancient Islamic cultural values. As a result the newly framed philosophy of gender equality which came into being in the new

Soviet era began to be challenged. During the transition period a clear trend toward reform in the social system emerged.

Despite the fact that the constitution reflected principle of equality between men and women in Central Asian Republic, state authorities started supporting patriarchy which stressed the women's traditional role as mothers and homemakers.

The statutory provisions have tried to empowered and uplift Uzbek women by giving them certain rights but the traditional societal framework is hampering their growth. Females are also more unreasonably affected by the negative aspects of the socio-economic transformation happening currently in the country. Many factors like insufficiency, unemployment, limited resources illiteracy, marginalization and domestic violence result in the exploitation of womenfolk in Uzbekistan .It is by the decree of government that's women are granted equal rights but the society is not in favour of empowering women in this male-dominated society. Aware of this the government, non-governmental organizations and other civil society organizations are taking initiatives in creating awareness about the equal rights, status and duties of women.

4.1.4 Current Scenario

Gender equality is an important area which is being attended too in most countries, and is also one of the United Nations Millennium Development Goals (MDGs).Sustainable Development Goals to be attained by the UN by 2030 has also incorporated gender equality. UN Development Program in Uzbekistan is taking many initiatives in empowering and development women of the land, despite this fact the statistics indicate that more adequate economic and social reforms have to be made and implemented to uplift the status of women in Uzbekistan.

Women and men are equal in number in Uzbekistan .Yet, in the cities women dominate over men and in the villages men are more women live around five years longer than men on an average, and only 17% of them are involved in crime.(Table -1) The statistics reveal disparity in socio-economic participation of women. There is significant gender inequality in education in Uzbekistan. According to statistics only 36.5 per cent of the 258.4 thousand students who enter universities are women. Women mainly are interested in studying liberal arts and pedagogy-over 50% and 60% respectively. Only 18 to 19% women study technical education in University. Resulting in gender imbalances in sectors such as public health, sports, education, and the arts, where women represent more than 70 per cent of employees It is often stated that "the work of a woman include teacher doctor and artist.' Furthermore, gender imbalances can be found in public administration and management, where women's representation is only 27%, while they make up only 19% of local government officials. It is worth noting that there are no Khokim women.(6 Khokim were selected from women's in the beginning of 2020).

(Chin, G. V. S., & Hoogervorst, T.)The authors have mentioned in their article that the literature also speaks that the magnitude to which a modern Peranakan woman could embrace western ways was limited. Following the modernity by females was accepted as long as it doesn't contradict with their traditional domestic roles, but the womenfolk behaved in any ways which fell outside the purview of traditional femininities, or deemed antithetical to the established gender norms was condemned as tjemar (polluted) and was subjected to the disciplinary forces of culture and society. Uzbekistan until now was no different.

Women empowerment is one of the key areas of concern in Central Asia. Government has created equal opportunities for women in education and health, which has affected the poverty rates. It has also helped in enhancing literacy rate of children and also helps in the physical and mental health all the children of Uzbekistan.

For every country it is important to express zero tolerance to gender biases .Government of Uzbekistan also promotes equal rights to women and is making efforts to alleviate poverty by encouraging girl child to study and also by giving them opportunity for employment.

UN also focuses on promoting projects to empower Women, realising her important role in family and creating meaningful societies. Uzbekistan's government, in collaboration with UNDP, has been making efforts to bring gender equality. Significant steps have also been taken in promoting women entrepreneurs, rising wakefulness of ensuring equal rights to women and incorporating gender dimensions in budgeting processes.

5. INITIATIVES TOWARDS WOMEN EMPOWERMENT IN UZBEKISTAN

Organizations such as Uzbekistan's Women's Commission, Uzbekistan's OSCE Project Coordinator, and the National Association of NGOs and Uzbekistan-India Friendship Society are all working to augment the women empowerment in Uzbekistan. The U.N institutions (UNDP, UNESCO, UNFPA and UNV) have been promoting joint program addressing women's socio-economic status and also initiating strategies to empower women across Uzbekistan. Many organizations carry on important initiatives and tasks in tackling gender inequality. Achieving a legal framework for empowerment of women in Uzbekistan would help women boost their socio-economic standing while improving society as a whole.

5.1 A Joint Project by Women's Committee of Uzbekistan and UNDP (2017)

Women's Committee of Uzbekistan A joint project "Empowering Women to Participate in Public Administration and Socio-Economic Life" is initiated by the Uzbekistan Women's Committee and UNDP. The purpose of this initiative is to increase women's social and political participation and reinforcing their contribution in public administration. (UNDP, 2017)The collaborative women's empowerment project began its actions in November 2017.

The strategic dimensions of the joint project are:

- Testing and expanding women's empowerment initiatives to ensure women active participation of women folk in social and financial life.
- Support in making the laws, draft legislation, strategy and theoretical papers on women empowerment in harmony with international human rights truces;
- Aid in steering training, seminars, symposia, other capacity-building activities.
- Building the atmosphere for institutional and cultural change. Encouraging the women to participate in country's socio-political life.
- Preparing draft legislation on women empowerment for women workers in ministries and public department.

In association with the Academy of Public Administration and other government organization the Women Committees are developing the training programs for women, civil servants and managers.

The project also imparts trainings in mathematics, physics, information technology, engineering, chemistry, biology and other natural sciences for girls also organizes the competitions to encourage them.

Project supports women owned ventures, public partnership initiatives for women's education and development of women entrepreneurs.

Grants are also provided to various regional universities, scientific laboratories, working with khokimiyats to ensure involvement of girls and women to take up the technical education and hone their skill and become self-reliant.

5.2 Women's Committee on Gender Equality Issues

Researches states that gender equality can be attended if the women are given more opportunity for monetary assistance or credit access, right to use the land, and employment openings (Morrison, et al, 2007). According to Kishore (1997) there is a positive correlation between gender inequality and low per capita income.

Uzbekistan has seen progress and recession both since independence in 1991in the issues of Gender equality. The constitution enshrines ideals of non-discrimination and equal rights for men and women. Uzbekistan's Women's Committee (WCU) is machinery which works for the women and various matters pertaining to her and is instrumental in encouraging gender equality.

Established in 1991, the Women's Committee aims to improve the status of women in society. The WCU, led by the deputy prime minister, has regional body with a compulsory role of a deputy head on issues related to women. The President's latest decree of February 2018 has provisions which further encourages WCU practices, and allows for more innovative and systemic gender mainstreaming strategies.

The WCU identified priority issues for urban women: "employment, job creation, business development and entrepreneurship skills." The key initiatives for rural women are improvement in social and civic services, and the necessity for having business which are family and home based.

5.3 Creation of Virtual Reception Office

Since the beginning of 2017 a step towards facilitating the interaction of women with the government on any issue of concern to them was initiated by WCU. In each administrative location, a virtual reception office was built to promote citizens ' communications with government. Every citizen can directly send inquiries to the Government; WCU conducts regular evaluations and looks into the appeals made to the virtual Reception Bureau by the women. The main issues concerning women are demands for legal, social, housing and financial support, as well as queries and suggestions about cultural behaviour, dress codes, marriages, and traditions.

5.4 Hotline for Women

The Women's Committee started a hotline in 2018 for the victims of domestic violence. They have to call on number 1146 to take assistance from a doctor, psychologist or legal advisor. The committee also started its first lodgings for domestic violence sufferers where they can get respite from physical or mental torture.

5.5 Publication of a Draft Law for Prevention of Sex Discrimination

In April 2018 the Women's Committee of Uzbekistan released a draft law aimed at preventing gender discrimination and improves the status of women in society. This draft legislation document is the first of its kind in Uzbekistan. This has included gender equality, discrimination and other issues related to women folk. It also describes measures for protecting women rights, and imposes punishments for their violation. President Shavkat Mirziyoyev signed a decree in 2018 aimed at improving support given to women's and strengthening the family institution. The legislation critiqued the existing situation of the rights of women and their role in state affairs. The decree also formed a center Oila ("Family"), which purposes to make the marriages strongly bonded, investigate reproductive health issues of women, explore problems faced by modern families and compile lists of low-income households. Oila center workers travel across the country, addressing the issues of domestic abuse with women and their own family members. Qila is also responsible for making the family institution stronger. Before Qila came into being, if anyone wanted to terminate their marriage they had to seek permission from their local council office but after formation of Oila, they have the authority over such decisions.

6. UNDP AND WOMEN EMPOWERMENT

6.1 Initiatives by UNDP

- Capacity Building and Skills Training

UNDP and its partners have empowered women through capacity building initiatives in various areas. UNDP has imparted training in capacity building and helped in enhancing managerial skills in all women in the small and medium-sized enterprise. These women have taken up various types of entrepreneurial activities. Work in this field has focused particularly on the Aral Sea region. (UNDP,2016). UNDP has also suggested economic policies which support the women. It has actively empowered women within Uzbekistan to make them self-reliant and empowered. The concept of gender budgeting has now been firmly introduced through the budget code.(UNDP,2014) The financial policymakers in association with UNDP have ensured that women empowerment initiatives have enough financial support it requires. Women-led businesses have provided the requisite support and assistance to find footholds in national and international marketplaces. Women's roles in business and government have been greatly enhanced through assistance from UNDP and other UN agencies in the Aral Sea bordering Republic of Karakalpakstan .The contribution made by UNDP in enhancing the skills and ability of women has ensured great participation of women in making decisions, and also the support given to infrastructure projects have drastically improved the lives of women and girls living in isolated communities of Uzbekistan. UNDP has supported more than 200 small-scale businesses which were majorly operated by all or many number of women workers. Training women in professional silk-weaving skills has helped to empower them with financial independence. (UNDP,2015).

- Promoting And Implementing Gender Budgeting

UNDP and the Ministry of Finance of Uzbekistan have started a joint project namely "Budget System Reform in Uzbekistan"(UNDP-2010-2016) Which is aimed at ensuring the efficiency, accountability and transparency of the budget system. During this project UN carried out an initial analysis of the gender sensitivity of the state budget of the Djizak region. Since 2011 gender budgeting methodologies have been promoted in Uzbekistan by UNDP. Gender budgeting is a study and measurement of public expenditure and revenue to see that the interests of both men and women are protected. It is viewed as a significant tool in creating a democratic It also helps in, proving efficient use of resources to achieve gender equality and humandevelopment.Gender budgeting emphasizes the adjustment of goals, not an increase in government expenditure, and provides opportunities for governments to pursue more equitable and sustainable development objectives.

- Business Forum of Uzbekistan (Phase III)(UNDP-2014-17)

One of the important objectives of this project was to Develop women entrepreneurship. Seminar was conducted where 60 representatives from 28 banks took part on the strategy for introducing gender financing in commercial banks in order to stimulate involvement of women in entrepreneurship.

6.2 Initiatives by the UN Women – (United Nations Entity for Gender Equality and Empowerment of Women)

The United Nations Entity for Gender Equality and Women's Empowerment (UN Women) was made to take the initiative to make progress towards fulfilling the needs of women and girls around the world. UN Women's formation in 2010 is viewed as a breakthrough move in advancing the overall goals of the United Nations on gender equality and women empowerment

UN Women's work is centred on the underlying conviction that gender equality is the cornerstone of sustainable development. Accordingly, UN Women supports UN Member States in enforcing universal standards to attain gender equality, and also collaborating with governments and civil society in formulating the legislation, strategy frameworks, programs and amenities necessary to implement these standards (UN women, 2015)

Based in Almaty, Kazakhstan, the UN Women multi-country office for Central Asia functions in four countries, including Uzbekistan, Kazakhstan, Tajikistan and Turkmenistan. It supports governments and civil society organizations in these countries in developing and implementing innovative strategies that aim to achieve gender equality, sustainability, and peace. UN Women's activities in Uzbekistan have been undertaken since 2010, and supported by a gender advisor. Its primary work areas include the following:

- Economic Empowerment of Women

UN Women supports efforts by the Uzbek Women's Committee to improve the economic and social standing of womenfolk in rural areas. This is accomplished by mobilizing rural communities to attend to monetary and social challenges which hinder development based on rights of gender. It also pays attention to enhancing standard of living of rural women and augmenting the capacity of Centres to give financial advice and educational assistance to rural women, to ensure that they have access to economic and financial services for these women.

- National Female Entrepreneurship Program in Uzbekistan.

UN Women is supporting Uzbekistan's Chamber of Commerce and Industry (CCIUz), together with the Uzbek Women's Committee in the creation of a "National Women's Entrepreneurship Program in Uzbekistan" (WED).UN Women's past experience in the country with implementing women's economic empowerment initiatives serves as the foundation for this complex initiative, which concentrates in particular on vulnerable women's groups, especially the rural women.

- Promoting special temporary measures in Uzbekistan

UN Women's key areas in Uzbekistan is tied to promoting gender equality, in the country's political domain. With technical support by the UN Women, participation of Uzbekistan's Women's Committee, National Human Rights Commission, parliamentarians, political parties, and NGOs guidelines are created and assured to be implemented to improve women's involvement in decision-making.

7. GOVERNMENT INTERVENTIONS ON WOMEN'S POLITICAL AND PUBLIC PARTICIPATION (UNDP, 2016-17)

Uzbekistan bans violence against women and prohibits on the-job discrimination. Since 2004, when the 30% quota for women was implemented in the candidate lists of political parties, the number of women in parliament has risen from 9.4% in 2014 to 16% in 2017.But still women are underrepresented at other levels of decision making (16 per cent 25 per cent), and women have not yet achieved the representation of at least 30 per cent required for them to have a noteworthy voice in decision-making.

7.1 The Development Strategy of Uzbekistan for 2017–2021

7.1.1 Employment and the Labor Market

Employment and creation of Jobs are a permanent state priority. The participation of women in the labor market or in commercial activity is not prohibited by any legislation. The 2017–2021 Development Strategy explicitly speaks about job creation for women and vocational college graduates.While women make up 49.6 percent of the population of Uzbekistan, their share of formal jobs (45.7 percent) is lower than that of men (54.3 percent).Women lead in lower-paid social sector jobs (in education, health care, social services, catering),(Table2) while men dominates in technical and other more profitable fields (construction, industry, transportation, communications, IT).Women majorly work in family owned business like farming or handicrafts, which have noteworthy prospects and are supported by the government. Since women are engaged in the household chores they get less chance to work in formal jobs or start-ups.

7.1.2 Gender Roles and Norms

All the laws in Uzbekistan are established on the principles of gender equality . Chapter 10,Article 46 of the Constitution of Uzbekistan ensures that

Women and men shall have equal rights. The laws which protects the rights of women conforms with international standards. Traditional gender roles prescribe the jobs of women and men in family and society, establish tacit and explicit guidelines and assign variousresponsibilities and duties to women and men.

Traditional notions of motherhood, babies, and family are commonplace in Uzbekistan. A woman who wants towork has an obligation to make work life balance.

Women's and men's professional choices and educational opportunities are based on gender stereotypes. There are more conservative gender norms in the rural areas. particularly in terms of the roles of women and marriageable age.

The President of the Republic of Uzbekistan's most recent decree (February 2018) defines measures aimed at radically improving assistance to women and the family as an institution, and also addressing the issues of gender inequality.

7.1.3 Property Rights and Access to Resources to Women by Asian Development Bank

While legislation provides equal rights for both women and men to own property, there are still noteworthy gender inequalities. Many people obtain homes by inheritance which historically is favouritism towards males. Just 22.3% comprises of female property out of total property registered with the national land and property Cadaster Agency Traditionally, rural families are run by men; thus maximum real estate is registered in their name. Community funds accumulate in the hands of the eldest man, normally a community living in law who manages the budget. The limited access by women to finance and assets is impacting their monetary opportunities and empowerment. To address these issues, Asian Developmental Bank ADB has funded an affordable housing initiative that, among other outcomes, gives women greater access to housing loans, thereby contributing to the gender balance in property rights. ADB seeks to go beyond isolated changes in women's lives and foster a pattern of fairer gender roles and gender equality.

7.1.4 EU-funded Project ACTED Uzbekistan

ACTED is an international French non-governmental organization (NGO) which started in 1993. It is committed to immediate humanitarian assistance to support those in urgent need and to protect the dignity of people, while co-creating opportunities for sustainable growth in the longer term and fulfilling the potential of people.

ACTED Uzbekistan has been implementing a EU funded project to strengthen women's rights through increased protection and self-employment since early 2018.

In the scope of this initiative, a pilot study is currently being undertaken across the country's various rural communities to recognize women vulnerable to domestic violence and to illustrate the history and behavioural patterns linked to domestic violence in the targeted areas.

7.1.5 Recommendations to Improve Gender Equality in Uzbekistan (As per UNDP-2014)

Countrywide promotional campaign using TV commercials, videos, and billboards that would show family relationships involving educated working women should be promoted. Egalitarian relationships within the family must also be given importance and should be promoted.Government and NGOs must hold interactive trainings for law enforcement officers to develop their dispute resolution skills and nurture no tolerance to domestic violence. Government Laws must define Equal Marriage Age for both males and females. Introduction of NGOs that can provide mediation for families so that the women folk are given assistance and support.

Education for all should be the most important mission of the Government. The Uzbek government and other development agencies must focus on developing a system of distance learning so as to encourage and promote education for women. Targeted Enrolment, Quotas, and Women's Scholarships must be promoted to carry out research in "Male" Majors. Steps must be taken to expand pre-schooling, particularly in rural areas, to educate women so that they get equal opportunities in labour market. Girls must be encouraged to go for higher education. Scholarships for women and seats reservation must be introduced in Colleges.

Fixed-Hours for each Working Day must be propagated through adequate Labour Laws in Public Organizations and Fair Recruitment practices, giving equal opportunities for all must be followed. Giving women equal opportunity is a moral and economic imperative and rescinding discriminatory laws is a vital first step (Shanta Devarajan, World Bank 2020)

Government shall implement measures in areas where women are less represented to include women in their working manpower.(Female Specialist Register, 30 Per Cent Female Employee Quota, Etc.). (The Committee on the Elimination of Discrimination against Women in the fifth periodic report of Uzbekistan, 2015)

Implementation of awareness campaigns with an emphasis on male audience aimed at eradicating stereotypes and increasing gender literacy among the general population.

Data must be obtained annually from individuals who are discriminated by sex and should be encourage equal consideration of the interests and needs of women and men in the implementation of government programs and policies.

8. CONCLUSION

There is a great discrepancy between the objectives stated by the government to enhance women empowerment and the actual state of affairs related to women's legal, economic, and cultural participation. The women of Uzbekistan are empowered on paper but face lot of gender biases in the labour market, education, business etc.

The laws promulgated by the government on gender equality are difficult to follow as the traditional perceptions about women and her gender specific roles and responsibilities are stronger in the minds of the society than legal regulations

The Uzbek government is making an effort to improve its image internationally by promoting its interest in preserving universal rights and values, including the equality of women and men. New government bodies promoting gender equality is not sufficient and moreover cultural resistance are strong which acts as a barrier in giving equal status to women. The current reforms in the legal system should be accompanied by reformation of social life and cultural habits and perception. The reforms on gender balance have to be supplemented by generating equal opportunities for women and preventing violence against them.

Women's rights are changing in Uzbekistan but at a slower pace, country still lacks domestic violence law and gender equality legislation is yet to be introduced.

REFERENCES

ADB. (2017). *Basic Statistics. Manila*. Https://Www.Adb.Org/Publications/Basic-Statistics-2017

Asian Development Bank (ADB). (2005). *Country Gender Assessment Uzbekistan*. Philippines: ADB.

Bum, S. M. (1995). *The Social Psychology of Gender*. McGraw-Hill College.

Cabinet of Ministers. (1998). *On the Establishment of the Oila National Scientific, Practical Centre (Decree No. 54). 2 February*. Http://Old.Lex.Uz/Pages/Getact.Aspx?Lact_Id=844011.

Chin, G. V. S., & Hoogervorst, T. (2017). From Soetji to Soendel: Negotiating race, class and gender in a Netherlands Indies newspaper. *Intersections: Gender and Sexuality in Asia and the Pacific, 41*.

Elliott, C. M. (2008). *Global empowerment of women: Responses to globalization and politicized religions*. Rutledge.

Hawk, J., & Mills, J. (2011). *The women's empowerment principles: Equality means business initiative. United Nations Global Compact* (2nd ed.). UN Women.

Human Development Report. (2016). Http://Hdr.Undp.Org/Sites/All/Themes/Hdr_Theme/Country-Notes/Uzb.Pdf

Ibrahim, S. (2013). Status Of Women In Uzbekistan. *Journal Of Humanities And Social Science, 10*(3), 47-55.

Kabeer, N. (2005). Gender equality and Women"s empowerment: A critical analysis of the third Millennium Development Goal. *Gender and Development, 13*(1), 13–36. doi:10.1080/13552070512331332273

Kishor, S. (1997). *Empowerment of women in Egypt and Link to the Survival and Health of their infants*. Paper presented at the Seminar on Female Empowerment and Demographic Process.

Morrison, A., & Biehl, L. (Eds.). (2007). *Too Close to Home: Domestic Violence in Latin America*. Inter-American Development Bank.

Pathak, K. N., & Tomar, J. S. (2012). *Skill- Up gradation in five year plans. Yojana, August 2012*. Ministry of Information and Broadcasting.

Rajput, P. (2001). Women's political participation in India: An agenda for empowerment. In P. Kapur (Ed.), *Empowering the Indian Women*. Ministry of Information and Broadcasting, Government of India.

Rappaport, J. (1987). Terms of empowerment/examples of prevention: Toward a theory for community Psychology. *The Journal of Psychology, 15*(2), 121–148. PMID:3604997

Sushama, S. (1998). Women and Empowerment- Approach and Strategies. Discovery Publishing House.

Tiwari, R. S. (2001). Feminism and globalization versus Indian women empowerment. In Modernity, Feminism and Women's Empowerment. Rawat Publication.

Wallerstein, N. (1992). Powerlessness, empowerment and health: Implication for Health promotion programs. *American Journal of Health Promotion, 6*(3), 197–205. doi:10.4278/0890-1171-6.3.197 PMID:10146784

Women's Rights in Uzbekistan, Briefing note to the UN Committee on the Elimination of Discrimination Against Women (CEDAW) Coalition of Uzbek women's rights NGOs Coordination by the Bureau of Human Rights and Rule of Law Uzbekistan (CEDAW Pre-session, Geneva, February 2009) @Strengthening Womens Political Participation-An Analysis of the impact of women's parliamentary networks in Europe and Central Asia –Report by UNDP. https://www.opendemocracy.net/en/odr/uzbekistan-gender-ineaulity-violence-en/ https://www.unwomen.org/en/about-us/about-un-women https://www.uz.undp.org/content/uzbekistan/en/home/presscenter/pressreleases/2017/11/20/wc-undp-will-promote-women-empowerment.html

Zimmerman, M. A. (1995). Psychological empowerment: Issues and illustrations. *American Journal of Community Psychology, 25*(5), 581-599. (https://www.gazeta.uz/oz/2020/03/11/women-mayors doi:10.1007/BF02506983

Chapter 8
3 R`s for Women Empowerment:
Respect, Recognition, and Remuneration – Women Labour Force Participation: Trends and Issues

Neeraja Vijay
Dr. M. G. R. Educational and Research Institute, India

Arti Chandani
https://orcid.org/0000-0001-7662-7967
Symbiosis Institute of Management Studies, Symbiosis International (Deemed University), India

Elumalayan S. V.
Dr. M. G. R. Educational and Research Institute, India

ABSTRACT

Women are no less than men. She herself is on par with a man. WO-MAN empowering is not only a verbal concept; it should be in practical life. She is no less than a man in any work assigned to her. She is always ill-treated as a weaker sex. But in the real life, she is more powerful than a man. Her commitment towards her work is always dedicated. She always tries to prove herself in any task assigned to her. This movement of women empowerment is not a new one. When you look back into the prehistoric period, women were treated as equal warriors, better half to men. They were strong enough in mind and soul. Then when and where did she lose her identity? Why is she treated as a weaker sex? Why she is deprived of her right to respect, recognition, and remuneration in the outer world with reference to her male colleagues? Through this chapter, the author is trying to shed light on the rights of a women, which she is deprived of since ages.

DOI: 10.4018/978-1-7998-3737-4.ch008

INTRODUCTION

In the global scenario only few countries are named as she nations. One such nation is India. A country which is always recognized for the respect given to women folk of their nation. A country which is named after as Bharath Matha[Mother]. It is often said that the status and position of women in society are the mirror images of their civilization, its progress and its shortcomings. In case of India, women have come a long way from women being warriors, saints and scholars in the Rig Vedic period, to the women who entered into armed forces, IT sector, politics, Entrepreneur, industry and other significant areas by effectively and efficiently managing their role. She also play role of a daughter, wife and mother irrespective of her education, position she hold in society. Women had to fight the traditional Indian male-dominated society to emerge as stronger and independent entity. While all these are positive developments, cases of rape, harassment at workplace and dowry deaths are rampant. Illiteracy and ignorance about her rights are still prevalent among a majority of the women. Through this paper the author want to throw a light to the aspects of women remuneration at work, recognition at workplace and family, respect she deserve. Women empowerment here is focused from prehistoric period to the present era.

- **Objective of this work:**
  - To understand the dimensions of Women Empowerment
  - To identify the missing pieces how and where the identity of women is lost.
  - To identify how to Rehabilitate the respect of women

BACKGROUND OF THIS STUDY

Women are the power of nation. In the present century the statistics tell that appx. 50% of the worlds working population are women. In a country like India women are always treated like goddess. India itself is called as **She** nation. Right from ancient times India is always regarded as a nation who respects women. They were empowered from age old times In earlier historic Epic of Mahabharata the great warriors were name after their mother like.Gangaputhra-Bhishma pitamaha, Kunth putra- first 3 brothers of pandavas(Dharmaraj, Arjuna, Bheem), Karna was named as Radhaiya as he was brought up by Radha, Anjani putra named after Hanuman, lord Krishna also called as Yashoda putra . India also worships goddess Lakshim, Saraswathi, Durga. Women in Pre-Vedic Period: Historical studies and the scriptures indicate that Indian woman enjoyed a comparatively high status during the early Vedic period (2000 B.C. to 1000 B.C.), surpassing contemporary civilizations in ancient Greece and Rome. The Aryans, who were mostly busy fighting wars, regarded woman as useful and productive members of society. The condition of Vedic Woman was good. Woman also enjoyed religious status like that of men, especially in Vedic initiation and studies. The Rig Veda provides ample evidence to prove that women were treated at par with men they had capacity to acquire the highest knowledge, even the absolute knowledge. During the Rig Veda period women were rendered the highest social status but this slowly started fading away. They were neglected and their status fell in the later Vedic and Epic period. They were not at all treated equally with men or were not enjoying equal rights and privileges as compared to men. Though the woman participated in each family ceremony with men but they only played a role as a silent observer not an active participant. However, changes into the status of woman introduced in 15th century. Saints and supporters of bhakti movement were expounded and spoken about equality of woman with men. Women constituted the keystone in the arch of Indian society.

A glance into Indian history reveals the facts of India great women warriors like Rani Rudramadevi fromWarangal (Telengana), Rani of Jansi Lakshmi Bai etc. Jijabai mother of great Chatrapati Shivaji who trained her son as a great warrior etc. Razia Sultana, Rudrama Devi, Rani Mangammal, Rani Velu Nachiyar, Chand Bibi. Abbakka Rani. Tarabai, Bibi Dalair Kau.etc who are icons of women empowerment.

Empowerment is a multi-faced, multi-dimensional and multi-layered concept. As such, it is not this or that, but is the action and interaction of various factors-physical, socioeconomic, political, mental, psychological, and attitudinal and so on. Women's empowerment could be described as a process in which women gain greater share of control over resources-material, human and intellectual like knowledge, information, ideas, and financial resources like money and access to money and control over decision making in the home, community, society and nation, and to gain power'.

Empowering Women is considered to be Smart Economics. Women Empowerment according to International Centre for Research on Women (ICRW) can be understood as:

"A woman is economically empowered when she has both the ability to succeed and advance economically and the power to make and act on economic decisions.

As women's empowerment is a vast field with a myriad of indicators, the prominent dimensions of women's empowerment are: economic contribution, education, government, health, and media. Each dimension is divided into categories of indicators used by national and international agencies.

Table 1. Dimensions of Women Empowerment

Dimensions	Category
Economic Contribution	Market Participation, Resource Equity
Education	Characteristics of population, Educational System
Governance	Representation, Electoral System and Process, Justice
Health	Access and utilization of health services,Disease and prevention, Environmental health, Fertility and population growth, Health care management, Health expenditures, maternal and infant health, Mental health and risk behaviour, nutrition, reproductive health, violence against women
Media	Equal treatment of media employees, Equal coverage in news reporting, equal expression of freedom of speech.

The women's economic empowerment comprises:

- economic advancement through increased income and return on labour;
- access to opportunities and life chances, such as skills development or job openings;
- access to assets, services and the support required to advance economically; decision-making authority in different spheres including household finances.
- Changes in gender relations between men and women in the household and/or the business.
- new skills; adapted business practices to accommodate women
- increases in, and expenditure of, women's income

- changes in women's and men's attitudes to the role of women in the workplace
- increases in decision making by women in businesses
- changes in women's self-reliance, self-confidence or status as a result of increased access

Benefits of Women Empowerment

Women empowerment adds to confidence of women in their ability to lead meaningful and purposeful lives. It removes their dependence on others and makes them individuals in their own right.

- They are able to lead their lives with dignity and freedom
- It adds to their self esteem
- It gives them a distinct identity
- They are able to gain positions of respect in society
- As they are financially independent they are able to spend on all their needs and desires
- They are able to make meaningful contributions to the well-being of society
- They act as capable citizens to make the country achieve enhanced Gross Domestic Product (GDP) growth
- They get fair and equitable access to resources of the country

The term "women's empowerment" has come to be associated with women's struggle for social justice and equality. Even in the prehistoric period women was treated at par with men. Lord Krishna had to take help of Sathyabhama to fight against the Evil power of Narakasura. Lord Shiva has make Goddess Parvati his better half. Empowerment of a woman should not be seen only in social justice but also in 360^0perspective.

The term empowerment refers to a range of activities from individual self-assertion to collective resistance, protest and mobilization that challenge basic power relations.In order to understand what is power' one has to understand its partner Ideology'. As Nath and Chatterjee stated that for true empowerment', what is most significant is the control of ideology, i.e., control over thoughts and perceptions that shapes individual beliefs, values and attitudes-ways of perceiving, thinking, feeling and analyzing. This control in turn confers decision making power which increases access to and control over resources.According to the Report of Government of India empowerment means moving from a position of enforced powerlessness to one of power. It would promote women's inherent strength and positive self-image.

The empowerment of the woman begins when she becomes aware of the socio-psycho-cultural injustice that is being done to her and also how gender inequality and inequity and gender and social-cultural, economic and political forces are affecting her adversely in every sphere of her life. It starts when she becomes fully aware of her positive self –image, self –esteem, positive rights and duties, of her capabilities and potentialities.

Thus to empower women in the real sense is to enable them to showcase and explore their talents, facilities, abilities and capacities, and to realize their full potentialities, and real identity as also freedom of thought, expression and action, and strength to handle every sphere of their lives. It is not only to make a women aware of their capacities, but also to provide them with the opportunities, facilities, and external and internal environment to utilize their inherent qualities and to develop in them self-confidence, self-esteem and social-psycho-economic self-reliance and self –dignity and the ability to raise a voice and fight against injustice, exploitation and violence done to her.

Empowerment of women in India heavily depend on many different variables that include Geographical location (urban/rural), educational status, social status (caste and class), and age. Policies on women's empowerment exist at the national, state, and local (panchayat) levels in various sectors, like health care, hospitality, education, economic opportunities, gender-based violence, and Political participation etc. However, there are significant gaps between policy advancements and actual practice at the operational level. As such, Women and girls have restricted mobility, access to education, access to health facilities, and Lower decision-making power, and experience higher rates of violence. Political participation is also hindered at the panchayat (local governing bodies) level and at the state and national levels, Despite existing reservations for women. The impact of the patriarchal structure can be seen in rural and urban India, although women's Empowerment in rural India is much less visible than in urban areas. This is a issue of concern though urbanization is in fast pace still many rural issues are not addressed properly.

- H. Subrahmanyam (2011) compares women education in India at present and Past. Author highlighted that there has a good progress in overall enrolment of girl students in schools. The term empower means to give lawful power or authority to act. It is the process of acquiring some activities of women.
- M. Bhavani Sankara Rao (2011) has highlighted that health of women members of SHG have certainly taken a turn to better. It clearly shows that heath of women members discuss among themselves about health related problems of other members and their children and make them aware of various Government provisions specially meant for them.
- Doepke M. Tertilt M. (2011) Does Female Empowerment Promote Economic Development? This study is an empirical analysis suggesting that money in the hands of mothers benefits children. This study developed a series of non cooperative family bargaining models to understand what kind of frictions can give rise to the observed empirical relationship.
- Duflo E. (2011) Women's Empowerment and Economic Development, National Bureau of Economic Research Cambridge The study argues that the inter relationships of the Empowerment and Development are probably too weak to be self sustaining and that continuous policy commitment to equally for its own sake may be needed to bring about equality between men and women.
- Sethuraman K. (2008) The Role of Women's Empowerment and Domestic Violence in child Growth and Under nutrition in a Tribal and Rural Community in South India. This research paper explores the relationship between Women's Empowerment and Domestic Violence, maternal nutritional status and the nutritional status and growth over six months in children aged 6 to 24 months in a rural and tribal community. This longitudinal observational study undertaken in rural Karnataka. India included tribal and rural subjects.
- Venkata Ravi and Venkatraman (2005) focused on the effects of SHG on women participation and exercising control over decision making both in family matters and in group activities.

ISSUES TO BE DISCUSSED

Making the World a Better Place

We are living in an age of women empowerment. Women the world over are working shoulder to shoulder with men. By and large, they are now empowered to take decision about different aspects of their life and profession they need to be recognized, respected and be paid remuneration at par with men for her work.

The Three Principles

Principle 1: Leadership Promotes Gender Equality

1. Affirm high-level support and direct top-level policies for gender equality and human rights.
2. Establish company-wide goals and targets for gender equality and include progress as a factor in managers' performance reviews.
3. Engage internal and external stakeholders in the development of company policies, programmes and implementation plans that advance equality.
4. Ensure that all policies are gender-sensitive – identifying factors that impact women and men differently – and that corporate culture advances equality and inclusion.

Principle 2: Equal Opportunity, Inclusion and Nondiscriminiation

1. Pay equal remuneration, including benefits, for work of equal value and strive to pay a living wage to all women and men.
2. Ensure that workplace policies and practices are free from gender-based discrimination.
3. Implement gender-sensitive recruitment and retention practices and proactively recruit and appoint women to managerial and executive positions and to the corporate board of directors.
4. Assure sufficient participation of women – 30% or greater – in decision-making and governance at all levels and across all business areas.
5. Support access to child and dependent care by providing services, resources and information to both women and men.

Principle 3: Health, Safety and Freedom from Violence

1. Taking into account differential impacts on women and men, provide safe working conditions and protection from exposure to hazardous materials and disclose potential risks, including to reproductive health.
2. Establish a zero-tolerance policy towards all forms of violence at work, including verbal and/or physical abuse, and prevent sexual harassment.
3. Strive to offer health insurance or other needed services – including for survivors of domestic violence – and ensure equal access for all employees.
4. Respect women and men workers' rights to time off for medical care and counseling for themselves and their dependents.
5. In consultation with employees, identify and address security issues, including the safety of women traveling to and from work and on company-related business.

6. Train security staff and managers to recognize signs of violence against women and understand laws and company policies on human trafficking, labour and sexual exploitation.

SOLUTIONS AND RECOMMENDATIONS

- Without women's empowerment, one cannot remove injustice and gender bias and inequalities.
- If women are not empowered, they cannot enjoy security and protection in life
- Empowerment acts as a powerful tool against exploitation and harassment of women
- It is a great means to get adequate legal protection for women
- If not socially and economically empowered, women cannot develop their own identity
- If women are not employed, the global economy will be adversely affected as women constitute a vast chunk of the world's population
- Women are highly creative and intelligent which makes it imperative to receive their contributions in socio-economic activities
- For a just and progressive society, women need to be provided equal opportunities for work.

CONCLUSION

Women make up 40 percent of the world's workforce. Many of the sectors that are critical for economic growth in some of the poorest countries rely heavily on women. Small and medium-sized enterprises (SMEs) with female ownership represent 30 percent to 37 percent of all SMEs (8 million to 10 million women-owned firms) in emerging markets. These businesses have unmet financial needs of between US$260 billion and US$320 billion a year. This is their biggest barrier to growth and development. Access to credit can open up economic opportunities for women, and bank accounts can be a gateway to the use of additional financial services. However, women entrepreneurs and employers face significantly greater challenges than men in gaining access to financial services

Women Empowerment helps to make the society and world a better place to live in and march forward on way to inclusive participation. It means increase happiness for the family and the organizations where women make a difference.To support her is to make a better place for her and her family to live.

Governments and financial institutions in each economy can work to identify obstacles such as the need for recognition of credit history and lack of collateral assets, and collaborate to put in place measures to ameliorate or remove the barriers to include the women in the development of economy.

REFERENCES

Ashraf, N., Karlan, D. S., & Yin, W. (2009). *Female Empowerment: Impact of a Commitment Savings Product in the Philippines*. Harvard Business School Working Paper, 09-100.

Banerjee, A., Duflo, E., Glennerster, R., & Kinnan, C. (2009). *The Miracle of Microfinance? Evidence from a randomized evaluation.* Center for Microfinance Working Paper 31.

Department for International Development, The Importance of Financial Sector Development for Growth and Poverty Reduction. (2004). Policy Division Working Paper.

Field, E., Jayachandran, S., & Pande, R. (2010). Do Traditional Institutions Constrain Female Entrepreneurship? A Field Experiment on Business Training in India. *The American Economic Review, 100*(2), 125–129. doi:10.1257/aer.100.2.125

GenderNet Issues Paper. (2011). *Women Economic Empowerment.* Author.

Jones, L. (2012). *Discussion Paper for an M4P Women's Economic Empowerment Framework. How can the Making Markets Work for the Poor Framework work for poor women and for poor men?* The Springfield Centre for Business in Development.

Lawson, S. (2008). *Women Hold Up Half the Sky*. Goldman Sachs Global Economics Paper No: 164.

Warth, L. (2009). *Gender Equality and the Corporate Sector.* United Nations Economic Commission for Europe (UNECE) Discussion Paper No.4. https://www.un.org/en/ecosoc/newfunct/pdf/womens_empowerment_principles_ppt_for_29_mar_briefing-without_notes.pdf

Chapter 9
An Observational Study on Women Empowerment in Marketing With Reference to Chennai City:
Successful Women Entrepreneurs in India in Business

M. Radhikaashree
Dr. M. G. R. Educational and Research Institute, India

Shalini M.
Dr. M. G. R. Educational and Research Institute, India

ABSTRACT

Women's empowerment is much developed compared with the past. Women are working alongside men and making their own decision making in the situations like education, profession career, and lifestyle. It is clear that women can add incrementally to a developing nation's economy. However, the regulatory regime, narrow thinking, and conflict of work-life balance are some of the obstacles that are hindering the growth of women entrepreneurship. The chapter is an attempt to discuss issues like growth of women entrepreneurs globally and in India and contribution of women entrepreneurs. In spite of several obstacles faced by women entrepreneurs like lack of trust by the other party on their capabilities, struggles of managing work-life balance, proving their worth in a patriarchal society, with the increasing potential of women entrepreneurship, several initiatives taken by different authorities and organisations all over the world are playing a pivotal role in encouraging and supporting women entrepreneurs in different parts of the world. Need of the hour is the change in the mindset of the people and increase in the confidence on the capabilities of women entrepreneurs.

DOI: 10.4018/978-1-7998-3737-4.ch009

INTRODUCTION

Empowerment is a stage of acquiring power in order to understand one's rights and also to perform his/her responsibilities in a most effective way. Empowerment is an active, multi-dimensional process which enables women to realize their potential and powers in all spheres of life.

Empowerment as a concept was introduced at the International Women's Conference in 1985 at Nairobi. The conference defined empowerment as a redistribution of social power and control of resources in favour of women. The different parameters of empowerment are – ƒ Enhance self esteem and self confidence in women. ƒ Build a positive image of women by recognizing their contributions to the society and economy. ƒ Develop in them an ability to think critically. ƒ Foster decision making and action through collective process ƒ Enable them to make informal choices in areas like education, employment and health. ƒ Ensure equal participation in the development process ƒ Provide information, knowledge and skill for economic independence. ƒ Enhance access to legal literacy and information related to their rights and entitlements in the society with a view to enhance their participation on an equal footing in all areas.

Women empowerment is an active, multi-dimensional process which enables women to realize their potential and powers in all spheres of life. The process should materialize only when there is a conducive environment for the enlightenment which is to be ensured first. Empowerment is enlightenment and there is no development without enlightenment; it is the quality of life measured not in terms of rising money incomes or longer life spans alone, rather by the autonomy and security enjoyed by women everywhere.

The United Nations Development Fund for Women includes the following factors in its definition of women empowerment. a) Acquiring knowledge and understanding of gender relation and the ways in which these relations may be changed. b) Developing a sense of self-worth, a belief in one's ability to secure desired changes and the right to control one's life. c) Gaining the ability to generate choices and exercise bargaining power. d) Developing the ability to organize and influence the direction of social change to create a more just, social and economic order nationally and internationally.

The key factor for determining success for marketing development is the status, position of women in the society. The women while doing the marketing, they must much concentrate on the creative spots don't effectively communicate this and provide no direct tie towards others. Its products support women to overcome from obstacles.

The key goal of empowerment in marketing to be recognizing women as intelligent customer and communicate to them as such, marketers should use this approach in a way that honours their company's message rather than simply jumping on a bandwagon.

Failure to do this reduces what could be a meaningful piece of marketing to something more closely resembling the "pink it and shrink it" gimmicks of years past.

To avoid this, marketers must present a message in which the company or product has a clear and relevant role. This is, of course, easier said than done, but marketers can start by focusing less on the nebulous objective of empowering women and instead push themselves to identify a real insight about the female audience that can be tied back to the company or product in a meaningful way.

Despite huge potential of women entrepreneurship and rapid economic growth, gender disparities in women's economic participation have remained deep and persistent globally and in India. Still in every economy there are fewer female than male entrepreneurs and they appear to show reluctance to scale their businesses or to enter new and less tested markets.

The present study has analysed issue like growth of women entrepreneurs globally and in India, contribution of women entrepreneurs towards sustainable economic development.

LITERATURE REVIEW

Charmes and Wieringa (2003) conceptualize women's empowerment in a similar way to Kabeer; they view empowerment as a progression from awareness to agency that depends on resources, education, political conditions and subjective factors, which influence the existence and consciousness of choice.

Alkire et al. (2013) These conceptualizations of empowerment contrast operationalizations of empowerment in the form of measuring decision-making.

Rao and Joshi (2014) as these represent an individualized and situational perspective of empowerment. Qualitative studies of debunk certain assumptions, e.g. that economic empowerment will lead to overall empowerment or that the participation in decision-making processes will empower women. These studies provide a more nuanced understanding of factors influencing and mediating empowerment. Such an understanding is further related to other concepts in gender and development research,.

Nazneen et al. (2011) depict how the term empowerment evolved in Bangladesh from the initially instrumental zed logic of international donors to a more nuanced understanding with multiple discourses on divergent meanings. They have concluded in their review of documents by NGOs, political parties, women's groups and donors in Bangladesh that empowerment is seen mostly as an individual, and not a collective or institutionalized, mechanism, focused on material means, rather than greater structural change. The authors visualized this in a double continuum of empowerment from individual to collective and from economic to political empowerment.

Sultan (2015) has researched women's perception of empowerment in Bangladesh and concluded with the need to "move beyond seeing women as victims or heroines, and engage with their everyday realities… to do more than give individual women economic opportunities to tackle deeper-rooted structural constraints that perpetuate inequalities."

WOMEN EMPOWERMENT THROUGH WOMEN ENTREPRENEURSHIP: SUCCESSFUL WOMEN ENTREPRENEUR IN INDIA

KiranMazumdar Shaw

She is the founder Chairman and Managing Director (CMD) of Biocon Limited.

She worked as a trainee brewer in Carlton and United Breweries, Melbourne and as a trainee maltster at Barrett Brothers and Burston, Australia. She started Biocon in 1978 and spearheaded its evolution from an industrial enzymes manufacturing company to a fully integrated bio-pharmaceutical company. Today Biocon under Shaw's leadership has established itself as a leading player in biomedicine research with a focus on diabetes and oncology. Kiran is also a member of the board of governors of the prestigious Indian School of Business and Indian Institute of Technology Hyderabad.Kiran received the prestigious Padma Shri (1989) and the Padma Bhushan (2005) from the government of India.

KanikaDewan: Designer of floor of IGI's Terminal 3

Dewan's family owned business, Bramco, headquatered in Bahrain,carried out the floor work for the airport.She started a vertically integrated design firm that would capitalize on the exclusive availability of exotic marbles and granite from Bramco's mines.

NeelamDhawan, Managing Director, Microsoft India

Leads Microsoft India. She is a graduate from St. Stephens College in 1980, and also passed out from Delhis Faculty Of Management studies in 1982. Then she was keen on joining FMCG majors like Hindustan Lever and Asian Paints, both companies rejected Dhawan, as they did not wish to appoint women for marketing and sales..

Simone Tata

Has been instrumental in changing a small subsidiary of Tata Oil Mills into the largest cosmetic brand in India – LAKME, synonymous today with Indian Fashion. She became a part of Lakme during 1961 and has been responsible for turning the company into one of the biggest brands of fashion in India. At present she is the Chairperson of Trent Limited, a subsidiary of Tata Group.

Sneha Roy and Sananada Mishra- Toptomato.in

Toptomato.in by Sneha Roy &Sananda Mishra is an online platform for ordering all household items. It's not a new concept but the founder aim to make it unique with its grocery subscription. The venture is self funded and the seed capital was about Rs. 5 Lakhs.

SUCCESS PERCENTAGE OF THE WOMEN ENTREPRENEUR IN BUSINESS

With the constant development in the Indian startup ecosystem, more and more women are chasing the entrepreneurial dream and succeeding in their ventures. This is empowering other Indian women who are still confined to the traditional homemaker role to think for themselves. However, a recent report states that only two Indian cities have made it to a ranking of the 50 most favorable global places for women to work. India's Silicon Valley, Bengaluru, ranked 40th, while Delhi came in at the 49th place. This survey was conducted by the tech giant Dell, and consultancy firm IHS Markit. The ranking—based on inputs from Indian female entrepreneurs, policymakers, venture capitalists, media, and academicians—measures a city's ability to attract and support women who want to grow their businesses.

According to the National Sample Survey, only 14% of the businesses in India are run by female entrepreneurs. Most of the companies are bootstrapped and run on a small scale. The global disparity is evident in a report which says nearly 126 million women have their own business across the globe with Indian women lingering around the 8 million mark; a paradoxical statement given that we are the second most populous nation in the world.

SOME INTERESTING STATISTICS ON WOMEN ENTREPRENEURS IN INDIA

- About 58% of the female entrepreneurs were in the age range of 20-30 when they started out.
- Nearly 73% of them report revenue of approximately Rs.10 lakhs in a financial year.
- Almost 57% of these women started out solo i.e. without any other member.
- About 35% of the women had a co-founder.
- Roughly 71% of the Indian female entrepreneurs employ five people or less.

In a country like India where most of the women aren't encouraged to think big (especially the rural parts of the nation), there are some who have soared higher than one would expect from a constrictive setup. These wonder women are inspiring other ladies to venture on the path of start-ups through the stories of their personal struggles and challenges. As a result, India is steadily rising up the ranks when it comes to a favourable start-up ecosystem with solid backing from the Government.

MAJOR CHALLENGES AND BARRIERS FACED BY WOMEN ENTREPRENEURS

Inspite of having great potential women still represent a minority of all entrepreneurs. Research shows that the number of women-owned firms continues to rise at rates exceeding the national average, yet they remain smaller than the average firm. The question is why women entrepreneurs still represent a minority portion. Some of the major barriers faced by Women Entrepreneurs in the Indian and Global context are summarised as below:

1. **Financing difficulty due to negative investors' perception:** Investor's perception about investing in women owned business is negative.
2. The report estimates that the total financial requirement for women entrepreneurs was $158 billion in 2012 but they only had access to around $42 billion from formal lenders. Finance is regarded as "life-blood" for any enterprise, be it big or small. However, women entrepreneurs suffer from shortage of finance on two counts.Firstly, women do not generally have property on their names to use them as collateral for obtaining funds from external sources. Thus, their access to the external sources of funds is limited. Secondly, the banks also consider women less credit-worthy and discourage women borrowers on the belief that they can at any time leave their business. Given such situation, women entrepreneurs are bound to rely on their own savings, if any and loans from friends and relatives who are expectedly meager and negligible. Thus, women enterprises fail due to the shortage of finance.
3. **Higher dependence on owned capital than borrowed capital:** Women owned firms typically starts with less capital and therefore underperform in terms of assets, revenue, profitability and survival. For example the Kaufman Foundation, which collects annual information on US Firms start up began a survey of nearly 5000 new business launched in 2004 and traded their performance. The survey data shows that women tend to start business using more of their own money and less capital from outsiders.

4. **Difference in personal situations faced:** Women face different personal situations from men. Women are more effected than men by the conflicting demands of work and family life. In India, it is mainly a women's duty to look after the children and other members of the family. Man plays a secondary role only. In case of married women, she has to strike a fine balance between her business and family. Her total involvement in family leaves little or no energy and time to devote for business.

Support and approval of husbands seem necessary condition for women's entry into business. Accordingly, the educational level and family background of husbands positively influence women's entry into business activities.

5. **Regulatory regimes that don't undermine women:** Even at the beginning of the 21st century, women are hampered by laws that deny them the same rights as men. Laws like these are clearly costly in terms of economic development. For example:
    a. In Kuwait, women are prohibited to work after 8 pm.
    b. Restrictive labor laws of Senegal's have forced almost half of all workers into the unregulated sector of the economy and even in this sector,women are at a distinct disadvantage, earning only half of what men earn.
    c. In Swaziland, women require the permission of husband or father to open a bank A/C or a business to obtain passport or to enforce a contract.
6. *Limited Mobility:* Unlike men, women mobility in India is highly limited due to various reasons. A single woman asking for room is still looked upon suspicion. Cumbersome exercise involved in starting an enterprise coupled with the officials humiliating attitude towards women compels them to give up idea of starting an enterprise.
7. **Networking:** Social networks have an impact on the likelihood of successful entrepreneurial endeavour. Many of the problems women face appear to relate to women's relative lack of exposure to the world of business. It has been noted that women's business networks are poorly developed as social assets yet effective networking can provide significant advantages for women entrepreneurs (Linehan and Scullion, 2008) by helping to provide a competitive edge in business.The confidence to travel across day and night and even different regions and states are less found in women compared to male counterparts. This shows the low level of freedom of expression and freedom of mobility of the women entrepreneurs.

WOMEN EMPOWERMENT: WINDS OF CHANGE

Women empowerment has become the buzzword today with women working alongside men in all spheres. They profess an independent outlook, whether they are living inside their home or working outside. They are increasingly gaining control over their lives and taking their own decisions with regard to their education, career, profession and lifestyle.

With steady increase in the number of working women, they have gained financial independence, which has given them confidence to lead their own lives and build their own identity. They are successfully taking up diverse professions to prove that they are second to none in any respect.

But while doing so, women also take care to strike a balance between their commitment to their profession as well as their home and family. They are playing multiple roles of a mother, daughter, sister, wife and a working professional with remarkable harmony and ease. With equal opportunities to work, they are functioning with a spirit of team work to render all possible co-operation to their male counterparts in meeting the deadlines and targets set in their respective professions.

Women empowerment is not limited to urban, working women but women in even remote towns and villages are now increasingly making their voices heard loud and clear in society. They are no longer willing to play a second fiddle to their male counterparts. Educated or not, they are asserting their social and political rights and making their presence felt, regardless of their socio-economic backgrounds.

While it is true that women, by and large, do not face discrimination in society today, unfortunately, many of them face exploitation and harassment which can be of diverse types: emotional, physical, mental and sexual. They are often subjected to rape, abuse and other forms of physical and intellectual violence.

Women Are the Largest Untapped Reservoir of Talent in the World

It is undeniable that women empowerment in the corporate world has a crucial direct impact on the economic growth and simultaneous national development. In India, where Women representation in the corporate scenario stands at 30.55% the reservoir of women leadership is certainly untapped. But with many organizations leading the change in the past decade, India's corporate world is inclusive of women holding significant positions in top-notch organizations.

While the country's top women leaders are heads of major corporations: SchaunaChauhan, CEO of Parle Agro, Aisha Sequiera, Country head and head of investment banking at Morgan Stanley, and KiranMazumdar Shaw, CMD of Biocon, a globally recognized biopharmaceutical enterprise. It is motivating to see how women leaders have impacted the corporate world. The most successful and influential women in today's Indian corporate are: Neeru Sharma, co-founder of Infibeam, RadhikaGhaiAggarwal, co-founder of ShopClues and Suchi Mukherjee, founder and CEO of Limeroad, are all well-equipped to face the challenge corporate world throws at them with the education that empowered them to thrash the stereotypes and gender biases.

Today, in India, companies like Adobe India, Indigo are not just empowering women by providing them with employee benefits. They have created a work culture that understands and encourages women to be as active as a man by providing them with the necessary training and stimulating their capabilities by enrolling them in women leadership programmes.

The need for women's empowerment is felt because of the status they have in society since the beginning. There is a need to redefine the status of women in the society. A change can be brought through the constitution and supportive legislations. The Constitution of India gives a women status equal to men. There have been attempts to reserve seats for women in political bodies. This is no doubt a step in the right direction. Women have the ability to judge for themselves and take right decisions. However merely allowing for reservation of women in Panchayat and legislative bodies without empowering women individually falls short of actual emancipation. Women have been excluded from centers of power as a result of systematic conspiracy by patriarchal thought most common in India KhapPanchayat that has relegated women to an allotted and confined space. A reorientation of our attitudes towards women has to be carefully guided for their real emancipation from the patriarchal domination.

Figure 1. Women empowerment growth in India

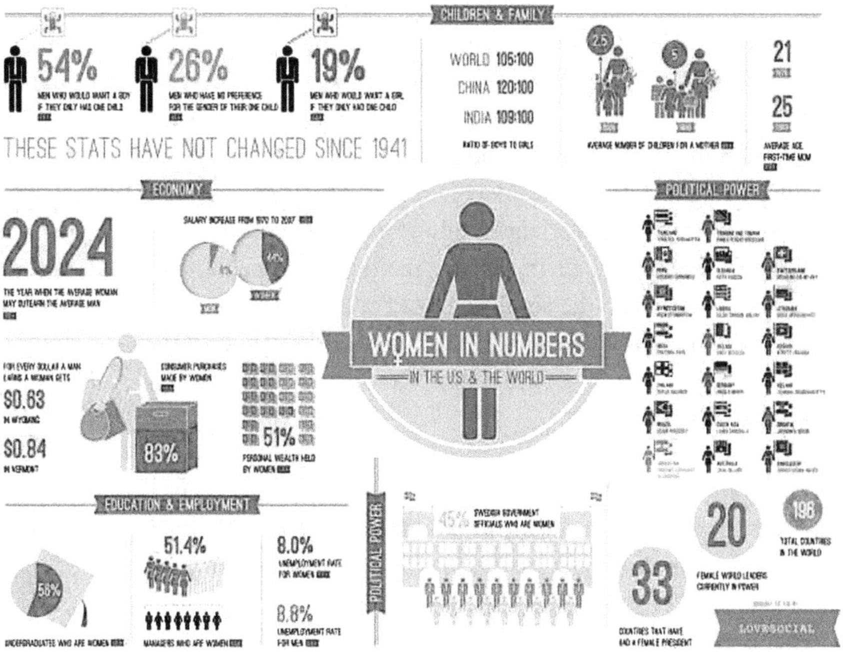

Figure 2. Need for women empowerment

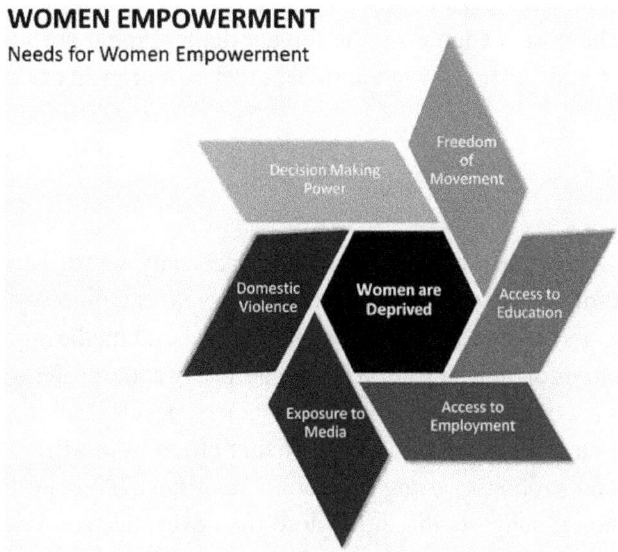

The impoverished and illiterate status of most women in society is due to their inability to attain sufficient levels of economic power. To sustain any level of empowerment women have to be educated to be aware of their rights and privileges in a modern society. It is only when they become aware of their status in society that they will be able to take full advantage of the concessions offered to them as a corrective measure.

Verizon's "Inspire Her Mind"

While the content of Verizon's "Inspire Her Mind" ad fits within the category of female-empowerment marketing, this ad focuses more directly on the opportunity women have to affect the future of science and technology.

A message like this could easily fall into the category of the generic public service announcement=. Instead, the ad tells a powerful story that feels as much like a recruitment effort as anything else, leveraging the topic to communicate Verizon's authority in innovation-related fields while showcasing the important role that women can have in shaping the future of the industry and, in turn, the company.

Verizon's ability to demonstrate the significance of women's empowerment in a way that also communicates its authority in innovation-related fields makes this ad successful.

Feminism Is Not a Trend

But with the range of products and services marketed to women as 'empowering' now being stretched to mundane tasks such as washing your hair or having a drink of water, have we reached peak empowerment? "There is times when I think if I see that word one more time I will explode," says Pashley, in her typically honest style. "Feminism is not a trend," she adds.

Visibility is crucial; as when audiences don't see themselves reflected by brands the message is that they aren't valued. Yet for many products and services not only are they ignoring or stereotyping vast swathes of their audiences, but they aren't creating products to meet their needs, thus missing out on huge commercial opportunities. "Women want to be seen by brands – look at products such as the Apple Health Tracker, which didn't track periods when it launched," says Pashley.

For the car industry the costs of ignoring the female demographic are high. "Crash test dummies have long been based on a male torso, so women suffer greater injuries in car crashes," explains Pashley

CONCLUSION

Women empowerment, in the truest sense, will be achieved only when there is attitudinal change in society with regard to womenfolk, treating them with proper respect, dignity, fairness and equality. The rural areas of the country are, by and large, steeped in a feudal and medieval outlook, refusing to grant women equal say in the matters of their education, marriage, dress-code, profession and social interactions.

Women entrepreneurs are transforming families and society, besides making contributions to business development. The rising number of women entrepreneurs around the world suggests that there might be more attention to social problems, using economic solutions. Michelle Bachelet, United Nations Women's Executive Director, suggests that now more than ever the world needs to unleash women's entrepreneurship to make our economies and societies stronger.

Today's women are taking more and more professional and technical degrees to cope up with market need and are flourishing as designers, interior decorator, exporters, publishers, garment manufacturers and still exploring new avenues of economic participation.

It is perhaps for these reasons that Government Bodies, NGO's, Social Scientists, Researchers and international agencies have started showing interest in the issues related to entrepreneurship among women in India. At the same time, it is also recognised that their challenges are immense and complex. For women entrepreneurs, starting and operating a business involves considerable risks and difficulties because of the narrow and orthodox mindset of the society.

REFERENCES

Alkire, S., Meinzen-Dick, R., Peterman, A., Quisuimbing, A. R., Seymour, G., & Vaz, A. (2013). The Women's Empowerment in Agriculture Index. *World Development*, *52*, 71–91. doi:10.1016/j.worlddev.2013.06.007

Charmes, J., & Wieringa, S. (2003). Measuring Women's Empowerment: An assessment of the Gender-related Development Index and the Gender Empowerment Measure. *Journal of Human Development*, *4*(3), 419–435. doi:10.1080/1464988032000125773

Guérin, I., Kumar, S., &Agier, I. (2013). Women's Empowerment: Power to Act or Power over Other Women? Lessons from Indian Microfinance. *Oxford Development Studies, 41*(sup1), S76-S94.

Joshi, D. (2014). Feminist Solidarity? Women's Engagement in Politics and the Implications for Water Management in the Darjeeling Himalaya. *Mountain Research and Development*, *34*(3), 243–254. doi:10.1659/MRD-JOURNAL-D-13-00097.1

Kabeer, N. (1999). Resources, Agency, Achievements: Reflections on the measurement of women's empowerment. *Development and Change*, *30*(3), 435–464. doi:10.1111/1467-7660.00125

Nazneen, S., Hossain, N., & Sultan, M. (2011). National Discourses on Women's Empowerment in Bangladesh: Continuities and Change. *IDS Working Papers, 2011*(368), 1-41.

Stauss, B., Chojnacki, K., Decker, A., & Hoffmann, F. (2001). Retention effects of a customer club. *International Journal of Service Industry Management*, *12*(1), 7–19. doi:10.1108/09564230110382745

Sultan, M. (2015). *Women's perception of empowerment: Findings from the Pathways of Women's Empowerment Programme*. Presentation at the ADB Regional Seminar on Women's Employment, Entrepreneurship and Empowerment: Moving forward on imperfect pathways, Bangkok, Thailand.

Section 3
Well-Being for Inclusive Growth

Chapter 10
A History of the United States Women's Bureau 1917–1930:
Economic Opportunity and Immigration

Adam I. Attwood
https://orcid.org/0000-0002-4718-9272
Austin Peay State University, USA

ABSTRACT

This chapter provides historical analysis of the United States Women's Bureau focusing on its role in women's rights, immigration, and economic advancement in the United States from 1917-1930. The decade of the 1920s dawned on August 18, 1920 with the ratification of the Nineteenth Amendment to the United States Constitution granting women the right to vote in every state. But there was another, less known victory that had already occurred on June 5, 1920, one that was pivotal in the trajectory of the next phase of the women's rights movement throughout the 1920s: House Resolution 13229.

INTRODUCTION

This chapter examines the topic of women's advancement in the workforce of the United States from 1917-1930. This timeline is emphasized because the federal office that became known as the Women's Bureau was founded in 1917 under the name Women in Industry Service which was later renamed the Women's Bureau in 1920. This unit of the federal government initiated a new trend in women's rights as this office accelerated the focus on economic advancement of women in the United States throughout the 1920s. The analysis in this chapter end in the year 1930 because that was when the Great Depression started. Also, Mastracci (2004) evaluated the Women's Bureau's role after 1930, but not its first decade of existence. There has been a gap in the literature on the early history of the United States Women's Bureau (1917-1930) and its contribution to the policy changes that affected women's labor rights. This chapter is an original historical analysis using primary and secondary sources that fills that gap. The objective of this analysis is to identify contributions of the United States Women's Bureau to labor policy

DOI: 10.4018/978-1-7998-3737-4.ch010

affecting American women and immigrant women to the United States from 1917-1930. This adds to an understanding of the changing role of labor policy toward women in the United States both from a social perspective and an economic perspective.

BACKGROUND

Josephine Schain wrote in 1918 that "a tremendous obligation rests upon the coming generation of women, those who inherit these new opportunities" (p. 120). Two years later those opportunities culminated in the largest women's rights victory in popular living memory up that time in the United States of America. The decade of the 1920s dawned on August 18, 1920, with the ratification of the Nineteenth Amendment to the United States Constitution granting women the right to vote in every state (Ayers, Gould, Oshinsky, & Soderlund, 2012). But another victory had already occurred on June 5, 1920—one that was pivotal in the trajectory of the next phase of women's rights movement throughout the 1920s: House Resolution 13229—"An Act To establish in the Department of Labor a bureau to be known as the Women's Bureau" (also known as USC 41 Stat. L., 987, see United States House of Representatives, 1920).

Congress initially authorized the formation of Women in Industry Service in late 1917 with official formation in 1918 because of "the present emergency" (Weber, 1923, p. 1). That emergency was the labor vacuum caused by so many men fighting in the First World War. The unit Women in Industry Service was renamed the Women's Bureau in June 1920 indicating its full bureau status within the United States Department of Labor. Women filled the labor vacuum during the last year of the First World War. This set a precedent upon which "women's organizations successfully lobbied Congress to establish the bureau permanently" on June 5, 1920. According to Weber (1923), the Women's Bureau was successful in convincing Congressman P. P. Campbell. He expressed his support for House Resolution 13229 by arguing that it was "wise" and "humane" for women to be in charge of their work methodology (Women's Bureau, n.d.; Weber, 1923, p. 1).

The findings of the Women's Bureau and the perspective of Italian immigrant George La Piana about the integration of immigrant women into the American workforce relative to native-born women are the focus. The contributions of the Women's Bureau to the study of immigrant and native-born women from 1920-1930 have only just begun to be studied by scholars. The gendered cultural change that began in the 1910s and 1920s is also suggested in the unique papers of George La Piana who wrote about part of the situation of Italian immigrants within the same temporal context. Most articles that analyze the women's bureau focus on the Bureau's contributions from after the Second World War (see Mastracci, 2004). This chapter adds to the literature by analyzing the Women's Bureau from its founding in 1917 up to 1930 that are its formative, precedent-setting years.

The Annual Reports of the Women's Bureau from 1920-1930 focused on generally young "wage-earning women" and female European immigrants, during the popular countercurrent of "Americanization." The Annual Reports of the Director of the Women's Bureau and the Bulletins of the Women's Bureau from the 1920s portray a time of upward mobility and increasing employment opportunities for women. The Women's Bureau analyzed the immigrant laborers' economic integration into American society from different perspectives—one bureaucratic and the other personal (United States Department of Labor, 1930; United States Department of Labor, 1921, p. 3; Manning, 1930; Gullett, 1995; Olneck, 1989; La Piana, n.d., 1916a, 1916b).

WOMEN'S RIGHTS AND THE WOMEN'S BUREAU

Personal Backgrounds and Legislating the Women's Bureau

La Piana, as a Roman Catholic priest and Harvard faculty member, is important to this discussion for his personal view of women immigrants during the late 1910s to 1930. The term "Americanization" can be traced back to at least 1930 within the context of women's immigration, as evidenced by Caroline Manning's (1930) annual report for the Women's Bureau. La Piana's letters and the Women's Bureau reports suggest the issue of Americanization and fiscal advancement are linked together, so this is analyzed in relation to women's gainful employment not so much in direct comparison, but rather in parallel for their respective personal and bureaucratic perspectives.

Originally from the hamlet of Piana degli Albanesi, Palermo Province of Sicily, La Piana emigrated to the United States in 1913 and joined the faculty of Harvard Divinity School two years later. Boston became his new home. While rising to civic prominence in Boston's North End with his social work, he also became an officer in the Family Service League. La Piana's career reached its zenith when he was made the John H. Morison Professor of Church History in 1932. He wrote about immigrant life and aspirations in addition to Roman Catholic Church history, because those were ideas that he was familiar with at a personal and professional level. Many immigrants came to America from western Europe and so many were likely Catholic or knew Catholics at some social level. Transplanting themselves in their new home brought some of the old ways, but change was inevitable as they mixed with other immigrants and native-born Americans (La Piana, n.d., 1916a, 1916b, "George La Piana, 1978-1972").

Prior to the passage of the Nineteenth Amendment and the formation of the Women's Bureau as an exemplar of a women's government program, there was contention over the direction of equal rights. The Daughters of the American Revolution typified an ironic view because of their focus on "immediate acculturation" of immigrants by "Americaniz[ing]" them with "'an imperious…conformity'" (Gullett, 1995, p. 77). Counter to this view was the more well-known view of Jane Addams (1923) and Josephine Schain (1918). The contentiousness was in tandem with "the Red Scare of 1919-20," which made the atmosphere politically precarious (Dumenil, 1998, p. 82). Addams claimed in her book *A New Conscience and an Ancient Evil* that some industrial sectors featured slave-like conditions that poor girls had to endure for little pay (see Addams, 1923). Ultimately, this activist mentality was mirrored by the Women's Bureau under Mary Anderson's leadership, and Schain's (1918) view was victorious as both men and women increasingly saw gender equality as essential for social and economic advancement.

The ratification of the Nineteenth Amendment came to a tie-breaker vote in 1920. The junior senator from Tennessee, Harry Burn, who was 26 years of age voted to break the tie in favor of woman suffrage after receiving a dramatic letter from his mother, Febb King Ensminger Burn, urging him to "vote for suffrage!" (Burn, 1920, as quoted in Grunwald and Adler, 2005). The Nineteenth Amendment is the most well-known policy victory of the early twentieth century, but the formation of the Women's Bureau was a women's movement victory almost forgotten. It formed on July 9, 1918 as a temporary "war agency of the Department of Labor under the name of "Women in Industry Service." The Secretary of Labor stipulated that the Service had "the duty of 'developing standards and policies to ensure the effective employment of women while conserving their health and welfare'" (Weber, 1923, pp. 1-2). Women in Industry Service was renamed the Women's Bureau after passage of H.R. 13229 on June 5, 1920.

The agency's duty was expanded into a mandate: "to formulate standards and policies which shall promote the welfare of wage-earning women, improve their working conditions, increase their efficiency, and advance their opportunities for profitable employment" (United States Department of Labor, Women's Bureau, 1920). The code phrases in their new mandate that probably most pleased the U.S. Department of Labor included "increase their efficiency" and "profitable." The semantics of the mandate are significant because the Women's Bureau was specifically representing economic considerations as the basis of women's role in the labor force. In other words, a type of feminism had entered the bureaucratic mainstream for the first time. The feminism of the Women's Bureau emerged as unified and hierarchical. It is what this researcher calls Federal-Bureaucratic Feminism. It functioned above the factionalized casual women's clubs (see Gullett, 1995; Haarsager, 1997; Mastracci, 2004).

New Trend in the 1910s and 1920s With Employment

The Women's Bureau focused on economics as a key to gender equalization through the financial security of gainful employment, arguing that "authentic data on women workers" was critical for a society to overcome stagnation. The United States made great gains during the tenure of the Bureau, because of women's "recent entrance into the wage-earning arena" (United States Department of Labor, Women's Bureau, 1930, p. 6).

Mary van Kleeck was appointed the director of Women in Industry Service and Mary Anderson named assistant director to take "charge"—Congressman Campbell was suggesting the Women's Bureau take an activist approach. At the end of 1931, the Bureau had a staff of 50, all of whom (except the director) were hired after successful completion of the Civil Service Examination. Its most notable accomplishment "was the formulating of standards to govern the employment of women" (United States Department of Labor, Women's Bureau, 1930, pp. 2, 4). Mary van Kleeck resigned in 1919 and Mary Anderson was subsequently elevated to director. She was retained by United States President Warren Harding and approved by the Senate after the war-time agency Women in Industry Service was changed to the permanent Women's Bureau (United States Department of Labor, Women's Bureau, "Fact Finding," 1930).

While the professional sector was the most prestigious gain in women's employment, many jobs for women were also added in the industrial sector. The largest concentration was in manufacturing, specifically the automobile factory occupation and the electrical supply occupation. Just over half the women employed in the mid-1920s were employed in the industrial sector (see Dempsey, 1922; United States Department of Labor, Bureau of Labor Statistics, 1927). In 1927 the Women's Bureau compiled the 1914 to 1924 manufacturing employment records from Ohio into a case study of women's employment in the region. Ohio had the third largest employment figure for the manufacturing industry in the United States (see United States Department of Labor, Women's Bureau, 1927). The study showed that in Ohio "women fared better, proportionally, than did men between 1919 and 1924." Despite the "depression" of 1920-1921 and 1924, women did not lose their jobs at as high a rate as men did. In fact, a remarkable shift occurred in the employment landscape: "women, who in 1919 constituted 15.8 per cent of all wage earners, and who recovered somewhat from the depression following, though men did not, were 16.8 per cent of all wage earners in 1924." Gainfully employed women were able to get manufacturing jobs in relatively large numbers and hold on to more of them proportionally than men in the early 1920s. The figures indicated what one manufacturer had astutely commented in 1921: factory and milling work was "'as much a woman's job as a man's'" (van Kleeck, 1921, p. 3).

Van Kleeck was the "head of the department of industrial studies of the Russell Sage Foundation," while Anderson's career began as a labor leader in Chicago. Prior to Anderson's appointment as assistant director of Women in Industry Service, she was the leader of the Boot and Shoe Workers' Union, Local 94. She was also on the Executive Board of the Women's Trade Union League of Chicago. In 1910 she supported a strike led by the United Garment Workers of America (see Walkowitz, 1990; Women's Trade Union League of Chicago, 1910).

Anderson (1926) authorized Women Bureau reports on powerful industries such as the agricultural business. One such "Letter of Transmittal" prefaced an Autumn 1923 report on the "survey of women employed in seasonal industries in the State of Washington" (Anderson, 1926, p. ix). The report was a case study of the agro-industrial labor of women. Anderson's (1926) Letter of Transmittal officially indicated her approval of what was a relatively harsh report that documented "problems" with how agricultural female workers were sometimes treated in relation to their general "welfare" in work hours. In other words, the Bureau considered work hours in relation to personal or family duties to be an important factor that employers should consider without threatening to dismiss employees for certain personal family commitments (see United States Department of Labor, Women's Bureau, 1925).

FINDINGS

Findings: The Civil Service Examination and Work Access Toward Equal Access

The issue of women's eligibility for the Civil Service examination was of special importance. According to Mastracci (2004), Mary van Kleeck did not encourage Women in Industry Service to become an enforcement agency. However, Anderson (1926) embraced the enforcement mentality. She recognized that the prevailing discrimination against women taking the examination was keeping many women out of Federal bureaucratic occupations. So, it was on this issue that Anderson first steered the Bureau toward enforcement. Women had been barred on most occasions from taking the examination because of conservative power groups within the government. The Women's Bureau contended that the few women who were given an exception to take the examination performed well (see United States Department of Labor, Women's Bureau, 1920). Anderson emphasized the importance of the Civil Service examination in her "Letter of Transmittal" prefacing the Bureau's report "Women in the Government Service." Anderson exercised the Bureau's policy-making mandate (see Nienburg, 1920; Anderson, 1926). She set as a top priority to get the legislature to open the Civil Service examination to all qualified women, because this would assure a larger female voice in other policy concerns relating to women's employment. The Bureau argued its cause in its report "Women in the Government Service," submitted on November 5, 1919 to the Civil Service Commission. Only "10 days after receiving the report, the Civil Service Commission passed a ruling opening all examinations to both women and men" (Nienburg, 1920, p. 7). This major policy victory so early in the existence of the Women's Bureau was important because it marked a political victory directly attributable to this precedent-setting federal agency run for and by women. Anderson's vindication in taking the Bureau in a more aggressive direction than her predecessor quickly became apparent when the federal government was declared shortly thereafter to be "the greatest employer of women in the country" (United States Department of Labor, Women's

Bureau, 1920, pp. 3-4). Women demonstrated that they were both qualified to take the examination and could pass just as the men did. Women's influence in the federal government expanded with this policy victory and enlarged their numbers in the professional career category of employment.

The prestige of the Women's Bureau had increased substantially as it gained power. The United States Department of Labor appropriated $40,000 to the Women's Bureau for its first year of operation. The next year, director Mary Anderson and staff secured a near doubling of its annual appropriation to $75,000 (United States Department of Labor, Women's Bureau, 1921). This was a prodigious increase in funding for such a young bureau, especially when considering that there was a national recession during 1920 and 1921 (United States Department of Labor, Women's Bureau, 1929). The United States Department of Labor was impressed by the fiscal situation. By 1925 it was written "that the volume of work the [B]ureau is called upon to perform increases with each year of its existence" (United States Department of Labor, Women's Bureau, 1925, p. 1). Evidently the Department tended to agree early in the Bureau's history when considering its fiscal appropriations.

Under Anderson's leadership, the Women's Bureau was secure in probing the federal labor laws and pushing Congress toward policy reform to promote women's employment (United States Department of Labor, Women's Bureau, 1924). The conclusion of the Bureau's investigations in 1927 was upbeat. It had been of "genuine assistance" in getting standards agreed upon within the federal government to have female workers placed under labor contracts that could improve their efficiency. These contracts included the Bureau's recommended standards on hours, wages, and working conditions (United States Department of Labor, Women's Bureau, 1927, p. 4). This labor law review process began during the war years and continued during the 1920s to include an eight or nine-hour workday, standard mealtimes, and sanitary working conditions with safety equipment readily available. State industrial commissions also agreed to establish health protection protocols for women doing night work. Most economically notable was the provision that wages were to be "based on occupation and not on sex nor race" (United States Department of Labor, Women's Bureau, 1927, p. 4). In August of 1918, the Women's Bureau (then known as Women in Industry Service), succeeded in getting state industrial commissions to agree to women's health protection controls during night work. Summarizing the Bureau's first five years of accomplishments, Weber (1923) noted that he saw the significance of the history of the Bureau as an agency that "cooperated" at the federal, state, and local levels to influence policies and legislation that favored better labor standards for women's job protection. The maintenance of local employment flexibility and the use of statistical analysis to suggest a funneling of female workers to districts that were facing labor shortages augmented the Bureau's substantial analyses.

According to Smith (1925) and Dempsey (1922), both employees of the Women's Bureau, women's employment increased with the help of the Women's Bureau. They claimed that women comprised 21.2 percent of the United States workforce in 1920. Although women had been employed in industrial labor jobs, there was a shift of gainfully employed women into professional careers. Of all Americans gainfully employed in 1880, 14.7 percent were women. By 1920 that percentage had risen to 21.1 percent. 43.3 percent of "professional" jobs—as defined by the Women's Bureau—were held by women in 1920. She first noted that the original census data showed a total of 1,693,361 Americans employed in "professional" jobs. Of that number women comprised 43.3 percent. Florence Patteson Smith (1925) arrived at even higher percentage by combining the original census data from the U.S. Bureau of the Census with her own analysis of the "public serv[ice]" positions that women held. Smith's (1925) combination of "extraction of minerals and public serv[ice] jobs" raises the total number of Americans employed in professional jobs to 2,143,889. Of this number, women accounted for 2,186,924, or 47.4 percent. By combing these data, she posited that women may even have comprised an astounding 47.4 percent of the total professional jobs in 1920 (Smith, 1925, p. 6). The largest gainful occupational category for women was the domestic services at 67.1 percent. There was a downturn of professional employment between 1910 and 1920 because of the occupational skewing that the First World War created. The economic depression after the war caused an overall drop of the proportion of women in gainful employment, but the recovery of the 1920s reversed the downward trend, preparing the labor market for an infusion of immigrant women who would work for lower wages for employers more accustomed to wage-earning women of any national origin (see Smith, 1925; Dempsey, 1922).

To be "gainfully occupied" was to be a "wage-earner," or better yet, a salaried employee. Gainful occupations suggested professionalism. In either case, maximum production value was key for employers. And women employees knew that advancement was possible. Mary Veronica Dempsey (1922) drew attention to the census data for proof of this: "every time a woman invaded an occupation hallowed for generations as a pursuit for men only, attention was called to the fact by the woman's coworkers and in some cases by the press" (p. 1). One manufacturer commented in 1921 that factory and milling work was "'as much a woman's job as a man's'" (quoted in van Kleeck, 1921, p. 3). An increase in the numbers of gainfully employed women necessitated a shift in some of the men's perspective towards gainfully employed women. Dempsey (1922) noted that the media attention surrounding historically male-dominated occupations created the false impression that "vast numbers of women were taking up gainful employment for the first time" (p. 2). The census statistics, however, showed that "21.3 per cent of all women 16 years of age and over were employed in nonagricultural pursuits in 1920, as compared with 20.7 per cent similarly employed in 1910" (Dempsey, 1922, p. 2). Specific occupational percentages showed that there was a 13.6 percent decrease of women in "domestic and personal service," a 140.4 percent increase of women in "clerical occupations," and a 38.5 percent increase in women employed in "professional service" in 1920 relative to 1910. The study continued by noting that the number of gainful occupations that women were hired for showed little sign of decreasing (see Dempsey, 1922, pp. 2-3, 28). Dempsey (1922) suggested that this was an indication that women's office occupations were at least remaining relatively constant with 1920 beginning with 8,549,511 women 10 years of age and over gainfully employed. A two-fold change occurred during the Bureau's early years. First, women had indeed been gainfully employed for many years despite the popular misconception and, second, the Women's Bureau's research empowered it to draw upon the factual evidence about women's employment.

The increase in the number of women in professional service occupations showed an overall arc of increase from 1910 to 1930. Professional services included such positions as "bookkeepers and cashiers, teachers, [and] saleswomen" (Dempsey, 1922, p. 3). These jobs were the most prestigious because of the power and salary of this level of work as well as the financial self-sufficiency. They also generally required political connections and advanced education but hard work from entry level can lead to promotions (see Table 1 and Table 2). Wage parity was out of balance, however. The largest employer of women throughout the 1920s for professional services was always the federal government. Mary Anderson was at the forefront of women's advancement in the government apparatus. As a bureaucrat, her contribution to the women's movement was "an important achievement both in the status of the [B] ureau and in the advancement of the position of women" (United States Department of Labor, Women's Bureau, 1931, pp. 3-4).

Female professionals advanced their pay rate towards that of men by 1925, largely in federal occupations—no small part of which was the Women's Bureau itself. Female representation in the professional careers increased to such an extent that by 1929 the demand for the Bureau's study of female professionals was high and so they were paid according to that market demand (United States Department of Labor, Women's Bureau, 1929). Anderson was paid a salary of $5,000 per year and she was also given an assistant who was paid $3,500 per year (see House Resolution 13229 as quoted in United States Department of Labor, Women's Bureau, 1922). These salaries placed Anderson and her assistant in the upper economic class. And this was being accomplished despite "the depression of 1920-1921" (United States Department of Labor, Women's Bureau, 1929, p. 13). This is another indication that the Women's Bureau had influence within the federal bureaucracy and especially President Warren Harding's administration.

Findings: Gainfully Employed Immigrant Women Recognized

In this section, specific examples of issues in which the Women's Bureau studied women immigrants. George La Piana's papers are analyzed in conjunction with the Bureau's for a case study on the different views of a bureaucracy and an individual on the woman immigrant's employment in American society. The majority of his analysis centers on Italian immigrants, so this is a focal point in which specific mention of Italian and western European immigrants by the Women's Bureau will be compared for analysis.

President Harding addressed the first ever Women's Industrial Conference in January of 1923 by declaring his personal convictions about gainfully employed women:

Long before women were called to that broader participation in public affairs which is now both their duty and the public's advantage I was personally strongly convinced of the great benefits which would be derived from a more insistent expression and more general consideration of women's point of view in relation to social and industrial concerns. (Quoted in United States Department of Labor, Women's Bureau, 1923, pp. 2-3)

His precedent-setting support for feminist activity suggested that the Women's Bureau and women laborers had reached a new level of public support from the executive branch of the United States government. The Conference of 1926 was the second Bureau-sponsored conference of its kind in which the Bureau focused on "the investigation of foreign-born women in industry [which] was begun in December 1924" (United States Department of Labor, Women's Bureau, 1926, pp. 2, 10). Considering the influence gained from the success of the first Women's Industrial Conference in 1923, the one in 1926 continued the Bureau's influence beyond the technically narrow economic purpose of the U. S. Department of Labor and into the social aspects of economic change. Having established itself with years of economic analyses of gainfully employed women, the Bureau commented on the socioeconomics of immigrant women.

The *Tenth Annual Report of the Director of the Women's Bureau: Fiscal Year Ended June 30, 1928* unequivocally stated that immigrant women were "of interest and importance and in harmony with the purposes and duties of the Women's Bureau" (United States Department of Labor, Women's Bureau, 1928, p. 8). Women entered the professional ranks more than in any other previous era. According to historian Daniel Walkowitz, "the immigrant origins of the [female social worker] staff were highly visible [in New York City]" (Walkowitz, 1990, p. 1056). This immigrant background in large urban areas assisted in professionals' ability to understand the most recent immigrants who often prompted new words for the results of their integration. La Piana specifically notes, for example, that to find work some immigrants paid "a tip to a boss." This was "common among Italian" workers in the United States. The situation was irregular in their native country, however, so immigrants made a new word for their new type of boss in America: "'la bossatura'" (La Piana, 1916a, p. 8). Regardless of the ethical dimension to this fee system, it featured a person—*la bossatura*—who, as an immigrant, sought profit like most of the recent immigrants.

In 1924, the Women's Bureau conducted field research of "foreign-born women in industry" (United States Department of Labor, Women's Bureau, 1926, p. 10) by conducting interviews and analyzing the "facts and figures on questions vitally affecting wage-earning [native-born and foreign-born] women, and to formulate practical standards for wage-earning women in industry in each of the 48 States" (United States Department of Labor, Women's Bureau, 1924, p. 2). This endeavor was accomplished with the help of "progressive managers," despite popular anti-immigrant sentiments (see Goldberg, 1999, p. 153; Harwood, 1986, p. 202). The Women's Bureau published large portion of the Philadelphia and Lehigh Valley study in 1930, having interviewed 2,146 European immigrant women (see Manning, 1930, p. 3).

A new trend in immigrant women's gainful employment was that they were able to earn high enough wages to be relatively self-supporting. President Harding told the Women's Industrial Conference of 1923:

The revolutionary change that has taken place in the status of women in the world of business and affairs has not only justified but necessitated that broader and more intimate activity of women in behalf of the particular phases of public and social interests . . . very definite public benefit. (United States Department of Labor, Women's Bureau, 1923, pp. 2-3)

Married women began to be at least co-supporters with their husbands in financial matters. Co-support with the husband went beyond the basic contributions to the family income. Some women became the main source of family income, especially when the husband was unemployed or irregularly employed because of injury or illness. Even when the husband was working regularly as a co-supporter, the women's wage was a significant portion of the family income (Manning, 1930). A certain amount of independence was possible for women with the increasing wage trends of some unskilled and semi-skilled jobs. Wage increases were quite noticeable for semi-skilled immigrant women (Manning, 1930). Angelina of Italy, for example, began as a laundry worker earning $3.15 per week when she came to America. She had ambition for more than this, however, and sought a career position in a dress shop. She began earning $10 at a dress shop and then $12. She worked very hard, having "not lost a day except for holidays and layoffs of a week or so each summer. She was proud of the money she earned." Three years after advancing to $12 per week she was promoted to forelady at $13 per week. Her fiancé at the time had a wage of $14 per week, and for Angelina, "the girls whispered about it with awe" (quoted in Manning, 1930, p. 15). Angelina was making almost as much as her fiancé and she was sending money back to the old country where she had family depending on her financial support. Five years after her promotion to forelady, her husband could not work because of illness, so she supported her two children on her own wage (see Manning, 1930).

La Piana (1916a, 1916b) contended that emigrants to America came because they had "the knowledge of the existence of the other market in which wages are higher" (1916b, p. 5). This is part of what La Piana contends was a three-step process in why his European contemporaries emigrated to America. The first two steps before "knowledge of the existence of the other market in which wages are higher" were: "existence of two markets in which the wages and means are different" and the two markets have "a system of communication" (La Piana, 1916b, p. 5). So, after realizing that they could make more money in America, they emigrated. La Piana was suggesting that immigrants are basically capitalists—a philosophical fit for the America of the "Roaring Twenties." A shift had taken place in the intervening years between 1916 and Manning's (1930) report. The Italian migrant had become more inclined to acculturate, and successive generations lost their ancestral linguistic dialect. La Piana wrote that America was the "best field" for Europeans to begin anew. Italians were especially "led to come to America" if their lands were not yielding sufficiently (La Piana, 1916b, p. 5).

The Women's Bureau workers who interviewed Italian and other European immigrants found many very receptive to the attention. This is shown in the sheer amount of data procured by Women's Bureau interviewers. Although some of the data indicated depressed immigrant women, there were many who could be seen as happy to have the economic opportunity that was available in the United States. La Piana (1916a, 1916b) remarked on what he saw of the Italian laborer class, and not necessarily on what he personally believed about America. This is relevant because it adds to a portrait of the immigrant experience in gainful employment. In other words, economic realities are linked with social constructs. La Piana found that Sicilians from remote villages were not "enthusiastic for America" because they did "not find this country beautiful, and for him [the Sicilian/Italian immigrant] the most wonderful things of America are the elevated trains, the subway, and the breweries" (La Piana, 1916a, p. 7). Angelina of Italy, for example, suggested this in her career-oriented outlook during her interview with the Women's Bureau employee. Her success outside of the home caused "whispers" among some, but the suggestion from the interview context of the Women's Bureau was that many immigrant women quietly approved (see Manning, 1930, p. 15).

The Bureau's substantial case study of Philadelphia and Lehigh Valley in 1927-1928 was "based on interviews with foreign-born women in and near Philadelphia and in the Lehigh Valley" (United States Department of Labor, Women's Bureau, 1927, p. 16). The composite statistics were representative of Ohio largely because this state had 3,321,963 women gainfully employed at the time of the 1920 census. Florence Patteson Smith (1925) concluded that:

earnings of women interviewed . . . were higher in the Lehigh Valley than in Philadelphia; 29 per cent of the women in the Lehigh Valley, in contrast to 17 per cent of those in Philadelphia, earned as much as $20 a week. . . . The median of the week's earnings for all women reporting on this was $15.35 in Philadelphia and $16.75 in the Lehigh Valley. (Smith, 1925, p. 10; United States Department of Labor, Women's Bureau, 1928, p. 10)

The median weekly income in the Lehigh Valley was $1.40 higher than in Philadelphia. This is significant because immigrant women were not necessarily confined to the urban areas for gainful employment.

One-sixth of the textile employees in Philadelphia were foreign-born women. In the United States as a whole in 1920, "of the 1,930,341 women employed in manufacturing and mechanical industries, more than one in every five was foreign born," according to Caroline Manning (1930, p. 3). The clothing industry was one of the largest of the industrial employers of women. The immigrant women whom the Bureau interviewed frequently worked for wages so that they could feed their families. The stories of these women were "of great courage and enduring patience" according to Manning (1930), the industrial supervisor of the Women's Bureau. One interviewee, named Jeanie, was 21 years old when she came to the United States. She got a job in a textile factory because she was efficient and agreed to the low wage. After she became a mother, she had to quit her job. She eventually found a company that allowed her to work from home making clothes (see Manning, 1930, p. 138). This was a notable change in labor relations because of women's ability to directly exercise some control over their work conditions and home life. As discussed by Walch (1994), home ownership was one of the "dominant values of American society" (p. 68), which in turn was in parallel with immigrants' aspirations.

While the Philadelphia and Lehigh Valley case study revealed a generally promising economic development, the study also inadvertently echoed the issue of what has been called "urban-rural conflict" by some historians (see Eagles, 1989; Brown, 1994/2008, p. 97). There was a disparity in wages between urban Philadelphia and the rural Lehigh Valley. This situation was not uncommon to immigrant women from southern Europe. The issue of rural-urban boarders was important to immigrants' social integration because in Sicily and southern Italy "the custom of keeping boarders is unknown" (La Piana, 1916a, p. 13). Immigrant populations began to house individuals together who were not of the same family. Internal immigration from urban to rural districts was not uncommon because of economic incentives (see Eagles, 1989; Brown, 1994/2008).

Findings: Socioeconomic Nuance for the Upwardly Mobile Immigrant Woman

Americanization has been known as a loosely defined movement that seeks to assimilate immigrants into the English language by eliminating immigrant language and culture. Gayle Gullett, in her article on the role of women's clubs in Americanization campaigns in California, suggests that workplace competition between native-born and immigrants in the 1920s occasionally fueled what had been called an "imperious" phenomenon (Gullett, 1995, p. 77). Goldberg (1999) argued that so-called "old-stock" Americans' fear of immigrant economic competition in the first couple of decades of the twentieth century added to the negative connotations of the term (Goldberg, 1999, p. 153). La Piana (1916a, 1916b), however, did not think of Americanization as a negative phenomenon. He defined Americanization as a "higher standard of living," (La Piana, 1916a, p. 3) because the United States was generally seen as a place with economic opportunity. Olneck (1989) came closest of the secondary sources to paralleling La Piana's (1916a) definition of the phenomenon. Despite the "upsurge of nativist sentiment" in the 1920s, Olneck (1989) contended that Americanization courses were not necessarily a clunky imperialist endeavor, but, rather, a refined attempt to make sure immigrants knew that "self-reliance," among other qualities, was a part of the American character. Therefore, immigrants could see Americanization as a less threatening "symbolic" process of cultural integration rather than assimilation (Olneck, 1989, pp. 399, 408).

Regardless of which side—nativist or immigrant—invoked the term, each had an economic basis for doing so. The motivation for economic empowerment brought immigrants into competition with some native-born citizens because of a *perception* of competition even if actual competition was not necessarily there (Gullett, 1995; Goldberg, 1999). Masao Suzuki (1995) noted that some immigrant groups were highly successful with acculturation, and they "improved their occupational status both in terms of the growing proportion of gainfully employed in 'middle-class' occupations and in terms of a declining proportion of unskilled workers" (pp. 890-891). Expanding fiscal power among immigrant communities was seen by native-born wage-earners as a threat to their job security. Polling percentages during the 1920s indicated an anti-immigrant sentiment among urban and rural districts (Eagles, 1989). There was a growing discontent in the United States Congress in 1920-1921 that increased isolationist tendencies briefly. Most notable of the anti-immigration legislation was the National Origins Act (1921) and the Johnson-Reed Act (1924). Both temporarily restricted immigration via draconian quotas, nearly barring immigration completely from several countries for a time (see Kyvig, 2004, p. 173).

Immigrant women who did make it into the county before the anti-immigration laws found it difficult, but not impossible, to acculturate in order to abate some of the resentment from native-born workers. The Women's Bureau found in its Philadelphia and Lehigh Valley case study that "[o]nly 60 per cent of the women were able to speak English. . . . Less than a third of the women could read English, and one in seven could not read at all" (United States Department of Labor, Women's Bureau, 1928, p. 8). This finding was used to support what was ostensibly the attitude of some "[o]rganized women [who] began supporting Americanization efforts" (Gullett, 1995, p. 73), because more women's organizations temporarily became concerned with the notion that some immigrant groups were not seen as fully assimilating into American culture (Ngai, 1999).

The Bureau again addressed the Americanization phenomenon in its reports that were sympathetic to the female immigrant, because immigrant women were part of its mandate (see United States Department of Labor, Women's Bureau, 1928, p. 8).

The Women's Bureau interviewed immigrant women to get their perspective in their own words. The 1930 report stated that,

after talking with women who for years have done some of the heaviest and most disagreeable tasks in our factories and mills, but whose hearts and minds still dwell in the Carpathian Mountains, Americanization seems little more than a strange word and a vague ideal as yet far from attainment. (Manning, 1930, pp. 2-3)

George La Piana crystallized the meaning of the term 'Americanization' from his Italian immigrant perspective. Writing about how the immigrants he knew thought of Americanization as meaning a "higher standard of living," he continued to say that the term was a "problem" because it seemed "like a body without a soul" (La Piana, 1916b, p. 21). He suggested—much like the quote found in the Women's Bureau's 1930 report (see Manning, 1930)—that some immigrants still had their "soul" set in the Carpathian Mountains. They were still thinking of their ancestral home in Europe. Nevertheless, the domestic tradition of Italian women was surprisingly flexible in its new American surroundings. Despite widespread nostalgia for their country of birth, La Piana (1916b) suggested that immigrant women recognized the economic "environment" of their new country as the pivotal item for immigrants to acculturate into if they were to be accepted and achieve financial security.

The older generation of Italian women thought that once a woman "learned how to prepare the oatmeal she was already Americanized." (La Piana, 1916b, p. 20) The first generation seemed to emphasize assimilation more often than not, at least from La Piana's (1916b) perspective. Even if culinary acculturation seemed cursory, it was noteworthy for its tendency to be an item quickly to be assimilated into the popular culture. Food adoption was a visible sign that the immigrant was integrating into local society. If Italian immigrant women deemed the action of cooking oatmeal as evidence of their successful acculturation, then native-born women's acceptance of Italian food evidenced their acceptance of the newcomers. This diffused some of the tension in urban and rural areas. La Piana went so far as to claim that "many Americans were Italianized because they liked macaroni and spaghetti almost with the same enthusiasm [as] Italians themselves" (La Piana, 1916b, p. 20). Fostering familiarity was seen as a positive for economic advancement and component of acculturation (La Piana, 1916b, p. 1, p. 20).

The threat of "single capital consideration," according to La Piana (1916a, p. 4), was that "to americanize [sic] the Italian immigrants, we have to put them in a favourable [sic] condition" (La Piana, 1916a, p. 4). In other words, the environment had to be favorable economically for acculturation. La Piana (1916a) suggested that equalizing pay would assist immigrants' integration in their new society, though, at first, they would likely work for less. As La Piana (1916a) wrote, they would initially "atone for their coming" (pp. 21, 202).

Successfully assimilating immigrants meant different things to different people. Gullett (1995) and Graham and Koed (1993) echoed the same concept in suggesting that champions of Americanization in 1910s and 1920s, including many women's clubs such as those in California, over-emphasized aggressive assimilation. Olneck (1989) claimed that school coursework successfully "resulted in individual regeneration" and "ultimately in collective transformation" of the immigrant into an American (pp. 409-410). But trying to force assimilation was not nearly so successful, according to La Piana (1916a, 1916b), although he did agree with the women's clubs that declared education to have been the "crucial point" for immigrants' integration and economic advancement (La Piana, 1916a, p. 20). He suggested that the women's clubs and charities were rarely well-situated to address immigrants' situation through their programs. But when they were successful, acculturation took the form of education that benefited immigrant's employment prospects. So "willed learning," as noted by Olneck (1989, p. 409), was successful if immigrants obtained jobs. With greater work abilities came greater cultural integration, because the immigrants became invested in their new country. The aggressive acculturation campaigns of the Daughters of the American Revolution (DAR) left out the dynamics that different immigrants brought to the United States. Many native-born citizens adopted immigrant foods, for example. America's tradition of individualization historically undermined the very acculturation that the DAR tried to accomplish (see Gullett, 1995, p. 77; Graham & Koed, 1993, pp. 28-29). For some it was through the medium of food and for others it was through leaving the domestic sphere for the workplace.

The Women's Bureau reports used interviews and cliometrics as the main method of investigation. According to Gullett (1995), the Daughters of the American Revolution, the California Federation of Women's Clubs, and the General Federation of Women's Clubs "demanded that the newcomers [female immigrants] learn from them how to become acceptable women citizens" (p. 73).The Women's Bureau, however, decided not to "demand" uncompromising consistency from immigrants. Instead, the Women's Bureau maintained its mandate of "promot[ing]" women immigrants with statistically grounded reports (see United States Department of Labor, Women's Bureau, 1920, p. 3). In keeping with its mandate, the Women's Bureau espoused flexibility as opposed to the rigid Americanization agenda of several prominent women's clubs of the time (see Gullett, 1995, pp. 73, 77; Haarsager, 1997, p. 316).

Caroline Manning (1930) oversaw a report that indicated how female immigrants were integrating into the work force through acceptance of—at first—comparatively low wages that got them hired. This finally gave them the opportunity for advancement once they had established themselves in the workplace. She built further upon Mary Veronica Dempsey's report of 1922. Dempsey's (1922) study of businesses that employed 1,000 or more women and men in 1910 and 1920 revealed a situation that was unanticipated during its time: "the changes in rate of increase or decrease for the two sexes were entirely disproportionate, and in by far the greater number of cases the women took the lead in the rate of increase" (p. 4). Although men were still numerically higher in number in gainful occupations, women's disproportionate increase in industrial employment indicated the growing opportunities for women in the workforce. Dempsey (1922) deduced that women had "enlarged their field of work by entering in greater numbers occupations in which formerly they had but scant representation" (p. 4). This increase led to friction with some conservative employers, as indicated by one of the Women's Bureau's interviewees. Jeanie, an immigrant woman who was 21 years of age, quickly got a job in a textile factory but was eventually told by her employer that "she was earning too much" (as quoted in Manning, 1930, p. 138). This was an industrialist's admission that there was an economic shift in favor of young immigrant women, as had been indicated in Dempsey's report. That mentality from industrialist would change.

Economic advancement continued, and the Women's Bureau continued to study and support women's economic opportunity (United States Department of Labor, Women's Bureau, 1923, 1924, 1925, 1926, 1927, 1928, 1929).

An ironically unintended consequence of the anti-immigrant legislation of 1920-1921 was that such legislation benefited some young female immigrants already in the United States. Oshima (1984) noted that "the annual average of immigrants fell from 856,000 in 1900-1915 to 356,000 in 1915-1930" (p. 163). This downward trend put pressure on the manufacturers to find "unskilled labor" and spurred the drive for "the substitution of machines for unskilled labor throughout the 1920s" (Oshima, 1984, p. 164). However, employers in the manufacturing sector were not able to adapt to mechanization in a day or a year; therefore, they became eager for the dwindling supply of inexpensive unskilled labor caused by the anti-immigration laws, hence immigrant women were suddenly becoming more employable (Oshima, 1984). This phenomenon was being uncovered at the time by what this researcher calls Federal-Bureaucratic Feminists such as Mary van Kleeck—first director of what became the Women's Bureau—in her book *Women and Machines* (van Kleeck, 1921). She wrote that there was a "drift of women . . . to novel adventures in mechanics" (p. 4). Van Kleeck was referring to the growing number of women employed in manufacturing industries throughout the 1910s into 1920. The types of jobs available to women increased proportionally to the point where employability considerations were nearly "sexless." And even when gender was considered, "the fact is impressive that of the firms questioned in 1919 who had recruited women for [industrial] job[s] during the war, more than half were retaining them" (van Kleeck, 1921, pp. 5-6). This upward employability change was to prove lasting even for immigrant women.

The Women's Bureau had "Unpublished data [that] show[ed] that nearly four-fifths of [immigrant women] were under 25 years of age when they arrived" and "indeed, they lost little time in finding a job" (Manning, 1930, p. 135). This trend was evidence that many of those immigrants who did succeed in getting admitted into the United States were female (Oshima, 1984). They were able to take advantage of the legislated immigration squeeze of 1921-1924 that tended to exclude as many men as women from entering the United States. The prevention of further immigration increased the demand for inexpensive unskilled labor—primarily those immigrants who had made it into the country. Consequently, the mechanizing manufacturers hired those who fit their criteria of a large pool of labor who could be paid low wages. This workforce model increasingly trended towards young female immigrants (Oshima, 1984; Manning, 1930). In 1920 there were "1,930,341 women employed in manufacturing and mechanical industries" out of a total of 8.5 million employed women. 21.1 percent of the American work force was women in 1920 (Manning, 1930, p. 3). Although this percentage was down from 1910, the proportion of downturn was less than that of men—2.3 percent as opposed to 3.1 percent, according to Smith (1925, p. 5). By 1930, 10 million women were employed in America, according to Women's Bureau report "Fact Finding with the Women's Bureau" (United States Department of Labor, Women's Bureau, 1930a, 1930b). This large proportional statistic suggested that those groups previously frowned upon for arbitrary reasons or archaic social conventions were especially prime labor markets, because they were eager for gainful employment. Initially, employers were more likely to lay off men than women because of the economic priority of cutting costs.

SOLUTIONS AND RECOMMENDATIONS

If a group of people want to advance their economic interests, a solution is to work within the existing legal framework, which is what happened with the case study of the Women's Bureau. Using the existing legislative process can work with determination, organization, and advocacy.

FUTURE RESEARCH DIRECTIONS

The concept of Federal-Bureaucratic Feminism can be explored further through additional studies of economic advancement of women and male allies. Equality in federal influence can be studied more through case studies of government agencies.

CONCLUSION

Immigrants came to America primarily for economic advancement. La Piana's discussion of acculturation in the late 1910s showed immigrants not always afraid of the acculturation, but rather welcoming it if acculturation promoted their own economic advancement. Some immigrant women's native-born peers rose in the ranks of gainful employment along with them. La Piana (1916a) summarized the situation during the interwar years: "[immigrants, both men and women] are here to make money" (p. 7). Those women immigrants interviewed by the Women's Bureau in the 1910s and 1920s seemed to want to start a new life in which women could and would enforce their rights to earn money and advance in the workforce. The United States Women's Bureau was a precedent-setting unit within the U.S. Department of Labor that promoted and accelerated the advancement of women's rights by researching the issues under its mandate, interviewing people affected by policy, and promoting legislative action.

REFERENCES

Addams, J. (1923). *A new conscience and an ancient evil.* Macmillan. Open Collections Program, Widener Library, Collections Development Department, Harvard University. http://nrs.harvard.edu/urn-3:FHCL:436848

Anderson, M. (1926). *Women in the fruit-growing and canning industries in the State of Washington* [Letter of Transmittal]. United States Department of Labor, Women's Bureau. Washington, DC: Government Printing Office. Immigration to the United States, 1789-1930, Open Collections Program, Baker Library, Harvard University. http://ocp.hul.harvard.edu

Ayers, E. L., Gould, L. L., Oshinsky, D. M., & Soderlund, J. R. (2012). American passages: A history of the United States (4th ed.). Wadsworth Cengage.

Brown, M. E. (1994/2008). Parents and children fundamental questions about immigrant family life. In T. Walch (Ed.), *Immigrant America: European ethnicity in the United States* (pp. 89–102). Routledge.

Burn, F. K. E. (2005). 1920: August, Febb Burn to Harry Burn. In L. Grunwald & S. J. Adler (Eds.), *Women's letters: America from the Revolutionary War to the present* (p. 489). The Dial Press. (Original work published 1920)

Dempsey, M. V. (1922). *The occupational progress of women: An interpretation of census statistics of women in gainful occupations* (Bulletin of the Women's Bureau, no. 27). United States Department of Labor, Women's Bureau. Government Printing Office. http://nrs.harvard.edu/urn-3:HBS.BAKER:123561

Dumenil, L. (1998). Re-shifting perspectives on the 1920s: Recent trends in social and cultural history. In J. E. Haynes (Ed.), *Calvin Coolidge and the Coolidge Era* (pp. 63–96). Library of Congress.

Eagles, C. W. (1989). Congressional voting in the 1920s: A test of urban-rural conflict. *The Journal of American History*, *76*(2), 528–534. doi:10.2307/1907989

George La Piana. 1878-1972. (n.d.). [Immigration to the United States, 1789-1930]. Open Collections Program, Harvard University. http://ocp.hul.harvard.edu/immigration/people_lapiana.html

Goldberg, D. J. (1999). *Discontented America: The United States in the 1920s*. The Johns Hopkins University Press.

Graham, O. L. Jr, & Koed, E. (1993). Americanizing the immigrant, past and future: History and implications of a social movement. *The Public Historian*, *15*(4), 24–49. doi:10.2307/3378635

Gullett, G. (1995). Women progressives and the politics of Americanization in California, 1915-1920. *Pacific Historical Review*, *64*(1), 71–94. doi:10.2307/3640335

Haarsager, S. (1997). *Organized womanhood: Cultural politics in the Pacific Northwest, 1840-1920*. University of Oklahoma Press.

Harwood, E. (1986). American public opinion and U.S. immigration policy. *The Annals of the American Academy of Political and Social Science*, *487*(1), 201–212. doi:10.1177/0002716286487001013

Kyvig, D. E. (2004). *Daily life in the United States 1920-1940: How America lived through the 'Roaring Twenties' and the Great Depression*. Ivan R. Dee.

La Piana, G. (1916a, January 17). *Andover-Harvard Theological Library, Harvard Divinity School, Cambridge (Papers, 1878-1972 inclusive, Manuscripts MS 104/11, folders 5-18, mass. sequence 54-74)* [Social Work Among Italian Immigrants]. Open Collections Program, Baker Library, Harvard University. http://nrs.harvard.edu/urn-3:DIV.LIB:828929

La Piana, G. (1916b, October). *Andover-Harvard Theological Library, Harvard Divinity School, Cambridge (Papers, 1878-1972 inclusive, Manuscripts bMS 104/11, Folders 5-18, mass. sequence 32 of 325)* [Italians in America]. Open Collections Program, Baker Library, Harvard University. http://nrs.harvard.edu/urn-3:DIV.LIB:828929

La Piana, G. (n.d.). *Andover-Harvard Theological Library, Harvard Divinity School, Cambridge (Papers, 1878-1972 inclusive, Manuscripts MS 104/11, folders 5-18, mass. sequence 75-89)* [Italian Woman at home]. Open Collections Program, Baker Library, Harvard University. http://nrs.harvard.edu/urn-3:DIV.LIB:828929

Manning, C. (1930). *The immigrant woman and her job (Bulletin of the Women's Bureau, no. 74). United States Department of Labor, Women's Bureau*. Government Printing Office. Open Collections Program, Baker Library, Harvard University. http://nrs.harvard.edu/urn-3:HBS.BAKER:452545

Mastracci, S. H. (2004). Backstage and spotlight activism: One survival strategy of the Women's Bureau and its price. *Labor History*, *45*(1), 85–99. doi:10.1080/0023656042000202990

Matthews, J. V. (2003). *The rise of the new woman: The women's movement in America, 1875-1930*. Ivan R. Dee.

Ngai, M. M. (1999). The architecture of race in American immigration law: A reexamination of the Immigration Act of 1924. *The Journal of American History*, *86*(1), 67–92. doi:10.2307/2567407

Nienburg, B. M. (1920). *Women in government service (Bulletin of the Women's Bureau, no. 8). United States Department of Labor, Women's Bureau*. Government Printing Office. Open Collections Program. Baker Library, Harvard University. http://nrs.harvard.edu/urn-3:HBS.BAKER:136884

Olneck, M. R. (1989). Americanization and the education of immigrants, 1900-1925: An analysis of symbolic action. *American Journal of Education*, *97*(4), 398–423. doi:10.1086/443935

Oshima, H. T. (1984). The growth of U.S. factor productivity: The significance of new technologies in the early decades of the twentieth century. *The Journal of Economic History*, *44*(1), 161–170. doi:10.1017/S0022050700031429

Schain, J. (1918). *Women and the franchise*. Chicago: A.C. McClurge & Company. Open Collections Program, Harvard University, Schlesinger Library on the History of Women in America. http://nrs.harvard.edu/urn-3:RAD.SCHL:134371

Smith, F. P. (1925). *Facts about working women: A graphic presentation based on census statistics and studies of the Women's Bureau (Bulletin of the Women's Bureau, no. 46)*. Government Printing Office. Open Collections Program. Baker Library, Harvard University. http://nrs.harvard.edu/urn-3:HBS.BAKER:477001

Suzuki, M. (1995). Success story? Japanese immigrant economic achievement and return migration, 1920-1930. *The Journal of Economic History*, *55*(4), 889–901. doi:10.1017/S0022050700042200

United States Department of Labor. Women's Bureau. (1920). *Second Annual Report of the Director of the Women's Bureau for the Fiscal Year Ended June 30, 1920*. Washington, DC: Government Printing Office. Open Collections Program, Baker Library, Harvard University. http://nrs.harvard.edu/urn-3:HBS.BAKER:508406

United States Department of Labor. Women's Bureau. (1921). *Third Annual Report of the Director of the Women's Bureau for the Fiscal Year Ended June 30, 1921*. Washington, DC: Government Printing Office. Open Collections Program, Baker Library, Harvard University. http://nrs.harvard.edu/urn-3:HBS.BAKER:508406

United States Department of Labor. Women's Bureau. (1922). *Fourth Annual Report of the Director of the Women's Bureau for the Fiscal Year Ended June 30, 1922*. Washington, DC: Government Printing Office. Open Collections Program, Baker Library, Harvard University. http://nrs.harvard.edu/urn-3:HBS.BAKER:508406

United States Department of Labor. Women's Bureau. (1923). *Fifth Annual Report of the Director of the Women's Bureau for the Fiscal Year Ended June 30, 1923*. Washington, DC: Government Printing Office. Open Collections Program. Baker Library, Harvard University. http://nrs.harvard.edu/urn-3:HBS.BAKER:508406

United States Department of Labor. Women's Bureau. (1924). *Sixth Annual Report of the Director of the Women's Bureau: Fiscal Year Ended June 30, 1924*. Washington, DC: Government Printing Office. Open Collections Program. Baker Library, Harvard University. http://nrs.harvard.edu/urn-3:HBS.BAKER:508406

United States Department of Labor. Women's Bureau. (1925). *Seventh Annual Report of the Director of the Women's Bureau: Fiscal Year Ended June 30, 1925*. Washington, DC: Government Printing Office. Open Collections Program. Baker Library, Harvard University. http://nrs.harvard.edu/urn-3:HBS.BAKER:508406

United States Department of Labor. Women's Bureau. (1926). *Eighth Annual Report of the Director of the Women's Bureau: Fiscal Year Ended June 30, 1926*. Government Printing Office. Open Collections Program. Baker Library, Harvard University. http://nrs.harvard.edu/urn-3:HBS.BAKER:508406

United States Department of Labor, Bureau of Labor Statistics. (1927). *Handbook of Labor Statistics, 1924-1926*, 439. Government Printing Office. http://ocp.hul.harvard.edu/ww/

United States Department of Labor. Women's Bureau. (1927). *Ninth Annual Report of the Director of the Women's Bureau: Fiscal Year Ended June 30, 1927*. Government Printing Office. In *Women Working, 1800-1930*. Open Collections Program. Baker Library, Harvard University. http://nrs.harvard.edu/urn-3:HBS.BAKER:508406

United States Department of Labor. Women's Bureau. (1928). *Tenth Annual Report of the Director of the Women's Bureau: Fiscal Year Ended June 30, 1928*. Government Printing Office. In *Women Working, 1800-1930*. Open Collections Program. Baker Library, Harvard University. http://nrs.harvard.edu/urn-3:HBS.BAKER:508406

United States Department of Labor. Women's Bureau. (1929). *Eleventh Annual Report of the Director of the Women's Bureau: Fiscal Year Ended June 30, 1929*. Government Printing Office. In *Women Working, 1800-1930*. Open Collections Program. Baker Library, Harvard University. http://nrs.harvard.edu/urn-3:HBS.BAKER:508406

United States Department of Labor. Women's Bureau (1930a, December 9). *Fact Finding with the Women's Bureau* (Women's Bureau Bulletin, no. 84). St. Louis Federal Reserve, Discovery Economic Center. https://fraser.stlouisfed.org/title/5392

United States Department of Labor. Women's Bureau. (1930b). *Twelfth Annual Report of the Director of the Women's Bureau: Fiscal Year Ended June 30, 1930*. Government Printing Office. In *Women Working, 1800-1930*. Open Collections Program. Baker Library, Harvard University. http://nrs.harvard.edu/urn-3:HBS.BAKER:508406

United States Department of Labor. Women's Bureau. (1931). *Activities of the Women's Bureau of the United States* (Bulletin of the Women's Bureau, no. 86). St. Louis Federal Reserve, Discovery Economic Center. https://fraser.stlouisfed.org/files/docs/publications/women/b0086_dolwb_1931.pdf

United States House of Representatives. (1920). *41 Stat. L., 987 – An Act to Establish in the Department of Labor a bureau to be known as the Women's Bureau*. https://uscode.house.gov/statviewer.htm?volume=41&page=987

van Kleeck, M. (1921). *Women and machines*. The Consumer's League of the City of New York. Open Collections Program. Baker Library, Harvard University. http://nrs.harvard.edu/urn-3:HBS.BAKER:500055

Walch, T. (Ed.). (1994). *Immigrant America: European ethnicity in the United States*. Routledge.

Walkowitz, D. J. (1990). The making of a feminine professional identity: Social workers in the 1920s. *The American Historical Review*, *95*(4), 1051–1075. doi:10.2307/2163478

Weber, G. A. (1923). *The Women's Bureau: Its history, activities, and organization*. The Johns Hopkins Press. Open Collections Program, Widener Library, Harvard University. http://nrs.harvard.edu/urn-3:FHCL:123612

Women's Bureau. (n.d.). In *Women Working, 1800-1930*. Open Collections Program, Harvard University. http://ocp.hul.harvard.edu/ww/

Women's Trade Union League of Chicago. (1910, October 29). *Official report of the Strike Committee: Chicago Garment Workers' Strike*. Women's Trade Union League of Chicago. Open Collections Program, Widener Library, Harvard University. http://nrs.harvard.edu/urn-3:FHCL:458789

KEY TERMS AND DEFINITIONS

Americanization: A form of acculturation in the United States during the first half of the 20th century.

Federal-Bureaucratic Feminism: A term coined in this chapter to mean a feminism by employees of the federal government to promote gender equality through the power and influence of the federal government.

Women's Bureau: A unit of the United States Department of Labor that began in 1917 as the Women in Industry Service and then as a Bureau in 1920 to promote the economic advancement of women.

Chapter 11
Factors Affecting the Motivation and Productivity at the Workplace:
A Case of Female University Teachers

Zeeshan Maqsood
University of Sialkot, Pakistan

Iqra Sardar
https://orcid.org/0000-0002-7568-3008
Riphah International University, Islamabad, Pakistan

Bezon Kumar
https://orcid.org/0000-0003-4489-431X
Rabindra University, Bangladesh

ABSTRACT

This chapter mainly explores the significant factors influencing the motivation and productivity of female university teachers in the workplace. This chapter uses primary data and several methods in achieving the objectives. This chapter finds that all the factors considered in the study have a significant impact on the motivation and productivity of female university teachers. The analysis also reveals that almost all the factors of motivation, work environment, and productivity have a relationship with one another. More specifically, this chapter finds that female teachers get motivation and increase their productivity when they are satisfied with their basic needs, job safety, work environment gets support from their families, get self-determination and get supportive behavior from the supervisor. Therefore, this chapter calls for policymakers to take proper initiatives in increasing female university teachers' motivation and productivity by considering the above factors.

DOI: 10.4018/978-1-7998-3737-4.ch011

INTRODUCTION

The performance of an organization depends on the working of its employees. If employees are well motivated and giving a good response to their job, the organization will perform well in the market. An organization can flourish when its employees work with full zeal and honesty (Kwapong, et al. 2015). It is a general tendency that an employee performs better when he/she gets appreciation and motivation for his/her work. Many researchers researched on motivation and productivity of employees. Most of the researches are on the employees of industries or other organizations. However, a very few researches is found on the productivity of female university teachers. The core contribution of this paper is to focus on this gap and aim at finding the factors affecting female university teachers' performance at the workplace and their interrelationship.

From the earlier literature, it is found that there are many factors affecting the motivation and productivity of employees. However, this paper focuses on five new factors of job performance i.e. motivation and productivity of female university teacher in the study area. The way how these five factors are affecting teachers' performance is shown in Figure 1.

Figure 1. Factors affecting job performance
Source: Author's creation based on literature

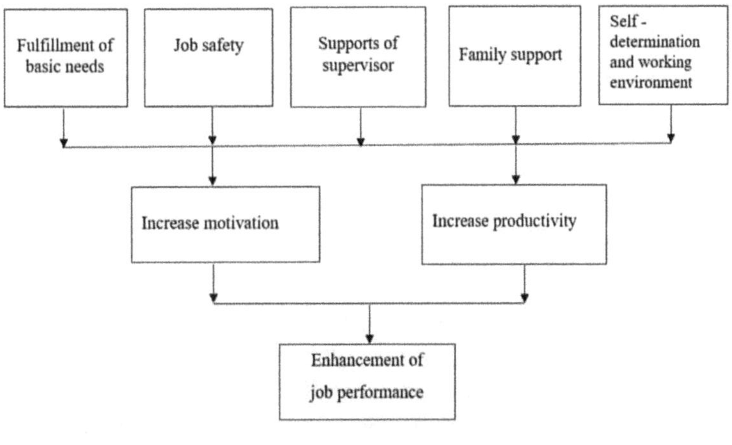

These five factors are considered to be helpful to motivate the teachers at their workplace to enhance their performance. The fulfillment of the basic needs at the workplace is very important. When an employee is satisfied from basic needs (teachers' satisfaction from their salary package, suitable working hour, working conditions and extra benefits by the institution) and the job safety (annual holidays with pay, job security, retirement benefits, location of institute and so on), he/she will work more confidently to make his/her job more secured.

Productivity, the generation of goods and services with the minimum quantity of effort, measures how well an organization or individual, industry, country transfers the efforts and stuff, labor, materials, machines and so on into goods and services. Attitude of a teacher is the quality which enables him/her to make a significant change in the lives of students (Gourneau, 2005). Many teachers are desirous of being successful teachers who will be kept in mind lovingly by their students. Some want to have a chance to be an improved teacher than the level they qualified. Female Teachers' attitude during teaching show how well they can manage the students, motivate the students and they be satisfied with their job.

The workplace is a place where a duty is accomplished. Physical features of a workplace environment have a direct impact on teachers' productivity. It is typically involved with the other factors related to the physical work environment of employees, such as furniture of office, proper natural ventilation, productive and organized environment. Similarly, behavioral work environment factors are related to people, students and colleagues' behavior; respect for each other; social circle and friendly environment. These can affect the employees' performance. The main objectives of the study are as follows:

1. To explore the demographic features of the female teachers.
2. To find out the factors affecting motivation and productivity of the female teachers.
3. To check the interrelationship between different factors.

The study is important for all the educational institutions for their development and better results. The finding of this paper may be helpful for the university itself and other educational institutions for improving their employees' performance which can produce quality graduates. The findings of this paper may contribute to the national development and achieve the Sustainable Development Goals (SDGs).

LITERATURE REVIEW

This section describes an insight into the factors affecting an employee's motivation and productivity in the workplace. From the earlier literature, it is found that different researchers have used different methods and found different findings which have been discussed below. Aiyetan and Olotuah (2006) conducted a study to find out the relationship between motivation and productivity of the workers of industry in Nigeria. From the study, it was found that salaries of the workers were very low and promotion chances in that industry were very rare. That is why the workers preferred financial incentives rather than non-financial incentives. Therefore, to increase their productivity, it was necessary to increase their salaries and holidays with pay. Haynes (2008) conducted a study to examine the impact of office comfort on workplace occupiers' productivity found that there was a significant impact on workplace productivity by placing greater stress on office environment comfort systems. Office user perceptions can also be managed by keeping occupiers informed of any issue which affects their comfort.

Stella (2008) conducted a study to find out the causes of the unsatisfactory performance of workers and the identification of motivational factors so that they could be included in plans to improve the performance of the employees. Findings of the analysis indicated that supervision, working condition, job security, and performance evaluation must be the baseline to motivate the employees. One hygiene factor, i.e.; 'salary' was playing the critical performance of the employees' dissatisfaction. Marufa and Uzhenyu (2017) recommended that the university should improve on awarding of extrinsic motivators and to also streamline the heavy workloads of academics so that administrative issues should be tackled largely by the support staff. Inuwa (2016) depicts that there is a positive and significant relationship between job satisfaction on the performance of non- academic staff of the University. Akhtar and Iqbal (2017) uncovered that there was a positive relationship between teacher's intrinsic motivation and extrinsic motivation and job performance. Nwakasi and Cummins (2018) found that if employees are supported, the productivity of the employees is enhanced exponentially. On the other hand, Nabi, et al. (2017) indicate that if employees are positively motivated, it improves both their effectiveness and efficiency drastically for achieving organizational goals. While Kwapong et al. (2015) confirms a significant positive correlation between motivation and performance among teaching staff of Ghanaian polytechnics, Viseu, et al. (2016) found that organizational culture was the most studied variable associated with teacher motivation and most studies in this area were published between 2010 and 2014.

Sommerfeldt (2010) conducted a study to recognize the factors that motivate the Queensland police to perform well at their workplace. Factor analysis exposed five factors that motivate the police, these are feeling valued, achievement, workplace relationship, work itself, salary and terms and conditions of service. It was proposed that Police leaders must use these five motivational factors in their service policies as planning tools to improve the quality of work. Chandrasekar (2011) conducted a study to find the relationship between employees and workplace environment and found that there was a close relationship between work, workplace, and tools of work. The researcher also suggested that managers of the organizations should focus on personal motivation and infrastructure of the work environment to increase the employees' productivity.

Cristini (2011) recommended an analytical framework to differentiate between the causes of work motivation made by modern workplace practices and developed the theoretical conditions for the most favorable amount of organizational dedication to rise in presence of such practices.

They found that practices providing significant empowerment on powerful intrinsic motivators- forgiven pay and working conditions, they made stronger employees' attachment to the ðrm and identification with its values. Alhaji (2012) researched on the overall success of an organization and found that motivated employees tried their best to increase their participation and contributed more to the overall success of the organization. Leblebici (2012) conducted a study on the impact of workplace quality on employees' productivity. Results showed that workplace environment affects employee performance but the behavioral workplace environment had great an effect on employees' performance. Rashid (2012) conducted a study to identify the factors which motivate the employees and to check the difference between private and public sector employees' motivational constructs in Banking. Results showed that public sector employees were motivated by work contents and they had experience in work-life balance. Private sector employees were more motivated by financial rewards, promotions, and a friendly environment. Private Bank employees were more satisfied than public sector banks employees.

Although there are many studies on the motivation and productivity of employees around the world, studies in the context of Pakistan using primary data is very scant. In addition, this paper has examined five new variables to examine the motivation and productivity of female university teachers in Pakistan is a virgin area which makes this study more constructive and worthy.

MATERIAL AND METHODS

Study Area and Sample Size

This is mainly a case study based on primary data. For the study, the University of Haripur was considered as the study area. The university had five faculties having 159 faculty members. For the selecting sample, a stratified random sampling technique was used because the population was heterogeneous, and also sampling frame was available. In this case, the population was divided into two strata according to the mode of their service as regular and contract faculty. From each stratum proportionate number of female teachers was interviewed with a well-structured questionnaire from February to March 2019. From the population, sample size was determined by the formula stated by Taro Yamane shown below.

$$n = \frac{N}{1 + Ne^2}$$

where, n = the sample size, N= the population size and e = rate of precision (0.05).

$$n = \frac{159}{1 + 159\left(0.05^2\right)} = 114$$

The distribution of population and sample respect to faculties are presented in the following table.

Table 1. Distribution of sample size by faculty and job category

Faculties	Regular		Contract		Total	
	P	S	P	S	P	S
Faculty of Arts	19	13	04	3	23	16
Faculty of Computing	05	4	10	7	15	11
Faculty of Science	33	24	35	25	68	49
Faculty of Management	15	11	13	9	28	20
Faculty of Social Science	17	12	08	6	25	18
Total	89	64	70	50	159	114

Note: P = Size of Population and S = Size of Sample

Reliability Analysis

In doing research, checking the reliability of data is very important because the test of reliability minimizes the error of measurement which leads to internal consistency. There are many methods of checking the reliability of data, Cronbach's Alpha method is quite popular which is also known as the coefficient of reliability (or consistency). The standardized formula of Cronbach's alpha is stated as follows:

$$\alpha = \frac{N \cdot \overline{c}}{\overline{v} + \left(N - 1\right) \cdot \overline{c}}$$

where N is equal to the number of items, C-bar is the average inter-item covariance among the items and V-bar equals the average variance.

From the above formula, it is clear that if the number of items is increased, the value of Cronbach's alpha increases. Additionally, if the average inter-item correlation is low, the alpha will be low. As the average inter-item correlation increases, Cronbach's alpha increases as well (holding the number of items constant). When alpha is more than 0.7 then the questionnaire items as well as data is considered to be more reliable.

Item Analysis

The item analysis was made to find out the discriminating items for different factors of motivation and productivity at the workplace of the female teachers. For this analysis the formula used is given as follows:

$$T = \frac{\bar{X}_{H-\bar{X}_L}}{\sqrt{\frac{\Sigma(X_H - \bar{X}_H)^2 + \Sigma\,(X_{L-\bar{X}_L})^2}{n\left(n-1\right)}}}$$

$\bar{X}_H$ = Mean of upper 25% of scores for an item.
$\bar{X}_L$ = Mean of lower 25% of scores for an item.
$\Sigma(X_H - \bar{X}_H)^2$ = Sum of squares of deviations for upper 25% of scores.
$\Sigma\,(X_{L-\bar{X}_L})^2$ = Sum of squares of deviations for lower 25% of scores.
n = Number of observations in lower or upper 25% of the data.

RESULTS AND DISCUSSIONS

This section presents the estimated results of collected data by applying different methods.

Reliability Analysis

Before analyzing data, the study performed the reliability test of data for all variables except demographic variables. The result of the reliability test is shown in Table 2.

Table 2. Reliability test

Cronbach's Alpha	No. of items
0.950	78
Source: Field survey, 2019	

Table 1 shows that the estimated value of Cronbach's alpha is 0.950 which interprets that the data obtained with the help of this questionnaire is reliable.

Descriptive Analysis

This section presents a descriptive analysis of some characteristics of female teachers. The result is analyzed with SPSS 23 and presented in tabular form by using frequency, percentage, mean, maximum, minimum, and median.

Table 3. Distribution of female teachers by level of education and seniority

Attributes	Categories	Frequency	Percentage
Education Level	Graduate	6	5
	Post Graduate	63	55
	Ph.D	45	40
Seniority Level	Professor	3	3
	Associate Professor	4	3
	Assistant Professor	51	45
	Lecturer	46	40
	Teaching Assistant	10	9

Source: Field survey, 2019

Table 3 shows that 5% of the teaching faculties were holding a Graduate degree, 55% had a Post Graduate degree and 40% had done their Doctorate in different fields. This finding explains that the ratio of Post Graduate female teachers was more than that of Graduate and Ph.D degree holders. Furthermore, the study finds that 3% were Professors, 3% were Associate Professors, 45% Assistant Professors, 40% Lecturers, and 9% were Teaching Assistants. It reveals that the ratio of lecturer in the study area was greater than other ranks among teachers.

Table 4. Distribution of female teachers by age and income

Variables	Mean	Median	Minimum	Maximum
Age	33.63	33.00	22	54
Income	88,491.23	75,000.00	30,000	2,00,000

Source: Field survey, 2019

Table 4 reveals that the minimum age of female teachers was 22 years while the maximum age was 54 years. The average age of female teachers in the study area came out to be 33.63 years and the median age was 33 years. The minimum income of teachers was Rs.30,000/- while the maximum income was Rs.2, 00,000/-. The average income of female teachers was Rs.88, 491.23 and the median was Rs.75, 000/-. It indicates that the majority of the female teachers were young and 50% of the female teachers with income up to 75,000/-.

Item Analysis

To find out the discriminating items for different factors of motivation and productivity at the workplace of the university female teachers in the study area item analysis is employed. Item analysis is utilized for five factors affecting motivation and productivity of university female teachers are presented in following the tables.

Table 5 shows that the t-values for all items were more than 1.75, so it can be concluded that the basic needs as regards financial incentives, current salary package, working hours, working conditions, medical, transportation and insurance benefits of almost all the female teachers were fulfilled. They were satisfied with their jobs and motivated to work for the progress of the institution. Thus, it can be concluded that the fulfillment of basic needs have a significant effect on the motivation of female teachers.

Table 5. Item analysis for basic needs

Statements	Mean of Lower 25% Scores	Mean of Upper 25% Scores	Sum of Squares of Lower 25% Scores	Sum of Squares of Upper 25% Scores	T-Values
Motivation due to financial incentives	2.29	4	23.71	30	6.41
Motivation due to current salary package	2.71	4.36	45.71	16.43	5.73
Suitability of working hours	3.11	4.11	56.68	26.68	3.01
Satisfaction with the working conditions	2.21	4.36	28.71	18.43	8.6
Satisfaction with medical, transportation and insurance benefits	2.21	4.36	28.71	22.43	8.24

Source: Field survey, 2019

Item analysis for job safety shown in Table 6 reveals that the job safety as regards satisfaction with annual holidays with pay, security at the workplace, retirement benefits, workplace being near to home and no gender discrimination, almost all the female teachers were satisfied and motivated to work for the progress of the institution. Thus, it can be concluded that job safety have significant effect on the motivation of female teachers.

Table 6. Item analysis for job safety

Statements	Mean of Lower 25% Scores	Mean of Upper 25% Scores	Sum of Squares of Lower 25% Scores	Sum of Squares of Upper 25% Scores	T Values
Satisfaction with Annual holidays with pay	3.29	4.36	37.71	12.43	4.15
Security at workplace	2.93	4.11	45.86	22.68	3.92
Satisfaction with the retirement benefits	2.61	3.64	28.68	28.43	3.77
Workplace is near to home	1.5	4.21	19	24.71	11.36
No gender discrimination at workplace	2.36	4.43	24.43	8.86	9.86

Source: Field survey, 2019

Item analysis for supervisor support concludes that with almost all the female teachers are agree with the factors of supervisor support as regards fair to all employees, satisfied from support, recognition of good work, encouragement on taking honest feedback, confidence on sharing plans, guides for professional development, motivation from supervisor's appreciation, and feeling motivation on getting rewards. They were satisfied with their supervisor and were motivated to work for the progress of the institution. Thus, it can be concluded that supervisor support had a significant effect on the motivation of female teachers.

Table 7. Item analysis for supervisor support

Statements	Mean of Lower 25% Scores	Mean of Upper 25% Scores	Sum of Squares of Lower 25% Scores	Sum of Squares of Upper 25% Scores	T Values
Supervisor Fair to all employees	1.89	4.54	14.68	20.96	12.17
Satisfied from support of supervisor	2.07	4.93	19.86	1.86	16.86
Supervisor always recognized the good work	2.21	4.93	21.43	1.86	15.84
Encouraged to take honest feedback from supervisor	2.54	4.68	26.71	6.11	9.84
Confident to share plans with supervisor	2.21	4.68	26.71	6.11	12.3
Supervisor guides for professional development	2.79	4.68	42.71	6.11	7.5
Motivated from Supervisor appreciates me	2.04	4.36	20.96	18.43	10.16
Motivated to get rewards	3.18	4.64	50.11	6.43	5.35

Source: Field survey, 2019

Table 8 shows that almost all the female teachers were agreed with family support for the motivation at the workplace as regards satisfaction with the job, salary package, support of family as a sign of motivation. They were satisfied with their family and were motivated to work for the progress of the institution. Thus, it can be concluded that family support have a significant effect on the motivation of female teachers.

Table 8. Item analysis for family support

Statements	Mean of Lower 25% Scores	Mean of upper 25% Scores	Sum of Squares of Lower 25% Scores	Sum of Squares of Upper 25% Scores	T Values
Family satisfied with job	3.11	4.89	32.68	2.68	8.25
Family satisfied with salary package	2.71	4.82	29.71	6.11	9.68
Family is the sign of motivation	3.07	4.86	45.86	5.43	6.86
Family support has a great impact	3.29	4.79	41.71	6.71	5.93

Source: Field survey, 2019

As shown in Table 9 Item analysis for self-determination, it concluded that almost all the female teachers agreed with the factors of the self-determination as regards struggle to achieve important things, use expertise to show work more valuable and work hard to get higher designation. They were satisfied and motivated to work for the progress of the institution. Thus, it can be concluded that self-determination have significant effect on the motivation of female teachers.

Table 9. Item analysis for self determination

Statements	Mean of Lower 25% Scores	Mean of Upper 25% Scores	Sum of Squares of Lower 25% Scores	Sum of Squares of Upper 25% Scores	T Values
Struggle to achieve important things	2.96	4.89	28.96	2.68	9.43
Use expertise to show work more valuable	3.07	5	33.86	0	9.12
Work hard to get higher designation	2.96	4.93	32.96	1.86	9.13

Source: Field survey, 2019

As shown in Table 10 Item analysis for the physical environment, it concluded almost all the female teachers agreed with the factors of the physical environment as regards working alone, productive and organized, finding innovative things, old established procedure, colleagues have respect for each other, away from student's noise, natural ventilation of the office room, furniture of office room, disturbance due to noise and lunch break hours almost all the teachers were satisfied. They were motivated to work for the progress of the institution. Thus, it can be concluded that the physical environment have a significant effect on the motivation of teachers.

Table 10. Item analysis for physical environment

Statements	Mean of Lower 25% Scores	Mean of Upper 25% Scores	Sum of Squares of Lower 25% Scores	Sum of Squares of Upper 25% Scores	T Values
Prefer to do work alone	2.61	3.79	24.68	44.71	5.64
Work environment makes employees productive and organized	2.75	3.96	41.25	28.96	3.98
Work environment encourages to find innovative things	2.96	3.93	42.96	33.86	3.02
In work environment everything is running according to old established procedure	3.04	3.68	48.96	34.11	1.94
Colleagues have respect for each other	3.04	4.43	46.96	12.86	4.95
Office is far away from student's noise	2.43	4.07	28.86	29.86	5.9
Satisfied with natural ventilation of office room	2.25	4.39	47.25	18.68	7.26
Satisfied with the furniture of office room	2.07	3.93	37.86	25.86	6.41
Student's noise disturbs me	2.64	3.75	40.43	49.25	3.2
Satisfied with lunch break hours	2.86	4.57	35.43	12.86	6.76

Source: Field survey, 2019

Item analysis for behavioral shown in Table 11 shows that all the female teachers agreed with the factors of behavioral level of interaction and distraction as regards: always help students, discuss their lessons, attentiveness students during lecture, knowledge of the things that going on during lecture, friendly behavior with students, visiting the office for queries, attending different events, big social circle, respecting the advice of other's point of view and conflict among colleagues. They were satisfied and were motivated to work for the progress of the institution. Thus, it can be concluded that the behavioral environment have significant effect on the motivation of female teachers.

Table 11. Item analysis for behavioral

Statements	Mean of Lower 25% Scores	Mean of Upper 25% Scores	Sum of Squares of Lower 25% Scores	Sum of Squares of Upper 25% Scores	T Values
Always help students in their work	3.68	4.82	36.11	4.11	4.95
Students easily discuss their lessons	3.75	4.86	36.11	4.11	5.02
Students are attentive during lecture	3.32	4.75	32.11	7.25	6.27
Know about the thing that goes on during lecture	3.98	4.82	36.11	4.11	4.95
Behavior with students is friendly	3.46	4.93	33	1.86	7
Students always visit office for queries	3.5	4.96	35	0.96	6.88
Always used to attend different events	3.25	4.86	17.25	5.43	9.24
Have a big social circle	3.36	4.79	36.4	8.71	5.85
Respect the advice of others	3.29	4.93	31.71	1.86	7.8
Always enquire about the point of view of the colleagues	3	4.82	30	10.11	7.9
Can recognize conflict among colleagues	3.11	4.93	20.68	1.86	10.6

Source: Field survey, 2019

As shown in Table 12 item analysis for the impact of professional development, it concludes that there was a significant effect of the factors of professional development as regards workshops, qualification program, participation in a network of female teachers, research, professional literature and engaging in informal dialogue, over the motivation and productivity of female teachers. Thus, it can be concluded that professional developments have a significant effect on the productivity of female teachers.

As shown in Table 13 Item analysis for attitude as a teacher, it can be concluded that almost all the female teachers agreed with the attitude as a teacher as regards; satisfaction with the job, making significant educational change, tackling with most difficult and unmotivated students and knowledge of the techniques of getting through the students. They were satisfied with their attitude and were motivated to work for the progress of the institution. Thus, it can be concluded that the attitude of a teacher had a significant effect on productivity.

Table 14 reveals that almost all the female teachers agreed with the factors of performance and development culture as regards female teachers feel valued and supported, prepared to take the risk and try new things, performance and development culture and needs and concerns. They were satisfied and motivated to work for the progress of the institution. Thus, it can be concluded that performance and development have a significant effect on the productivity of female teachers.

Table 12. Item analysis for impact of professional development

Statements	Mean of Lower 25% Scores	Mean of Upper 25% Scores	Sum of Squares of Lower 25% Scores	Sum of Squares of Upper 25% Scores	T Values
Courses/workshops	2.11	3.75	20.68	5.25	8.87
Qualification program	1.5	3.61	21	6.68	10.97
Participation in a network of female teachers	1.54	3.36	20.96	30.43	6.98
Research	1.54	3.71	22.96	5.71	11.2
Professional literature	2.04	3.86	40.96	5.43	7.347
Engaging in informal dialogue	2.07	3.68	43.86	12.11	5.88

Source: Field survey, 2019

Table 13. Item analysis for attitude as a teacher

Statements	Mean of Lower 25% Scores	Mean of Upper 25% Scores	Sum of Squares of Lower 25% Scores	Sum of Squares of Upper 25% Scores	T Values
Satisfied with job	3	4.86	24	3.43	9.75
Making significant educational difference in the lives of students	3.14	4.89	21.43	2.68	9.8
Can make progress with the most difficult and unmotivated students	3.25	4.89	25.25	2.68	8.5
Know that how to get through to students	3.42	4.89	24.86	2.67	7.65

Source: Field survey, 2019

Table 14. Item analysis for performance and development culture

Statements	Mean of Lower 25% Scores	Mean of Upper 25% Scores	Sum of Squares of Lower 25% Scores	Sum of Squares of Upper 25% Scores	T Values
University has a culture where female teachers feel valued and supported	2.75	4.75	45.25	7.25	7.6
Female teachers are prepared to take risk and try new things	2.79	4.54	24.71	12.96	7.84
University has a performance and development culture	2.86	4.71	39.43	5.71	7.6
University responsible for needs and concerns	2.43	4.71	26.86	7.71	10.75

Source: Field survey, 2019

Item analysis for workplace satisfaction shown in Table 15 interprets that almost all the female teachers agreed with the factors of workplace as regards basic needs, job safety, supervisor support, family support, self-motivation, physical work environment, behavioral work environment, professional development, attitude as a teacher and performance and development culture. They were satisfied and motivated to work for the progress of the institution. Thus, it can be concluded that workplace satisfaction have a significant effect on the productivity of female teachers.

Table 15. Item analysis for workplace satisfaction

Statements	Mean of Lower 25% Scores	Mean of Upper 25% Scores	Sum of Squares of Lower 25% Scores	Sum of Squares of Upper 25% Scores	T Values
Basic needs	2.79	4.64	26.71	16.43	7.8
Job safety	2.89	4.64	28.68	18.4	7
Supervisor support	2.75	4.46	29.25	25	6.38
Family support	3.68	4.71	42.11	9.71	3.93
Self -motivation	3.57	4.86	38.86	5.43	5.2
Physical work environment	2.96	4.71	26.96	9.71	7.94
Behavioral work environment	2.75	4.82	31.25	6.107	9.3
Professional development	3.72	4.57	18.11	16.86	6.5
Attitude as a teacher	3.25	4.86	33.25	3.43	7.3
Performance and development culture	2.96	4.64	36.96	12.42	6.57

Source: Field survey, 2019

From the analysis, it is found that most of the female teachers got motivation from the underlying five factors and most of them wanted to involve themselves in more professional development. Through the descriptive analysis it is found that the motivation and productivity of teachers of the University of Haripur are significantly affected by the factors. According to Aiyetan and Olotuah (2006), the most motivating factors are self-determination and increases in income these could lead towards higher productivity of the organization. Motivated teachers are productive, when female teachers of any institute are motivated and productive at their workplace then they will produce the efficient products.

CONCLUSION

The study broadly focuses on the factors affecting the motivation and productivity of the female teachers at the workplace. Besides the study also explores the demographic features of the respondents and the interrelationship of the significant factors affecting female teachers' performance. Using primary data and several methods, this paper finds some interesting results.

Firstly, this paper finds that the ratio of regular female teachers was more than contract staff. Most of the female teachers got motivation from self-determination who believed in themselves. Secondly, female teachers also motivated by their supervisor and family support which implies that if the supervisor and family have supportive behavior they can do their work with full attention and interest. Teachers also motivated by their work environment. Thirdly, the findings of this paper reveals that the productivity of female teachers depends on the attitude of a teacher. The study also discusses different factors having effects on motivation and productivity of female teachers at the workplace. Since motivation is an encouragement for the female teachers and through motivation productivity of the workplace can enhance. For extracting higher output, the supervisor should support their employees and increase salaries of employees could also lead the institute towards the horizon.

Based on the findings, the study recommends that providing the satisfactory working environment, handsome salaries, good motivation to the female teachers are the effective tools to improve their performance. Since time and budget were limited, the study was carried out in a particular area. Thus, this paper suggests researchers to carry out further study for exploring the pros and cons of this issue. Moreover, the paper expects that these findings may be the well representative to take policies in improving female teachers' performance not only in the study area but also at the national level.

ACKNOWLEDGMENT

This paper has not received any grants from any government and non-government organizations. However, authors of this paper are duly acknowledged to BK School of Research for providing technical supports.

REFERENCES

Abbasi, M. N., Malik, A., Chaudhry, I. S., & Imdadullah, M. (2011). A study on student satisfaction in Pakistani universities: The case of Bahauddin Zakariya University, Pakistan. *Asian Social Science*, *7*(7), 209. doi:10.5539/ass.v7n7p209

Akhtar, J. H., & Iqbal, I. (2017). Impact of motivation on teachers' job performance: A case study of a public sector university. *Journal of Educational and Social Research*, *4*(1), 53–71.

Alhaji, I. A. (2012). Does motivational factor influence organizational commitment and effectiveness? A review of literature. *E3 Journal of Business Management and Economics, 3*(1), 1-9.

Arif, B., & Farooqi, Y. A. (2014). Impact of work life balance on job satisfaction and organizational commitment among university teachers: A case study of University of Gujrat, Pakistan. *International Journal of Multidisciplinary Sciences and Engineering, 5*(9), 24-29.

Awang, Z., Ahmad, J. H., & Zin, N. M. (2010). Modelling job satisfaction and work commitment among lecturers: A case of UiTM Kelantan. *Journal of Statistical Modeling and Analytics*, *1*(2), 45–59.

Chandrasekar, K. (2011). Workplace environment and its impact on organizational performance in public sector organizations. *International Journal of Enterprise Computing and Business Systems, 1*(1), 1-19.

Cristini, A. (2011, October). *Employees' motivation and high performance workplace practices.* In European Economic Association and Econometric Society. 2011 Parallel Meetings, Malaga, Spain.

Danish, R. Q., & Usman, A. (2010). Impact of reward and recognition on job satisfaction and motivation: An empirical study from Pakistan. *International Journal of Business and Management*, *5*(2), 159. doi:10.5539/ijbm.v5n2p159

Fatima, N., & Sahibzada, S. A. (2012). An empirical analysis of factors affecting work life balance among university teachers: The case of Pakistan. *Journal of International Academic Research*, *12*(1), 16–29.

Forson, M., & Essel, J. (2012). *Impact of motivation on the productivity of employees at GTBank Ghana* (Doctoral dissertation).

Hardré, P. L., & Kollmann, S. L. (2012). Motivational implications of faculty performance standards. *Educational Management Administration & Leadership, 40*(6), 724–751. doi:10.1177/1741143212456913

Inuwa, M. (2016). Job satisfaction and employee performance: An empirical approach. *The Millennium University Journal, 1*(1), 90–103.

Jaskiewicz, W., & Tulenko, K. (2012). Increasing community health worker productivity and effectiveness: A review of the influence of the work environment. *Human Resources for Health, 10*(1), 38. doi:10.1186/1478-4491-10-38 PMID:23017131

Kwapong, L. S. A., Opoku, E., & Donyina, F. (2015). The effect of motivation on the performance of teaching staff in ghanaian polytechnics: The moderating role of education and research experience. *International Journal of Education and Research, 3*(11), 35–48.

Leblebici, D. (2012). Impact of workplace quality on employee's productivity: Case study of a bank in Turkey. *Journal of Business. Economics, 1*(1), 38–49.

Marufa, E., & Uzhenyu, D. (2017). Motivation of university academic staff in zimbabwe. a case study of Zimbabwe open university (2009 – 2014). *IOSR Journal of Business and Management, 19*(9), 78–86.

Nabi, M. N., Islam, M. M., Dip, T. M., & Hossain, M. A. (2017). Impact of motivation on employee performances: A case study of Karmasangsthan Bank Limited, Bangladesh. *Arabian Journal of Business and Management Review, 7*(1), 1–8.

Nadim, M., Chaudhry, M. S., Kalyar, M. N., & Riaz, T. (2012). Effects of motivational factors on teachers' job satisfaction: A study on public sector degree colleges of Punjab, Pakistan. *The Journal of Commerce, 4*(4), 25.

Naqvi, S. M. H., Khan, M. A., Kant, A. Q., & Khan, S. N. (2013). Job stress and employees' productivity: Case of Azad Kashmir public health sector. *Interdisciplinary Journal of Contemporary Research in Business, 5*(3), 525–542.

Nisar, A., Zafar, M. I., Mahmood, B., Sohail, M. M., Sher, F., & Safdar, M. R. (2012). Pay benefits and workplace milieu effecting job satisfaction level of university teachers: A case study of Punjab University. *International Journal of Asian Social Science, 2*(10), 1815–1831.

Nwakasi, C. C., & Cummins, P. A. (2018). Teacher motivation and job satisfaction: A case study of north west Nigeria. *Global Jurnal of Educational Research, 17*(2), 103–112. doi:10.4314/gjedr.v17i2.2

Rasheed, M. I., Aslam, H. D., & Sarwar, S. (2010). Motivational issues for teachers in higher education: A critical case of IUB. *Journal of Management Research, 2*(2), 1. doi:10.5296/jmr.v2i2.349

Rashid, S., & Rashid, U. (2012). Work motivation differences between public and private sector. *American International Journal of Social Science, 1*(2), 24–33.

Santo, S. A., Engstrom, M. E., Reetz, L., Schweinle, W. E., & Reed, K. (2009). Faculty productivity barriers and supports at a school of education. *Innovative Higher Education*, *34*(2), 117–129. doi:10.100710755-009-9098-z

Sommerfeldt, V. (2010). *An identification of factors influencing police workplace motivation* (Doctoral dissertation). Queensland University of Technology.

Viseu, J., Jesus, S. N. D., Rus, C., Canavarro, J. M., & Pereira, J. (2016). Relationship between teacher motivation and organizational variables: A literature review. *Systematic Literature Review*, *26*(63), 111–120.

Chapter 12
International Remittances, Household Welfare, and Women Empowerment:
Evidence From Bangladesh

Bezon Kumar
https://orcid.org/0000-0003-4489-431X
Rabindra University, Bangladesh

Syed Rashid Ali
https://orcid.org/0000-0002-7234-2371
Department of Economics, University of Karachi, Pakistan

Md. Golam Kibria
https://orcid.org/0000-0001-9976-1114
Noakhali Science and Technology University, Bangladesh

ABSTRACT

This chapter explores the impact of international remittances on household welfare and women empowerment in Bangladesh. In doing so, primary data and several methods are used. Firstly, this chapter constructs a household welfare index and women empowerment index to measure the level of household welfare and women empowerment, respectively. Secondly, this chapter uses a one-way ANOVA test to analyze respondents' socio-economic features. Finally, linear regression is applied to examine the impact of international remittances on household welfare. This study finds that international remittances have an influence on household welfare improvement but no influence on women empowerment in the study area. This chapter also finds that if a household receives international remittances, the level of household welfare may be increased by Tk. 3167.49. Therefore, this chapter calls for the policies for larger inflows of remittances and its proper utilization in productive purposes.

DOI: 10.4018/978-1-7998-3737-4.ch012

INTRODUCTION

The mobility of human beings is the fact of life. People move to survive sometimes voluntarily and sometimes by force and this movement is called migration. People who migrate are called migrants. Migration may be happened both within and outside the country. The basic decision of a person's migration is made by many reasons like unemployment, nepotism, religion, racial clash, law and order situation, desire to uplift the standard of living, and so on (Todaro and Smith, 2012). These migrants are now living and working abroad and sending their earnings to their families in home countries either in the form of goods or cash, known as remittance (Kumar et al. 2018). Bangladesh is one of the largest labor exporting countries which exports huge human resources abroad and receives remittances every year. The wave of migration from Bangladesh started in the 1970s when countries from the Gulf region started for looking toward cheap labor exporting countries. According to the Household Income and Expenditure Survey 2010, about 8.7 million households depend on remittances in Bangladesh. This remittance helps households in many ways. It generates employment opportunities, empowers women, increases savings and investment rates, improves the balance of payments, and reduces poverty, and so on (Kumar, 2019c; Adams, 2005 and Bruyan 2005). Remittance in Bangladesh is utilized on consumption, investment, or savings and for charity or community initiatives which plays a crucial role in improving the standard of living. However, the relationship between international remittances and household welfare (household consumption expenditure) is not clear in Bangladesh's perspective stated in Figure 1.

Figure 1. Relationship between remittances and consumption expenditure
Source: World Development Indicator

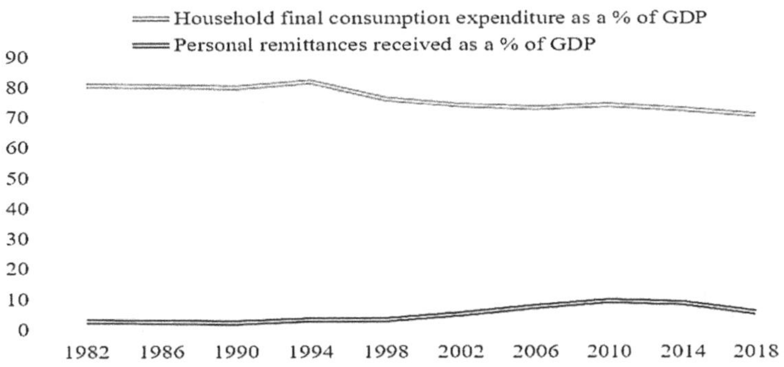

Figure 1 reveals that both remittances and consumption expenditure remain the same until 1995. From 1995, consumption expenditure starts to decrease at a little bit rate while remittance starts to increase. Beyond, 2014 both remittance and household consumption expenditure starts to fall again where the rate of falling of remittances is greater than that of consumption expenditure. This scenario reveals that there is no specific directional relationship between remittances and household consumption expenditure. Therefore, an empirical investigation is required to carry out on this issue.

Welfare is an arguable issue because many countries required some kind of indicator to measure their economic, social, cultural, and environmental progress in the world. Many studies have used gross domestic product (GDP) to measure only economic activity of a country (Costanza et al., 2009 and Stiglitz et al., 2010) because the gross domestic product was never intended to quantify social or monetary welfare but nowadays it is the most generally used indicator for representing human welfare (Marcuss and Kane, 2007). There is considerable evidence in the economic literature that remittances are the direct link of economic welfare in the home country.

In the new economics of labor migration, Taylor (1999) argued that migration is the plan of a household for different income enhancing strategies, and remittance is the tool that helps the household to overcome income reducing difficulties. Remittance also creates a multiplier effect on income, employment, and production in the home countries. International remittances also influence the power of taking deciding for women in the absence of a man of the family. Here is the era of women empowerment. Most of the countries of the world are now empowering their women by involving them in decision making. Women empowerment refers to increasing the spiritual, political, social, educational, gender, or economic strength of individuals and communities of women (Narayan, 2002). Women empowerment has five components: women's sense of self-help; their right to have and determine choices; their right to have access to opportunities and resources; their right to have the power to control their own lives, both within and outside the home; and their ability to influence the direction of social change to create more just social and economic order, nationally and internationally.

The role of remittance for women's empowerment and wellbeing got much attention in recent days. People from all walks of life emphasize the importance of women's role in social welfare, social discipline, politics, economic stability, and remittances have the potential to transform the economic role of women, within the household and the larger community. Figure 2 shows the behavior of various indicators of Bangladeshi women concerning remittances. As remittances increases, Bangladeshi women's participation in industrial and services sectors are increasing and there is a declining trend in the agricultural sector while numbers of women employers remain stable. This trend confirms the positive impact of remittances on the economic, social, and political lives of Bangladeshi women.

Figure 2. Remittances and women empowerment indicators in Bangladesh (1991-2019)
Source: World Development Indicator

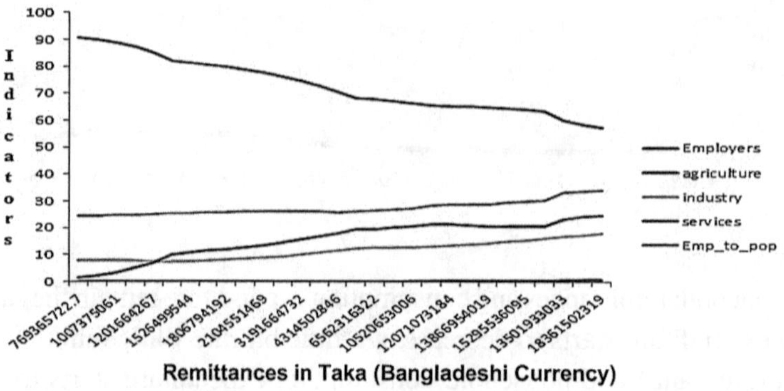

According to the International Organization for Migration, remittances help to increase women's participation in household financial decision-making processes. Men are more interested to invest the remittance money while women spend most of this foreign money on consumption, education, or the health of family members, especially on children.

Many studies confirm the positive effect of remittances on economic and social welfare in Bangladesh. The huge flow of remittances helps Bangladesh in reducing poverty and unemployment, improving foreign exchange reserves, the condition of balance of payment, and social status. GDP's role in establishing a distinction between the positive effects of welfare and the negative effects of welfare is ambiguous (Talberth et al., 2007). So many new indexes have been developed which are an alternative to GDP to adjust these shortcomings in human welfare measurement even some studies proposed a series of indicators instead of relying on just one indicator (Smith et al., 2013).

Nowadays, it is observed that household welfare is being measured by per capita household expenditure due to the non-availability of proper welfare measuring index or formula (Abbas et al., 2014 and Raihan, et al., 2009). However, the present study is different in a way that it is the first research in which a newly constructed welfare index is used to measure household welfare. At the same time, most of the studies have measured women empowerment by considering either social or economic aspects while this paper measures considering both aspects. Broadly speaking, the core contribution of this study is that it measures the household welfare and women empowerment using newly constructed welfare index and women empowerment index, respectively. Besides, this paper explores the impact of international remittances on household welfare. This paper may be helpful for the researchers and policymakers to measure household welfare and women empowerment and to implement the policies to improve household welfare and women empowerment by international remittances.

LITERATURE REVIEW

There is an increasing trend in the economic literature to evaluate the welfare effects of remittances. Many studies confirm that remittances are necessary for the economic and social uplift of households left behind. Remittances are either used as consumption or investment. After consumption, remittances are mainly utilized as an investment in education, livestock, farming, and cottage industries. Similarly, the migrant family is benefited by remittances because remittances are a sizable source of revenue for the families left behind.

Some studies have revealed that remittance has a positive effect on household asset accumulation and household welfare (Kumar, 2019a, and Kangmennaang et al., 2018). The degree of influence is much higher for international remittances compared to internal remittances although internal and external remittances have a significant influence on poverty reduction, increasing consumption expenditure (Wadood and Hossain, 2017). At the same time, the study also reveals that remittances do not influence education and health care. Ahmed et al. (2018) showed that the inflow of international remittances made positive and significant changes in the household economic situation and household expenditure which interprets that that international remittances have positive and significant impacts on household welfare. Similarly, Haider et al. (2016) indicated that remittance has a statistically significant positive impact on attributing food and aggregate consumption expenditure in addition to savings behavior in the selected rural areas of the south-west region of Bangladesh. Interesting findings have been found by Cuong and Linh (2018) that migration does not affect household welfare but remittance has.

Many studies report the positive impact of remittance on poverty reduction (Kumar, 2019c, and Adams, 2005). Adams (2005) reported a strong positive association between remittances and poverty reduction. They analyzed the 74 low and middle-income countries and found that on average 1.97 percent poverty reduction if remittances increase on average by 10 percent. Some studies find remittances and income equalities have both positive and negative relationships. On the other hand, Kumar (2019b) explained that international remittances have a negative and significant impact on education while international remittances have positive and significant on health. On the other hand, Adam (2005) found that healthcare and educational expenditure increases in the household of international migrants. Indeed remittances and welfare are positively related as discussed by Koc and Onan (2001). Their study examined the remittances and welfare association in Turkey and finds a direct association between remittances and household welfare. This study also confirms the direct and indirect effects of income on production, income inequality, and poverty. They conclude that 80% of remittances are being used for the improvement of their living standard in Turkey. Remittances are also a source of income for saving and investment. Remittances help meeting up the basic needs for food and cash. It also serves as a payment for irrigation and other agricultural needs.

Remittance has been a key driver of economic wellbeing and poverty reduction in Bangladesh. The migrants send back billions of dollars which is also beneficial to the families. Remittance plays a persuasive role in socio-economic development and enhancing human welfare in developing countries. Remittance enables Bangladesh to reduce poverty and to achieve sustainable development. Bruyan, (2005) also confirmed that remittance increases the personal saving and investment capabilities of Bangladeshi people. Kapur (2004) examined the welfare effect of remittances on Bangladeshi households. The study finds remittance as an influencing tool to smooth consumption, reduce poverty, investment in real estate, investment in capital stock, and education. These are all long term implications of economic welfare. Mustafa and Ali (2018) concluded that the economic performance of home countries has a positive impact on remittance which creates a welfare effect in the home country. Similarly, Kumar et al. (2018) exhibited that remittances of Bangladeshi migrants utilize mostly on household food consumption. Hildebbrandt and Mckenzie (2005) showed that in Mexican migrant households, there is a high birth-weights and lower infant mortality ratio. But this study also confirms that Mexican migrant children have less healthcare preventative opportunities than non-migrant households. Kumar (2019a) found that the average gross per capita expenditure of remittance-receiving households is three times higher than that of non-recipient households which interprets that recipient households enjoy a higher level of welfare.

The remittances have proven to be the beneficial flow of income to migrant's family members who left behind and this foreign money is used as consumption and different types of investment purposes. Many studies confirmed that remittances are positively related to poverty reduction, education enrolment, growth, saving and investment, and the BOP situation in Bangladesh (Kumar, 2019c and Chowdhury, 2011). According to the Global Economic Prospects, remittance has decreased the poverty headcount ratio by 6 points in Bangladesh during 1990-2006 (Barua, et al., 2007). Besides, Kumar (2019c) proved that the probability of a household being poor is alleviated by 28.07 percent if the household receives remittance. Fakir and Abedin (2020) studied the nature of Bangladeshi women empowerment when primary male migrated and find that migration of the primary male, on average, empowers the women left behind, by providing them with opportunities to manage assets, finances, and the right to exercise greater physical autonomy. Remittances are also a source of investment for the families left behind. Many emigrant wives invest remittances money in income-generating activities to earn some extra money for rainy days (Ramirez et al. 2005) even in Bangladeshi context; migrant husband discusses the different family matter and social-economic issues with their wives who left behind which shows the women empowerment in a family context (Debnath and Selim 2009). Mahapatro et al. (2017) found that remittance-receiving families prefer to use this foreign money on education and health care instead

Figure 3. Indicators of measuring women empowerment in Bangladesh
Source: Adopted from Hashemi et al (1996)

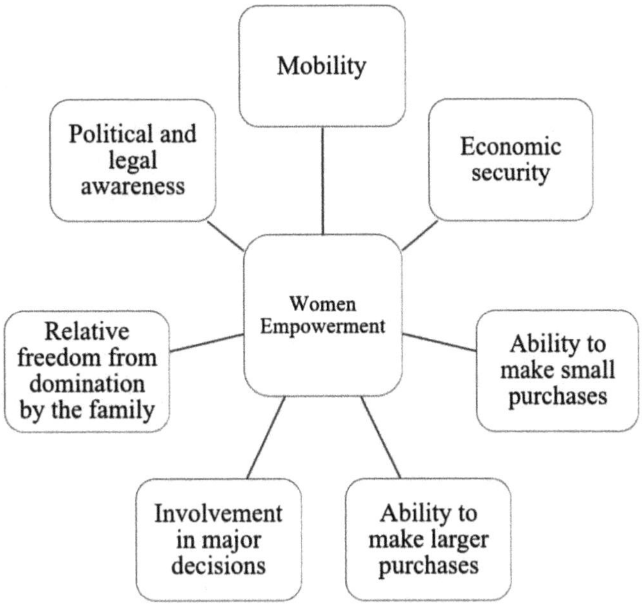

of food consumption in India. They further confirm that remittance and development have a positive relationship which proves that remittances enhance household well-being. Hashemi et al (1996) used eight indicators to measure women empowerment of Bangladesh as depicted in Figure 3.

Ullah (2017) described the relationship between remittances and families left behind. This study discussed how women being empowered financially, socially, and politically by using different indicators like women's position, human development outcome of the left-behind family members, gender, and intra-household relationship. The study confirms that women, in the absence of her husband, make decisions and this capacity and freedom make them empowered. Hadi (2001) explained that women have more controlling and deciding positions in family issues which are less prevalent in the male-dominated society. The migration transfers the secular views which also change the women's position in the male-dominated or traditional society. These foreign adopted views bring changes in the traditional position of women and make them empowered by doing jobs, mobility, getting better health care, reproductive decision, and child education.

Keeping in view the literature, this study is organized to assess the impact of international remittances on household welfare and women empowerment in Bangladesh.

DATA AND METHODS

This study mainly uses primary data that are collected from *the Naogaon* district of Bangladesh. The rationale for selecting this district as the study area is that every year many people of this district migrate abroad searching for better livelihoods and sends remittances to their families. However, there is no particular research on the impact on international remittances on household welfare and women empowerment in *the Naogaon* district of Bangladesh. For selecting samples, this paper employs a multi-stage random sampling technique. There are 11 police stations in this district from which *Atrai* and *Raninagar* police stations are selected randomly. From each police station, two unions are selected. In the next step, from each union three villages are selected. In this stage, the total number of remittance recipient and non-recipient households of the selected villages are collected from each union council office. Finally, twenty percent of households from both types of household heads from each village are selected randomly for interview. In this way, a total of 408 household heads and chief female family members are interviewed face to face from June to August 2019 with a well-structured questionnaire. The distribution of the sample is presented in the following table.

Table 1. The distribution of sample by village

Police Station	Union	Village	Remittance Recipient Households		Remittance Non-recipient Households	
			Population	Sample	Population	Sample
Atrai	Bhopara	Bhopara	78	15	114	23
		Tilabodury	65	13	110	22
		Teghory	35	7	95	19
	Panchupur	Panchupur	88	18	124	25
		Gurnoi	38	8	88	18
		Biharipur	45	9	105	21
Raninagar	Bargacha	Bargacha	60	12	119	24
		Gohelapur	45	9	109	22
		Malsun	79	16	120	24
	Mirat	Mirat	72	14	125	25
		Dhonpara	66	13	136	27
		Ataikula	28	6	94	18
Total number of sample				140		268

After collection, data are checked, sorted, and edited, and finally used for analysis. Data are analyzed through MS Excel 2010, SPSS 23, and Stata 14.2.

DESCRIPTIVE ANALYSIS

Before analyzing the impact of international remittances on household welfare, this paper analyzes the descriptive statistics of the socio-economic features of sampled households. To analyze descriptive statistics, this paper applies the One Way ANOVA test, and findings are presented in tabular and graphical form.

Measurement of Household Welfare

Although many scholars have measured household welfare ever before, most of them have used the per capita household consumption expenditure directly as a proxy variable of a household which predicts crude results (Kumar, 2019a; Raihan et al., 2009 and Abbas et al. 2014). Therefore, this paper has constructed a new welfare index having five components. This index is the simple arithmetic mean of five distinct components of household consumption expenditure. The formula of household welfare is stated as follows.

$$HW = \frac{1}{12}\left(\frac{EF + ENF + EH + EE + EI}{N}\right) \tag{1}$$

Where,

HW = Household welfare
EF = Expenditure on food (Tk. /year)
ENF = Expenditure on non-food (Tk. /year)
EH= Expenditure on housing (Tk. /year)
EE= Expenditure on education (Tk. /year)
EI= Expenditure on investment (Tk. /year)
N = Household size
12 = Number of months in a year

The above formula gives the level of household welfare or household per capita expenditure per month. The higher the value of the index reveals the higher the level of welfare and vice versa.

Women Empowerment Index

To measure the impact of international remittances on women empowerment, this paper constructs a women empowerment index newly which measures the empowerment among the women of remittance recipient and non-recipient households in the study area. This index is constructed with ten distinct indicators following Sultana, et al. (2013) and Mahmud, et al. (2012). The indicators of the index reveal that women of a household take the decision in the followings- working outside home for money, buying furniture, spending family savings, using contraceptives, having children, visiting doctor for self, taking a loan, visiting father's house, having children's education and visiting doctor for the children. These indicators are measured with five points likert scale such as strongly disagree = 1, disagree = 2, neither agree nor disagree = 3, agree = 4, and strongly agree = 5. The women empowerment index is measured through the following formula.

$$WEI = \frac{\sum_{i=1}^{\nu} R_i}{ST} \tag{2}$$

Where,

WEI = women empowerment index,

R_i = rating given by the students to a particular indicator,

S = maximum rate of the likert scale (here it is 5) and

T = total number of indicators (here it is 10).

The estimated value of the women empowers the index ranges from 0 to 1. In this study, the value ranges from 0 to 0.50 is assigned a lower level of empowerment while value ranges from 0.51 to 0.75 and 0.76 to 1.00 are assigned as a medium and higher level of empowerment, respectively.

Linear Regression Analysis

After being informed with the level of household welfare, this paper estimates the extent to which international remittances impact household welfare. In doing so, this paper formulates a linear functional relationship between household welfare and a set of explanatory variables. Equation 3 states that relationship as follows:

$$HW_i = f(P_i) \tag{3}$$

Where, $HW_{i,}$ dependent variable, is household welfare and P_i is a set of explanatory variables that affect the dependent variable. As the dependent variable is continuous, the paper applies a linear regression model estimated through OLS method following Raihan, et al. (2009) and Abbas, et al. (2014). Econometrically the equation 3 can be formed as:

$$HW_i = \delta P_i + \varepsilon_i \tag{4}$$

More specifically, the Equation 4 can be written as:

$$HW_i = \delta_0 + \delta_1 EDU + \delta_2 HHS + \delta_3 OCP + \delta_4 ILS + \delta_5 LNS + \delta_6 PCI + \delta_7 REM + \varepsilon_i \tag{5}$$

Where, HW_i is household welfare measured by the household welfare index, δ_0.....δ_7 are parameters to be estimated and ϵ_i is the stochastic disturbance term. The explanatory variables used in regression model are explained in Table 2 which have been adopted from earlier literature.

RESULTS AND DISCUSSION

Socio-economic and Demographic Features of Households

This section presents the socio-economic and demographic features such as education, household size, occupation, income from livestock, land size, per capita income and per capita expenditure of remittance recipient and non-recipient households. These features are analyzed with a one way ANOVA test to check the statistically significant variation in different features by different categories of households. This test is performed through SPSS 23.00 and the result is presented in the following table.

Table 3 shows that the mean years of education of remittance recipient households' heads are 4.76 years while it is 5.31 years for non-recipient households and this variation is statistically significant at 5 percent level of significance. On the other hand, it is found that household size is higher for remittance non-recipient households than compared to recipient households and this variation is significant at 5 percent level of significance. Like education and household size, income from livestock, land size, per capita income, and per capita expenditure are also statistically significant. Contrarily, occupation is statistically insignificant. The table also shows that per capita expenditure is higher for remittance recipient households than that of non-recipient households and the variation is significant at 1 percent level of significance. This variation explains that remittances have a significant influence on household welfare.

Table 2. Description of explanatory variables used in regression model

Name of Variables	Type	Measurement	Expected Sign
Education (EDU)	Continuous	Schooling of household head (years)	+
Household size (HHS)	Continuous	Total number of family members	-
Occupation (OCP)	Dummy	1 if the profession of household head is non-agricultural, otherwise 0	+
Income from livestock (ILS)	Continuous	Monthly income of the household from livestock (Tk.)	+
Land size (LNS)	Continuous	Total amount of cultivable land (*bighas* = 33.33 decimals)	+
Per capita income (PCI)	Continuous	Monthly per capita income of household (Tk.)	+
Remittance (REM)	Dummy	1 if the household receives international remittances, otherwise 0	+

Table 3. Features of remittance recipient and non-recipient households

Variables	Mean		F	Sig.
	Remittance Recipient Households	Remittance Non-recipient Households		
Education**	4.76	5.31	3.23	0.032
Household size**	5.18	5.05	2.76	0.050
Occupation (non-agriculture)	0.29	0.31	0.12	0.193
Income from livestock*	2760.12	5670.87	11.31	0.025
Land size**	4.57	3.67	7.22	0.031
Per capita income*	9435.21	4972.77	41.22	0.000
Per capita expenditure*	3553.12	2133.57	51.39	0.001

Note: * and ** means 1 and 5 percent level of significance
Source: Field survey, 2019

Sector-wise Distribution of Household Expenditure

For meeting up their needs, both the remittance recipient and non-recipient households expense their annual income in different sectors like food, non-food, housing, education, health, and investment. The percentage distribution of sector-wise household expenditure per year is presented in Figure 4.

Figure 4. Percentage distribution of sector-wise household expenditure
Source: Field survey, 2019

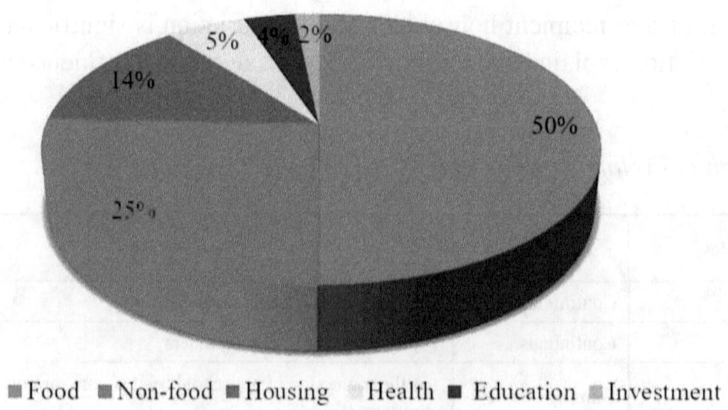

Figure 4 shows that households in the study area expense 50 percent of their total household expenditure for the consumption of food purposes only. Secondly, households expense on non-food sectors which is 25 percent of their total annual household expenditure. Despite expensing in the education sector is quite important for their benefit, the expense only 4 percent of their total annual expenditure while they expense 14 percent in the housing sector. From this figure, it is also found that households in the study area expense least in investment sectors which only 2 percent. These findings reveal that a majority of the expenditure is expensed for consumption purposes and remittance is not utilizing in productive purposes like an investment in the business, farm, buying vehicles, child's education, and so on. If the remittance is utilized in such productive purposes, it would be more beneficial for enhancing household welfare.

Level of Household Welfare

The level of household welfare is measured by the household welfare index. The estimated findings are presented in the following table which shows the percentage of households concerning different levels of household welfare (monthly per capita household expenditure). Table 4 reveals that most of the remittance recipient households (47.56%) enjoys a moderate level of household welfare while most of the remittance non-recipient households (42.67%) enjoys a lower level of household welfare.

Table 4 also reveals that the percentage of households enjoying a higher level of welfare is greater for the remittance recipient group than the remittance non-recipient group. From Table 4, it is also found that the majority of households (41.48%) in the study area enjoy a moderate level of household welfare. This scenario reveals that international remittances have a significant influence on household welfare. These findings can be interpreted by the fact that remittance recipient households can expense more on buying their basic needs with remittances results in a higher level of household welfare of the remittances recipient households.

Table 4. Level of household welfare

Levels of Welfare	Households in Percentage		
	Remittance Recipient	Remittance Non-recipient	Total
Lower level (Tk. 2500 and below)	19.14	42.67	34.60
Moderate level (Tk. 2500 to Tk. 5000)	47.56	38.30	41.48
Higher level (Tk. 5001 and above)	33.30	19.03	23.92

Source: Field survey, 2019

Level of Women Empowerment

The level of women empowerment is measured by the women empowerment index. The estimated findings are presented in the following table which shows the percentage of women for different levels of empowerment.

Table 5. Level of women empowerment

Levels of Empowerment	Women in Percentage		
	Remittance Recipient	Remittance Non-recipient	Total
Lower level (0.50 and below)	58.69	44.70	49.48
Medium level (0.51 to 0.75)	25.61	36.29	32.51
Higher level (0.76 and above)	15.70	19.01	18.01

Source: Field survey, 2019

Table 5 reveals that most of the women in the study area have a lower level of empowerment. Between two groups of women, women from remittance recipient households (58.69 percent) are more in the lower level of empowerment than that of remittance non-recipient households (44.70 percent). Contrarily, the percentage of women from remittance non-recipient households are higher in a medium and higher level of empowerment that remittance recipient households. The above table also shows that the majority of women (49.48 percent) in the study area have a lower level of empowerment. This paper finds that international remittance does not influence women's empowerment. These findings can be interpreted by the fact that most of the migrant households are poor and their literacy rate is relatively lower than non-migrant households. As a result, women from non-migrant households are more able to take decisions in their daily life activities than that of women from migrant households.

Impact of International Remittances on Household Welfare

The linear regression model for measuring the extent to what international remittances impact on household welfare is analyzed with Stata 14.2 and the result is presented in Table 6.

Table 6. Impact of international remittances on household welfare

Variables	Coefficient	Robust Std. Err.	t-Ratio	P>|t|
Constant	1052.85	923.55	1.14	0.27
Education***	1807.76	789.41	2.29	0.00
Household size	-604.19	622.88	-0.97	0.46
Occupation	297.77	192.11	1.55	0.04
Income from livestock***	762.86	169.15	4.51	0.01
Land*	1687.25	286.46	5.89	0.06
Per capita income**	1422.85	364.83	3.90	0.02
Remittance***	3167.49	748.82	4.23	0.00

F (7, 400) = 27.17; Prob > F = 0.000; R^2 = 0.89; Root MSE = 2261.3; DW = 1.97
Note: ***, ** and * means 1%, 5% and 10% level of significance.
Source: Field survey, 2019

Table 6 shows that the value of R^2 is 0.89 indicates that explanatory variables of the model explain the dependent variable by 89 percent. Elsewhere, the F-statistic value is 22.17 with Prob>F = 0.000 brings out that the model is completely good at fitted. This paper takes robust standard error action for clarifying the heteroscedasticity problem in the data. The study also exercises VIF to detect multicollinearity problems and explicitly reveals a negative result. The Durbin Watson test (DW = 1.97) expresses that no autocorrelation problem exists in the model. The study finds that all variables exhibit the expected signs while education, income from livestock, land, per capita income, and remittance are statistically significant.

The estimated coefficient of education is 1807.76 which exhibits that the welfare or monthly per capita household expenditure may be increased by Tk. 1807.76 if the level of education of household head is increased by one year. This finding is statistically significant at 1 percent level of significance. The dynamic explanation may be that the higher level of education of household head enhances the level of consciousness about of family's betterment. As a result, households expense more in productive purposes and enjoy better welfare.

The monthly per capita household expenditure or welfare may be increased by Tk. 762.86 if a unit of income from the livestock of the households and this finding statistically significant at a 1 percent level of significance. The interpretation may be that households can expense more in household consumption purposes when they earn more income from livestock cultivation like cow, goat, buffalo, and ship. A similar finding is found by Abbas, et al. (2014) and Raihan, et al. (2009).

Similarly, the monthly per capita household expenditure may be increased by Tk. 1687.25 if the household head holds an extra unit of land. This finding is significant at 10 percent level of significance and can be interpreted by the fact that households with large size of land can produce crops, vegetables, fisheries, and livestock. This can build a strong basement for household expenditure.

This paper also finds that the level of household welfare may be increased by Tk. 1422.85 if the household's per capita income is increased by one unit. This is significant at a 5 percent significance level and the interpretation may be that households with high per capita income can expense more in different purposes like food, non-food, housing, education, health treatment, and investment. The result is in line with Abbas, et al. (2014) and Raihan, et al. (2009).

The coefficient of remittance reveals that the level of household welfare may be increased by Tk. 3167.49 if a household receives international remittances which are significant at a 1 percent level of significance. The rational explanation may be that remittance recipient households can easily meet their basic needs and can invest in productive purposes also with the blessings of remittance. Abbas, et al. (2014) and Raihan, et al. (2009) found a similar finding.

CONCLUSION AND POLICY RECOMMENDATIONS

The study mainly focuses on three distinct questions. First, what is the level of welfare among remittance recipient and non-recipient households? Second, what is the level of empowerment among women of remittance recipient and non-recipient households? Third, what is the impact of international remittances on household welfare? To find out the answer to these questions, this paper uses primary data are collected from 408 households and several statistical and econometric methods, and finds three interesting findings.

First, this paper finds that most of the households (41.48 percent) enjoy a moderate level of welfare. Besides, this paper also finds that the rate of households enjoying a higher level of welfare is greater for remittance recipient households than remittance non-recipient households. This emanates that international remittances have a significant impact on household welfare. This paper also finds that households in the study area expense about 50 percent of their total household expenditure only in the consumption of food purposes while 2 percent in investment purposes. This reveals that households are not utilizing expenditure or remittances in productive purposes like an investment in business and farming. Second, this paper finds that the majority of the women (49.48 percent) in the study area have a lower level of empowerment. Moreover, it is found that the percentage of women from remittance non-recipient households is greater in a moderate and higher level of empowerment. This emanates that international remittances do not influence women's empowerment. Third, this study finds that if a household receives international remittances, the welfare of that household may be increased by Tk. 3167.49.

Therefore, this paper calls for policymakers to consider international remittances as an effective tool to enhance household welfare in Bangladesh. Since the time and budget for this study was limited, the study area and sample size were small. Thus, this paper also suggests to carry out further study on it broadly so that the findings may be more general.

ACKNOWLEDGMENT

This study has not taken any grants from any government and non-government organizations. However, authors are duly acknowledged to BK School of Research for providing technical and software assistance.

REFERENCES

Abbas, K., Sabir, H. M., Shehzadi, A., & Abbas, Q. (2014). Impact of Workers' Remittances on Household Welfare in District Jhang (A Case Study of Tehsil 18 Hazari). *Journal of Financial Economics, 2*, 131–135.

Adams, H. R. (2005). *Remittances, household expenditures and investment in Guatemala.* World Bank Policy Research Working Paper 3532.

Ahmed, R., Saha, J. K., Begum, M., & Haque, M. S. (2018). Impact of foreign remittances on household welfare in Sylhet region of Bangladesh. *Journal of Business and Economic Management, 6*, 22–32.

Barua, S., Majumder, M., & Akhtaruzzaman, D. (2007). *Determinants of Workers' Remittances in Bangladesh: An Empirical Study.* Policy Analysis Unit (PAU), Bangladesh Bank Working Paper No. WP, 713.

Bruyn, D. T. (2005). Dynamics of Remittance Utilization in Bangladesh. IOM Migration Research Series, No. 18. UN.

Chowdhury, M. B. (2011). Remittances flow and financial development in Bangladesh. *Economic Modelling, 28*(6), 2600–2608. doi:10.1016/j.econmod.2011.07.013

Costanza, R., Hart, M., Talberth, J., & Posner, S. (2009). Beyond GDP: The need for new measures of progress. *The Pardee Papers*.

Cuong, N. V., & Linh, V. H. (2018). The impact of migration and remittances on household welfare: Evidence from Vietnam. *Journal of International Migration and Integration, 19*(4), 945–963. doi:10.100712134-018-0571-3

Debnath, P., & Selim, N. (2009). Impact of short term male migration on their wives left behind: A case study of Bangladesh. *Gender and Labour Migration in Asia, IOM*, 121-151.

Fakir, A. M., & Abedin, N. (2020). Empowered by Absence: Does Male Out-migration Empower Female Household Heads Left Behind? *Journal of International Migration and Integration*, 1–25.

Hadi, A. (2001). International migration and the change of women's position among the left-behind in rural Bangladesh. *International Journal of Population Geography, 7*(1), 53–61. doi:10.1002/ijpg.211

Haider, M. Z., Hossain, T., & Siddiqui, O. I. (2016). Impact of remittance on consumption and savings behavior in rural areas of Bangladesh. *The Journal of Business, 1*(4), 25–34. doi:10.18533/job.v1i4.49

Hashemi, S. M., Schuler, S. R., & Riley, A. P. (1996). Rural credit programs and women's empowerment in Bangladesh. *World Development, 24*(4), 635–653. doi:10.1016/0305-750X(95)00159-A

Hildebrandt, N., & McKenzie, D. (2005). *The effects of migration on child health in Mexico.* Working Paper No. 3573. World Bank.

Kangmennaang, J., Bezner-Kerr, R., & Luginaah, I. (2018). Impact of migration and remittances on household welfare among rural households in Northern and Central Malawi. *Migration and Development, 7*(1), 55–71. doi:10.1080/21632324.2017.1325551

Kapur, D. (2004). *Remittances: The New Development Mantra?* (No. 29; G-24 Discussion Paper Series). United Nations Conference on Trade and Development.

Koc, I., & Onan, I. (2001). The impact of remittances of international migrants on the standard of living of the left-behind families in Turkey. Hacettepe University Institute of Population Studies, 6100.

Kumar, B. (2019a). Remittances, poverty and welfare: Evidence from Cumilla, Bangladesh. *American Journal of Data Mining and Knowledge Discovery*, *4*(1), 46–52. doi:10.11648/j.ajdmkd.20190401.17

Kumar, B. (2019b). The impact of international remittances education and health in Bangladesh. *International Journal of Science and Qualitative Analysis*, *5*(1), 6–14. doi:10.11648/j.ijsqa.20190501.12

Kumar, B. (2019c). The impact of international remittances on poverty alleviation in Bangladesh. *Remittances Review*, *4*(1), 67–86. doi:10.33182/rr.v4i1.665

Kumar, B., Hossain, M. E., & Osmani, M. A. G. (2018). Utilization of international remittances in Bangladesh. *Remittances Review*, *3*(1), 5–18. doi:10.33182/rr.v3i1.424

Mahapatro, S., Bailey, A., James, K. S., & Hulter, I. (2017). Remittances and household expenditure patterns in India and selected states. *Migration and Development*, *6*(1), 83–101. doi:10.1080/21632324.2015.1044316

Mahmud, S., Shah, N. M., & Becker, S. (2012). Measurement of women's empowerment in rural Bangladesh. *World Development*, *40*(3), 610–619. doi:10.1016/j.worlddev.2011.08.003 PMID:23637468

Marcuss, D., & Kane, R. E. (2007). US national income and product statistics born of the Great Depression and World War II. *Bureau of Economic Analysis: Survey of Current Business*, *87*, 32–46.

Mustafa, K., & Ali, S. R. (2018). The macroeconomic determinants of remittances in Pakistan. *International Journal of Business Management and Finance Research*, *1*, 1–18.

Narayan, D. (Ed.). (2002). Empowerment and poverty reduction - a sourcebook. Washington, DC: The World Bank.

Raihan, S., Khondker, B. H., Sugiyarto, G., & Jha, S. (2009). *Remittances and household welfare: a case study of Bangladesh.* ADB Economics Working Paper-189.

Ramírez, C., Domínguez, M. G., & Morais, J. M. (2005). *Remittances, Gender and Development.* Working Paper. United Nations International Research and Training Institute for the Advancement of Women.

Smith, L. M., Case, J. L., Smith, H. M., Harwell, L. C., & Summers, J. K. (2013). Relating ecosystem services to domains of human well-being: Foundation for a U.S. index. *Ecological Indicators*, *28*, 79–90. doi:10.1016/j.ecolind.2012.02.032

Stiglitz, J. E., Sen, A., & Fitoussi, J. P. (2010). Mismeasuring Our Lives: Why GDP Doesn't Add Up. The New Press.

Sultana, A. M., Hed, N. M., & Leh, F. C. (2013). Measuring empowerment between working and non-working women: Malaysian perspective. *Asian Journal of Humanities and Social Studies*, *1*, 415–421.

Talberth, J., Cobb, C., & Slattery, N. (2007). The Genuine Progress Indicator 2006: A Tool for Sustainable Development. *Oakland: Redefining progress*, 31.

Taylor, J. B. (1999). A historical analysis of monetary policy rules. In *Monetary policy rules* (pp. 319–348). University of Chicago Press. doi:10.7208/chicago/9780226791265.001.0001

Todaro, M. P., & Smith, S. C. (2012). *Economic Development*. Pearson.

Ullah, A. A. (2017). Male Migration and 'Left–behind Women: Bane or Boon? *Environment & Urbanization Asia*, *8*(1), 59–73. doi:10.1177/0975425316683862

UNDP. (2000). *Human Development Report 2000*. United Nations Development Program.

Wadood, S. N., & Hossain, A. (2017). Microeconomic impact of remittances on household welfare: Evidences from Bangladesh. *Business and Economic Horizons*, *13*(1), 10–29. doi:10.15208/beh.2017.02

Chapter 13
Janani Suraksha Yojana:
An Ardent Approach to Empower Rural Women for Institutional Deliveries – Inclusive Growth Strategy in Healthcare

Vijayetta Sharma
Indian School of Business, Mohali, India

ABSTRACT

Health of the mothers is of prime concern for growth of any country, and their level of empowerment can be significantly related to the place of delivery selected for birth of a child. Janani Suraksha Yojana (JSY) is an astute attempt towards safeguarding maternal health by Government of India under the flagship health programme, National Rural Health Mission, to promote institutional deliveries among the poor pregnant women. Safe deliveries at the institutions are an indicator of women empowerment and inclusive growth, which paves the way towards economic growth by securing the health and well-being of mothers in rural areas, thereby sustaining productive capacities of women. The chapter assesses the rise in proportion of institutional deliveries among JSY beneficiaries with increased awareness under JSY in Punjab, after carefully assessing the situation of maternal health prevailing in the world, India, and state of Punjab. Further, policy measures have been recommended to augment women's health and empowerment, an inclusive economic growth parameter of country's growth trajectory.

INTRODUCTION

Women's empowerment is a public health imperative asserts Dr Poonam Khetrapal Singh, WHO Regional Director for South-East Asia, and has a substantial impact on public health and wellbeing (WHO, 2018). Women empowerment is also a matter of significance for ushering an era of inclusive growth in the country. Services espoused for maternal health care; a critical area of women's health invariably determines the level of empowerment of women in an economy. Maternal health care is measured to a great extent in the advocation of institutions for delivery and ensuring skilled birth attendance along

DOI: 10.4018/978-1-7998-3737-4.ch013

with provision of financial incentives. Further, reduction in maternal mortality through the government's efforts of financial and social intermediation have exclusive impact on women's health, which increases their productive capacity, accelerating the pace of inclusive economic growth in the country. To a great deal of demise a visible proportion deliveries still occur in the homes, often in the presence of a birth attendant who is unskilled due to lack of governments efforts to reach these families, low level of health-related knowledge and awareness among these communities, lack of decision-making power with no trigger from the health system and ongoing service gaps in the health programmes. Deliveries at home in the hands of unskilled professionals is the leading cause of deaths among the pregnant women, particularly in rural areas where skilled birth attendance is lacking (Sara, Haji and Gebretsadik, 2019) and poor accessibility to health services (Petra, 2003) which compels women to deliver at home.

As per Joint UNICEF/WHO database, 2019 based on population based national household survey data and routine health systems of skilled health personnel assisting in delivery, India accounts for 81 percent of births assisted by a skilled birth attendant which is less than the world average of 87.04 percent with the neighbouring countries like china at 99.9 percent. Metcalfe and Adegoke, 2013 highlighted that South Asia has the lowest rates of skilled birth attendance in the world. The factors that influence non accessibility to the health facility for child delivery arise from physical to financial concerns, education, obstetric history and cultural barriers, awareness of danger signs and perception on low quality of care given at the government health centres. Regrettably, large number of women could not have died of the preventable causes of death, if they would have been taken to the health centre. Institutional delivery guarantees skilled attendance at birth as well as access to emergency obstetric care which provides mental succour of being at safe place, if emergency arises. Keeping all this in view, ensuring institutional delivery is the primary restorative measure to accelerate maternal health, reduce mortality count and inclusive coverage of every woman in the health service network. Therefore, it becomes the utmost priority of the government to take necessary steps to encourage women for institutional delivery to save their lives of the preventable causes of death and start an era of inclusive growth in healthcare paradigm, particularly women's health.

INCLUSIVE ECONOMIC GROWTH AND MATERNAL HEALTHCARE

If we look at the mandate of inclusive economic growth it entails to provide and abridge essential services broadly with respect to health and education to the poor sections of the society, hand holding them to the concrete platform of growth trajectory and escalate the economic progress of the country. Further in order to substantiate inclusive growth paradigm, the rural areas of the country essentially need to be targeted while proving the services in health, education and other schemes to eradicate poverty. The economic progress in broader terms is measured in terms of real GDP and per capita income. However, the inclusive economic progress of any country relies to much extent on development of the social sector, progress in the welfare schemes, reduction in regional disparities and dismantling the deleterious edifice of disease, ill health and poverty. In other words, the inclusive growth aims at distributing the benefits of development to disadvantaged sections of society residing in rural area of the country.

India's rank in the human development index stands at 129 out of 189 countries in 2019 with HDI value of 0.647 which represents inequalities in key elements of human development such as health, education, dignity and respect for human rights (Human Development Report, 2019). There is an increase in one rank from 130 to 129 for the year 2019 (The Hindu Business line, 2019). In 2018 the scores experience a drastic fall of almost 27 percent against a world average of 20 percent (Financial Express, 2018). The expenditure on social services which include health and education increased by 1.5% of GDP during the 2014-20 period. Out of pocket expenditure as a percentage of total health expenditure declined from 64.2% in 2013-14 to 58.7% in 2016-17 (GoI, Economic Survey, 2019-20). States spent 63% of its budget on developmental purposes, allocated during 2015-20. Developmental expenditure consists of social services, which includes expenditure on education, health, water supply and sanitation, housing, urban development, and welfare of backward communities. During the 2015-20 period out of 24% of budget on human development, states on an average have spent 5.3% of their budget on health and family welfare, after the highest spending of 16% towards education. Further, the central government transfers the grants-in-aid to states which are tied in nature, i.e., they are linked to specific schemes and expenditure avenues, including National Health Mission and allied schemes (Institute for Policy Research Studies, 2019).

The maternal health scheme in the form of JSY aims to augment economic development by bringing financial and physical stability in the health of mothers during pregnancy and child birth, by assuring cash assistance for institutional delivery and provision of caring support through a network of wide-ranging health service institutions and skilled health providers. The relation of maternal health scheme JSY to economic development and inclusive growth can be seen in Figure 1.

Figure 1. Maternal health and Economic development
Source: Author's compilation

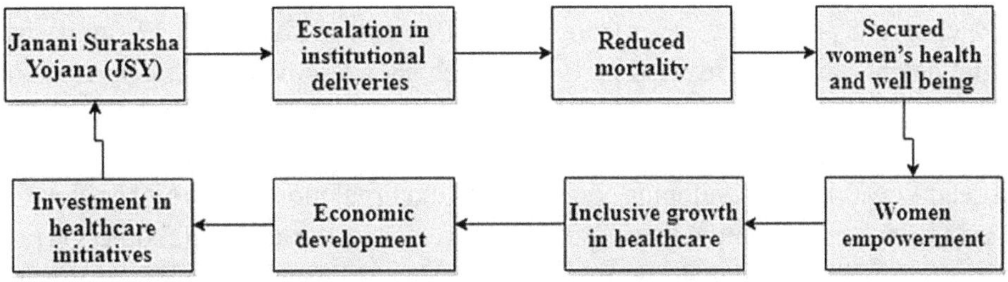

Realizing the importance of health care schemes propelled by the government which secures welfare along with cash assistance, it is desirable to look at the adversity prevailing around maternal health and the indicators of maternal health status in the world, India and the study area Punjab.

Maternal Health Statistics

If we look at the mortality estimates as per the latest trends, world over 295,000 deaths were witnessed among mothers out of which 94 percent of all maternal deaths occurred in low and lower middle-income countries. Africa and South East Asis accounted for the maximum proportions of these deaths (See Table 1). Every day in 2017, approximately 810 women died from preventable causes related to pregnancy and childbirth. It has repeatedly been reinforced by WHO, UNICEF and other national health agencies that institutional deliveries and skilled care before, during and after childbirth can save the lives of women and newborns (WHO, 2019). Hence, depending upon the region-specific concerns of different territories

Table 1. Estimates of maternal mortality ratio (MMR) per 100000 live births, 2017

WHO Regions	MMR Point Estimate and Range of Uncertainty Interval (UI:80%)			Number of Maternal Deaths	Lifetime Risk of Maternal Death 1 in
	Lower UI	Middle UI	Upper UI		
Africa	480	525	629	192000	39
Americas	55	57	62	8500	850
South-East Asis	132	152	180	53000	280
Europe	12	13	14	1400	4300
Eastern Mediterranean	138	164	217	30000	170
Western Pacific	36	41	49	9800	1400
World	199	211	243	295000	190

Source: World Bank (2019).

and some common denominators of health, a wide-ranging incidences of mortality has emerged across the globe, as may be seen in Table 1.

The situation of India in reducing mortality is not very pleasant, it has missed the Millennium Development Goal (MDG) target of 108 maternal mortality ratio (MMR) by 2015 and is committed to lower it to 100 by 2020 as per National Health policy, 2017 and a further commitment to reduce its maternal mortality ratio to less than 70 per one lakh live births by 2030 stands as part of achieving SDGs (WHO, 2017) The Sample Registration System (SRS) 2015-2017 bulletin for MMR released in November 2019 witnessed a decline of 8 points (6.2%) i.e. from 130 in 2014-15 to 122 in 2015-17 signifying that nearly 2,000 maternal deaths have been averted per year, which shows some progress signs according to the bulletin.

With respect to the rural health scenario, the World Health Organization has emphasized that 99% of all maternal deaths occurred in developing countries and maternal mortality is higher in women living in rural areas and among poorer communities (WHO, 2019). Hence, the health of mothers is prime concern in the rural areas of developing countries and calls for urgent policy action to restore the declining care indices and bring in inclusive growth coverage with respect to maternal health. Governments of these developing countries from time to time take steps to provide relief to the mothers facing dire situations in critical times of childbirth. Further in order to restore maternal health, ensuring institutional delivery have been the major concern of government of every country so that the emergency situations are handled by safe and experienced health professional. As per the available data from various government reports, there has been a rise in institutional deliveries and skilled birth attendance in India to almost double the percentage since 2005, considering the efforts of *Janani Suraksha Yojana*. The growth has also been clearly followed in the rural areas of the country, specifically the state of Punjab, as may be seen in Table 2 and Table 3. However as per the available figures the proportion of skilled birth attendance is greater to the institutional deliveries pointing towards the assistance given by health professional in deliveries outside the health institutions or in household setting.

Table 2. Institutional Delivery

Data source	India		Punjab	
	Total	Rural	Total	Rural
NFHS - 3 (2005-06)	38.7	28.9	51.3	47.6
DLHS - 3 (2007-08)	46.9	37.8	63.1	59.5
CES (2009)	72.9	68	60.3	54.1
DLHS - 4/AHS-III (2012-13)	74.62	70.6	82.7	81.8
NFHS -4 (2015-16)	78.9	75.1	90.5	91.5

Janani Suraksha Yojana

Janani Suraksha Yojana (JSY) is an astute attempt towards safeguarding maternal health by Government of India under the much-lauded flagship health programme - National Rural Health Mission to promote institutional deliveries among the poor pregnant women, ensure inclusive coverage of women in health service network to usher economic development. It is a 100% centrally sponsored conditional cash transfer scheme dovetailed with escort, transport and referral services which motivates poor pregnant women in rural areas for institutional delivery. The primary objective of the programme is to reduce maternal and neonatal mortality to commence an era of healthy mothers and children, free from disease or preventable deaths.

The primary objective of JSY scheme is to achieve an upsurge in institutional deliveries to provide necessary obstetric care and reduce maternal mortality. As part of provisions of JSY, the beneficiaries are counselled by Accredited Social Health Activist (ASHA) to select an institution for delivery and ensure that everyone sticks to it by proving a proper connect and accompanying the beneficiary to the health centre throughout the pregnancy cycle. While deciding the institution, ASHA keeps note of the ANC reports of beneficiaries, proximity or the specific preference given by the beneficiary as voiced to them by neighbours/ family/friends for quality attendance at childbirth (Janani Suraksha Yojana, 2005).

To understand the rise in institutional deliveries, the study of JSY initiative in the State of Punjab, India has been conducted.

Table 3. Safe Delivery - Births Assisted by Health Personnel

Data source	India		Punjab	
	Total	Rural	Total	Rural
NFHS - 3 (2005-06)	46.6	37.5	68.2	67.1
DLHS - 3 (2007-08)	52.3	43.3	76.9	74.3
CES (2009)	76.2	71.7	66.7	61.5
DLHS - 4/AHS-III (2012-13)	81.82	78.51	97	97.2
NFHS -4 (2015-16)	81.4	78	94.1	95

METHOD AND MATERIALS

Th purpose of the study is to analyse the rise in proportion of institutional deliveries among maternal health beneficiaries with increased awareness under JSY in Punjab, India. Two district from the state of Punjab, one high performing i.e. district Ropar and one low performing i.e. district Mohali has been selected for the purpose of the study (NRHM, 2013). The state of Punjab is a high performing state in India, as per the performance index devised by National Rural Health Mission (NRHM), one of the largest and most ambitious programmes to revive health care in India towards the objective of inclusive growth and development.

A sample of 232 *Janani Suraksha Yojana* (JSY) beneficiaries has been selected i.e.116 women from each district based on probability proportionate to size sampling. While collecting data for the sample, equal representation has been ensured from each block of the districts. The data has been collected through a structured interview schedule supplemented by qualitative observations to know the responses for place of delivery and year of childbirth. The year of childbirth corresponds to the total enrolments to the scheme in a particular year, who took benefits of JSY. Chi-square test of association has been applied to check the association between place of delivery and districts. Results have been discussed for institutional deliveries among JSY beneficiaries and level of awareness which translated into enrolment to JSY, since its inception.

RESULTS

Table 4 gives an account of place of delivery of maternal heath beneficiaries under JSY i.e. home or institution.

Table 4. Place of delivery

S. No.	Place of Delivery	District Ropar		District Mohali		χ2	p-Value
		Number	Percentage	Number	Percentage		
1	Home delivery	12	10.34	2	1.72	7.6016	.005832**
2	Institutional delivery	104	89.66	114	98.28		
Total		**116**	**100.00**	**116**	**100.00**		

Source: Computed from primary data, p-value ≤ 0.01 is significant to denote**

The data interestingly highlights that there are visibly greater proportion of institutional deliveries i.e. around 90% in district Ropar and 98.28% in district Mohali among the JSY beneficiaries, considered primarily, as evident from the responses given by the beneficiaries, result of the awareness drive initiated under JSY.

Most of the beneficiaries contended that the first thing ASHA exhorted to them while registering for the scheme was to compulsorily deliver their baby at the government health centre by making available the option of nearby health centres which they could select. They were also guided about the need for going to the health centre and made conversant of the various emergency situations that might arrive during the intrapartum phase which require skilled birth attendant. The beneficiaries upon enquiring also enumerated the obstetric care precautions that a health centre could provide to tackle emergency situation as contrary to delivery at home by unskilled traditional attendants. The beneficiaries who delivered their babies at the health centre attested full conviction to the importance of skilled birth assistance at the institution, saving life in case of emergency, rationalistic efforts by the community health workers and the cash assistance for the noble work. However, despite the concerted policy measure by the government through JSY some cases of home delivery have come to light.

HOME AS DELIVERY PLACE

During interactions with the beneficiaries, some worth mentioning factors that triggered and intensified home delivery apart from financial or personal constraints, lack of conveyance, predominance of family traditions, fear and stress on part of the pregnant lady, were the following:

1. Late introduction of scheme in some villages, mostly in 2008, and not available at the time of delivery in the year 2006, 2007- the intended inception years of JSY.
2. Non-availability, and no timely availability of medical staff at some PHC. In such cases, families advised the pregnant ladies in their vicinity for home delivery to avoid any inconvenience.
3. Service enthused ANMs, who from PHC went to the beneficiary's home to assist in delivery.
4. Some of the pregnant women who went to their maternal home, opted for home delivery as they were not conversant with the ASHA or health centre of that village or did not want to take the heed to search for the same as their mothers hold trust in traditional birth helpers, *"Dai's"*- who were old and experienced village ladies.

From the foregone discussion, it can be said that the causes of home deliveries does not entirely accrue to the will of concerned pregnant lady but a number of factors such a family pressures, dominance of old traditions, fear of assistance from the unknow attendants, outlying health centre, non-availability of scheme, lack of transport facility, old beliefs, change of locality i.e. registration to scheme and delivery, information on non-availability of medical staff etc; which acts as deterring factors in achieving exclusive coverage for institutional deliveries and reduce mortality count.

LEVEL OF AWARENESS TO SCHEME

To know the benefits accrued by the prospective maternal health beneficiaries from JSY, it is pertinent to know whether the level of awareness with the scheme got transformed to actualize gains from the scheme not only till registration or ANC but delivery at institution. To this respect, the trend in increase or decrease in number of beneficiaries with year, who gave birth to child after availing the scheme has been analysed. Thus, the data for the year of childbirth by maternal health beneficiaries has been inured to know the benefits availed by them and to notice the enrolment trend with respect to the year cumulatively.

Table 5 provides the year of childbirth of maternal health beneficiaries who availed the JSY scheme.

Table 5. Year of childbirths of JSY beneficiaries

S. No.	Year of Childbirth of JSY Beneficiaries	District Ropar			District Mohali		
		Number	Percentage	Cumulative Frequency	Number	Percentage	Cumulative Frequency
1	2006	1	0.86	1	3	2.59	3
2	2007	1	0.86	2	2	1.72	5
3	2008	2	1.72	4	10	8.62	15
4	2009	6	5.17	8	3	2.59	13
5	2010	14	12.07	22	11	9.48	24
6	2011	13	11.21	27	29	25	40
7	2012	15	12.93	42	6	5.17	46
8	2013	24	20.69	39	10	8.62	16
9	2014	29	25	68	34	29.31	50
10	2015	11	9.48	40	8	6.9	42
Total		**116**	**100**	**156**	**116**	**100**	**158**

Source: Computed from primary data

It can be noted from the data that most of the JSY beneficiaries i.e. 25% from district Ropar and 29% from district Mohali had child delivery in the year 2014. The beneficiaries who delivered their babies in later years stated that they were aware of the scheme ahead of time as their relatives and neighbours applauded about the accrued benefits, so they were disenchanted to avail the scheme and deliver their babies in safer environment, displaying as feeling of being empowered. As evident in Table 5, there has been increase in child births with increase in years, which shows that more and more women enrolled to the scheme with every passing year. The least number of deliveries were witnessed in the year 2006 and 2007- the initial years of the start of the scheme. This is due to the reason that people were reluctant to enroll to the scheme and deliver in health centre fearing the social repercussions of deviation from centuries followed home delivery system prevalent in the villages, which hold trust on traditional *Dai's*. And in many areas, the scheme started late i.e. in the year 2008, as communicated by many beneficiaries.

An ANM of a PHC remarked, in this regard:

"The people come readily to the health centre enquiring about the dates of ANC, delivery etc., and there has been perceptible shift in institutional deliveries over the years. In 2006, when the scheme started, I used to accompany the ASHA, introducing her to the village people and propagating about benefits of delivery at health centre, but we got a lot rejection from the village folks. But with the change of time, trust of people has shifted from home delivery to visiting institution for every pregnancy related enquiry and all deliveries are at health centre in my village, which invariably exhibits a sense of women empowerment."

Thus, it can be stated that an increasing trend in enrolment with year of childbirth is witnessed which shows increase in registration for the scheme with rise in awareness. As the awareness increased among the rural women more and more women enrolled for the JSY scheme and availed provision of the scheme. Presumably equivalent number of child births in the villages would have occurred, especially in years preceding 2009, but the women did not enroll to the scheme due to lack of awareness or reluctance so the data is reflecting a lesser percentage of births especially from 2006 to 2009 i.e. the initial years of the start of scheme.

In the nutshell, from the above analysis, it can be stated that there has been rise in institutional deliveries with the awareness created by the JSY. Greater number of beneficiaries opted for institutional delivery with the prime concern of their safety, availability of skilled attendance at birth and for a sense of satisfaction that is generated as part of belongingness to the larger community of JSY that receives care and safety precautions on priority. The chi-square result ($\chi 2= 7.6016$, p-value < 0.01) was found to be highly significant which revealed that there is association in proportion of responses among beneficiaries belonging to district Ropar and district Mohali with delivery place. Greater number of beneficiaries from district Ropar insured delivery at institution than district Mohali. Hence, it can be stated that there has been rise in institutional deliveries among maternal health beneficiaries with increased awareness under JSY in Punjab.

CONCLUSION AND RECOMMENDATIONS

The JSY has achieved a surmounting success in vying the rural women for institutional delivery thereby saving their lives by providing skilled assistance during the intrapartum phase, through the meticulous approach and concerted efforts of various stakeholders. There have been increase in enrolment to the JSY scheme through increase in awareness which has resulted as a result of tiresome efforts of community health workers who spend restless days by visiting house to house and propagating the benefits of the scheme. It can veritably be emphasised that JSY has led to accelerated economic growth via espousing the rural areas in the network of inclusive growth paradigm; saving the lives of women, providing them needed facilities at the crucial junction of child birth and securing their productive capacity for economic activity on one hand, and economic development in terms of an improved score in health indicators such as MMR, Institutional deliveries, Skilled birth assistance on the other. Further, as the institutional deliveries guarantees reduced mortality, saving the life of each women endows them with empowerment which guarantees inclusive growth in healthcare and securing a way forward for inclusive economic development.

However, in order to achieve further surge in institutional deliveries, the policy measures of the government should encapsulate the socio-economic, cultural and administrative lags that has resulted in home delivery by many pregnant women. The institutional mechanism for taking care needs to be strengthened so that no pregnant woman returns or move to next health centre due to non-availability of care options or assistance. Behaviour change initiatives need to strengthen so that the Dai families are brought to the service network and used as a means to advocate for institutional deliveries. An augmented counselling by the community health workers would yield greater results by changing the behavioural difficulties, family pressures and spurious belief sets which debar the pregnant women moving to institution for delivery. A national database to chart out home deliveries should be prepared, with the inputs of ASHA or ANM of the regions to have greater clarity on home delivery front and remove the bottlenecks. Further, a satisfactory honorarium for the service delivery for the ASHA with minimum base pay should be devised for achieving greater effectiveness. At last, institutional delivery is not the end, however it is a means to measure the progress on MMR; the health of women emerges a prime concern after the child birth, therefore an effective post birth interventions should be propelled with full zeal and fervour so that they emerge as empowered mothers and their well-being truly symbolises the inclusive growth parameter of the country to achieve an escalated economic progress.

REFERENCES

Express, F. (2018). *India's economic growth not inclusive enough, inequality rises*. Retrieved March 15, 2020, from https://www.financialexpress.com/economy/indias-economic-growth-not-inclusive-enough-inequality-rises/1358413/

Government of India. (2007). National Family Health Survey (NFHS- 3) 2005-06. Ministry of health and family welfare.

Government of India. (2009). Coverage Evaluation Survey (CES). Ministry of health and family welfare.

Government of India. (2010). District Level Household and Facility Survey (DLHS-3) 2007-08. Ministry of health and family welfare.

Government of India. (2013). District Level Household and Facility Survey (DLHS-4) 2012-13. Ministry of health and family welfare.

Government of India. (2017). *National Health Policy*. Ministry of health and family welfare. Retrieved March 15, 2020, from http://www.cdsco.nic.in/writereaddata/National-Health-Policy.pdf

Government of India. (2017). National Family Health Survey (NFHS- 4) 2015-16. Ministry of health and family welfare.

Government of India. (2020). *Economic Survey 2019-20*. Ministry of Finance, Department of Economic Affairs. Retrieved March 15, 2020, from https://www.prsindia.org/sites/default/files/parliament_or_policy_pdfs/Economic%20Survey%202019-20%20Summary.pdf

Human Development Report. (2019). *Beyond income, beyond averages, beyond today: Inequalities in human development in the 21st century*. United Nations Development Programme.

Institute for Policy Research Studies. (2019). *State of State Finances*. Government of India. Retrieved March 15, 2020, from https://www.prsindia.org/sites/default/files/parliament_or_policy_pdfs/State%20of%20State%20Finances%202019-20.pdf

Metcalfe, R., & Adegoke, A. A. (2013). Strategies to increase facility-based skilled birth attendance in South Asia: A literature review. *International Health*, *5*(2), 96–105. doi:10.1093/inthealth/ihs001 PMID:24030109

NRHM. (2013). *District data: NRHM index*. Collected from the NRHM state office of Punjab.

Office of Registrar General. (2019). *Special bulletin on Maternal mortality in India 2015-17*. Sample Registration System.

Petra, S. (2003). Maternal Mortality in a Contemporary Social Background. *Transylvanian Journal of Multidisciplinary Research in Humanities*, *8-9*, 173–190.

Sara, J., Haji, Y., & Gebretsadik, A. (2019). Determinants of Maternal Death in a Pastoralist Area of Borena Zone, Oromia Region, Ethiopia: Unmatched Case-Control Study. *Obstetrics and Gynecology International. Article ID, 5698436*. Advance online publication. doi:10.1155/2019/5698436 PMID:30805003

The Hindu Business Line. (2019). *India rises one rank to 129 in human development index, Economy*. Retrieved March 15, 2020, from https://www.thehindubusinessline.com/economy/india-moves-up-one-rank-129-in-human-development-index/article30249584.ece

UNICEF/WHO. (2019). *Joint database of skilled health personnel based on population based national household survey data and routine health systems*. Retrieved March 15, 2020, from https://data.unicef.org/topic/maternal-health/delivery-care/

WHO. (2018). *Women's empowerment is a public health imperative: WHO*. South-East Asia. News. Statement. India. Retrieved March 15, 2020, from https://www.who.int/ southeastasia/news/detail/07-03-2018-women-s-empowerment-is-a-public-health-imperative-who

WHO. (2019). *Maternal mortality*. Newsroom, Factsheet, September 19. Retrieved March 15, 2020, from https://www.who.int/news-room/fact-sheets/detail/maternal-mortality

WHO. (2017). *Fact sheets on sustainable development goals: health targets*. Maternal health, Media centre, World Health Organization.

World Bank. (2019). *Trends in maternal mortality 2000 to 2017: Estimates by WHO, UNICEF, UNFPA, World Bank Group and the United Nations Population Division*, 2. Washington, DC: World Bank Group.

Yojana, J. S. (2005). *Features & frequently asked questions and answers*. Ministry of health and family welfare, Government of India. https://nhm.gov.in/WriteReadData/l892s/97827133331523438951.pdf

Chapter 14
Menstrual Untouchability: Socio-Psychological Factors Perpetuating the Social Evil

Gaurav Joshi
https://orcid.org/0000-0002-3166-514X
Laxman Singh Mahar Government PG College, Pithoragarh, India

Sunita Bhatt Joshi
Prosecution Wing, Pithoragarh, India

ABSTRACT

This chapter presents an enquiry into the scourge of menstrual untouchability, which still pervades a large section of Indian society. An attempt has been made to understand the underlying dynamics of the social evil of menstrual untouchability through anecdotal evidence gathered through unstructured theme-based interviews of respondents in Uttarakhand, India. Social norms and the pressure to abide by them have been found major reasons for propagation of menstrual untouchability. The practice of menstrual untouchability has been found to be much less rigidly observed in urban communities and single adult-women households. Isolation during menstrual periods and consequent respite from household chores has also been discovered as a reason for some women submitting themselves to this practice. All these insights have formed the basis for suggestions made to rid the society of evil of menstrual untouchability.

INTRODUCTION

Article 17 of the Indian Constitution forbids the practice of untouchability and makes it a punishable offence (Kashyap, 2008 & Laxmikanth, 2004). Discrimination on the basis of birth was rampant in India since centuries and had divided the people along the caste lines. So, outlawing this social evil was perhaps seen as a necessary precondition to laying the foundation of a just and egalitarian Indian society. Special provisions were also made- including reservation in education and employment- to ameliorate the condition of those who had been at the receiving end of this evil custom all this while.

DOI: 10.4018/978-1-7998-3737-4.ch014

All these efforts bore fruit-albeit not as spectacularly as our founding fathers would have liked- and significant sections of the Indian society have now got rid of this inhumane practice. However, untouchability on the basis of gender- a comparatively less prevalent phenomena than that on the basis of birth, still no less inhumane- has never been targeted with the same zeal. Many sections of the Indian society, for instance, still treat menstruating women as untouchable labelling them to be impure (Garg & Anand, 2015).

It was the Sabarimala controversy that suddenly woke up the general society to the scourge of this discrimination faced by women because of their gender. Sabarimala is a temple complex located inside the Periyar Tiger Reserve in Kerala. It is the seat of the revered Hindu deity Lord Ayyappa, who is believed to be a celibate by his devotees. As such, menstruating women, those in the age group of 10-50, are not allowed to enter the temple. This practice has been going on since time immemorial and has general sanction from the community, including from many of the women falling in this age group and therefore most affected by this discriminatory tradition. In 1991, a law suit was filed against this practice in Kerala High Court, which upheld the custom. However, in 2018, this ruling was overturned by a Supreme Court (SC) bench, comprising five judges including the then Chief Justice, with a 4-1 split decision. The bench declared restriction on entry of women in the 10-50 age group as unconstitutional and discriminatory. Hearing a review petition against this ruling, the SC has recently – in November 2019- referred the case to a larger bench for a more thorough examination.

Sabarimala is no exception however. Discrimination against menstruating women extends much beyond to social sphere also. In one such instance in February 2020, residents of a girls' hostel- a part of an institute of higher learning- in Kutch (Gujarat) were allegedly forced to strip to prove that they were not menstruating.

Thus, discrimination against menstruating women- mostly in matters pertaining to religion but also in the social sphere - is a phenomenon rampant in India (Puri & Kapoor, 2006). In some communities, for instance, women, who have entered the age of menarche- the onset of menstrual periods- face a lot of humiliation at the hands of their own family members as well as the larger society. They are considered 'impure' during the 4-5 days of their menstrual periods (Garg & Anand, 2015) and are forbidden from even touching others. If, accidentally, they happen to touch someone, the person has to perform proper purification rituals like bathing or sprinkling cow urine- considered holy- on himself. This menstrual untouchability also manifests itself in various other ways.

Women are not allowed to go to temples, participate in religious functions or touch the deities- even in their own houses- during their menstrual periods. They are also forbidden from entering the kitchen or cooking food (Puri & Kapoor, 2006). They cannot even touch the utensils till the menstrual periods continue. In some places, they are even shunted out of the house for the duration of their menstrual periods and made to stay put in unhygienic conditions in the cowshed or a ramshackle shelter built specially for this purpose.

The authors of this article have made an attempt to understand this phenomenon of Menstrual Untouchability and its various aspects in detail. They have relied extensively on unstructured 'theme-based' in-depth interviews-supplemented by passive observations in some instances- as research tool for this purpose. The data has been collected primarily from Kumaon region in the Uttarakhand state. The ensuing paragraphs document their findings.

WHAT IS MENSTRUATION?

Menstruation- also known as 'period' or 'monthly'- is a naturally occurring process in females, which takes place every 21 to 40 days, during which blood is discharged from the inner lining of uterus through the vagina. The duration of discharge may vary from 3 to 7 days among different women. Change in the hormone levels in the body is the reason behind menstrual cycle. Most women report pain-which may vary from mild to severe- while some may also experience heavy bleeding during their menstrual periods. Other associated symptoms include acne, feeling tired, irritability and general mood swings.

Females start menstruating around the age of 8 to 15 years- this signals fertility and is known as Menarche. Women tend to stop menstruating temporarily during pregnancy and permanently after Menopause which occurs around the age of 45 to 55 years.

MENSTRUATION AND CULTURE

Different cultures have different beliefs associated with the natural process of menstruation. In some cultures, menstruating women were considered powerful and sacred (Janowitz, 2002). In some others, they were thought to possess special psychic skills and strength to heal the sick (Biziou, 2010). In ancient Rome, for instance, menstruation was considered to bestow special powers on women making them capable of even healing the sick and destroying the enemies. Hunter-gatherer societies of Africa view menstruation positively unlike some other cultures which treat it as ritually unclean. Still others consider it a private affair and prescribe keeping it hidden from public glare.

Sikhism and Buddhism (except certain branches of Japanese Buddhism) see menstruation for what it is- a natural phenomenon- and condemn any discrimination towards menstruating women (Shahi, 2018). They are allowed to attend worship and enter holy places without any bar. Most Christian denominations don't prescribe any special rituals for menstruating women. Islam is also very accommodative towards menstruating women- they are excused from offering prayers and observing fasts. They are advised not to enter mosque during menstrual periods but can attend public gatherings and festivities. However, sexual intercourse during menstrual period is strictly forbidden and the responsibility for this has been laid on the male partner also.

Menstruation also finds mention in *Ayur Veda* and Hindu religious texts like *Dharma-Shastra*, however, principally, in connection with its health and societal implications respectively. It is claimed that Hinduism does not specifically impose any restrictions on menstruating women. It does not even consider it a purely private affair: in some South Indian Hindu communities, the onset of first period (Menarche) is marked by family members with ceremonial celebrations- *Ritu Kala Sanskaram* or *Ritu Siddhi* – and the girl child is showered with gifts including her first *sari*, presented to her by her maternal uncle. The wearing of this *sari* in the later half of the ceremony marks her passage into womanhood (Munan, 2012). Likewise, *Ambubachi Mela* – the annual fertility festival held in the north-eastern state of Assam during the monsoons (around June) celebrates the yearly menstruating course of Goddess Kamakhya.

Thus, Hinduism, to begin with was quite liberal in its treatment of menstruating women. It is speculated that over the course of time, some rules - against entering temples, doing household chores, indulging in sexual intercourse or touching others during menstrual periods- were introduced for the convenience of menstruating women. These rules were formulated with sound reasoning: menstrual periods are physically draining for women; not needing to walk all the way to the temple or to do household chores would have allowed menstruating women some time for rest and recuperation. Similarly, sexual intercourse during menstrual periods does not have much procreational value – it is highly unlikely to result in pregnancy- in addition to increasing the risk of infection from a sexually transmitted disease. Injunction against touching others was possibly to reduce opportunities for social interaction to not let menstruating woman's mood-swings have an impact on her relationships with others.

It is unfortunate, therefore, that these recommendatory prescriptions- adherence to which was left to individual's own discretion- acquired deep roots and an obligatory hue with the passage of time. So much so that they have now transformed into a social malice prompting derogatory treatment of women during their menstrual periods. As of today, menstrual untouchability is practised not only in India -especially in the north - but is also widespread in Nepal.

The following paragraphs- based mostly on first person accounts - bring out the various aspects of this practice.

SUMI' S CASE: SOCIETAL PRESSURE FORCING CONFORMITY

Sumi (name changed on the request of the respondent) is a Class 'B' government servant since 2013 and currently posted in Pithoragarh- a remote hill district in Uttarakhand. She has had her schooling from Tanakpur, an easily accessible and therefore relatively more developed town in the Uttarakhand plains. Her family started looking for a suitable groom for her soon after she got posted to Pithoragarh. Eventually, she got married in 2016 into a family that was based in Pithoragarh itself. Since this meant that she could simultaneously fulfill her familial and professional obligations, she was very happy when her marriage got fixed.

Her in-laws had settled in a roadside village on the outskirts of the Pithoragarh town- hardly 5 kilometres from the town centre. Having constructed the house on the ancestral land only a few years back, they had shifted to the village from their rented residence in the town centre. The extended family members were also settled nearby in their own separate dwellings.

Sumi's in-laws' were a nuclear family with her husband being the lone son and his only sister already married off. Sumi's husband had a government job. Her father-in-law was also a retired government servant while her mother-in-law, though a full-time housewife, had been a Science graduate. In this sense, Sumi was getting married into an educated family. This was the reason why Sumi was even more appalled by what happened just two days after her marriage was solemnised.

Sumi recalls that all the guests had left by then and it was the first time that she had got the opportunity to sit and have a chat with her mother-in-law. In the middle of the chat, her mother-in-law mentioned in passing that the extended family members- who lived nearby- were very conservative and that they observed the practice of keeping the women isolated for the duration of her menstrual periods. She didn't go into details as she probably assumed Sumi to be aware of such a practice which was widespread in most places in Uttarakhand. Sumi had indeed witnessed this custom in various places but her own family had never followed it. She was not expecting anything different in her in-laws' household also. But, the mother-in-law then asked to let her know in advance when Sumi's menstrual periods were due so that proper arrangements could be made.

Initially, it occurred to Sumi that her in-laws do observe the segregation rules during menstrual period. As such, and also as a new bride, she had almost decided to comply when her husband intervened. Her husband happened to overhear them and came inside the room. He was visibly disturbed and asked his mother in a raised voice to explain the reason for this 'sudden' change of household rules. He asked his mother as to why this practice was never observed earlier in his growing up years when he was a child and their family lived in the town. The mother-in-law responded with the argument that they had no choice but to stick to the customs & traditions dutifully observed by the other more conservative members of their extended family, and in whose neighbourhood they had been living. '*Jaisa desh waisa bhesh*' (In Rome, do what the Romans do), she concluded.

Later, her husband explained to Sumi that he had no memory of his family observing menstrual segregation though he could recall having seen women in the extended family-back in the village- being forced into isolation for a few days every month. So, he was upset at the thought that his mother would allow such a regressive practice to be observed in their family. It was this reason which made him argue with his mother on the issue.

However, it all ended well for Sumi. The matter was put to rest after that. Sumi's guess is that the unexpected opposition from her own son was most likely the reason behind her mother-in-law's decision to not discuss the matter ever again.

Sumi's case succinctly brings out an important aspect: the favourable attitude of extended family members, neighbours and the larger society towards menstrual untouchability has a role in the continuation and propagation of this practice. Sumi's mother-in-law's response to her son's objections attest to the veracity of this argument.

Existing academic literature on 'Conformity' and 'Group Norms' in Social Psychology point in the same direction. People feel obligated to follow the social norms- mostly unwritten and unspoken- of the group to which they belong in order to retain their membership (Cialdini, 1994). Violating these norms attracts reprisals from other members in the group ranging from mild (rebuke, expression of displeasure etc.) to severe (boycott and expulsion). Members tend to abide by the group norms to avoid such a fate (Baron, 2006). This regulation of member-behaviour also keeps the group intact and enhances group cohesion.

Sumi's mother-in-law never had to witness menstrual untouchability herself while the family earlier resided in the town. Having moved back to the village, where the local community practised menstrual untouchability much more religiously, she felt obligated to introduce the practice in her own family to avoid being ridiculed and harassed by the extended family, neighbours and other community members.

This came to light when the authors interviewed her within a few weeks of their interaction with Sumi. The fact that the authors had already had an interaction with Sumi was withheld from her on purpose. Sumi's mother-in-law, in fact, narrated the tale- independently verified by the authors later- of an elderly couple acquainted with her.

This couple- both husband and wife in their 70s- lived in a nearby village in their ancestral residence. They had three sons. Each of the sons had well-paying jobs and was settled in different cities with their wives and children. They had tried to convince their parents to come to stay with them but the elderly couple was reluctant. On their insistence, and partly owing to their own old age & physical condition, however, the couple had now employed a maid for the routine household work. The maid was in her 30s; more importantly, from the same caste as theirs- this not by accident but by design; the couple had been particularly careful about this. She belonged to a poor family and lived with her husband and child in the same village. She would come every day for two hours and finish the chores. The elderly couple had, however, decided not to have the maid cook for them.

The birthdays of two of their sons and marriage anniversary of the third happened to fall on the same date. That day, every year, the couple would perform a brief *pooja* (ceremonial worship) and host a special feast for the neighbours. It was no different the year when they hired the maid- the *pooja* was offered and dinner was prepared for the invitees. The neighbours did pay a visit, but declined to have the food. Allowing the maid to work in their house even during her menstrual periods, and *chhoot* (impurity) arising from this was quoted as the reason. And this was stated unequivocally, not in any euphemistic or oblique manner- as though their decision to not have food at the couple's place was to send across a stern message rather than to preserve their own piety. The message was that the couple should not have allowed the maid to work in their house during her menstrual periods. The elderly couple bowed to this pressure. Now, the maid doesn't visit the couple's household for 4-5 days every month presumably because she is having her menstrual periods. The neighbours have also resumed attending the dinner that the couple invites them to every year.

The authors found that there was another reason for perpetuation of the practice of menstrual untouchability.

SUBMISSION TO MENSTRUAL UNTOUCHABILITY: A FUNCTION OF WHERE ONE LIVES!

Researches have documented how villages generally have more closely knitted communities than urban areas. Residents of a small village are more likely to know one another; many a times, they are also connected by ties of kinship. In any case, they demonstrate a higher level of participation in one-another's life. Therefore, village life exerts a greater pressure on the residents to stick to the norms of general conduct (Swain, 2009). Individuals in such communities are also more likely to display a norm-congruent behaviour as the deviations would not go unpunished. On the other hand, residents in a city generally don't even know who their neighbours are. Evidently, there would be more opportunities for the urban residents to indulge in norm-deviant behaviours without worrying too much about the consequences.

This would mean that even if menstrual untouchability is widespread in the general society and the social norms support it, it would be more prevalent in the villages than in the urban spaces. To put it differently, the norm-congruent behaviours (practice of menstrual untouchability) would be more readily demonstrated by rural folks; more instances of norm-deviation (disregard for the practice) would be observed among the town residents.

It comes as no surprise, therefore, that it was this realisation which made Ambedkar criticize Mahatma Gandhi's prescription for restructuring the society in free India and rather propose an alternative model. The Gandhian model advocated self-sufficient & autonomous villages capable of managing all their affairs independently (Gandhi, 1962). Baba Saheb Ambedkar opposed this model and denounced villages as cesspool of ignorance, casteism, discrimination and oppression. Instead, he campaigned for the cities to be made the fulcrum of community life in free India as he thought of them as 'melting pots' where difference of caste, community and gender give way to a more egalitarian society. The authors' observations- that menstrual untouchability is much more rigidly practised in villages than in urban areas - prove that Ambedkar was indeed correct.

Does this mean that the place of residence can also impact the loyalty with which a family observes the practice of menstrual untouchability? Yes. This fact revealed itself when the authors interacted with the Sanwals of Lucknow in Uttar Pradesh.

The head of the Sanwal family is an elderly gentleman nearing ninety. He tells the authors that having landed a job there, he migrated to Lucknow with his wife and mother in 1970s from their ancestral village in Almora (Uttarakhand). The society was more conservative then and segregation of menstruating women during their menstrual periods was fairly common. His own mother was particular about not allowing his wife inside the kitchen during her menstrual period. But once they settled in Lucknow, this age-old practice in their household gradually gave way.

MENSTRUAL UNTOUCHABILITY: WHO BOW TO SOCIETAL PRESSURE? WHO DON'T? AND WHY?

In their interaction with Sumi's husband, the authors came to know of his strong views against the practice of menstrual untouchability, which according to him, "was a tool of oppression used against the weaker gender". This was on expected lines considering what Sumi had told the authors while narrating her story.

However, what came as surprise was that his views were shared by his mother- Sumi's mother-in-law - also. She had made it clear to us that she thought of the practice of menstrual untouchability as demeaning for women. It was apparent that the fear of admonition by extended family members had driven her to propose daughter-in-law Sumi's isolation during menstrual periods shortly after his son's marriage.

So, though the mother-son duo shared the antipathy for the practice of menstrual untouchability, they exhibited remarkably different behaviours in actual life. The son's behaviour was congruent with his negative attitude towards the practice- he went to the extent of joining issues with his mother to ensure that his wife did not have to suffer the ignominy of menstrual untouchability. On the other hand, despite privately holding a negative attitude towards the practice, the mother tried to introduce it into her family after her son's marriage. Thus, the attitude-behaviour link – was found to be very weak in her case.

The authors' in-depth interview of her revealed the reason. She had a small social circle- most of her interactions were with the extended family members and other neighbours in the village. The son had friends and acquaintances outside the village also and therefore, had a considerably lesser proportion of his social interactions with the extended family members and neighbours. As such, Sumi's mother-in-law had more to lose than her son if she invited the ire of extended family members by violating the norms held by them as sacrosanct and non-negotiable. This explains her anxiety not to appear as a deviant to them.

The authors found support for this in literature on Attitude also. Behaviour of an individual towards an attitude object doesn't entirely depend on his own attitude (Kotler, 2003). It has instead been found to be moderated by the attitude of 'important others' in his life towards that object (Sheth, 1974). In Sumi's mother-in-law's case, her negative attitude towards the practice of menstrual untouchability was weakened, to a large extent, because of the favourable attitude of the extended family members in her neighbourhood who, owing to being integral part of her social circle, were 'important' to her. This was why she insisted on introducing the practice in her own household also despite privately holding views to the contrary.

In finally bowing to her son's wish also, she made it clear that he was also an 'important other' - much more important to her than the other 'important others' in the extended family and neighbourhood.

On the other hand, her son- owing to a much larger proportion of acquaintances outside the extended family also- did not perceive the extended family members to be so central to his existence. In other words, his extended family members were not 'important others' in his life and therefore the moderating effect of their favourable attitude towards menstrual untouchability was not strong enough to impact his own behaviour. Therefore, his behaviour was in tune with his negative attitude towards menstrual untouchability.

Another aspect that struck the authors was Sumi's own ambivalence towards the practice of menstrual untouchability. Considering that she was the one who would have faced the consequences had her mother-in-law had her say, it was remarkable that Sumi was 'almost ready to comply'- to do her mother-in-law's bidding. She did not assert her opposition to the practice of menstrual untouchability. The emotions that she reported experiencing on the prospect of segregation during menstrual periods were also no way as intense as her husband's. Part of this could be attributed to- as she herself narrated to the authors- her inhibition as a new bride. Still, her acquiescence puzzled the authors until they came across Meenu (name changed on request) and had a long interaction with her.

MEEK SUBMISSION TO MENSTRUAL UNTOUCHABILITY... OR DRAWN IN BY PROSPECTS OF LEISURE

Meenu, 40, a high school graduate and a single parent, lives with her two adolescent sons and mother-in-law in Almora. Her husband, a government servant, died around 15 years ago. Faced with this sudden adversity, Meenu took up the job of office attendant offered to her in the same office on compassionate grounds. Meenu tells the authors that her mother-in-law has always been particular about the practice of isolating women in the family for the duration of their menstrual periods. She herself had religiously observed this practice before her menopause set in and insisted that her daughter-in-law (Meenu) remain loyal to this age-old custom. And Meenu obliges, not because of any deep-rooted belief in the inherent logic of this practice but because it affords her 4-5 days of rest every month. On the days, when she is isolated because of her menstrual periods, she is forbidden from entering the kitchen. Most of the household chores are instead performed by her mother-in-law. This is a welcome break for her from household work which, being a working women, she finds extremely draining specially when combined with her familial responsibilities as a mother of two growing up children.

Kamla (name changed) attests to this fact. She had had her schooling from a predominantly rural area in Pithoragarh around 70 kilometres from the main town. She, then pursued engineering from a government institution in Pithoragarh and soon got married. She affirms that she doesn't mind being isolated during her menstrual periods as long as it keeps her away from the household work.

Sumi also sounded only mildly critical of the practice of menstrual untouchability in her conversation with us. This indifference could, therefore, possibly be the result of her conflicting feelings: she might have felt relieved on being spared the ignominy of being treated as an untouchable during her menstrual periods owing to her husband's assertive opposition; at the same time, she might be ruing the fact that she missed out on the opportunity of having periodic breaks from the household chores which she would have enjoyed had her mother-in-law had her say. This, though, could not be independently verified with Sumi.

Nonetheless, their interaction with Meenu and Kamla has given the authors anecdotal evidence that the prospect of opportunity to relax, owing to isolation during menstrual periods, blunts the opposition to menstrual untouchability among at least a few of those women who are at the receiving end of this practice.

This revelation also made the authors curious to investigate what happens in families with only one adult female member? Who performs the household chores when she is kept in isolation during her menstrual periods? Do the male members take over the work? To find this, interacting with families with limited support for arguments trying to rationalise the practice of menstrual untouchability would not have made much sense. Such families cannot be expected to remain loyal to the practice when it starts interfering with their daily routine- when the lone female member is not available for household chores owing to isolation during her menstrual periods.

So, the authors tried to interview a conservative family in Haldwani (Nainital) originally hailing from Gwaldam, a small town in Chamoli district in Uttarakhand. The Mishra family- including the octogenarian head of the household, his son, daughter-in-law and two grandchildren aged 10 & 12 years - still pays visits to its ancestral village every year to perform worship, despite having settled in Haldwani now. Mishras are deeply religious: they have a dedicated room-albeit small- for worship. The authors could also see the *tulsi* planted in their front-yard with an earthen lamp underneath it when they visited them. The authors also noticed the daughter-in-law spontaneously reaching out for the corner of her *sari* and covering her head, a traditional practice in this part of the world signalling deference, when her father-in-law happened to enter the room where she was chatting with us.

QUEST FOR CONVENIENCE UNDERMINES LOYALTY TO CUSTOMS

She tells us that she was the only lady in an all-male household when she joined the family after her marriage, her mother-in-law having been dead long ago. She categorised her family as relatively conservative in many ways; in fact, she strictly advised the authors against even mentioning the issue of menstrual untouchability with her father-in-law. Still, she avers that she was never subjected to the practice of menstrual untouchability in her marital home. On probing further, she admits that her being the only women could have been the reason for that- 'who will cook food, send the children to school and tend to *pitaji* (father, referring to her father-in-law),' she poses the question. That they resided in a city, however, meant that they could do away with the practice of menstrual untouchability in their family without having to worry about the backlash from the community. When the authors posed the question whether this would have been acceptable back in Gwaldam, she answered circuitously: she disclosed that the family has a tacit understanding, not to make any mention of this in front of their relatives from Gwaldam, when they come on visits occasionally. Thus, the authors could see that the loyalty to menstrual untouchability was tempered by the desire for convenience even in relatively conservative households.

ERADICATING MENSTRUAL UNTOUCHABILITY

Menstrual untouchability is indeed humiliating to those women who are subjected to it. It also causes them emotional trauma. The authors have seen that menstrual untouchability is more widespread in rural areas than in urban spaces and that nuclear families tend to be less dogmatic about this practice than bigger joint families. This leads the authors to believe that the current trend of disintegration of Indian joint households into nuclear families- because of various reasons- and large scale rural to urban migration in search of education, health and employment opportunities shall contribute to this social evil gradually wearing itself out. Nevertheless, efforts need to be made to hasten its demise and rid the society of this evil practice.

This requires attitudinal shift among the community members. However, bringing about attitude change among adults is difficult to accomplish. This is truer for the attitudes linked to cultural & religious practices which are strongly held by individuals (Ciccarelli & Meyer, 2008). Therefore, the authors believe that the ideal target group for attitude change interventions should be the young children in the impressionable age group of 12-18 years. Discussion on menstrual untouchability can be combined with sex education or modules on reproductive systems. Encouraging scientific outlook and rational thinking and inculcating respect for women and love for values of equality in the courses on Moral Science can also prepare the students to grow up to reject this strongly entrenched degrading custom.

Sensitivity training programmes- including role plays and self-counterconditioning - can be run among those in the larger community who are loyal supporters of the practice of menstrual untouchability. In the former, male participants are asked to assume the role of women and enact the various problems faced by them owing to menstrual untouchability in a freewheeling psycho-drama. This sensitises them towards the physical and mental agony faced by women on being discriminated against owing to their menstrual state.

In self-counterconditioning, the participants- originally supporters of menstrual untouchability- are asked to collect information from different sources and list the ways in which menstrual untouchability is harmful for the society and why it needs to be eradicated.

Religious propaganda can also be used to change community attitude towards menstrual untouchability. The legend of Goddess Kamakhya, discussed in preceding paragraphs, for instance, can be used to counter the negative connotation associated with menstruation and the wrong perception that menstruating women are unclean.

Role Modelling can also be a useful tool to engender behaviour changes in the larger community. Well known personalities- from arts & music, sports, cinema, politics etc.-can be asked to speak out against menstrual untouchability. This would encourage their followers to think and act along the same lines.

Lastly, just as *Sati* and child-marriages were declared illegal, the legislatures can also consider outlawing the practice of menstrual untouchability as a violation of the Fundamental Right to Equality.

CONCLUSION

The authors have found that menstrual untouchability is more widespread in rural areas than in urban areas. In the communities in which menstrual untouchability has acquired the force of a widespread social custom, the fear of admonishment by the community members forces even the independent minded individuals, otherwise sceptical of the utility and propriety of this practice, into compliance. This is how menstrual untouchability is able to sustain and propagate itself. However, the threat of this social sanction doesn't work on those who don't deem acceptance by community members as central to their existence. One reason for tacit acceptance of menstrual untouchability by some women is that it allows them a break from the drudgery of household chores. The authors also found single adult-women households- with no female member to perform the household chores in event of the menstruating women being isolated- to be much less loyal to the practice of menstrual untouchability owing to practical concerns. This understanding of the dynamics of menstrual untouchability has informed the suggestions proposed by the authors towards the end to eradicate this social evil.

REFERENCES

Baron, R. A. (2006). *Psychology*. Pearson Education, Inc.

Biziou, B. (2010). *The Joy of Family Rituals: Recipes for Everyday Living*. Cosimo, Inc.

Cialdini, R. B. (1994). *Interpersonal Influence* (S. Shavitt & T. C. Brocks, Eds.). Allyn & Bacon.

Ciccarelli, S. K., & Meyer, G. E. (2008). Psychology: South Asian Edition. New Delhi: Dorling Kindersley (India) Private Limited.

Gandhi, M. K. (1962). *Village Swaraj* (H. M. Vyas, Ed.). Navjivan Publishing House.

Garg, S., & Anand, T. (2015). Menstruation Related Myths in India: Strategies for Combating It. *Journal of Family Medicine and Primary Care*, *4*(2), 184–186. doi:10.4103/2249-4863.154627 PMID:25949964

Janowitz, N. (2002). *Magic in the Roman World: Pagans, Jews and Christians*. Taylor & Francis. doi:10.4324/9780203457641

Kashyap, S. C. (2008). *Our Constitution: An Introduction to India's Constitution & Constitutional Law*. National Book Trust.

Kotler, P. (2003). *Marketing Management*. Pearson Education, Inc.

Laxmikanth, M. (2004). *Indian Polity. Chennai: McGraw Hill Education*. Private Limited.

Morgan, C. T., King, R. A., Weisz, J. R., & Schopler, J. (1993). *Introduction To Psychology*. Tata McGraw-Hill Publishing Company Limited.

Munan, H. (1991). Culture Shock! Malaysia: A Guide to Customs and Etiquette. Graphic Arts Centre.

Puri, S., & Kapoor, S. (2006). Taboos & Myths Associated With Women Health Among Rural & Adoloscent Girls In Punjab. *Indian Journal of Community Medicine*, *31*, 168–170.

Shahi, M. K. (2018). *Period & Emotion: Educate Yourself and your Family*. Evincepub Publishing.

Sheth, J. N. (1974). Consumer Behaviour: Theory & Application. Boston: Allyn & Bacon.

Swain, S. (2009). *Applied Psychology: India-specific & Cross-cultural Approaches*. New Vishal Publications.

KEY TERMS AND DEFINITIONS

Attitude: Way of thinking and feeling towards a person, object or idea which oftentimes determines one's behaviour towards these.

Conformity: Act of displaying obedience to the generally accepted rules of conduct of the group to which one belongs.

Menarche: The first menstrual period experienced by a female. It is a signal of the female body having acquired the capacity to reproduce.

Menopause: Refers to the permanent cessation of menstrual periods in females around the age of 45-55 years. It also signals the loss of capacity to reproduce naturally.

Menstrual Untouchability: A form of discrimination, practised against menstruating women during their menstrual periods, which forbids them from having physical contact with anybody. It generally also entails physical isolation, bar on entering places of worship and kitchen and prohibition of engaging in sexual intercourse.

Menstruation: A naturally occurring biological phenomena in 10- 50 year old females which entails 3-7 days of intermittent vaginal bleeding; it repeats itself every 21-40 day and, hence, also referred to as 'monthly' or period.

Norm-Congruent Behaviour: Behaviour aligned with the existing rules of conduct in the larger society and therefore, likely to result in social approval.

Norm-Deviant Behaviour: Behaviour which violates the existing rules of conduct in the society and therefore may attract social sanction in form of humiliation, reprimand, boycott, etc.

Right to Equality: One of the six fundamental rights granted to the citizens by the Indian constitution. It entails equality before law, prohibits discrimination, prescribes equal treatment in matters of education and employment and outlaws the practice of untouchability.

Social Norms: Established rules -mostly unspoken- of conduct in a society which the individual members are expected to abide by. Individuals learn them by observing fellow members and follow them to obtain approval of the larger society.

Tulsi: An aromatic plant considered holy in the Hindu religion.

Chapter 15
The Plight of the Orang Asli Women in Malaysia: Promoting Wild Edible Plants Through Street Food

Rachel Thomas Tharmabalan
Sunway University, Malaysia

ABSTRACT

In the past, Orang Asli women and men were considered equal, even though their roles were very different. As modernization slowly crept into their lifestyles, the gender divide has gotten a lot bigger and the paternalistic culture has taken a hold of many. Some researchers have said the skewed depictions was influenced by both Christianity and Islam, whereby women were considered to be created by supernatural powers alongside the male species. However, there have been accounts of women being the village chief, but as more anthropologists targeted their research on the Orang Asli, the role of a women in the decision making process slowly got relegated. Hence, this review aims to provide the role of Orang Asli women in educating the general public on the usage of wild edibles found in Malaysia and how it could be incorporated into street food to preserve traditional dietary culture. Some of the key challenges, plans, and practical applications are discussed to improve rural development and prepare a holistic mediation guideline to buffer the health and safety of the population.

INTRODUCTION

Based on current estimates, the amount of indigenous people that can be found worldwide roughly accounts for 370 million people and is spread across 90 countries. Each indigenous groups have their own specific customs and what differentiates them from the mass population is the way they live, their economic and social relationships and also the stratification of their society (UN, 2018). The term Orang Asli, which literally translates to 'original people' was first introduced by both the government and sociology researchers on how to identify these indigenous people. Based on the Federal Constitution of

DOI: 10.4018/978-1-7998-3737-4.ch015

Malaysia, the term can also be applied and referred to as the Aboriginal people of Malaysia. However, the term indigenous people of Malaysia is more broadly used when identifying this particular group of people. During the time of the British Occupation, they were categorized into three main groups namely Negrito, Senoi/Semai and Proto-Malay to ease administration purposes and govern them (Edo, 2006).

Currently, among Orang Asli families, women are thought to be the primary care giver for their households; and nothing more than that, which has contradicted many reports on them being midwives, paving way for them to be shamans and spiritual leaders in their own rights. However, in the 1940's a paradigm shift happened and shamans that exist today are all man. As a consequence of this, the social standing of a women from the Orang Asli people has been deteriorating, more so in the last few decades. When it comes to making decisions that would affect the nuclear family unit and the village, the man acts as both the representation of the women and their children.

To make matters worse, similarly to their identity, the role of women has been enforced upon the dominant society rather than it being defined on their own. A quick survey among the urban population, when asked about the Orang Asli yielded many negative perceptions both in terms of identity and the servitude role a woman plays in their family. When being compared to other indigenous groups in West Malaysia, the Orang Asli do not have enjoy any special rights or privileges. This has led to their lack of representation, marginalization, being poverty stricken and also their poor living conditions especially among the Orang Asli women. As their land rights have been abused by various government and private agencies, many do not own any land, though forest reserves has been gazetted in the Aboriginal People's Act.

Past literature has reiterated that in comparison to many other hunter-gathering societies, there were no gender divisions between the Orang Asli. All activities to ensure continuous survival were deemed to be equal. No one gender, were superior to the other, though there were some tasks that were more gender oriented such as hunting. Marriage was seen as a tie that allowed both sexes to form a self-sufficient economic unit. However, the shift from hunter gathering lifestyles to a cash economy came about through various governmental policies forcing the Orang Asli to assimilate with the dominant culture which allowed them to understand the value of money that seemed to slowly seep into their non-violent and materialistic culture. Wood from trees and exotic animals from the jungle have become prized goods and raw materials for various industries. The prices of some of these goods started increasing in value and many men succumbed in trade participation, gathering large amount of forest material for sale (Howell, 2006). When the Orang Asli men started have started receiving kickback from the sales of these resources, it caused a further divide between gender roles. The amount obtained has allowed them to exert an authoritarian like position in their own families. The women were further relegated and had to take up more male-dominated role which were often carried out by their husbands as they were away for longer periods of time due to depletion of forest resources causing them to venture in further into the forest. Since women were not the ones earning money, they had to rely on their husbands to purchase groceries and materialistic goods to feed the mouths of their chilren and them.

That is not to say that the women took a backseat in providing for their families. Orang Asli women were engaged in foraging and were well educated when it came to the usage of medicinal plants (Gianno, 2006). They also fished in the nearby rivers for additional protein. When it came to durian and mango season, the women took an active role in plucking them. Many different varieties of mangoes and durians are gathered using lengthy bamboo poles. Their skill and agility in handling these plants are based on experience. These poles are then attached to a hand woven basket with jagged ends to agitate the fruits to fall into the bag. Sometimes, the women and the children travel downwards to the main highway to sell their fruits and vegetables which experience on over harvest so as to rely less on their husbands for a sustenance income.

About the same time when finding prized woods and exotic animals started dwindling, a lot of their lands had been taken away from them, to pave way for development projects. Their problems do not cease to end as once they are uprooted from their ancestral hand, the traditional way of life is also left behind as they go hand in hand, more so among the women as they are not used to working such long hours in farms. Not forgetting to mention that their nutritional levels has also been negative affected with women being more susceptible than man especially in common health problems such as goitre, anaemia and being malnourished (Baer, 2006). A rural nutrition report highlighted that when it came to equality, women are considered to be subordinate, have limited access to education thus translating to harder labour and being underpaid. With proper laws being set in placed, as well as educating the women when it came to nutrition and childbirth, the health problems experience by them could be prevented in the first place.

Before the severity of the discrimination faced by the orang Asli women reaches a point of no return, it is important to highlight their contribution not just taking into account the welfare of their families but also to the society in terms of leadership roles, their work ethics and just basic human rights as it cannot be denied that the key role in ensuring the continuity of both culture and tradition food system is highly dependent on the women. Take for example in Japan, where farm stays are booming due to the role that the women play in ensuring cultural traditions are being maintained. Hence, the objective of this study is to highlight how Orang Asli can play a vital role women in educating the general public on the usage of wild edibles found in Malaysia and how it could be incorporated into street food to preserve traditional dietary culture. As times have changed in the Orang Asli settlements, the women are currently singlehandedly responsible for raising the kids and putting food on the table. More can be done to help empower the women in this field, so that they will not be further left behind from society by introducing various activities such as cooking, or the weaving of mats as part of a centralized feature in promoting tourism and helping the general public gain awareness that can help boost the morale of the women. Helping the Orang Asli women build their self-confidence and creating awareness is one thing with the help of governmental and no-governmental agencies, but the benefits that will come about from this include preservation of culture and ensuring that the tradition does not die is also highlighted in this review.

WILD EDIBLE PLANTS

The growing unease over the multifaceted matter of food security global challenge in the world whereby the demand for food will increase by up to 60% in the year 2050 (Maarten Elferink and Florian Schierhorn, 2016). Addressing the predicament of starvation, malnutrition and obesity is the result of a maturing understanding that the genetic base of most human caloric intake from plants is alarmingly limited. The three main staples (rice, maize and wheat) contributes 60% of the world's food energy intake. Prescott-Allen (1990), has emphasized, that the genetic diversity is what allows them to adapt to the environment.

Long gone are the days when researchers have focused their attention solely on these staple crops to multiply its production to meet the increasing and ever changing global food demands. Many have come to recognize that the preferable equilibrium to tackle this problem is to connect research and development of both staple and traditional plants. Oil palm, kiwi fruit were at some point were treated value-less and only occupied specific functions in the local output and consumption systems, but they now have an important role in the economy and livelihood of agrobiodiversity –rich countries, that not only benefits the government but also the poor people. As such, traditional plants represent an unparalleled opportunity to test the prevalent agricultural system in a more absolute manner than accomplished by organic and other alternative food movements. Most of these traditional plants have a comparative advantage in marginal lands, where they have been naturally selected to withstand stress conditions and can therefore contribute to low-input sustainable production systems.

There is a lack of consensus definition and what these plants should be referred to. For the purpose of this paper. I'll define them as wild edibles that have not been previously classified as major crops, have previously been under-researched, currently occupy low levels of utilisation and are mainly confined to rural areas. Rural populations of the world are the primary consumers and agents of preservation for neglected and underutilized plants. And knowledge and classification of these plants are often locked up in indigenous knowledge.

Sustainable nutrition is what is needed is the key to maintain food security and given the common threads linking food, health, and environmental well-being in traditional societies, there is no better time than now to remember and restore indigenous plants. The lay of the land in Malaysia is perfect to cultivate these crops hence making it more advantageous as availability is a key point in molding people's outlook towards these neglected and underutilized species. Introducing these orphan species into urban diets would not only increase the opportunity to produce nutrient-rich food but simultaneously enhances the environmental capacity for future generations to supply themselves.

STREET FOOD

Street food can be defined as foods that are ready to eat and beverages made and sold on the streets or food courts. It is easily available and can be found almost anywhere. In Malaysia, although street food caters to the low and middle income groups, it has been recently reported that many vendors are millionaires apart from providing a main source of income for thousands of Malaysians who come from disadvantageous backgrounds.

It represents the local culture that exist in multiple ways. Creating street food requires creativity. Malaysia being a melting pot of various Asian cuisines, have caused much of these street food to assimilate contributing to an irresistible culinary repertoire. A quick comparison between the Hokkien Mee sold in China and the ones here, are two completely ubiquitous versions with the latter being made out of prawn broth based. The flock mentality is always applied when it comes to street food. The crowded a stall is, the better the food sold.

On an international level, street food around the world not only showcases a country's culture but it also features various dishes from particular continents and countries, therefore allowing customers to sample an assortment of dishes made from around the world like Japan, Korea even the United States. During the recent Ramadan Market, malay vendors were seeing selling takoyaki (a type of Japanese street food) as youths these days are more adventurous with the types of food they consume (The Star, 2017). Therefore, making a point that in order to appeal to the young, street food has to be renewed to make it richer.

The famous Penang Char Koay teow dish which which recently ranked 14th on the World Street Food Top 50 list at the World Street Food Congress 2017 features "taugeh" also known as bean sprouts and chives (World Street Food Congress, 2017). Chives though low in calories still lack a lot of much needed nutrients, however the opposite can be said about bean sprouts. Micronutrients is necessary to ensure proper functioning of every system in the body and is crucial for good health. Substituting this with other wild edibles not only boosts nutritional status of urban population but also preserves agrobiodiversity (Wang, et al., 2016). As deforestation is becoming more rampant in certain parts of Malaysia to pave way for urbanization and industrilization, safeguarding some of these species which are slowly being lost and demand laborious efforts to gather could be prevented, if there is a need to keep this safe. This would also then create a need to start cultivating and domesticating these plants thus relegating its status from neglected.

THE ROLE OF ORANG ASLI WOMEN

As, both men and women are regarded as equal (Tijah, Thambiah and Leong, 2000). Women were kept busy by gathering food and division of labour was unheard off. Men could easily take care of children and cook food for them if need be. A women's work was generally to forage for vegetables, gather firewood, weave baskets and handicrafts, take care of children. These activities were not considered to be lower nor were their contributions deemed irrelevant (Dentan,2000). Many researchers have attributed resettlement strategies that have led to them leading sedentary lifestyles has caused a lot of a women's impact and the role she plays in the society to dwindle in the past 30-40 years or so since the introduction of monetary economy. Fast forward to present times, the women have stopped gathering firewood and the collection of vegetables is done only when needed as the landscapes of their settlements have changed. Household chores is taking precedence as they spend most of their time indoor in the confinement of their own home. This is not to say that the women cannot earn and play a role in providing for their families, but with the type of work they are able to do, their contributions would not be as significant as their husbands. Also the Islamization policy which stereotypes both sexes according to their gender has led them to accept some of these power imbalances (Gouda, 2016).

It cannot be denied that the key role in ensuring the continuity of tradition food system is highly dependent on the women (Nicholas, 2013). When subsistence economy were in play, the women played an active role in ensuring good dietary practices among the villagers as well as earning an income whenever the need arose to buy food items or daily necessities that cannot be found in the jungle.

As times have changed, the women are currently singlehandedly responsible for putting food on the table. They are also the ones who are involved in deciding what types of that will be consumed by the household and are also involved in home gardening. The responsibility of earning an income is solely based on the man, however more can be done to help empower the women in this field. On one hand, women have become more sedentary as taking care of household chores, laundry, looking after the children is a full time job. Making cooking lessons as part of a centralized feature in promoting tourist and helping the general public gain awareness of the cooking methods that can be used will definitely help boost the morale of the women.

INCORPORATING THESE PLANTS INTO STREET FOOD

Globalization has taken many forms over the past decade, and is now dominantly taking over the food industry around the world, especially in developing countries. For the first time in the year 2000, the number of people suffering from obesity worldwide has surpassed the number of undernourished people (WHO/FAO, 2004). For many developing countries, this presents a so-called "double burden" of coping for over- and under-nourishment. Being reliant on staple crops worldwide has caused many nutrient inadequacies worldwide (Von Grebmer et al., 2014). Take a look at Vietnam, for example. Many of its women and children lack vitamin A and calcium until the recent development of golden rice which became a cost effective tool for combating hidden hunger in the population (Stein, 2008). Studies have shown that this is attributed back to the diet as they consume carbohydrate rich rice which tends to have lower amounts of these nutrients (Hefferon, 2014). Not forgetting that urban folks prefer to dine out, as the prices of groceries and main commodities are constantly on the rise thus causing a surge in the demand for cheap and ready to eat food. According to (Noor, 2002), more choices are presented to people now compared to the yesteryears. Coupled together with the dependence on convenience, highly processed fast food over the past 30-40 years or so which has also spurred on this phenomenon.

With gastronomic tourism booming over the past decade or so, a lot of it has to do with the increase fascination in street food (American Culinary Traveler Report, 2013) Mandala Research). Since, countries in all regions have experimented with numerous mechanisms to combat this obesity wave, the results achieved so far have been inadequate, therefore more light can be shed on the role street food could play in reversing this trend.

Street food could also be considered an alternative to fast food especially if you're ordering a take away meal and it is an integral part of local culture in every country (Aquino. 2015). People from various walks of like converge and have meals together in hawker centres or along various make shift stalls. Even when it comes to drinks, vendors use plastic bags with its edges tied to raffia so that customers can have it on a go. The same can be said about take away noodles and soups. Nasi lemak and various other rice and fried noodle dishes are wrapped in banana leaves with newspapers being the outermost covering. It does not only add aroma to a dish but also imparts a sweet, subtle flavour which can be detected among those eating it. Westerners are enthralled at the variety of local food offered in many 3rd world countries and this has caused hamburger too seems to succumb to the invasion, bombardment attack" seems to fade away. So much so, that Anthony Bourdain is about to open a hawker food centre right smack in New York City that would be costing about 6o million USD to build (Eater NY, 2017).

On the other hand, a real sit down hawker experience is not everyone's cup of tea. Safety and sanitation issues are still a concern, particularly among tourist. Colourful melamine plates, bowls and cutleries are washed using dirty dishwater in huge buckets usually nearby drains.

Since street food tend to use a lot of vegetables which are localized, an economical and easy way to combat these and enhance the health status of urban population is to ingest wild edibles as compared to commercially cultivated crops.

Traditional plants or plants from the jungle are micronutrient rich and low in calories (Singh et al. 2013; Amizi Ayob, 2016). They are very adaptable to various climate conditions and require very little attention for it to thrive. As of now, consumption of wild edibles is still within its respective communities (Mpala, 2015). A lot more research has been done to delve deeper on the roles played by these traditional plants, hence generating interest to restore these plants in to various culinary aspects. Opportunities exist for these plants to impart a nutrient rich diet to support holistic health among the urban populations as well as it safeguard the loss of knowledge and the dietary transition experience by many from around the world (Ghosh- Jerath, 2015).

Hence, one of the best ways to promote its utilization is by incorporating these vegetables into street food. As most of these vegetables can be obtained all year long, specifically in the orang Asli villages, there will always be a supply, especially if the demand grows.

It is a known fact that many of these traditional plants are rich in antioxidants and micronutrient (Ebert, 2014). Some even have healing properties which are usually only known by rural communities (Chivenge, 2015). Mixing some of these leafy vegetables is a great way to add taste and enhance flavour apart from improving health when cooking various dishes. In local Malaysian cuisine, herbs and spices are used to help brighten up and give it a very eclectic flavour to sculpt out a lasting impression on consumers.

Famous Street food like Assam laksa which is considered to be a true amalgam is a rice noodle fish soup dish which uses tamarind, ginger flowers, bird's eye chillies and cucumber matchstick to impart its rich flavour (Eckhardt, 2009). Amalgamating wild edibles will not only boost up its nutritional value but also kick up its flavour a notch. As most of these wild edibles are usually obtained fresh, more will be needed in a dish to give it a flavourful kick as its taste is not as concentrated compared to dried vegetables. To feature some of these vegetables, dishes which have a soup base is a lot easier on the palate and to experiment with it in comparison to a whole dish. It would give time for consumers to adapt to new flavours and taste brought about by these wild edibles.

As it might be difficult to obtain these plants, street vendors can start growing their own home garden and have a fresh supply of these vegetables. It is not only unique but the heritage associated with these plants can be preserved. Eventhough it might be challenging in the beginning to start utilizing these plants, it is not impossible. Vietnam is the best example when it comes to blending fresh herbs and vegetables native to their own country in their meals and street food. It is used to flavour every meal and sometimes up to 8-10 different herbs can be found in one single dish (Smith, 2014). Comparing Vietnamese cuisine to Thai, Malaysian and Indonesian food, Vietnamese dishes tend to be less oily yet still maintaining its richness. The way all four flavours are balanced requires great precision. Pho a common staple among Vietnamese and has gathered the praise of Westerners as far as a pho burrito has been created is seasoned with both wintery spices and hot- weather herbs which constitutes its garnishes (Munchies, 2017). Resent research done by Datassential MenuTrends (2017), have showed that many restaurants around the world has increased the use of fresh herbs over a one year and four-year trend in the United States alone. If restaurants are starting to follow these trend, it wouldn't be hard for street food vendors to start sourcing out locally grown produce and experimenting with their dishes.

WHAT NEEDS TO BE DONE?

The plight of the orang Asli women have been highlighted by various scholars especially after the sedentization lifestyle was introduced (Lim and Chee, 1998).When Orang Asli women are allowed to take centrefold in sharing the knowledge and practices that have been used from generation to generation, this would then empower them to take up an active role in the community. This will indirectly lead to the strengthening of the orang Asli culture which will then ease in the incorporation process of the knowledge stream.

On the other hand, for farming to take precedence, there is a need to build a bridge between food production and utilization (Hawjes and Ruel, 2011). For these plants to be turned into food, inputs from both man and nature are required. As history has shown, food systems worldwide are very agile and adaptable, and widely influenced by human cultures that's why the ever evolving food chain from a plant based diet to a protein rich diet. Food ways also builds on social cohesion and in ways reflect the community, wealth and the legal aspects surrounding them (Choe et al., 1993). The population generally tend to have subdue concern over the growing environmental threats that is happening. A quick study done among Malaysians showed that many understand the impact of climate change but do little to counteract and prevent this from escalating (Ahmad et al., 2012) Knowledge is key when it comes to making more informed choices. However, as many still fail to realize the importance of sustainable diets, this makes it difficult for them to alter their food preferences

In order for these vegetables to be incorporated and the poor's man food perception to be eliminated, sensory evaluation in terms of acceptability has to be done. Each person perceives sensory quality in many varied ways, therefore affecting their family's food selection. Some of the sensory ques which affect their decision are sight, smell, taste and texture (McCrickerd and Forde, 2015). As these vegetables are obtained from, the wild, it usually dries out pretty quickly. Preserving its freshness is an ultimate key as texture and appearance are critical traits in deciding its suitability. One of the major stumbling blocks which makes these plants extremely hard to break the barrier of main stream crops is due to the misconception that many people still regard them as poor man's food. Individuals are not very keen on sampling and supplementing their diets with these wild edibles are very little is known about its nutritional and quality aspects.

As cooking destroys a lot of the macro and micronutrient content, it is crucial to (determine) the types of cooking methods used to maintain its quality. Selecting vegetables which are fresh and budding are typically best due to its high moisture content. Studying the safety of these plants in terms of biological hazard is also best in terms of assessing its suitability.

One of the reasons why wild edibles could combat obesity is due tot the fact that it usually has a low caloric content as well as a much lower glycaemic index (Darkwa and Darkwa, 2013). All these are essential in weight lost. Irregular bowel movement is another reason why people tend to put on more weight. The high fibre content found in these plants will help to prevent constipation and promote regular trips to the bathroom. Coupled together with the fact that it has a low glycemic index, it can also reduce blood sugar spike. As Malaysians tend to prefer a diet that is rich in sugar and salt, this could offset the destructive consequences of consuming food high in saturated fat and sugar, thus reducing the risk of non-communicable disease.

As many of the urban population are not accustomed to the wild edibles and ferns, cooking activities should then be organized that will allow the general public to appreciate the food that has been prepared by the Orang Asli women and they might learn a thing of two which can then be used in their own personal cooking back home. Helping the Orang Asli build their self-confidence and creating awareness is one thing, but the benefits that will come about from this include preservation of culture and ensuring that the tradition does not die. As these are unique experiences that cannot be found in the city centre, participants would need to travel to these settlements and experience the Orang Asli way of life for a short while. The money obtained from programmers like these could help with rebuilding efforts.

PROMOTING WILD EDIBLES IN STREET FOOD

In order to start utilizing these crops and shifting towards a healthier lifestyle and a more balanced diet, increased effort needs to be done by the government and non-governmental agencies to ensure a successful progress. Table 1 shows the various keys, plan and practical application that needs to executed based on the conceptual framework given. The different subtopics are needed to make sure the objectives are achievable and the best way to make these information known is by publishing it in top tier journals or newspaper articles as it can reach to the public at a faster rate.

For the nutritional objective to be realized, the government has to allocate more funding to pave way for in depth and extensive research to identify the main macro and micronutrients. As there are many forgotten plants, identifying crops which have the highest nutritional value is crucial in identifying crops for the future. In terms of planning, the results obtained will then be used to educate children and the public. The best way to organize healthy food campaigns and promoting sustainable nutrition over the radio, television and newspapers as it can reach to the public at a faster rate. This then generates public awareness on the value of wild foods and the role it could play in terms of alleviating Non-communicable diseases. Once that is accomplished, street vendors will start following the buzz and experimenting with these wild eats. When they start doing that, it advocates the connection between maintaining a healthy weight and eating food from the wild.

The next objective will be the environmental effects. The key in preventing further biodiversity loss is to start equipping and training the public about the importance of preserving our biodiversity which is unique as Malaysia is situated on the equator. For this to happen, the link between food security, climate change and how it's impacting biodiversity needs to be explained in a simpler way so that even lay men can understand. In addition, there is also a need to distinguish these plants in terms of status. This can then be followed by broadcasting this issue on public forums or publishing this information in top tier journals.

Maintaining cultural heritage is an important key to ensure that the people's sense of age old tradition will not be forgotten and then ultimately lost. One way in preserving their sense of identity is to start learning how these vegetables are used or featured in their meals. A lot can be learned on how they combine certain vegetables with other types of food stuff. The Greek people living on the island in Ikiria, have various types of mountain tea made out of dried herbs such as wild rosemary, sage and oregano which acts as a diuretic and helps maintain their blood pressure. Recording the practices on how food is concocted to create a finished dish should also be done as many a times, not all vegetables can be combined together due to their various effects.

Social cohesion is an important concept which needs to have a more serious take as this paper focuses on traditional plants. One thing which cannot be denied is how these wild vegetables once used to be centered around the lives of the older generation. Since traditional culture Is slowly fading away, more studies needs to be done to revive and strengthen the ties that should not be broken in multi-ethnic Malaysia. The food culture is huge in Malaysia. But it's sad to see that there are more cafes mushrooming up in every state and that features more western cantered dishes instead of local eats. Some argue that there is a market for western cuisine as you can find street food in every nook and crannie. But if you really study the big picture, there aren't many upper class cafes which feature Malaysian dishes as millennials consider it to be cheap and of much lower class. Once the roles have been identified, these information could be the foundation of capacity development which then leads to increase the accessibility of these plants.

In terms of economic development, the rural, indigenous people and the much more older malay folk tend to live a very simple and basic life without much luxurious items. Once these plants become more well known, there will start to be a demand. And when this happens, it could help create an alternative source of income for the neglected folks, particularly the women through the sales of these crops. This in turn will spark more research among agricultural scientist to start developing some of these species into much more resilient crops, thus motivating the ethnic consumers to start domesticating these crops. A spillover effect will then take place, and when that happens, the government should allow small scale farming to be done. The benefits are endless as we are cultivating plants that are unique to our own country.

To encourage indigenous people to take up farming, the government should also start providing benefits in terms of providing lands and start-up capital. The orang Asli have been a forgotten community for ages, this will help develop their community and hopefully help improve the educational level of their children. The government has provided them the infrastructure needed such as schools, hospitals. But still more can be done as they were the pioneers of the land by making it more accessible. The government also have to look into various measures to encourage the usage of wild edibles among street vendor by providing these vegetables at a lower rate in the beginning so that they will be willing to try some of these plants in their food.

Table 1. Keys, plans and practical applications in promoting wild edibles in street food

Objective	Key	Plan	Practical Application
Nutritional	Funding more research on the nutritional status and benefits of these plants apart from enhancing its yield	Educating children and women as well as publish about the potential benefits. Generating public awareness on the value of wild foods and the roles they could play in terms of maintaining holistic health by tapping the knowledge held by Orang Asli women Organizing health food campaigns	Street vendors should then start experimenting with these vegetables Advocating the connection between maintaining health weight and eating food from the wild
Environmental	Educating the people about the importance of biodiversity Essential to classify plants based on their status (extinct, facing extinction, plenteous, availability, accessibility)	Expounding the link between food security climate change and loss of biodiversity in terms of sustainable conservation	Broadcasting and publication of environmental issues and concerns
Cultural	Maintaining cultural heritage by transferring traditional knowledge from older generations to the young ones	Recording traditional knowledge and practices, encompassing all facets of underutilized foods in the community	Start incorporating these plants in their
Social	Socio-cultural analysis on how these foods are centered around their lives and the role it plays to strengthen social cohesion	Publicize information on past application of these plants Capacity development to elevate knowledge	Increasing accessibility of these plants
Economic	Help the orang Asli women generate an alternative source of income through the sales of the crops	Help develop some of these species into new crops thus motivating both the orang Asli men and women to domesticate these crops	Allowing small scale farming
Progress/growth	Providing benefits in terms of lands, capital, if farmers start growing these plants	Incentives are given based on the output Value addition for certain types of plants	Motivation by providing bait to street vendors to start utilizing these pants

CONCLUSION

To preserve age old traditions and to retain a form of cultural identity, these traditional plants should be the centre of a meal, therefore traditional cooking should also be documented. Promoting the usage of traditional plants can only be accomplished by emphasising their importance as well as supplementing further opportunities to boost their consumption. In terms of improving the nutritional status of these particularly vulnerable group, exploiting the agrobiodiversity found in their own backyards will pave the way for scientist, agriculturalist and the urban population to look into measures to utilize these plants.

When that happens, it will spark off a chain reaction that significantly emphasizes the reliability and productivity of traditional food systems whilst essentially contributing to a more food secure and nutritionally sound families, which in turns fulfil market demands while establishing well connected value chains, at the same time generating an alternative source of income which can help improve lifestyle and sustenance of the Orang Asli. When taking into consideration the big picture as a whole, the development of value chains not only focuses on the food security aspect but also takes into account the effects of climate change and financial risks that is linked to a mono-cropping system. So in order for the urban class to shift away from the modern diet, a link between cultural identity and agricultural production should be renewed and restored.

REFERENCES

1F2017). *Chefs add fragrance and flavor with fresh herbs*. Nation's Restaurant News. Available at: http://www.nrn.com/whats-hot/chefs-add-fragrance-and-flavor- fresh-herbs

Amizi Ayob, M., Nutman, A., Lee, L. H., Alias, A., Khamis, S., Hafiz Boon, N. E. F., ... Soon, J. M. (2016). Indigenous Plants and Tuber as Alternative Food Sources for Temiar Communities During Flood seasons. *Advances in Environmental Biology, 10*(1), 93–100.

Aquino, J.P.L., Pedalgo, C.C., Zafra, A.R.N., & Tuzon, T.P. (2015). The Perception of Local Street Food Vendors Of Tanauan City, Batangas On Food Safety. *Laguna Journal of International Tourism and Hospitality Management, 3*(1).

Baer, A. (2016). The Health of Orang Asli Women. In *Orang Asli Women of Malaysia*. Centre for Orang Asli Concerns.

Chivenge, P., Mabhaudhi, T., Modi, A., & Mafongoya, P. (2015). The potential role of neglected and underutilized crop species as future plants under water scarce conditions in sub-Saharan Africa. *International Journal of Environmental Research and Public Health, 12*(6), 5685–5711. doi:10.3390/ijerph120605685 PMID:26016431

Choe, S. T., Capella, L. M., & Arnold, D. R. (1993). Acculturation, Ethnic Consumers And Food Consumption Patterns. *Journal of Food Products Marketing, 1*(4), 61–79. doi:10.1300/J038v01n04_05

Copil, T. K., Thambiah, S., & Rosalind, L. Y. L. (2000). *The Ungendered God: An Investigation into Gender Relations in Semai Religion and Cosmology*. Paper presented at the National Conference "Wanita Malaysia dalam Alaf Baru, Petaling Jaya, Malaysia.

Darkwa, S., & Darkwa A.A. (2013). The Use of Indigenous Green Leafy Vegetables in the Preparation of Ghanaian Dishes. *Food Processing & Technology, 4*, 286.

Dentan, R. K. (2000a). The Semai of Malaysia. In L. Sponsel (Ed.), *Endangered Peoples of East and Southeast Asia* (pp. 208–232). Greenwood Publishing Group.

Eater, N. Y. (2017). *Bourdain Doesn't Want His Big NYC Market to Be Just For 'Gringos'*. Available at: https://ny.eater.com/2017/2/6/14521340/bourdain-market-gringos-dystopia

Ebert, A. (2014). Potential of Underutilized Traditional Vegetables and Legume Crops to Contribute to Food and Nutritional Security, Income and More Sustainable Production Systems. *Sustainability*, *6*(1), 319–335. doi:10.3390u6010319

Edo, J. (2006). *Retorik Pembangunan Orang Asli Dalam Malaysia Menangani Perubahan Dan Pembangunan*. Universiti Malaya Press.

Elferink & Schierhorn. (2016). *Global Demand for Food is Rising. Can We Meet it?* https://hbr.org/2016/04/global-demand-for-food-is-rising-can-we-meet-it

Gianno, R. (2016). What Happened to the Female Midwives? Gender, Childbirth, and Change in Semelai Society. In *Orang Asli Women of Malaysia*. Centre for Orang Asli Concerns.

Global National Security and Intelligence Agencies Handbook. (2015). *Volume 1 Strategic information and contacts*. International Washington Publications.

Hawkes, C., & Ruel, M. T. (2011). Value chains for nutrition. Academic Press.

Hefferon, K. (2015). Nutritionally Enhanced Food Crops; Progress and Perspectives. *International Journal of Molecular Sciences*, *16*(2), 3895–3914. doi:10.3390/ijms16023895 PMID:25679450

Howell, S. (2016). Chewong Women in Transition: The Effects of Monetization on a Hunter- Gatherer Society. In *Orang Asli Women of Malaysia*. Centre for Orang Asli Concerns.

IFPRI. (2020). *International Conference ''Leveraging Agriculture for Improving Nutrition and Health.''* New Delhi, India: IFPRI.

Mpala, C., Dlaminia, M., & Sibandaa, P. (2013). The Accessibility, Utilisation and Role of Indigenous Traditional Vegetables in Household Food Security in Rural Hwange District. *International Open & Distance Learning Journal*, *1*(3), 40–48.

Munchies. (2017). *This Pho-Stuffed Burrito Is Better than It Sounds*. Available at: https://munchies.vice.com/en_us/article/vvq7b9/this-pho-stuffed-burrito-is-better-than-it-sounds

Prescott-Allen, R., & Prescott-Allen, C. (1990). How Many Plants Feed the World? *Conservation Biology*, *4*(4), 365–374. doi:10.1111/j.1523-1739.1990.tb00310.x

Singh, S., Singh, D. R., Singh, L. B., Chand, S., & Dam Roy, S. (2013). Indigenous Vegetables for Food and Nutritional Security in Andaman and Nicobar Islands, India. *International Journal of Agriculture and Food Science Technology*, *4*(5), 503–512.

Stein, A., Sachdev, H., & Qaim, M. (2008). Genetic Engineering for the Poor: Golden Rice and Public Health in India. *World Development*, *36*(1), 144–158. doi:10.1016/j.worlddev.2007.02.013

The Star. (2017). *Japanese delight meets Malaysian innovation - Nation | The Star Online*. Available at: http://www.thestar.com.my/news/nation/2017/06/02/japanese- delight-meets-malaysian-innovation/

Von Grebmer, K., Saltzman, A., Birol, E., Wiesmann, D., Prasai, N., Yin, S., Yohannes, Y., Menon, P., Thompson, J., & Sonntag, A. (2014). *Global Hunger Index*. International Food Policy Research Institute.

Wang, Y. J., Wang, Y. L., Sub, X. D., Caiji, Z. M., Yang, J. B., Cui, D., Cao, G. L., Ma, X. D., Han, B., Xue, D. Y., & Han, L. Z. (2016). Influence of ethnic traditional cultures on genetic diversity of rice landraces under on-farm conservation in southwest China. *Journal of Ethnobiology and Ethnomedicine*, *12*(1), 51. doi:10.118613002-016-0120-0 PMID:27788685

World Street Food Congress. (2017). http://wsfcongress.com/award-2017- winners/

Compilation of References

10Future of Business Survey. (2018). *Explore the Future of Business.* https://eu.futureofbusinesssurvey.org/manager/Storyboard/RHViewStoryBoard.aspx

11Catalyst, Historical List of Women CEOs of the Fortune Lists: 1972-2018. (2018). Academic Press.

12Thornton, G. (2018). Women in Business: Beyond Policy to Progress. Academic Press.

13Eastman, M. T. (2017). Women on Boards: Progress Report. MSCI.

14UNESCO. (n.d.). https://unesdoc.unesco.org/images/0026/002615/261593E.pdf

15UNESCO. (2018). *Gender parity index*. UIS (UNESCO Institute of Statistics).

16 OECD. (2017b). *OECD Science, Technology and Industry Scoreboard 2017: The Digital Transformation.* OECD Publishing. doi:10.1787/9789264268821-

17International Labour Organization (ILO). (2017). Economic Impacts of Reducing the Gender Gap (What Works Research Brief No. 10). ILO.

18ILOSTAT. (2017). World Employment and Social Outlook: Trends for Women. Geneva: Author.

19ILOSTAT. (2018). *World Employment and Social Outlook: Trends*. Geneva: Author.

1F2017). *Chefs add fragrance and flavor with fresh herbs*. Nation's Restaurant News. Available at: http://www.nrn.com/whats-hot/chefs-add-fragrance-and-flavor- fresh-herbs

1Global Gender Gap Report. (n.d.). In *Wikipedia*. https://en.wikipedia.org/wiki/Global_Gender_Gap_Report

20Life Expectancy. (n.d.). *Global Health Observatory (GHO) data*. Available from: https://www.who.int/gho/mortality_burden_disease/life_tables/situation_trends_text/en/

21 Compare, G. B. D. (2016). *Data visualization hub*. Institute for Health Metrics and Evaluation, University of Washington. Available from https://vizhub.healthdata.org/gbd-compare

22Gender and Blindness. (2002). *Gender and health information sheet*. Geneva: World Health Organization. Available from: https://www.who.int/gender-equity-rights/knowledge/a85574/en

23Statnews. (2018). https://www.statnews.com/2018/08/01/gender-inequality-health-care-leadership-women/

24WHO. (n.d.). https://www.who.int/reproductivehealth/publications/monitoring/maternal-mortality-2015/en/

25 OECD. (2015). *The ABC of Gender Equality in Education: Aptitude, Behaviour, Confidence*. OECD Publishing. doi:10.1787/9789264229945-

26Global Entrepreneurship Monitor Report. (2017). Global Entrepreneurship Monitor.

27OECD Calculations Based on OECD. (2017). *Survey of Adult Skills (PIAAC).* www.oecd.org/skills/piaac/

28GVI. (n.d.). https://www.gvi.co.uk/blog/why-is-gender-equality-important/

29 OECD. (2017a). *Entrepreneurship at a Glance 2017.* OECD Publishing. doi:10.1787/entrepreneur_aag-2017-

2IMF. (n.d.). https://www.imf.org/external/pp/ppindex.aspx

30PwC. (2017). *Women in Work Index.* https://www.pwc.co.uk/services/economics-policy/insights/women-in-work-index.html

31McKinsey & Company. (2015). The Power of Parity: How Advancing Women's Equality Can Add $12 Trillion To Global Growth. Author.

3WIR. (2018). https://wir2018.wid.world

4IPU. (n.d.). http://archive.ipu.org/parlinee/WomenInParliament.asp?REGION=All&typesearch=1&LANG=ENG

5World Bank. (n.d.a). https://globalfindex.worldbank.org

6World Bank. (n.d.b). https://documents.worldbank.org/curated/en/926401524803880673/Women-Business-and-the-Law-2018

7Intel. (n.d.). https://www.intel.com/content/dam/www/public/us/en/documents/pdf/women-and-theweb.pdf

8GSMA. (2018). *Connected Women – The Mobile Gender Gap Report 2018.* https://www.gsma.com/mobilefordevelopment/wpcontentuploads/2018/03/GSMA_The_Mobile_Gender_Gap_Report_2018_Final_210218.pdf

9GSMA. (n.d.). https://www.gsma.com/mobilefordevelopment/connected-women/the-mobile-gender-gap-report-2018/

Abbasi, M. N., Malik, A., Chaudhry, I. S., & Imdadullah, M. (2011). A study on student satisfaction in Pakistani universities: The case of Bahauddin Zakariya University, Pakistan. *Asian Social Science*, *7*(7), 209. doi:10.5539/ass.v7n7p209

Abbas, K., Sabir, H. M., Shehzadi, A., & Abbas, Q. (2014). Impact of Workers' Remittances on Household Welfare in District Jhang (A Case Study of Tehsil 18 Hazari). *Journal of Financial Economics*, *2*, 131–135.

Adams, H. R. (2005). *Remittances, household expenditures and investment in Guatemala.* World Bank Policy Research Working Paper 3532.

ADB. (2017). *Basic Statistics, Manila.* Https://Www.Adb.Org/Publications/Basic-Statistics-2017

Addams, J. (1923). *A new conscience and an ancient evil.* Macmillan. Open Collections Program, Widener Library, Collections Development Department, Harvard University. http://nrs.harvard.edu/urn-3:FHCL:436848

Ahmed, R., Saha, J. K., Begum, M., & Haque, M. S. (2018). Impact of foreign remittances on household welfare in Sylhet region of Bangladesh. *Journal of Business and Economic Management*, *6*, 22–32.

AIPEG. (2017). *Gender Inequality in Indonesia. A report prepared in a collaboration between the Australian-Indonesian Partnership for Economic Governance (AIPEG), the Australian Department of Foreign Affairs and Trade (DFAT) and Monash University's Centre for Development Economics and Sustainability.* CDES.

Akhtar, J. H., & Iqbal, I. (2017). Impact of motivation on teachers' job performance: A case study of a public sector university. *Journal of Educational and Social Research*, *4*(1), 53–71.

Akter, S., Rutsaert, P., Luis, J., Htwe, N. M., San, S. S., Raharjo, B., & Pustika, A. (2017). Women's empowerment and gender equity in agriculture: A different perspective from Southeast Asia. *Food Policy*, *69*, 270–279. doi:10.1016/j.foodpol.2017.05.003

Alhaji, I. A. (2012). Does motivational factor influence organizational commitment and effectiveness? A review of literature. *E3 Journal of Business Management and Economics, 3*(1), 1-9.

Ali, M. (2015). Effect of Gender Inequality on Economic Growth: Case of Pakistan. *Journal of Economics and Sustainable Development, 6*(9), 10-10.

Alisjahbana, A. S., & Manning, C. (2006). Labour market dimensions of poverty in Indonesia. *Bulletin of Indonesian Economic Studies*, *42*(2), 235–261. doi:10.1080/00074910600873674

Alkire, S., Meinzen-Dick, R., Peterman, A., Quisuimbing, A. R., Seymour, G., & Vaz, A. (2013). The Women's Empowerment in Agriculture Index. *World Development*, *52*, 71–91. doi:10.1016/j.worlddev.2013.06.007

Amizi Ayob, M., Nutman, A., Lee, L. H., Alias, A., Khamis, S., Hafiz Boon, N. E. F., ... Soon, J. M. (2016). Indigenous Plants and Tuber as Alternative Food Sources for Temiar Communities During Flood seasons. *Advances in Environmental Biology*, *10*(1), 93–100.

Anand, A. (2019). Indian healthcare at a crossroads (Part 1): Deteriorating doctor-patient relationship. *The National Medical Journal of India*, *32*(1), 41–45. http://www.nmji.in/article.asp?issn=0970-258X;year=2019;volume=32;issue=1;spage=41;epage=45;aulast=Anand#ft22 PMID:31823941

Anderson, M. (1926). *Women in the fruit-growing and canning industries in the State of Washington* [Letter of Transmittal]. United States Department of Labor, Women's Bureau. Washington, DC: Government Printing Office. Immigration to the United States, 1789-1930, Open Collections Program, Baker Library, Harvard University. http://ocp.hul.harvard.edu

Apostolopoulos, N., Al-Dajani, H., Holt, D., Jones, P., & Newbery, R. 2018). Entrepreneurship and the Sustainable Development Goals. In Entrepreneurship and the Sustainable Development Goals (Contemporary Issues in Entrepreneurship Research, Volume 8) (pp. 1-7). Emerald Publishing Limited.

Aquino, J.P.L., Pedalgo, C.C., Zafra, A.R.N., & Tuzon, T.P. (2015). The Perception of Local Street Food Vendors Of Tanauan City, Batangas On Food Safety. *Laguna Journal of International Tourism and Hospitality Management, 3*(1).

Arif, B., & Farooqi, Y. A. (2014). Impact of work life balance on job satisfaction and organizational commitment among university teachers: A case study of University of Gujrat, Pakistan. *International Journal of Multidisciplinary Sciences and Engineering, 5*(9), 24-29.

Ashraf, N., Karlan, D. S., & Yin, W. (2009). *Female Empowerment: Impact of a Commitment Savings Product in the Philippines.* Harvard Business School Working Paper, 09-100.

Asian Development Bank (ADB). (2005). *Country Gender Assessment Uzbekistan*. Philippines: ADB.

Asian Development Bank. (2013). *Gender Equality in the Labor Market in Cambodia*. International Publications: Cornell University ILR School.

Asiati, Aji, Ngadi, Triyono, Ningrum, Edi, Aruan, & Purba. (2018). Transformasi Digital dan Ketenagakerjaan di Indonesia. P2K-LIPI, Jakarta.

Asli, A., & Nour, H. (2018). Female Entrepreneurship in Morocco, Obstacles and Ways to Overcome Them. *6th International OFEL Conference on Governance, Management and Entrepreneurship. New Business Models and Institutional Entrepreneurs: Leading Disruptive Change. April 13th - 14th, 2018, Dubrovnik, Croatia, Governance Research and Development Centre (CIRU)*, 390-401.

Association of American Medical Colleges. (2018). An exploration of the recent decline in the percentage of U.S. medical school graduates with education debt. *Analysis in Brief, 18*(4). Retrieved from https://www.aamc.org/system/files/reports/1/september2018anexplorationoftherecentdeclineinthepercentageofu.pdf

Awang, Z., Ahmad, J. H., & Zin, N. M. (2010). Modelling job satisfaction and work commitment among lecturers: A case of UiTM Kelantan. *Journal of Statistical Modeling and Analytics, 1*(2), 45–59.

Ayers, E. L., Gould, L. L., Oshinsky, D. M., & Soderlund, J. R. (2012). American passages: A history of the United States (4th ed.). Wadsworth Cengage.

Baer, A. (2016). The Health of Orang Asli Women. In *Orang Asli Women of Malaysia*. Centre for Orang Asli Concerns.

Baldwin, M., & Johnson, W. G. (1992). Estimating the employment effects of wage discrimination. *The Review of Economics and Statistics, 74*(3), 446–455. doi:10.2307/2109489

Baliamousne-Lutz & McGullivray. (2007). Does Gender Inequality Reduce Growth in Sub Saharan African and Arab countries? *African Development Review*, 224–242.

Banerjee, A., Duflo, E., Glennerster, R., & Kinnan, C. (2009). *The Miracle of Microfinance? Evidence from a randomized evaluation.* Center for Microfinance Working Paper 31.

Baron, R. A. (2006). *Psychology*. Pearson Education, Inc.

Barretto, H. (1989). *The Entrepreneur in Microeconomic Theory: Disappearance and Explanation.* Routledge.

Barsh, J., & Yee, L. (2012). Unlocking the full potential of women at work. *McKinsey & Company/Wall Street Journal.*

Barua, S., Majumder, M., & Akhtaruzzaman, D. (2007). *Determinants of Workers' Remittances in Bangladesh: An Empirical Study.* Policy Analysis Unit (PAU), Bangladesh Bank Working Paper No. WP, 713.

Bawakid, K., Rashid, O., Mandoura, N., Shah, H., & Mugharbel, K. (2018). Professional satisfaction of family physicians working in primary healthcare centers: A comparison of two Saudi regions. *Journal of Family Medicine and Primary Care, 7*(5), 1019–1025. https://www.ncbi.nlm.nih.gov/pmc/articles/PMC6259539/ PMID:30598950

Bhattacharjee, Hnatkovsa, & Lahiri. (2015). The Evolution of Gender Gaps in India. *India Policy Forum, 11*(1), 119-156. https://faculty.arts.ubc.ca/vhnatkovska/Research/GenderGap.pdf

Biziou, B. (2010). *The Joy of Family Rituals: Recipes for Everyday Living*. Cosimo, Inc.

Blackden, M., Canagarajah, S., Klasen, S., & Lawson, D. (2007). Gender and Growth in Africa: Evidence and Issues. In Advancing Development: Core Themes in Global Development. WIDER and UNU-WIDER Research Paper No. 2006/37.

Blank, R. M, (2010). *Women-Owned Businesses in the 21st Century*. Report prepared by US. Department of Commerce, Economics and Statistics Department, for White House Council of Women and Girls.

Blau, F. D., & Kahn, L. M. (2001). *Understanding International Differences in The Gender Pay Gap*. NBER Working Paper No.8200. National Bureau of Economic Research.

Bloom, D. E., Canning, D., Fink, G., & Finlay, J. E. (2007). Fertility, Female Labor Force Participation, and Demographic Dividend. *Journal of Economic Growth, 14*(2), 79–101. doi:10.100710887-009-9039-9

Bobula, J. (1980). Work patterns, practice characteristics, and incomes of male and female physicians. *Journal of Medical Education, 55*, 826–833. PMID:7420390

Bodur, S. (2001). Job satisfaction of health care staff employed at health centres in Turkey. *Society of Occupational Medicine, 52*(6), 353-355. Retrieved from https://bit.ly/37EsEhF

Bovier, P., & Perneger, T. (2004). Predictors of work satisfaction among physicians. *European Journal of Public Health, 13*(4), 299–305. doi:10.1093/eurpub/13.4.299 PMID:14703315

Boyle, P. (2020). *U.S. physician shortage growing*. Association of American Medical Colleges. Retrieved from https://www.aamc.org/news-insights/us-physician-shortage-growing

Brown, M. E. (1994/2008). Parents and children fundamental questions about immigrant family life. In T. Walch (Ed.), *Immigrant America: European ethnicity in the United States* (pp. 89–102). Routledge.

Bruhn, M., & Zia, B. (2011). *Stimulating managerial capital in emerging markets: the impact of business and financial literacy for young entrepreneurs*. The World Bank. doi:10.1596/1813-9450-5642

Bruyn, D. T. (2005). Dynamics of Remittance Utilization in Bangladesh. IOM Migration Research Series, No. 18. UN.

Buchbinder, S., Melick, C., & Powe, N. (2001). Managed care and primary care physicians' overall career satisfaction. *Journal of Health Care Finance, 23*(2), 35–44. PMID:11794755

Bum, S. M. (1995). *The Social Psychology of Gender*. McGraw-Hill College.

Burke, M. (2004). Generational difference survey report. Society for Human Resource Management. Alexandria, VA: SHRM Research Department.

Burn, F. K. E. (2005). 1920: August, Febb Burn to Harry Burn. In L. Grunwald & S. J. Adler (Eds.), *Women's letters: America from the Revolutionary War to the present* (p. 489). The Dial Press. (Original work published 1920)

Cabinet of Ministers. (1998). *On the Establishment of the Oila National Scientific, Practical Centre (Decree No. 54). 2 February.* Http://Old.Lex.Uz/Pages/Getact.Aspx?Lact_Id=844011.

Cabot, R. (2015). Women in medicine. *Journal of the American Medical Association, 314*(10), 1076. doi:10.1001/jama.2014.11972 PMID:26348764

Cabrera-Gil-Grados, E. M., & Mauricio, D. (2017). *Factors affecting the success of women's entrepreneurship: a review of literature*. Academic Press.

Cagatay, N., & Ozler, S. (1995). Feminization of the labor force: The effects of long-term development and structural adjustment. *World Development, 23*(11), 1883–1894. doi:10.1016/0305-750X(95)00086-R

Cao, X. (2011). The Chinese Medical Doctor Association: A new industrial relations actor in China's Health Services? *Relations Industrielles. Industrial Relations, 66*(1), 74–97. doi:10.7202/1005106ar

Cennamo, L., & Gardner, D. (2008). Generational differences in work values, outcomes and person-organization values fit. *Journal of Managerial Psychology, 23*(8), 891–906. doi:10.1108/02683940810904385

Center for Studying Health System Change. (2008). *Health tracking physician survey*. Retrieved from http://www.hschange.org/CONTENT/1085

Central Bureau of Statistics. (2019). *Keadaan Angkatan Kerja di Indonesia Agustus 2018 (Labor Force Situation in Indonesia August 2018)*. BPS-Statistics Indonesia.

Cepeda, L. (2013). Gender Wage inequality in Indonesia. In T. W. Bank (Ed.), *Presentation*. The World Bank Office Jakarta.

Chandrasekar, K. (2011). Workplace environment and its impact on organizational performance in public sector organizations. *International Journal of Enterprise Computing and Business Systems, 1*(1), 1-19.

Chandra, T. (2019). *Literacy in India: The Gender and Age Dimension. ORF Issue Brief No. 322*. October, Observer Research Foundation.

Chant, S. (2010). Gender and Export Manufacturing in the Philippines: Continuity or change in female employment? The case of the Mactan Export Processing Zone. *Journal of Gender. Place and Culture.*, *2*(2), 147–176. doi:10.1080/09663699550021991

Charmes, J., & Wieringa, S. (2003). Measuring Women's Empowerment: An assessment of the Gender-related Development Index and the Gender Empowerment Measure. *Journal of Human Development*, *4*(3), 419–435. doi:10.1080/1464988032000125773

Chevalier, A. (2007). Education, Occupation and Career Expectations: Determinants of the Gender Pay Gap for UK Graduates. *Oxford Bulletin of Economics and Statistics*, *69*(6), 819–842. doi:10.1111/j.1468-0084.2007.00483.x

Chin, G. V. S., & Hoogervorst, T. (2017). From Soetji to Soendel: Negotiating race, class and gender in a Netherlands Indies newspaper. *Intersections: Gender and Sexuality in Asia and the Pacific, 41.*

Chivenge, P., Mabhaudhi, T., Modi, A., & Mafongoya, P. (2015). The potential role of neglected and underutilized crop species as future plants under water scarce conditions in sub-Saharan Africa. *International Journal of Environmental Research and Public Health*, *12*(6), 5685–5711. doi:10.3390/ijerph120605685 PMID:26016431

Choe, S. T., Capella, L. M., & Arnold, D. R. (1993). Acculturation, Ethnic Consumers And Food Consumption Patterns. *Journal of Food Products Marketing*, *1*(4), 61–79. doi:10.1300/J038v01n04_05

Choudhry, M. T., & Elhorst, P. (2018). Female labour force participation and economic development. *International Journal of Manpower*, *39*(7), 896–912. doi:10.1108/IJM-03-2017-0045

Chowdhury, M. B. (2011). Remittances flow and financial development in Bangladesh. *Economic Modelling*, *28*(6), 2600–2608. doi:10.1016/j.econmod.2011.07.013

Cialdini, R. B. (1994). *Interpersonal Influence* (S. Shavitt & T. C. Brocks, Eds.). Allyn & Bacon.

Ciccarelli, S. K., & Meyer, G. E. (2008). Psychology: South Asian Edition. New Delhi: Dorling Kindersley (India) Private Limited.

Colaco, V., & Hans, V. (2018). *Women Entrepreneurship in India–Changes and Challenges*. Academic Press.

Collins. (1976). Rousseau's Philosophy (or Philosophies?) of Education. *The Irish Journal of Education*, *2*, 51-80.

Collins, K., Schoen, C., & Sandman, D. (1997). *The Commonwealth fund survey of physician experience with managed care*. Commonwealth Fund. Retrieved from http://www.cmwf.org/ programs/health_care/physrvy.asp

Commins, J. (2017). US physician workforce is getting old, fast. *HealthLeaders*. Retrieved from https://www.healthleadersmedia.com/strategy/us-physician-workforce-getting-old-fast

Copil, T. K., Thambiah, S., & Rosalind, L. Y. L. (2000). *The Ungendered God: An Investigation into Gender Relations in Semai Religion and Cosmology*. Paper presented at the National Conference "Wanita Malaysia dalam Alaf Baru, Petaling Jaya, Malaysia.

Cornford, F. M. (1941). The Republic of Plato. Oxford University Press.

Costanza, R., Hart, M., Talberth, J., & Posner, S. (2009). Beyond GDP: The need for new measures of progress. *The Pardee Papers*.

Cotter, D., Hermsen, J. M., & Vanneman, R. (2011). The end of gender revolution? Gender role attitudes from 1977 to 2008. *American Journal of Sociology*, *117*(1), 259–289. doi:10.1086/658853 PMID:22003521

Cristini, A. (2011, October). *Employees' motivation and high performance workplace practices.* In European Economic Association and Econometric Society. 2011 Parallel Meetings, Malaga, Spain.

Cunningham, M., Beutel, A. M., Barber, J. S., & Thorton, A. (2005). Reciprocal relationships between attitudes about gender and social contexts during young adulthood. *Social Science Research, 34*(4), 862–892. doi:10.1016/j.ssresearch.2005.03.001

Cuong, N. V., & Linh, V. H. (2018). The impact of migration and remittances on household welfare: Evidence from Vietnam. *Journal of International Migration and Integration, 19*(4), 945–963. doi:10.100712134-018-0571-3

Czaja, S., Charness, N., Fisk, A., Hertzog, C., Nair, S., Rogers, W., & Sharit, J. (2006). Factors predicting the use of technology: Findings from the Center for Research and Education on Aging and Technology Enhancement. *Psychology and Aging, 21*(2), 333–352. doi:10.1037/0882-7974.21.2.333 PMID:16768579

Danish, R. Q., & Usman, A. (2010). Impact of reward and recognition on job satisfaction and motivation: An empirical study from Pakistan. *International Journal of Business and Management, 5*(2), 159. doi:10.5539/ijbm.v5n2p159

Darkwa, S., & Darkwa A.A. (2013). The Use of Indigenous Green Leafy Vegetables in the Preparation of Ghanaian Dishes. *Food Processing & Technology, 4*, 286.

Das, M. (2000). Women entrepreneurs from India: Problems, motivations and success factors. *Journal of Small Business and Entrepreneurship, 15*(4), 67–81. doi:10.1080/08276331.2000.10593294

Davis, S. N., & Greenstein, T. N. (2009). Gender ideology: Components, predictors, and consequences. *Sociological Perspectives, 50*, 249–271. doi:10.1525op.2007.50.2.249

Debnath, P., & Selim, N. (2009). Impact of short term male migration on their wives left behind: A case study of Bangladesh. *Gender and Labour Migration in Asia, IOM*, 121-151.

Deléchat, C., Newiak, M., Xu, R., Yang, F., & Aslan, G. (2018). *What is Driving Women's Financial Inclusion Across Countries?* IMF Working Paper 18/38, International Monetary Fund.

Dempsey, M. V. (1922). *The occupational progress of women: An interpretation of census statistics of women in gainful occupations* (Bulletin of the Women's Bureau, no. 27). United States Department of Labor, Women's Bureau. Government Printing Office. http://nrs.harvard.edu/urn-3:HBS.BAKER:123561

Dentan, R. K. (2000a). The Semai of Malaysia. In L. Sponsel (Ed.), *Endangered Peoples of East and Southeast Asia* (pp. 208–232). Greenwood Publishing Group.

Department for International Development, The Importance of Financial Sector Development for Growth and Poverty Reduction. (2004). Policy Division Working Paper.

Dissanayake, K. (2018). Environmental effects on women-LED SMEs in Asia: From institutional perspective. *The Journal of Business, 5*, 1.

Doss, C., Meinzen-Dick, R., Quisumbing, A., & Theis, S. (2018). Woman in agriculture: Four Myth. *Global Food Security, 16*(1), 69–74. doi:10.1016/j.gfs.2017.10.001 PMID:29552461

Dumenil, L. (1998). Re-shifting perspectives on the 1920s: Recent trends in social and cultural history. In J. E. Haynes (Ed.), *Calvin Coolidge and the Coolidge Era* (pp. 63–96). Library of Congress.

Eagles, C. W. (1989). Congressional voting in the 1920s: A test of urban-rural conflict. *The Journal of American History, 76*(2), 528–534. doi:10.2307/1907989

Eater, N. Y. (2017). *Bourdain Doesn't Want His Big NYC Market to Be Just For 'Gringos'*. Available at: https://ny.eater.com/2017/2/6/14521340/bourdain-market-gringos-dystopia

Ebert, A. (2014). Potential of Underutilized Traditional Vegetables and Legume Crops to Contribute to Food and Nutritional Security, Income and More Sustainable Production Systems. *Sustainability*, *6*(1), 319–335. doi:10.3390u6010319

Edo, J. (2006). *Retorik Pembangunan Orang Asli Dalam Malaysia Menangani Perubahan Dan Pembangunan*. Universiti Malaya Press.

Elborgh-Woytek, K., Newiak, M., Kochhar, K., Fabrizio, S., Kpodar, K., Wingender, P., Clements, B., & Schwartz, G. (2013). *Women, Work, and the Economy: Macroeconomic Gains from Gender Equity. Staff Discussion Note 13/10*. International Monetary Fund.

Elferink & Schierhorn. (2016). *Global Demand for Food is Rising. Can We Meet it?* https://hbr.org/2016/04/global-demand-for-food-is-rising-can-we-meet-it

Elliott, C. M. (2008). *Global empowerment of women: Responses to globalization and politicized religions*. Rutledge.

Elmhirst, Siscawati, Basnett, & Ekowati. (2017). Gender and generation in engagements with oil palm in East Kalimantan, Indonesia: insights from feminist political ecology. *The Journal of Peasant Studies*, *44*(6), 1135-1157.

Emmons, S., Nichols, M., Schulkin, J., James, K., & Cain, J. (2006). The influence of physician gender on practice satisfaction among obstetrician gynecologists. *American Journal of Obstetrics and Gynecology*, *194*(6), 1728–1739. doi:10.1016/j.ajog.2006.03.012 PMID:16635457

Epstein, R., & Peters, E. (2007). Beyond information: Exploring patients' preferences. *Journal of the Medical Association*, *302*(2), 195–197. doi:10.1001/jama.2009.984 PMID:19584351

Erturk, K., & Cagatay, N. (1995). Macroeconomic consequences of cyclical and secular changes in feminization: An experiment at gendered macromodeling. *World Development*, *23*(11), 1969–1977. doi:10.1016/0305-750X(95)00090-Y

Esteve-Volart, B. (2009). *Gender discrimination and growth: Theory and evidence from India. mimeo*. York University.

Express, F. (2018). *India's economic growth not inclusive enough, inequality rises*. Retrieved March 15, 2020, from https://www.financialexpress.com/economy/indias-economic-growth-not-inclusive-enough-inequality-rises/1358413/

Fakir, A. M., & Abedin, N. (2020). Empowered by Absence: Does Male Out-migration Empower Female Household Heads Left Behind? *Journal of International Migration and Integration*, 1–25.

FAO. (2019). *Country Gender Assessment of Agriculture and the Rural Sector in Indonesia*. Food and Agriculture Organization of the United Nations Jakarta.

Fatima, N., & Sahibzada, S. A. (2012). An empirical analysis of factors affecting work life balance among university teachers: The case of Pakistan. *Journal of International Academic Research*, *12*(1), 16–29.

Feridhanusetyawan, T., Aswicahyono, H., & Perdana, A. A. (2001). The male-female wage differentials in Indonesia. *Economics Working Paper Series, 59*.

Field, E., Jayachandran, S., & Pande, R. (2010). Do Traditional Institutions Constrain Female Entrepreneurship? A Field Experiment on Business Training in India. *The American Economic Review*, *100*(2), 125–129. doi:10.1257/aer.100.2.125

Fitrania, S. N. (2013). *The Impact of Globalization on Gender Wage Gap in Indonesia: A Sub-National Level Analysis* (Master's Thesis). Tilburg University.

Ford, M., & Parker, L. (2008). Thinking about Indonesian Women and Work. In M. Ford & L. Parker (Eds.), *Women and Work in Indonesia* (pp. 1–16). Routledge. doi:10.4324/9780203932360

Forson, M., & Essel, J. (2012). *Impact of motivation on the productivity of employees at GTBank Ghana* (Doctoral dissertation).

Forsythe, N., Korzeniewicz, R. P., & Durrant, V. (2000). Gender inequalities and economic growth: A longitudinal evaluation. *Economic Development and Cultural Change*, *48*(3), 573–617. doi:10.1086/452611

Frank, E., McMurray, J., Linzer, M., & Elon, L. (1999). Career satisfaction of US women physicians: Results from the women physicians' health study. *Archives of Internal Medicine*, *159*(3), 1417–1426. doi:10.1001/archinte.159.13.1417 PMID:10399893

Franklin. (1747). *Proposals relating to the Education of Youth in Pennsylvania 1747*. National Humanities Center Resource Toolbox Becoming American: The British Atlantic Colonies, 1690-1763.

Gandhi, M. K. (1962). *Village Swaraj* (H. M. Vyas, Ed.). Navjivan Publishing House.

Garg, S., & Anand, T. (2015). Menstruation Related Myths in India: Strategies for Combating It. *Journal of Family Medicine and Primary Care*, *4*(2), 184–186. doi:10.4103/2249-4863.154627 PMID:25949964

Gaye, A., Klugman, J., Kovacevic, M., Twigg, S., & Zambrano, E. (2010). Measuring key disparities in human development: The gender inequality index. *Human Development Research Paper, 46*, 41.

GenderNet Issues Paper. (2011). *Women Economic Empowerment*. Author.

George La Piana. 1878-1972. (n.d.). [Immigration to the United States, 1789-1930]. Open Collections Program, Harvard University. http://ocp.hul.harvard.edu/immigration/people_lapiana.html

Gerteis, M., Edgeman-Levitan, S., Daly, J., & Delbanco, T. (1993). *Through the patient's eyes: Understanding and promoting patient-centered care*. Jossey-Bass.

Ghani, E., William, K., & Stephen, O. (2011b). *Spatial Determinants of Entrepreneurship in India*. NBER Working Paper 17514.

Gianno, R. (2016). What Happened to the Female Midwives? Gender, Childbirth, and Change in Semelai Society. In *Orang Asli Women of Malaysia*. Centre for Orang Asli Concerns.

Global National Security and Intelligence Agencies Handbook. (2015). *Volume 1 Strategic information and contacts*. International Washington Publications.

Goldberg, D. J. (1999). *Discontented America: The United States in the 1920s*. The Johns Hopkins University Press.

Goldin, C. (1994). *The U-shaped female labor force function in economic development and economic history*. NBER Working Paper No. 4707.

Government of India. (2007). National Family Health Survey (NFHS- 3) 2005-06. Ministry of health and family welfare.

Government of India. (2009). Coverage Evaluation Survey (CES). Ministry of health and family welfare.

Government of India. (2010). District Level Household and Facility Survey (DLHS-3) 2007-08. Ministry of health and family welfare.

Government of India. (2013). District Level Household and Facility Survey (DLHS-4) 2012-13. Ministry of health and family welfare.

Government of India. (2017). National Family Health Survey (NFHS- 4) 2015-16. Ministry of health and family welfare.

Government of India. (2017). *National Health Policy*. Ministry of health and family welfare. Retrieved March 15, 2020, from http://www.cdsco.nic.in/writereaddata/National-Health-Policy.pdf

Government of India. (2020). *Economic Survey 2019-20*. Ministry of Finance, Department of Economic Affairs. Retrieved March 15, 2020, from https://www.prsindia.org/sites/default/files/parliament_or_policy_pdfs/Economic%20Survey%20 2019-20%20Summary.pdf

Graham, O. L. Jr, & Koed, E. (1993). Americanizing the immigrant, past and future: History and implications of a social movement. *The Public Historian*, *15*(4), 24–49. doi:10.2307/3378635

Grembowski, D., Ulrich, C., Paschane, D., Diehr, P., Katon, W., Martin, D., Patrick, D., & Velicer, C. (2003). Managed care and primary physician satisfaction. *Journal of the American Board of Family Medicine*, *16*(5), 383–393. doi:10.3122/jabfm.16.5.383 PMID:14645328

Guérin, I., Kumar, S., &Agier, I. (2013). Women's Empowerment: Power to Act or Power over Other Women? Lessons from Indian Microfinance. *Oxford Development Studies*, *41*(sup1), S76-S94.

Guiso, L., Sapienza, P., & Zingales, L. (2003). People's opium? Religion and economic attitudes. *Journal of Monetary Economics*, *50*(1), 225–282. doi:10.1016/S0304-3932(02)00202-7

Gullett, G. (1995). Women progressives and the politics of Americanization in California, 1915-1920. *Pacific Historical Review*, *64*(1), 71–94. doi:10.2307/3640335

Gursoy, D., Maier, T., & Chi, C. (2008). Generational differences: An examination of work values and generational gaps in the hospitality workforce. *International Journal of Hospitality Management*, *27*(3), 448–458. doi:10.1016/j.ijhm.2007.11.002

Haarsager, S. (1997). *Organized womanhood: Cultural politics in the Pacific Northwest, 1840-1920*. University of Oklahoma Press.

Hadi, A. (2001). International migration and the change of women's position among the left-behind in rural Bangladesh. *International Journal of Population Geography*, *7*(1), 53–61. doi:10.1002/ijpg.211

Haider, M. Z., Hossain, T., & Siddiqui, O. I. (2016). Impact of remittance on consumption and savings behavior in rural areas of Bangladesh. *The Journal of Business*, *1*(4), 25–34. doi:10.18533/job.v1i4.49

Hakura, M. D. S., Hussain, M. M., Newiak, M. M., Thakoor, V., & Yang, M. F. (2016). *Inequality, gender gaps and economic growth: Comparative evidence for sub-Saharan Africa*. International Monetary Fund.

Hans, V. (2018). *Women Entrepreneurs in Modern Era–Opportunities*. Trends and Challenges.

Haque, N. (2007). *Entrepreneurship in Pakistan. Pakistan Institute of Development Economics*. Working Paper, 20.

Hardré, P. L., & Kollmann, S. L. (2012). Motivational implications of faculty performance standards. *Educational Management Administration & Leadership*, *40*(6), 724–751. doi:10.1177/1741143212456913

Harwood, E. (1986). American public opinion and U.S. immigration policy. *The Annals of the American Academy of Political and Social Science*, *487*(1), 201–212. doi:10.1177/0002716286487001013

Hashemi, S. M., Schuler, S. R., & Riley, A. P. (1996). Rural credit programs and women's empowerment in Bangladesh. *World Development*, *24*(4), 635–653. doi:10.1016/0305-750X(95)00159-A

Hawkes, C., & Ruel, M. T. (2011). Value chains for nutrition. Academic Press.

Hawk, J., & Mills, J. (2011). *The women's empowerment principles: Equality means business initiative. United Nations Global Compact* (2nd ed.). UN Women.

Hefferon, K. (2015). Nutritionally Enhanced Food Crops; Progress and Perspectives. *International Journal of Molecular Sciences, 16*(2), 3895–3914. doi:10.3390/ijms16023895 PMID:25679450

Hildebrandt, N., & McKenzie, D. (2005). *The effects of migration on child health in Mexico.* Working Paper No. 3573. World Bank.

Hojat, M., Gonnella, J., Nasca, T., Mangione, S., Vergare, M., & Magee, M. (2002). *Physician empathy: Definition, components, measurement, and relationship to gender and specialty.* Center for Research in Medical Education and Health Care. Retrieved from http://jdc.jefferson.edu/cgi/viewcontent.cgi?article=1003&context=crmehc

Holmén, M., Min, T. T., & Saarelainen, E. (2011). Female entrepreneurship in Afghanistan. *Journal of Developmental Entrepreneurship, 16*(03), 307–331. doi:10.1142/S1084946711001860

Hotelling, H. (1936). *Relation between two sets of variates.* Biometrica.

Howcroft, D., & Rubery, J. (2018). *Gender Equality Prospects and The Fourth Industrial Revolution.* https://policynetwork.org/opinions/essays/gender-equality-prospects-fourth-industrial-revolution/

Howell, S. (2016). Chewong Women in Transition: The Effects of Monetization on a Hunter- Gatherer Society. In *Orang Asli Women of Malaysia.* Centre for Orang Asli Concerns.

Human Development Report. (2016). Http://Hdr.Undp.Org/Sites/All/Themes/Hdr_Theme/Country-Notes/Uzb.Pdf

Human Development Report. (2019). *Beyond income, beyond averages, beyond today: Inequalities in human development in the 21st century.* United Nations Development Programme.

Hummel, C. (1993), Aristotle (384-322 B.C.). PROSPECTS: The Quarterly Review of Comparative Education, 23(1-2), 39-51.

Hunt, Prince, Dixon-Fyle, & Yee. (2018). *Delivering Through Diversity.* McKinsey & Company.

Ibrahim, S. (2013). Status Of Women In Uzbekistan. *Journal Of Humanities And Social Science, 10*(3), 47-55.

IFPRI. (2020). *International Conference "Leveraging Agriculture for Improving Nutrition and Health."* New Delhi, India: IFPRI.

Institute for Policy Research Studies. (2019). *State of State Finances.* Government of India. Retrieved March 15, 2020, from https://www.prsindia.org/sites/default/files/parliament_or_policy_pdfs/State%20of%20State%20Finances%202019-20.pdf

Inuwa, M. (2016). Job satisfaction and employee performance: An empirical approach. *The Millennium University Journal, 1*(1), 90–103.

Jabeen, S., & Ahmad, F. (n.d.). *Culture and Barriers to Women's Entrepreneurs in Pakistan.* Academic Press.

Janowitz, N. (2002). *Magic in the Roman World: Pagans, Jews and Christians.* Taylor & Francis. doi:10.4324/9780203457641

Jaskiewicz, W., & Tulenko, K. (2012). Increasing community health worker productivity and effectiveness: A review of the influence of the work environment. *Human Resources for Health, 10*(1), 38. doi:10.1186/1478-4491-10-38 PMID:23017131

Jones, L. (2012). *Discussion Paper for an M4P Women's Economic Empowerment Framework. How can the Making Markets Work for the Poor Framework work for poor women and for poor men?* The Springfield Centre for Business in Development.

Joshi, D. (2014). Feminist Solidarity? Women's Engagement in Politics and the Implications for Water Management in the Darjeeling Himalaya. *Mountain Research and Development*, *34*(3), 243–254. doi:10.1659/MRD-JOURNAL-D-13-00097.1

Jovic, E., Wallace, J. E., & Lemaire, J. (2006). The generation and gender shifts in medicine: An exploratory survey of internal medicine physicians. *BMC Health Services Research*, *5*(May), 55. doi:10.1186/1472-6963-6-55 PMID:16677387

Jurkiewicz, C., & Bradley, D. (2002). Generational ethics: Age cohort and healthcare executives' values. *HEC Forum*, *14*(2), 148–171. doi:10.1023/A:1020907731617 PMID:12141008

Kabeer, N. (1999). Resources, Agency, Achievements: Reflections on the measurement of women's empowerment. *Development and Change*, *30*(3), 435–464. doi:10.1111/1467-7660.00125

Kabeer, N. (2005). Gender equality and Women"s empowerment: A critical analysis of the third Millennium Development Goal. *Gender and Development*, *13*(1), 13–36. doi:10.1080/13552070512331332273

Kaiser Family Foundation. (2015). *Distribution of physicians by gender*. Retrieved from http://kff.org/other/state-indicator/physicians-by-gender/#table

Kaldenberg, D., Becker, B., & Zvonkovic, A. (1995). Work and commitment among young professionals: A study of male and female dentists. *Human Relations*, *48*(11), 1355–1377. doi:10.1177/001872679504801106

Kalim, A. (2019). Women Entrepreneurship the Emerging Workforce in 21st Century: Turning Challenges to Opportunities. *Proceeding of 2nd International Conference on Business Management.*

Kangmennaang, J., Bezner-Kerr, R., & Luginaah, I. (2018). Impact of migration and remittances on household welfare among rural households in Northern and Central Malawi. *Migration and Development*, *7*(1), 55–71. doi:10.1080/21632324.2017.1325551

Kapur, D. (2004). *Remittances: The New Development Mantra?* (No. 29; G-24 Discussion Paper Series). United Nations Conference on Trade and Development.

Kashyap, S. C. (2008). *Our Constitution: An Introduction to India's Constitution & Constitutional Law*. National Book Trust.

Katerndahl, D., Parchman, M., & Wood, R. (2009). Perceived complexity of care, perceived autonomy, and career satisfaction among primary care physicians. *Journal of the American Board of Family Medicine*, *22*(1), 24–33. doi:10.3122/jabfm.2009.01.080027 PMID:19124630

Keeton, K., Fenner, D., Johnson, T., & Hayward, R. (2007). Predictors of physician career satisfaction, work-life balance, and burnout. *Obstetrics and Gynecology*, *109*(4), 949–955. doi:10.1097/01.AOG.0000258299.45979.37 PMID:17400859

Keltgen, J. (2016). *The impact of generational and gender effects on physician satisfaction in the US* (Doctoral dissertation). University of South Dakota.

Khan, A. A. (2014). Factors affecting the performance of female entrepreneurship: evidence from Punjab, Pakistan. Pakistan.

Khan, G., Naveed, R. T., & Jantan, A. H. B. (2018). Status of Wonder Women: Challenges for Young Future Women Entrepreneurs in Pakistan. *International Journal of Experiential Learning & Case Studies*, *3*(1), 97–109. doi:10.22555/ijelcs.v3i1.1838

Kim, J., Lee, J. W., & Shin, K. (2018). Gender inequality and economic growth in Korea. *Pacific Economic Review*, *23*(4), 658–682. doi:10.1111/1468-0106.12181

Kishor, S. (1997). *Empowerment of women in Egypt and Link to the Survival and Health of their infants*. Paper presented at the Seminar on Female Empowerment and Demographic Process.

Klasen, S. (2002). Low Schooling for Girls, Slower Growth for All? Cross Country Evidence on the Effect of Gender Inequality in Education on Economic Development. *The World Bank Economic Review*, *16*(3), 345–373. doi:10.1093/wber/lhf004

Klasen, S., & Lamanna, F. (2009). The impact of gender inequality in education and employment on economic growth: New evidence for a panel of countries. *Feminist Economics*, *15*(3), 91–132. doi:10.1080/13545700902893106

Koc, I., & Onan, I. (2001). The impact of remittances of international migrants on the standard of living of the left-behind families in Turkey. Hacettepe University Institute of Population Studies, 6100.

Konrad, T., Williams, E., Linzer, M., McMurray, J., Pathman, D., Gerrity, M., Schwartz, M., Scheckler, W., Van Kirk, J., Rhodes, E., & Douglas, J. (1999). Measuring physician job satisfaction in a changing workplace and a challenging environment. *Medical Care*, *37*(11), 1174–1182. doi:10.1097/00005650-199911000-00010 PMID:10549620

Kotler, P. (2003). *Marketing Management*. Pearson Education, Inc.

Kumar, B. (2019a). Remittances, poverty and welfare: Evidence from Cumilla, Bangladesh. *American Journal of Data Mining and Knowledge Discovery*, *4*(1), 46–52. doi:10.11648/j.ajdmkd.20190401.17

Kumar, B. (2019b). The impact of international remittances education and health in Bangladesh. *International Journal of Science and Qualitative Analysis*, *5*(1), 6–14. doi:10.11648/j.ijsqa.20190501.12

Kumar, B. (2019c). The impact of international remittances on poverty alleviation in Bangladesh. *Remittances Review*, *4*(1), 67–86. doi:10.33182/rr.v4i1.665

Kumar, B., Hossain, M. E., & Osmani, M. A. G. (2018). Utilization of international remittances in Bangladesh. *Remittances Review*, *3*(1), 5–18. doi:10.33182/rr.v3i1.424

Kumari, R. (2018). Economic growth, disparity, and determinants of female labor force participation: A research agenda. *World Journal of Entrepreneurship, Management and Sustainable Development*, *14*(2), 138–152. doi:10.1108/WJEMSD-03-2017-0009

Kwapong, L. S. A., Opoku, E., & Donyina, F. (2015). The effect of motivation on the performance of teaching staff in ghanaian polytechnics: The moderating role of education and research experience. *International Journal of Education and Research*, *3*(11), 35–48.

Kyvig, D. E. (2004). *Daily life in the United States 1920-1940: How America lived through the 'Roaring Twenties' and the Great Depression*. Ivan R. Dee.

La Piana, G. (1916a, January 17). *Andover-Harvard Theological Library, Harvard Divinity School, Cambridge (Papers, 1878-1972 inclusive, Manuscripts MS 104/11, folders 5-18, mass. sequence 54-74)* [Social Work Among Italian Immigrants]. Open Collections Program, Baker Library, Harvard University. http://nrs.harvard.edu/urn-3:DIV.LIB:828929

La Piana, G. (1916b, October). *Andover-Harvard Theological Library, Harvard Divinity School, Cambridge (Papers, 1878-1972 inclusive, Manuscripts bMS 104/11, Folders 5-18, mass. sequence 32 of 325)* [Italians in America]. Open Collections Program, Baker Library, Harvard University. http://nrs.harvard.edu/urn-3:DIV.LIB:828929

La Piana, G. (n.d.). *Andover-Harvard Theological Library, Harvard Divinity School, Cambridge (Papers, 1878-1972 inclusive, Manuscripts MS 104/11, folders 5-18, mass. sequence 75-89)* [Italian Woman at home]. Open Collections Program, Baker Library, Harvard University. http://nrs.harvard.edu/urn-3:DIV.LIB:828929

Lagerlof, N. (1999). *Gender Inequality, Fertility, and Growth*. Department of Economics, University of Sydney.

Lahoti, R., & Swaminathan, H. (2013). *Economic Growth and Female Labor Force Participation in India.* Indian Institute of Management Bangalore, Working Paper, (414).

Lancaster, L., & Stillman, D. (2003). *When generations collide.* Harper Business.

Langwell, K. (1982). Factors affecting the incomes of men and women physicians: Further explorations. *The Journal of Human Resources, 17*(2), 261–275. doi:10.2307/145472 PMID:7130708

Lawson, S. (2008). *Women Hold Up Half the Sky.* Goldman Sachs Global Economics Paper No: 164.

Laxmikanth, M. (2004). *Indian Polity. Chennai: McGraw Hill Education.* Private Limited.

Leblebici, D. (2012). Impact of workplace quality on employee's productivity: Case study of a bank in Turkey. *Journal of Business. Economics, 1*(1), 38–49.

Leigh, J., Kravitz, R., Schembri, M., Samuels, S., & Mobley, S. (2002). Physician career satisfaction across specialties. *Archives of Internal Medicine, 162*(14), 1577–1584. doi:10.1001/archinte.162.14.1577 PMID:12123400

Li, T. M. (2015). *Social impacts of oil palm in Indonesia: A gendered perspective from West Kalimantan.* Occasional Paper 124. Bogor, Indonesia: CIFOR.

Lichtenstein, R. (1984). Measuring the job satisfaction of physicians in organized settings. *Medical Care, 22*(1), 56–68. doi:10.1097/00005650-198401000-00005 PMID:6694460

Linzer, M., Konrad, T., Douglas, J., McMurray, J., Pathman, D., Williams, E., Schwartz, M., Gerrity, M., Scheckler, W., Bigby, J., & Rhodes, E. (2000). Managed care, time pressure and physician job satisfaction: Results from the physician worklife study. *Journal of General Internal Medicine, 5*(7), 441–449. doi:10.1046/j.1525-1497.2000.05239.x PMID:10940129

Lo Sasso, A., Richards, M., Chou, C., & Gerber, S. (2011). The $16,819 pay gap for newly trained physicians: The unexplained trend of men earning more than women. *Health Affairs, 30*(2), 193–201. doi:10.1377/hlthaff.2010.0597 PMID:21289339

Lopes, M., Coelho, L., & Ferreira, V. (2015). *Civil Society Organisations and Gender Equality: Mainstreaming and Empowerment in the Public Policies towards Civil Society.* Paper for the ISTR Eight International Conference and 2nd EMES-ISTR European Conference, The Third Sector and Sustainable Social Change: New Frontiers for Research, organized by ISTR, EMES in partnership with CINEFOGO, Barcelona, Spain.

Loury, G. (1977). A dynamic theory of racial income differences. In P. Wallace & A. Lamond (Eds.), *Women, Minorities, and employment discrimination* (pp. 153–186). Heath.

Mahapatro, S., Bailey, A., James, K. S., & Hulter, I. (2017). Remittances and household expenditure patterns in India and selected states. *Migration and Development, 6*(1), 83–101. doi:10.1080/21632324.2015.1044316

Mahmud, S., Shah, N. M., & Becker, S. (2012). Measurement of women's empowerment in rural Bangladesh. *World Development, 40*(3), 610–619. doi:10.1016/j.worlddev.2011.08.003 PMID:23637468

Malamassam, A., Latifa, A., Setiawan, B., Hidayati, I., & Romdiati, H. (2017). *Optimalisasi Modal Manusia Tenaga Kerja Melalui Migrasi: Kasus Kota Batam.* LIPI.

Manning & Aswichyono. (2012). *Perdagangan di Bidang Jasa dan Ketenagakerjaan: Kasus Indonesia.* ILO.

Manning, C. (1930). *The immigrant woman and her job (Bulletin of the Women's Bureau, no. 74). United States Department of Labor, Women's Bureau.* Government Printing Office. Open Collections Program, Baker Library, Harvard University. http://nrs.harvard.edu/urn-3:HBS.BAKER:452545

Marcuss, D., & Kane, R. E. (2007). US national income and product statistics born of the Great Depression and World War II. *Bureau of Economic Analysis: Survey of Current Business*, *87*, 32–46.

Mariyono, Latifaha, & Dewia. (2013). *Diskriminasi Jender di Sektor Pertanian Pedesaan di Jawa dan Bali: Kasus Masyarakat Petani Sayuran*. Komnas perempuan dan Program Studi Kajian Gender Program Pascasarjana Universitas Indonesia.

Marmot, M. (2002). The influence of income on health: Views of an epidemiologist. *Health Affairs*, *21*(2), 31–46. doi:10.1377/hlthaff.21.2.31 PMID:11900185

Marufa, E., & Uzhenyu, D. (2017). Motivation of university academic staff in zimbabwe. a case study of Zimbabwe open university (2009 – 2014). *IOSR Journal of Business and Management*, *19*(9), 78–86.

Mastracci, S. H. (2004). Backstage and spotlight activism: One survival strategy of the Women's Bureau and its price. *Labor History*, *45*(1), 85–99. doi:10.1080/0023656042000202990

Matthews, J. V. (2003). *The rise of the new woman: The women's movement in America, 1875-1930*. Ivan R. Dee.

Mattis, M. C. (2004). Women entrepreneurs: Out from under the glass ceiling. *Women in Management Review*, *19*(3), 154–163. doi:10.1108/09649420410529861

McMurray, J., Linzer, M., Konrad, T., Douglas, J., Shugerman, R., & Nelson, K. (2000). The work lives of women physicians. *Journal of General Internal Medicine*, *15*, 372–380. PMID:10886471

Mead, N., & Bower, P. (2002). Patient-centered consultations and outcomes in primary care: A review of the literature. *Patient Education and Counseling*, *48*(1), 51–61. doi:10.1016/S0738-3991(02)00099-X PMID:12220750

Medscape. (2019). *International physician compensation report 2019: Do US physician have it best?* Retrieved from https://www.medscape.com/slideshow/2019-international-compensation-report-6011814#5

Metcalfe, R., & Adegoke, A. A. (2013). Strategies to increase facility-based skilled birth attendance in South Asia: A literature review. *International Health*, *5*(2), 96–105. doi:10.1093/inthealth/ihs001 PMID:24030109

Michie, S., Miles, J., & Weinman, J. (2003). Patient-centredness in chronic illness: What is it and does it matter? *Patient Education and Counseling*, *51*(3), 197–206. doi:10.1016/S0738-3991(02)00194-5 PMID:14630376

Mitchelmore, S., & Rowley, J. (2013). Entrepreneurial competencies of women entrepreneurs pursuing business growth. *Journal of Small Business and Enterprise Development*, *20*(1), 125–142. doi:10.1108/14626001311298448

Morgan, C. T., King, R. A., Weisz, J. R., & Schopler, J. (1993). *Introduction To Psychology*. Tata McGraw-Hill Publishing Company Limited.

Morrison, A., & Biehl, L. (Eds.). (2007). *Too Close to Home: Domestic Violence in Latin America*. Inter-American Development Bank.

Mpala, C., Dlaminia, M., & Sibandaa, P. (2013). The Accessibility, Utilisation and Role of Indigenous Traditional Vegetables in Household Food Security in Rural Hwange District. *International Open & Distance Learning Journal*, *1*(3), 40–48.

Mukherjee, P., & Mukhopadhyay, I. (2013). Impact of Gender Inequality on Economic Growth: A Study of Developing Countries. *IOSR Journal of Humanities and Social Science*, *13*(2), 61–69. doi:10.9790/0837-1326169

Multani, N., & Sanghvi, A. (2017). Women Workers in Agricultural Sector: A Literature Review. *IRA-International Journal of Management & Social Sciences*, *6*(1), 24–30.

Mulyoutami, E., Martini, E., & Khususiyah, N. (2012). *Agroforestry and Forestry in Sulawesi series: Gender, livelihoods and land in South and Southeast Sulawesi.* Working paper 158. Bogor, Indonesia: World Agroforestry Centre (ICRAF) Southeast Asia Regional Program.

Munan, H. (1991). Culture Shock! Malaysia: A Guide to Customs and Etiquette. Graphic Arts Centre.

Munchies. (2017). *This Pho-Stuffed Burrito Is Better than It Sounds.* Available at: https://munchies.vice.com/en_us/article/vvq7b9/this-pho-stuffed-burrito-is-better-than-it-sounds

Mustafa, K., & Ali, S. R. (2018). The macroeconomic determinants of remittances in Pakistan. *International Journal of Business Management and Finance Research, 1*, 1–18.

Nabi, M. N., Islam, M. M., Dip, T. M., & Hossain, M. A. (2017). Impact of motivation on employee performances: A case study of Karmasangsthan Bank Limited, Bangladesh. *Arabian Journal of Business and Management Review, 7*(1), 1–8.

Nadgrodkiewicz, A. (2011). *Empowering Women Entrepreneurs: The Impact of the 2006 Trade Organizations Ordinance in Pakistan.* Center for International Private Enterprise. Available at http://www.cipe.org/publications/fs/pdf/042911.pdf

Nadim, M., Chaudhry, M. S., Kalyar, M. N., & Riaz, T. (2012). Effects of motivational factors on teachers' job satisfaction: A study on public sector degree colleges of Punjab, Pakistan. *The Journal of Commerce, 4*(4), 25.

Naqvi, S. M. H., Khan, M. A., Kant, A. Q., & Khan, S. N. (2013). Job stress and employees' productivity: Case of Azad Kashmir public health sector. *Interdisciplinary Journal of Contemporary Research in Business, 5*(3), 525–542.

Narayan, D. (Ed.). (2002). Empowerment and poverty reduction - a sourcebook. Washington, DC: The World Bank.

Nasir, M., Iqbal, R., & Akhtar, C. (2019). Factors Affecting Growth of Women Entrepreneurs in Pakistan. *Pakistan Administrative Review, 3*(1), 35–50.

Nazneen, S., Hossain, N., & Sultan, M. (2011). National Discourses on Women's Empowerment in Bangladesh: Continuities and Change. *IDS Working Papers, 2011*(368), 1-41.

Ngai, M. M. (1999). The architecture of race in American immigration law: A reexamination of the Immigration Act of 1924. *The Journal of American History, 86*(1), 67–92. doi:10.2307/2567407

Nienburg, B. M. (1920). *Women in government service (Bulletin of the Women's Bureau, no. 8). United States Department of Labor, Women's Bureau.* Government Printing Office. Open Collections Program. Baker Library, Harvard University. http://nrs.harvard.edu/urn-3:HBS.BAKER:136884

Nisar, A., Zafar, M. I., Mahmood, B., Sohail, M. M., Sher, F., & Safdar, M. R. (2012). Pay benefits and workplace milieu effecting job satisfaction level of university teachers: A case study of Punjab University. *International Journal of Asian Social Science, 2*(10), 1815–1831.

Noble, S., & Schewe, C. (2003). Cohort segmentation: An exploration of its validity. *Journal of Business Research, 56*(12), 979–987. doi:10.1016/S0148-2963(02)00268-0

Noland, Moran, & Kotschwar. (2016). *Is Gender Diversity Profitable? Evidence from a Global Survey.* Peterson Institute for International Economics.

NRHM. (2013). *District data: NRHM index.* Collected from the NRHM state office of Punjab.

Nwakasi, C. C., & Cummins, P. A. (2018). Teacher motivation and job satisfaction: A case study of north west Nigeria. *Global Jurnal of Educational Research, 17*(2), 103–112. doi:10.4314/gjedr.v17i2.2

OECD. (2014). Gender Eguality in the "three Es" in the Asia/Pacific region. Society at a Glance Asia/Pacific 2014.

Office of Registrar General. (2019). *Special bulletin on Maternal mortality in India 2015-17*. Sample Registration System.

Olneck, M. R. (1989). Americanization and the education of immigrants, 1900-1925: An analysis of symbolic action. *American Journal of Education, 97*(4), 398–423. doi:10.1086/443935

Oshima, H. T. (1984). The growth of U.S. factor productivity: The significance of new technologies in the early decades of the twentieth century. *The Journal of Economic History, 44*(1), 161–170. doi:10.1017/S0022050700031429

Park, D., & Shin, K. (2012). *The Service Sector in Asia: Is It an Engine of Growth?* Asian Development Bank.

Parker, S. C. (2009). *The Economics of Entrepreneurship*. Cambridge University Press. doi:10.1017/CBO9780511817441

Parry, E., & Urwin, P. (2011). Generational differences in work values: A review of theory and evidence. *International Journal of Management Reviews, 13*(1), 79–96. doi:10.1111/j.1468-2370.2010.00285.x

Parvin, L., Rahman, M. W., & Jia, J. (2012). Determinates of women micro-entrepreneurship development: an empirical investigation in rural Bangladesh. *International Journal of Economics and Finance, 4*(5), 254-260.

Pathak, K. N., & Tomar, J. S. (2012). *Skill- Up gradation in five year plans. Yojana, August 2012*. Ministry of Information and Broadcasting.

Pathman, D., Konrad, T., Williams, E., Scheckler, W., Linzer, M., & Douglas, J. (2002). Physician job satisfaction, job dissatisfaction, and physician turnover. *The Journal of Family Practice, 51*, •••. https://www.mdedge.com/familymedicine/article/65406/physician-job-satisfaction-job-dissatisfaction-and-physician-turnover PMID:12160487

Patterson, N., & Mavin, S. (2009). Women entrepreneurs: Jumping the corporate ship and gaining new wings. *International Small Business Journal, 27*(2), 173–192. doi:10.1177/0266242608100489

Paul-Majumder, P., & Begum, A. (2000). *The Gender Imbalances in the Export Oriented Garment Industry in Bangladesh*. Policy Research Report On Gender And Development Working Paper Series No. 12. The World Bank.

Petra, S. (2003). Maternal Mortality in a Contemporary Social Background. *Transylvanian Journal of Multidisciplinary Research in Humanities, 8-9*, 173–190.

Pew Research Center. (2010). *Baby Boomers retire*. Retrieved from www.pewresearch.org/daily-number/baby-boomers-retire

Pew Research Center. (2014a). *Generation X: America's neglected middle child*. Retrieved from http://www.pewresearch.org/fact-tank/2014/06/05/generation-x- americas-neglected-middle-child/

Pew Research Center. (2014b). *Millennials in adulthood: Detached from institutions, networked with friends*. Retrieved from https://www.pewsocialtrends.org/2014/03/07/millennials-in-adulthood/

Pinagara, F. A., & Bleijenbergh, I. (2010). *Understanding the Low Proportion of Women in Employment in Indonesia: A System Dynamics Approach*. Academic Press.

Prescott-Allen, R., & Prescott-Allen, C. (1990). How Many Plants Feed the World? *Conservation Biology, 4*(4), 365–374. doi:10.1111/j.1523-1739.1990.tb00310.x

Psacharopoulos, G., & Patronos, H. A. (2004). Returns to Investment in Education: A Further Update. *Education Economics, 12*(2), 111–134. doi:10.1080/0964529042000239140

Puri, S., & Kapoor, S. (2006). Taboos & Myths Associated With Women Health Among Rural & Adoloscent Girls In Punjab. *Indian Journal of Community Medicine, 31*, 168–170.

Rahmatullah, M., & Zaman, F. (2014). Female Entrepreneurship in Bangladesh: Constraints, Motivation and Success. *Bangladesh e-Journal of Sociology*, *11*(2).

Raihan, S., Khondker, B. H., Sugiyarto, G., & Jha, S. (2009). *Remittances and household welfare: a case study of Bangladesh.* ADB Economics Working Paper-189.

Rajput, P. (2001). Women's political participation in India: An agenda for empowerment. In P. Kapur (Ed.), *Empowering the Indian Women*. Ministry of Information and Broadcasting, Government of India.

Ramírez, C., Domínguez, M. G., & Morais, J. M. (2005). *Remittances, Gender and Development.* Working Paper. United Nations International Research and Training Institute for the Advancement of Women.

Rappaport, J. (1987). Terms of empowerment/examples of prevention: Toward a theory for community Psychology. *The Journal of Psychology*, *15*(2), 121–148. PMID:3604997

Rasheed, M. I., Aslam, H. D., & Sarwar, S. (2010). Motivational issues for teachers in higher education: A critical case of IUB. *Journal of Management Research*, *2*(2), 1. doi:10.5296/jmr.v2i2.349

Rashid, S., & Rashid, U. (2012). Work motivation differences between public and private sector. *American International Journal of Social Science*, *1*(2), 24–33.

Reid, R., Friedberg, M., Adams, J., McGlynn, E., & Mehrotra, A. (2010). Associations between physician characteristics and quality of care. *Archives of Internal Medicine*, *170*(16), 1442–1449. doi:10.1001/archinternmed.2010.307 PMID:20837830

Rendall, M. (2013). *The Service Sector and Female Market Work: Europe vs US*. The University of Zurich.

Revenga, A., & Shetty, S. (2012). Empowering Women Is Smart Economics-Closing gender gaps benefits countries as a whole, not just women and girls. *Finance and Development-English Edition*, *49*(1), 40.

Richardson, A., & Burke, R. (1991). Occupational stress and job satisfaction among physicians: Sex differences. *Social Science & Medicine*, *33*(10), 1179–1187. doi:10.1016/0277-9536(91)90234-4 PMID:1767288

Rodriguez, A. V. (2018). Economic growth and gender inequality: An analysis of panel data for five Latin American countries. *CEPAL Review*, *2017*(122), 79–106. doi:10.18356/73d010ed-en

Roomi, M. A., & Parrott, G. (2008). Barriers to development and progression of women entrepreneurs in Pakistan. *The Journal of Entrepreneurship*, *17*(1), 59–72. doi:10.1177/097135570701700105

Roomi, M. A., Rehman, S., & Henry, C. (2018). Exploring the normative context for women's entrepreneurship in Pakistan: A critical analysis. *International Journal of Gender and Entrepreneurship*, *10*(2), 158–180. doi:10.1108/IJGE-03-2018-0019

Ryder, N. (1965). The cohort as a concept in the study of social change. *American Sociological Review*, *30*(6), 843–861. doi:10.2307/2090964 PMID:5846306

Saisana, M., & Philippas, D. (2012). Sustainable Society Index (SSI): Taking societies' pulse along social, environmental and economic issues. *Environmental Impact Assessment Review*, *32*, 94–106.

Santo, S. A., Engstrom, M. E., Reetz, L., Schweinle, W. E., & Reed, K. (2009). Faculty productivity barriers and supports at a school of education. *Innovative Higher Education*, *34*(2), 117–129. doi:10.100710755-009-9098-z

Sara, J., Haji, Y., & Gebretsadik, A. (2019). Determinants of Maternal Death in a Pastoralist Area of Borena Zone, Oromia Region, Ethiopia: Unmatched Case-Control Study. *Obstetrics and Gynecology International. Article ID, 5698436*. Advance online publication. doi:10.1155/2019/5698436 PMID:30805003

Sasser, A. (2005). Gender differences in physician pay tradeoffs between career and family. *The Journal of Human Resources*, *40*(2), 477–504. doi:10.3368/jhr.XL.2.477

Schain, J. (1918). *Women and the franchise.* Chicago: A.C. McClurge & Company. Open Collections Program, Harvard University, Schlesinger Library on the History of Women in America. http://nrs.harvard.edu/urn-3:RAD.SCHL:134371

Schumpeter, J. (1934). *The Theory of Economic Development.* Harvard University Press.

Seguino, S. (2000). Gender inequality and economic growth: A cross-country analysis. *World Development*, *28*(7), 1211–1230. doi:10.1016/S0305-750X(00)00018-8

Sen, G. (2007). Informal institutions and gender equality. In J. Ju¨ tting, D. Drechsler, S. Bartsch, & I. de Soysa (Eds.), Informal institutions: How social norms help or hinder development (pp. 49–72). Paris, France: OECD Set for Better Policies.

Setiawan, S. (2011). Kontribusi Industri Jasa dan Perdagangan Jasa Lintas Batas Bagi Rumusan Strategi Baru Pertumbuhan Ekonomi. *Catatan hasil pertemuan APEC SOM.*

Shahi, M. K. (2018). *Period & Emotion: Educate Yourself and your Family.* Evincepub Publishing.

Sherry, A., & Henson, R. K. (2005). Conducting and interpreting canonical correlation analysis in personality research: A user-friendly primer. *Journal of Personality Assessment*, *84*(1), 37–48. doi:10.120715327752jpa8401_09 PMID:15639766

Sheth, J. N. (1974). Consumer Behaviour: Theory & Application. Boston: Allyn & Bacon.

Silverstein, M., & Giarrusso, R. (2012). *Continuity and Discontinuity in Aging Families.* Johns Hopkins Univ. Press.

Singh, S., Singh, D. R., Singh, L. B., Chand, S., & Dam Roy, S. (2013). Indigenous Vegetables for Food and Nutritional Security in Andaman and Nicobar Islands, India. *International Journal of Agriculture and Food Science Technology*, *4*(5), 503–512.

Smith, Y. (2019). *Physician shortage. News-Medical.net.* Retrieved from https://www.news-medical.net/health/Physician-Shortage.aspx

Smith, F. P. (1925). *Facts about working women: A graphic presentation based on census statistics and studies of the Women's Bureau (Bulletin of the Women's Bureau, no. 46).* Government Printing Office. Open Collections Program. Baker Library, Harvard University. http://nrs.harvard.edu/urn-3:HBS.BAKER:477001

Smith, L. M., Case, J. L., Smith, H. M., Harwell, L. C., & Summers, J. K. (2013). Relating ecosystem services to domains of human well-being: Foundation for a U.S. index. *Ecological Indicators*, *28*, 79–90. doi:10.1016/j.ecolind.2012.02.032

Smola, K., & Sutton, C. (2002). Generational differences: Revisiting generational work values for the new millennium. *Journal of Organizational Behavior*, *23*(4), 363–382. doi:10.1002/job.147

Solberg, I. (2017). *Doctors' job satisfaction during early career and economic recession: Prospective and cross-national studies in Norway and Iceland.* Retrieved from https://www.duo.uio.no/handle/10852/57453

Sommerfeldt, V. (2010). *An identification of factors influencing police workplace motivation* (Doctoral dissertation). Queensland University of Technology.

Sparks, A. (2012). Psychological empowerment and job satisfaction between Baby Boomer and Generation X nurses. *Journal of Nursing Management*, *20*(4), 451–460. doi:10.1111/j.1365-2834.2011.01282.x PMID:22591147

Spector, N. (2018). The doctor is out? Why physicians are leaving their practices to pursue other careers. *NBC News*. Retrieved from https://www.nbcnews.com/business/business-news/doctor-out-why-physicians-are-leaving-their-practices-pursue-other-n900921

Stauss, B., Chojnacki, K., Decker, A., & Hoffmann, F. (2001). Retention effects of a customer club. *International Journal of Service Industry Management*, *12*(1), 7–19. doi:10.1108/09564230110382745

Stein, A., Sachdev, H., & Qaim, M. (2008). Genetic Engineering for the Poor: Golden Rice and Public Health in India. *World Development*, *36*(1), 144–158. doi:10.1016/j.worlddev.2007.02.013

Stevenson, L., & St-Onge, A. (2005). *Support for Growth-oriented Women Entrepreneurs in Tanzania*. ILO.

Stieger, T. L., & Wardell, M. (1995). *Gender and Employment in the Service Sector. Oxford Journals, 42(1).*

Stiglitz, J. E., Sen, A., & Fitoussi, J. P. (2010). Mismeasuring Our Lives: Why GDP Doesn't Add Up. The New Press.

Stotsky, J. G. (2006). *Gender and its Relevance to Macroeconomic Policy: A Survey* (No. 6-233). International Monetary Fund.

Strauss, V. (2014, January 10). America's oldest working teacher turns 100. *Washington Post*. Retrieved from http://www.washingtonpost.com/blogs/answer- sheet/wp/2014/01/10/americas-oldest-working-teacher-turns-100

Strauss, W., & Howe, N. (1997). *The fourth turning: What the cycles of history tell us about America's next rendezvous with destiny*. Broadway Books.

Subohi, A. (2006, Oct. 16). Competition driven sustained growth. *Daily Dawn*.

Suliman, A., Eltom, M., Elmadhoun, W., Noor, S., Almobarak, A., Osman, M., Awadalla, H., & Ahmed, M. (2017). Factors affecting job satisfaction among junior doctors working at teaching hospitals in River Nile State, Sudan. *Journal of Public Health and Emergency*, *1*(17), 79. doi:10.21037/jphe.2017.09.04

Sultan, M. (2015). *Women's perception of empowerment: Findings from the Pathways of Women's Empowerment Programme*. Presentation at the ADB Regional Seminar on Women's Employment, Entrepreneurship and Empowerment: Moving forward on imperfect pathways, Bangkok, Thailand.

Sultana, A. M., Hed, N. M., & Leh, F. C. (2013). Measuring empowerment between working and non-working women: Malaysian perspective. *Asian Journal of Humanities and Social Studies*, *1*, 415–421.

Surbakti & Devasahayam. (2015). *Women and Girls in Indonesia: Progress and Challenges*. UNFPA Indonesia Monograph Series: No.5.

Sushama, S. (1998). Women and Empowerment- Approach and Strategies. Discovery Publishing House.

Suzuki, M. (1995). Success story? Japanese immigrant economic achievement and return migration, 1920-1930. *The Journal of Economic History*, *55*(4), 889–901. doi:10.1017/S0022050700042200

Swain, S. (2009). *Applied Psychology: India-specific & Cross-cultural Approaches*. New Vishal Publications.

Swamy, Azfar, Knack, & Lee. (2001). Gender and Corruption. *Journal of Development Economics, 64*(1), 25-55.

Syed, J. (2010). *Women and small business entrepreneurship in Pakistan*. Academic Press.

Tabachnick, B. G., & Fidell, L. S. (2013). *Using multivariate statistics* (6th ed.). Pearson.

Tadjoeddin, M. Z. (2016). Productivity, wages and employment: Evidence from the Indonesia's manufacturing sector. *Journal of the Asia Pacific Economy*.

Talberth, J., Cobb, C., & Slattery, N. (2007). The Genuine Progress Indicator 2006: A Tool for Sustainable Development. *Oakland: Redefining progress*, 31.

Tam, H. (2011). U-shaped female labor participation with economic development: Some panel data evidence. *Economics Letters*, *110*(2), 140–142. doi:10.1016/j.econlet.2010.11.003

Taniguchi, K., & Tuwo, A. (2014). *New Evidence on the Gender Wage Gap in Indonesia*. Asian Development Bank Manila. doi:10.2139srn.2512096

Tannen, D. (1990). You just don't understand. Morrow: Academic Press.

Taragin, M., Wilczek, A., Karns, M., Trout, R., & Carson, J. (1992). Physician demographics and the risk of medical malpractice. *The American Journal of Medicine*, *93*(5), 537–542. doi:10.1016/0002-9343(92)90582-V PMID:1442857

Taylor, J. B. (1999). A historical analysis of monetary policy rules. In *Monetary policy rules* (pp. 319–348). University of Chicago Press. doi:10.7208/chicago/9780226791265.001.0001

The Complete works of Swami Vivekananda. (2002). Advaita Ashram.

The Hindu Business Line. (2019). *India rises one rank to 129 in human development index, Economy*. Retrieved March 15, 2020, from https://www.thehindubusinessline.com/economy/india-moves-up-one-rank-129-in-human-development-index/article30249584.ece

The Star. (2017). *Japanese delight meets Malaysian innovation - Nation | The Star Online*. Available at: http://www.thestar.com.my/news/nation/2017/06/02/japanese- delight-meets-malaysian-innovation/

Tiwari, R. S. (2001). Feminism and globalization versus Indian women empowerment. In Modernity, Feminism and Women's Empowerment. Rawat Publication.

Todaro, M. P., & Smith, S. C. (2012). *Economic Development*. Pearson.

Trask, B. S. (2010). Globalization and Families: Accelerated Systemic. *Social Change*. Advance online publication. doi:10.1007/978-0-387-88285-7_3

Tsani, S., Paroussos, L., Fragiadakis, C., Charalambidis, I., & Capros, P. (2013). Female labour force participation and economic growth in the South Mediterranean countries. *Economics Letters*, *120*(2), 323–328. doi:10.1016/j.econlet.2013.04.043

Tyssen, R., Palmer, K., Solberg, I., Voltmer, E., & Frank, E. (2013). Physicians' perceptions of quality of care, professional autonomy, and job satisfaction in Canada, Norway, and the United States. *BMC Health Services Research*, *13*(1), 516. doi:10.1186/1472-6963-13-516 PMID:24330820

U.S. Bureau of Labor Statistics. (2014). *Occupational employment & wage estimates*. Retrieved from http://www.bls.gov/oes/current/oes_nat.htm#29-0000

U.S. Bureau of Labor Statistics. (2019). Women had higher median earnings than men in relatively few occupations in 2018. *The Economics Daily*. Retrieved from https://www.bls.gov/opub/ted/2019/women-had-higher-median-earnings-than-men-in-relatively-few-occupations-in-2018.htm

Ulich, R. (1967). History of Educational Thought. Eurasia Publishing House(P) Ltd.

Ullah, A. A. (2017). Male Migration and 'Left–behind Women: Bane or Boon? *Environment & Urbanization Asia*, *8*(1), 59–73. doi:10.1177/0975425316683862

UNDP. (2000). *Human Development Report 2000*. United Nations Development Program.

UNICEF/WHO. (2019). *Joint database of skilled health personnel based on population based national household survey data and routine health systems.* Retrieved March 15, 2020, from https://data.unicef.org/topic/maternal-health/delivery-care/

United States Department of Labor. Bureau of Labor Statistics. (1927). *Handbook of Labor Statistics, 1924-1926*, 439. Government Printing Office. http://ocp.hul.harvard.edu/ww/

United States Department of Labor. Women's Bureau (1930a, December 9). *Fact Finding with the Women's Bureau* (Women's Bureau Bulletin, no. 84). St. Louis Federal Reserve, Discovery Economic Center. https://fraser.stlouisfed.org/title/5392

United States Department of Labor. Women's Bureau. (1920). *Second Annual Report of the Director of the Women's Bureau for the Fiscal Year Ended June 30, 1920.* Washington, DC: Government Printing Office. Open Collections Program, Baker Library, Harvard University. http://nrs.harvard.edu/urn-3:HBS.BAKER:508406

United States Department of Labor. Women's Bureau. (1921). *Third Annual Report of the Director of the Women's Bureau for the Fiscal Year Ended June 30, 1921.* Washington, DC: Government Printing Office. Open Collections Program, Baker Library, Harvard University. http://nrs.harvard.edu/urn-3:HBS.BAKER:508406

United States Department of Labor. Women's Bureau. (1922). *Fourth Annual Report of the Director of the Women's Bureau for the Fiscal Year Ended June 30, 1922.* Washington, DC: Government Printing Office. Open Collections Program, Baker Library, Harvard University. http://nrs.harvard.edu/urn-3:HBS.BAKER:508406

United States Department of Labor. Women's Bureau. (1923). *Fifth Annual Report of the Director of the Women's Bureau for the Fiscal Year Ended June 30, 1923.* Washington, DC: Government Printing Office. Open Collections Program. Baker Library, Harvard University. http://nrs.harvard.edu/urn-3:HBS.BAKER:508406

United States Department of Labor. Women's Bureau. (1924). *Sixth Annual Report of the Director of the Women's Bureau: Fiscal Year Ended June 30, 1924.* Washington, DC: Government Printing Office. Open Collections Program. Baker Library, Harvard University. http://nrs.harvard.edu/urn-3:HBS.BAKER:508406

United States Department of Labor. Women's Bureau. (1925). *Seventh Annual Report of the Director of the Women's Bureau: Fiscal Year Ended June 30, 1925.* Washington, DC: Government Printing Office. Open Collections Program. Baker Library, Harvard University. http://nrs.harvard.edu/urn-3:HBS.BAKER:508406

United States Department of Labor. Women's Bureau. (1926). *Eighth Annual Report of the Director of the Women's Bureau: Fiscal Year Ended June 30, 1926.* Government Printing Office. Open Collections Program. Baker Library, Harvard University. http://nrs.harvard.edu/urn-3:HBS.BAKER:508406

United States Department of Labor. Women's Bureau. (1927). *Ninth Annual Report of the Director of the Women's Bureau: Fiscal Year Ended June 30, 1927.* Government Printing Office. In *Women Working, 1800-1930.* Open Collections Program. Baker Library, Harvard University. http://nrs.harvard.edu/urn-3:HBS.BAKER:508406

United States Department of Labor. Women's Bureau. (1928). *Tenth Annual Report of the Director of the Women's Bureau: Fiscal Year Ended June 30, 1928.* Government Printing Office. In *Women Working, 1800-1930.* Open Collections Program. Baker Library, Harvard University. http://nrs.harvard.edu/urn-3:HBS.BAKER:508406

United States Department of Labor. Women's Bureau. (1929). *Eleventh Annual Report of the Director of the Women's Bureau: Fiscal Year Ended June 30, 1929.* Government Printing Office. In *Women Working, 1800-1930.* Open Collections Program. Baker Library, Harvard University. http://nrs.harvard.edu/urn-3:HBS.BAKER:508406

United States Department of Labor. Women's Bureau. (1930b). *Twelfth Annual Report of the Director of the Women's Bureau: Fiscal Year Ended June 30, 1930.* Government Printing Office. In *Women Working, 1800-1930.* Open Collections Program. Baker Library, Harvard University. http://nrs.harvard.edu/urn-3:HBS.BAKER:508406

United States Department of Labor. Women's Bureau. (1931). *Activities of the Women's Bureau of the United States* (Bulletin of the Women's Bureau, no. 86). St. Louis Federal Reserve, Discovery Economic Center. https://fraser.stlouisfed.org/files/docs/publications/women/b0086_dolwb_1931.pdf

United States House of Representatives. (1920). *41 Stat. L., 987 – An Act to Establish in the Department of Labor a bureau to be known as the Women's Bureau.* https://uscode.house.gov/statviewer.htm?volume=41&page=987

ValueWalk. (2019). *Professions in the world.* Retrieved from https://www.valuewalk.com/2019/03/top-10-most-respected-professions/

Van de Kerk, G., & Manuel, A. R. (2008). A comprehensive index for a sustainable society: The SSI-the Sustainable Society Index. *Ecological Economics, 66*(2-3), 228–242. doi:10.1016/j.ecolecon.2008.01.029

van Kleeck, M. (1921). *Women and machines.* The Consumer's League of the City of New York. Open Collections Program. Baker Library, Harvard University. http://nrs.harvard.edu/urn-3:HBS.BAKER:500055

Vaughan-Whitehead, D. (Ed.). (2016). *Long-term trends in the World of Work: What effects on inequalities and middle-income groups?* ILO and EC.

Viseu, J., Jesus, S. N. D., Rus, C., Canavarro, J. M., & Pereira, J. (2016). Relationship between teacher motivation and organizational variables: A literature review. *Systematic Literature Review, 26*(63), 111–120.

Von Grebmer, K., Saltzman, A., Birol, E., Wiesmann, D., Prasai, N., Yin, S., Yohannes, Y., Menon, P., Thompson, J., & Sonntag, A. (2014). *Global Hunger Index.* International Food Policy Research Institute.

Wadood, S. N., & Hossain, A. (2017). Microeconomic impact of remittances on household welfare: Evidences from Bangladesh. *Business and Economic Horizons, 13*(1), 10–29. doi:10.15208/beh.2017.02

Walch, T. (Ed.). (1994). *Immigrant America: European ethnicity in the United States.* Routledge.

Walkowitz, D. J. (1990). The making of a feminine professional identity: Social workers in the 1920s. *The American Historical Review, 95*(4), 1051–1075. doi:10.2307/2163478

Wallerstein, N. (1992). Powerlessness, empowerment and health: Implication for Health promotion programs. *American Journal of Health Promotion, 6*(3), 197–205. doi:10.4278/0890-1171-6.3.197 PMID:10146784

Wang, Y. J., Wang, Y. L., Sub, X. D., Caiji, Z. M., Yang, J. B., Cui, D., Cao, G. L., Ma, X. D., Han, B., Xue, D. Y., & Han, L. Z. (2016). Influence of ethnic traditional cultures on genetic diversity of rice landraces under on-farm conservation in southwest China. *Journal of Ethnobiology and Ethnomedicine, 12*(1), 51. doi:10.118613002-016-0120-0 PMID:27788685

Warth, L. (2009). *Gender Equality and the Corporate Sector.* United Nations Economic Commission for Europe (UNECE) Discussion Paper No.4. https://www.un.org/en/ecosoc/newfunct/pdf/womens_empowerment_principles_ppt_for_29_mar_briefing-without_notes.pdf

Weber, G. A. (1923). *The Women's Bureau: Its history, activities, and organization.* The Johns Hopkins Press. Open Collections Program, Widener Library, Harvard University. http://nrs.harvard.edu/urn-3:FHCL:123612

Wellalage, N., & Locke, S. (2017). Access to credit by SMEs in South Asia: Do women entrepreneurs face discrimination. *Research in International Business and Finance, 41*, 336–346. doi:10.1016/j.ribaf.2017.04.053

Whaley, N. (2018). 3 long-term effects the gender pay gap has on women. *Mic.* Retrieved from https://www.mic.com/articles/188833/3-long-term-effects-the-gender-pay-gap-has-on-women

Whitehead, A. L. (2012). Gender ideology and religion: Does a masculine image of god matter? *Review of Religious Research, 54*(2), 139–156. doi:10.100713644-012-0056-3

WHO. (2017). *Fact sheets on sustainable development goals: health targets.* Maternal health, Media centre, World Health Organization.

WHO. (2018). *Women's empowerment is a public health imperative: WHO.* South-East Asia. News. Statement. India. Retrieved March 15, 2020, from https://www.who.int/ southeastasia/news/detail/07-03-2018-women-s-empowerment-is-a-public-health-imperative-who

WHO. (2019). *Maternal mortality.* Newsroom, Factsheet, September 19. Retrieved March 15, 2020, from https://www.who.int/news-room/fact-sheets/detail/maternal-mortality

Winograd, M., & Hais, M. (2008). *Millennial makeover: MySpace, YouTube & the future of American politics.* Rutgers University Press.

Women's Bureau. (n.d.). In *Women Working, 1800-1930.* Open Collections Program, Harvard University. http://ocp.hul.harvard.edu/ww/

Women's Rights in Uzbekistan, Briefing note to the UN Committee on the Elimination of Discrimination Against Women (CEDAW) Coalition of Uzbek women's rights NGOs Coordination by the Bureau of Human Rights and Rule of Law Uzbekistan (CEDAW Pre-session, Geneva, February 2009) @Strengthening Womens Political Participation-An Analysis of the impact of women's parliamentary networks in Europe and Central Asia –Report by UNDP. https://www.opendemocracy.net/en/odr/uzbekistan-gender-ineaulity-violence-en/ https://www.unwomen.org/en/about-us/about-un-women https://www.uz.undp.org/content/uzbekistan/en/home/presscenter/pressreleases/2017/11/20/wc-undp-will-promote-women-empowerment.html

Women's Trade Union League of Chicago. (1910, October 29). *Official report of the Strike Committee: Chicago Garment Workers' Strike.* Women's Trade Union League of Chicago. Open Collections Program, Widener Library, Harvard University. http://nrs.harvard.edu/urn-3:FHCL:458789

World Bank. (2012). *Why the Manufacturing Sector Still Matters for Growth and Development in Indonesia. Policy Note.* The World Bank Office Jakarta.

World Bank. (2019). *Trends in maternal mortality 2000 to 2017: Estimates by WHO, UNICEF, UNFPA, World Bank Group and the United Nations Population Division,* 2. Washington, DC: World Bank Group.

World Street Food Congress. (2017). http://wsfcongress.com/award-2017- winners/

Worldometers. (2019). *Populations by gender, age, fertility rate, immigration.* Retrieved from https://www.worldometers.info/world-population/world-population-gender-age.php

Yojana, J. S. (2005). *Features & frequently asked questions and answers.* Ministry of health and family welfare, Government of India. https://nhm.gov.in/WriteReadData/l892s/97827133331523438951.pdf

Yunis, M. S., Hashim, H., & Anderson, A. R. (2019). Enablers and Constraints of Female Entrepreneurship in Khyber Pukhtunkhawa, Pakistan: Institutional and Feminist Perspectives. *Sustainability, 11*(1), 27. doi:10.3390u11010027

Zhou, M. (2019). Aging population a global challenge. *China Daily.* Retrieved from http://global.chinadaily.com.cn/a/201904/09/WS5cabe02da3104842260b50cb_1.html

Zimmerman, M. A. (1995). Psychological empowerment: Issues and illustrations. *American Journal of Community Psychology, 25*(5), 581-599. (https://www.gazeta.uz/oz/2020/03/11/women-mayors doi:10.1007/BF02506983

About the Contributors

Shailja Dixit did her PhD in Management and is a Gold Medallist in her Management Program. She is an ardent researcher and a passionate teacher. She believes in collaborative and purposeful teaching and learning. She has a vision that through this noble profession of teaching she can ignite many young minds and make this world a happy place. To pursue this vision, she has completed course on Social Entrepreneurship from The Wharton School of the University of Pennsylvania. She is working as Associate Professor in the Department of Management at Amity University, Lucknow, India. Her research interests include Women Entrepreneurship, Social Entrepreneurship, Consumer Research, Consumer Decision making, Branding. She has more than 30 research papers published in reputed peer reviewed journals. She is currently associated with many reputed Journals and she is working on various Research projects related to social well-being. She also has Two books to her credit.

Sana Moid is currently working as Assistant Professor with Amity University, in the department of Amity Business School and has a total teaching experience of 10 years. Her research interest includes Women Issues, Behavioral Finance, Forensic Accounting, and Women Entrepreneurship. Dr Sana has authored overl 8 research papers published in reputed peer reviewed indexed journals and is an active member of Indian Accounting Association and Indian Commerce Association. She is NET qualified in management. She has been invited as a resource person at several prestigious institutions and currently working on a Government Funded project as Co- Principal Investigator.

* * *

Devi Asiati was born in Bukittinggi, West Sumatera in June, 1967. She completed her bachelor degree at Faculty of Economics, Andalas University (1991) and Masters degree from Population and Employment Studies at the University of Indonesia (2004). Since 1994, Devi Asiati working as researcher at Research Center for Population, Indonesian Institute of Sciences (LIPI). She have been involved some research project focused on labor and employment. Some of the publications that have been published related to topics such as employment opportunities, quality of labor, small industries.

Adam I. Attwood is an Assistant Professor in the Department of Teaching and Learning at Austin Peay State University in Clarksville, Tennessee, United States. He currently teaches courses in educational psychology, classroom assessment, classroom management, and teaching in a diverse pluralistic society. He has taught history courses at the college level and was a teacher (grades 6-12) in Washington state and Missouri. He is the author of the book ***Social Aesthetics and the School Environment*** (2018), and he has several published journal articles and book chapters. He is a member of the American Educational Research Association.

Arti Chanadani, Associate Professor, has more than 21 years of teaching experience in the field of finance. she has published more than 30 journal article in National and International level and article. She is the editorial Board member for National and international Journals. She is also the guest editor for International Journal of pubic sector performance management of Inderscience.

Ozge Dinc-Cavlak earned her PhD degree in January 2019 from the Middle East Technical University (METU), consistently ranked among the highest in Turkey. She is now a research assistant of Business Administration Department at Ankara Hacı Bayram Veli University in Turkey. Her research area primarily is investigating individual decision making through using survey and experimental methods, and exploring the application of psychological models to business administration, mainly consumer behavior. She has published papers in international peer reviewed journals such as Natural Hazards Review. She has also done scientific research projects in METU

Nazima Ellahi is working as an Associate Professor/HoD, Department of Economics and Finance, Foundation University Islamabad, Pakistan. She is Certified Productivity Specialist (CPS) from APO (Japan) and Editor Foundation University Journal of Business & Economics. Dr. Ellahi is receiver of HEC's Best University Teacher Award for her teaching and research performance. She has authored several articles at internationally renowned journals, and presented her research across the world at various forums and received best research paper awards from two international conferences. She collaborates with various journals as a reviewer.

Satya Sekhar Gudimetla, M.Com, MBA, M.Phil, Ph.D, Associate Professor, Centre for Distance Learning, GITAM University, Visakhapatnam, has 20 years of teaching and research experience at Post Graduate level. He has published several books of which viz. 1) Financial Innovation-Theories, Models and Regulation, Vernon Press, USA, 2)The Indian Mutual Fund Industry, Palgrave Macmillan, London. 3) Mangement of Mutual Funds, Springer Nature, Germany, 4) Currency Risk Management, Vernon Press, USA are international publications. He has contributed lessons to the study material of 'Executive MBA Programme' of Andhra University, Visakhapatnam and also study material published by Centre for Distance Learning, GITAM University. Besides this, he has participated and presented papers in various national and international seminars. So far he has published 42 articles in various national and international reputed journals.

Alok Gupta earned his Master's Degree in Agriculture from the leading Agricultural University of Asia GBPUA&T, established by University of Illinois in India, in 1981 with distinction. After passing out the University, he joined a large Indian corporate business house as Forest Officer and subsequently moved to a Swiss Multi National Company CIBA-Geigy as Research and Development Officer. He finally joined Government in 1984 and worked for 35 long years with the Government sector at various senior positions in managing and administering Procurement, Production, and Marketing function on behalf of the Government. In his long and distinguished stint with the Government, he had very enriching experience of working for 20 long years with the European Community, the World Bank and other National and International Developmental / Donor Agencies in strengthening Agricultural Production base, Agri-business Management, Training and Technological Skill Up-gradation of farmers, and rural human resource development. Prof. Gupta never gave up his quest for knowledge and continued his academic pursuits including teaching and training. Apart from Master Degree in Agriculture, he also holds Master Degree in Business Administration, Master Degree in Rural Management, Master Degree in Agricultural Extension Management and Food Safety Management. He is presently holding position of Professor and Vice-Rector of Sharda University Uzbekistan.

Anviti Gupta joined as the founder Rector of Sharda University, Uzbekistan in 2019.She is a recipient of Vice Chancellor's Gold Medal for securing first position in Master of Arts (Psychology) and a Ph.D. in Applied Psychology from University of Lucknow, India. She also holds PG Diploma in Industrial Relations and Personnel Management and PG Diploma in Marketing and Sales Management from Bhartiya Vidhya Bhawan, Mumbai. Besides she has earned certificates in Clinical Hypnotherapy from California Hypnosis Institute, USA and EKAA. She is also a certified Counseling Psychologist from Christian Counseling Centre, Vellore, India. Prof Anviti Gupta has the ability to lead, develop and empower the team. She has over twenty three years of experience as an academician, academic administrator, trainer, researcher and a counseling Psychologist. She has been invited as an expert to deliver lectures by various organisations of repute. She has also been involved in designing and conducting various training programs at several government and private organisations. Has been a member of Board of Studies and has helped in designing the curriculum for various Programmes.

Gaurav Joshi, an engineering graduate with a PG Diploma in Management, is currently working as Assistant Professor (Business Administration) at LSM Government PG College, Pithoragarh, Uttarakhand. He has an experience of around 12 years.

Sunita Bhatt Joshi is a Master in Law from Kumaun University and is currently serving as Assistant Prosecuting Officer in Pithoragarh (Uttarakhand). She has an experience of more than 7 years.

Jaciel Keltgen earned a Ph.D. in political science with a specialty in healthcare administration. She is a former journalist and frequently serves as a media source for developments in the healthcare and retail industries. Dr. Keltgen teaches marketing, including healthcare and sport marketing, to undergraduate and graduate students at Augustana University in Sioux Falls, SD. Her research interests include generational behavior in the workplace, particularly job satisfaction in the healthcare setting, as well as the use of social media as a community-building strategy. Dr. Keltgen has won several best-paper awards for her work.

Md. Golam Kibria earned his Bachelor and Masters degree in Economics from Noakhali Science and Technology University, Noakhali-3814. His research interests include poverty, quality of life, globalization, environmental economics, trade, remittance, FDI, governance, institutional quality, and development. He published several research articles in international peer review journal and also has engaged in five ongoing research projects.

Bezon Kumar is now serving as a Lecturer in Economics at Rabindra University, Bangladesh. He started his career first at Varendra University as a Lecturer in Economics just after passing the Bachelor and Masters in Economics from the University of Rajshahi. Besides teaching, he is now working as a Director, BK School of Research. His expertise belongs to entrepreneurship, productivity, women empowerment, international migration, welfare, poverty, sustainable development, climate change, behavioral and psychological issues, and so on. He has several international peer-review journal articles and book chapters and he is currently engaged in three research projects. He also plays a role as the Reviewer and Editorial board member of some international journals. Mr. Kumar is also serving as an Editor of a multidisciplinary magazine named Saptasudha.

Ade Latifa was born in Surabaya, East Java in 1964. She's completed her Master degree from Women Study, University of Indonesia (1998). Since 1989, Ade Latifa working at Research Center for Population, Indonesian Institute of Sciences (LIPI) as a researcher, focuses on population issues studies. In the recent years, she has been involved in some research projects related to maternal and child health, poverty, food security, population mobility and health, and women organization. She has published several articles about gender such as: violence against women, climate change and women's reproductive health.

Qaisar Ali Malik is Associate Professor at Department of Business Administration, Foundation University Islamabad, Pakistan. He is Fellow Member of national professional accounting body (ICMA Pakistan). He holds two decades of extensive academic and allied experiences in the higher education sector. He has published over 30 papers in several national and international journals. He has attended and presented in several national and international conferences. His core theoretical, professional, and practical interests are in the areas of Financial Reporting & Analysis, Cost Management, Corporate Finance, Corporate Governance, Corporate Social Responsibility, Investment Analysis, Financial Inclusion and Firm Performance.

Zeeshan Maqsood is currently working as a lecturer at faculty of sciences, University of Sialkot in Pakistan. He has published 9 research papers in renowned journals. He has also reviewed 3 research papers of the renowned journals. He has five years of experience in the field of statistics related to teaching and research with varietal dynamics and his research focuses range applied multivariate statistics, multidisciplinary research, Social issues, non- parametric statistics, categorical analysis and other contemporary issues. He has arranged several trainings of university faculty on data analysis using Statistical software i.e: SPSS, R Language, Minitab and Stata.

Nawawi is a researcher at Research Center for Population, Indonesian Institute of Sciences (LIPI). He obtained PhD from School of Politics and International Studies, University of Leeds, the United Kingdom (2019). His interests relate to comparative labor politics, particularly in Asia. He is currently conducting research projects on Indonesian Migrant Workers in Korea sponsored by Korea Foundation and an individual research on Women Activist in Indonesia's Trade Unions.

Ngadi is a researcher at Research Center for Population, the Indonesian Institute of Sciences (LIPI) since 2005. He is a Ph.D candidate in Human Geography, the University of Tokyo, Japan. He obtained master degree from Population and Employment Studies at the University of Indonesia (2005). His research interests relate to population and labor mobility, employment and human resources, demographic change, and rural development. He has published more than 30 articles both as books and journals in national and international publisher.

Gayathri R. is currently an Assistant Professor at School of Management, SASTRA Deemed University in India. An excellent orator with a Doctorate in Economics (2013) from Bharathidasan University, India. Her areas of interest include International Business, Marketing and Business Ethics. She handles courses such as Economics and Marketing. She has a rich academic experience of 19 years in teaching and 7 years in Research. Her focus is on contemporary social research and she is a co-investigator in the funded project funded by the Ministry of Rural Development, Government of India. She has presented papers at international and national level conferences and seminars. She has published a number of research articles and case studies in referred Scopus indexed journals.

Syed Rashid Ali holds an M. Phil. in Economics from the Department of Economics, University of Karachi, Pakistan and has been teaching economics at the College of Accounting and Management Sciences (CAMS) since 2013. His teaching experience spans the last 15 years. As a teacher, Rashid has had the opportunity to teach in many colleges and universities. He is also the author/co-author in many quality research papers. Rashid firmly believes that success in education is about building relationships.

Iqra Sardar is now working as a Visiting Lecturer in Statistics, Department of Mathematics and Statistics, International Islamic University Islamabad, Pakistan. She has 5 years of experience in teaching at the university level besides doing research. She has a Master of Philosophy in Statistics from Riphah International University, Pakistan. She attended many national & International Seminars, Workshops, and conferences where she presented more than 7 research papers. Her research interests belong to Machine learning, Bayesian Statistics with modern computer-intensive methods and so on. She has several peer-reviewed journal articles and she is now engaged in some research projects.

Vijayetta Sharma is an ardent researcher in the areas policy and administrative sciences. She is triple gold medallist from Panjab University, India and has the credit of working in public policy courses at Indian School of Business, India. She has 9 years of experience in academics; teaching at Panjab University, affiliated colleges and Indian School of Business. Along with public policy she has experienced in composite domains at ISB in economics, strategy, marketing, organizational behavior, healthcare, statistics, law, analytics and entrepreneurship and worked with the renowned experts across the globe. She has presented more than 15 papers in national and international conferences and published many papers in books and journals. She holds UGC-NET and Phd in healthcare administration.

Rachel Thomas Tharmabalan is a Lecturer at School of Hospitality of Sunway University. She holds a Master's Degree in Food Technology from Universiti Sains Malaysia and is currently pursuing her PhD in ethnic studies at Universiti Kebangsaan Malaysia. Her research interests revolve around nutrition and well-being, revitalization of traditional food and forgotten crops and ethnic food.

Elumalayan V. is having 22 years of teaching experience and 6 years of Industry experience. He has published nearly 15 articles in journals and conferences at national and international level. He has been awarded best teacher award by various NGO'S.

Neeraja Vijay, M.Com, M.Phil, M.B.A. Ph.D is an inmate of Andhra Pradesh. She has been awarded Doctorate from Dr.MGR Educational and Research Institute, University. Chennai. She was awarded as "Accredited Management Teacher" by AIMA, New Delhi and Best Teacher award -2013 by NFED India. She has 20+ years of teaching experience. She has published more than 60 research papers at National and International level. She also published 20+ articles in SCOPUS database Journals. She is Editorial

Board member for various National and International journals. She is working as Professor & Deputy Head - Academics in Faculty of Management Studies at Dr.MGR Educational and Research Institute, University, Chennai, India.

C. Vijayabanu is currently an Associate Professor at School of Management, SASTRA Deemed University in India. She obtained her Ph.D. in Commerce-Human Resource Management in 2000 at Bharathidasan University, India. Her current research interests focus on the areas behavioral studies – Personality, Perception: attitudes & values. She handles courses such as Human Resource Management, organizational behavior and specialization courses such as Change Management, Training & Development, etc. She brings to her classes enriched knowledge of 5 years of Research & 21 years of academic experience. She has produced five doctoral scholars successfully and currently Guiding 2 Ph.D. scholar. She has presented papers at international and national level conferences and seminars. She has published number of research articles and case studies in referred Scopus indexed journals. She has served on the Editorial Review Boards of several academic journals, including Business theory and practice, Journal of Management Social Science and Humanities and Journal of Business Economics and Management.

Index

I

J

L

M

N

O

P

Q

R

S

T

V

W

www.ingramcontent.com/pod-product-compliance
Lightning Source LLC
LaVergne TN
LVHW080648011026
849160LV00014B/1355